Designing and Implementing Microsoft Azure Networking Solutions

Exam Ref AZ-700 preparation guide

David Okeyode

BIRMINGHAM—MUMBAI

Designing and Implementing Microsoft Azure Networking Solutions

Group Product Manager: Pavan Ramchandani

Publishing Product Manager: Prachi Sawant

Senior Editor: Athikho Sapuni Rishana

Technical Editor: Irfa Ansari

Copy Editor: Safis Editing

Project Coordinator: Ashwin Kharwa

Proofreader: Safis Editing

Indexer: Subalakshmi Govindhan

Production Designer: Joshua Misquitta

Marketing Coordinator: Marylou De Mello

First published: July 2023

Production reference: 1260723

Published by Packt Publishing Ltd.

Grosvenor House

11 St Paul's Square

Birmingham

B3 1RB

ISBN 978-1-80324-203-3

www.packtpub.com

This book is dedicated to the incredible individuals who continue to lovingly nurture me in the complex art of life: my father, Oluwagbenga; my mother, Oluwayemisi; my three sisters, Oluwapemi, Oluwagbolade, and Ajulooluwa; and my wife, Po Kei.

Additionally, a profound dedication goes to the individuals who patiently mentored me in the fields of networking, system administration, and security. I express my deepest gratitude to Tom Elgar, Rajeev Kapur, Ope Babayemi, Bara Mustafa, and Ross McKerchar.

– David Okeyode

Contributors

About the author

David Okeyode is the EMEA Chief Technology Officer for Azure at Palo Alto Networks. Before that, he was an independent consultant helping companies secure their Azure environments through private expert-level training and assessments. He also runs a specialized training company, Charis Cloud, that is focused on cloud security training for professionals and organizations. He has authored two other books on Azure security: *Penetration Testing Azure for Ethical Hackers* and *Microsoft Azure Security Technologies Certification and Beyond*. He has also authored multiple cloud computing courses for popular training platforms such as LinkedIn Learning. He holds over 15 cloud certifications across the Azure and AWS platforms, including the Azure Security Engineer, Azure DevOps, and AWS Security Specialist certifications.

He regularly speaks on cloud security at user groups and major industry events such as Microsoft Build, Microsoft Ignite, Azure Lowlands, Future Decoded, and the European Information Security Summit.

David is married to a lovely girl who makes the best banana cake in the world. They love traveling the world together!

About the reviewers

Michel Jatobá is a highly qualified and experienced professional with more than 10 years of experience in the cloud and infrastructure. He has an extensive understanding of technologies such as Office 365, EMS, and Azure, and has helped customers efficiently implement and improve their environments. With his technical skills (hard skills) and interpersonal skills (soft skills), Michel Jatobá is able to provide high-impact solutions for clients, ensuring project satisfaction and success.

I would like to thank everyone for their confidence in this project. Thanks to my family, who always support me; my wife, Luana de Barros; and my children, Luíza and Bento.

Leke Oluwatosin is a senior network and information security engineer, with over 15 years of relevant and progressive information technology experience, responsible for network and information security solution initiatives including network infrastructure design, security assessment, cloud security assessment, vulnerability management, and ongoing incident response.

He currently holds a master's degree in cybersecurity technology from the University of Maryland Global Campus and multiple expert-level vendor-focused certifications, such as CCIE and JNCIE, and vendor-neutral certifications, such as GIAC GCED, GDSA, and GCIH.

I'd like to thank the author for considering me worthy to provide my input to help readers learn about this technology and for making a positive impact in the technology community at large.

Table of Contents

Preface   xvii

Part 1: Design and Implement Core Networking Infrastructure in Azure

1

Azure Networking Fundamentals   3

Technical requirements	4	Task 1 – creating the dual-stack EngineeringVNet VNet and subnets	26
Understanding Azure VNet	4	Task 2 – verifying the creation of the dual-stack VNet and subnets	28
Azure VNet versus traditional networks	5		
Planning Vnet naming	6	Understanding private IP address assignment for subnet workloads	28
Planning VNet location	7		
Planning Vnet IP address spaces	8	Hands-on exercise – determining the VM location and sizes for future exercises	30
Planning Vnet subnet segmentation	11		
Working with platform services in subnets	15	Task 1 – determining the CPU quota limits for recommended subscription regions	31
Hands-on exercise – creating a single-stack VNet in Azure	17	Hands-on exercise – exploring private IP assignments	33
Task 1 – creating the CharisTech resource group	18	Task 1 – deploying VMs with dynamic and static private IP assignments	33
Task 2 – creating the CoreServicesVNet VNet and subnets	20	Hands-on exercise – cleaning up resources	36
Task 3 – verifying the creation of the VNet and subnets	24	Summary	36
Hands-on exercise – creating a dual-stack VNet in Azure	26	Further reading	36

2

Designing and Implementing Name Resolution 37

Technical requirements	38	Option 3 – Azure Private DNS	61
A hands-on exercise – provisioning resources for the chapter's exercises	38	A hands-on exercise – implementing Azure Private DNS	62
		Option 4 – Azure Private DNS Resolver and Azure Private DNS zones	73
Name resolution scenarios and options	42		
Internal name resolution scenarios and options	43	**External name resolution scenarios and options**	73
Option 1 – Azure-provided name resolution	44	A hands-on exercise – implementing Azure Public DNS	73
A hands-on exercise – exploring Azure-provided name resolution	46	**A hands-on exercise – clean up resources**	78
Option 2 – customer-managed DNS servers	50	**Summary**	78
A hands-on exercise – implementing a customer-managed DNS server	51	**Further reading**	79

3

Design, Implement, and Manage VNet Routing 81

Technical requirements	82	Hands-on exercise – route network traffic with a route table	97
Understanding the default routing for Azure VNet workloads	82	Implementing dynamic custom routing with BGP	108
Understanding default routing for dual-stack subnets	86	Hands-on exercise – implementing BGP dynamic routing with Azure Route Server	111
Hands-on exercise – provisioning resources for the chapter's exercises	86	Route selection and priority	117
Hands-on exercise – explore the default routing of Azure subnet workloads	90	**Hands-on exercise – cleaning up resources**	118
Modifying the default routing behavior	96	**Summary**	118
Implementing custom routing with user-defined routes	96	**Further reading**	118

4

Design and Implement Cross-VNet Connectivity   119

Technical requirements   120
Understanding cross-VNet
connectivity options   120
Connecting VNets using VNet
peering   121
Planning VNet peering implementation   121
Understanding VNet peering architecture
considerations   122
Understanding VNet peering and
transitive routing   123
Configuring VNet peering   124
VNet peering in a hub-and-spoke
architecture   124

Connecting VNets using a VPN
gateway connection   126
Understanding VPN Gateway architecture
considerations   128

Connecting VNets using a
vWAN   128
Hands-on exercise – provisioning
resources for the chapter   129

Task 1 – initializing the template
deployment in GitHub   130
Hands-on exercise – implementing
cross-region VNet connectivity
using the vWAN   132
Task 1 – creating a vWAN   132
Task 2 – creating a virtual hub in each
VNet location in the vWAN   135
Task 3 – connecting the VNets to the
regional virtual hubs   140
Task 4 – verifying effective routes on the
VNets and the virtual hubs   143
Task 5 – verifying the connectivity
between the VNets   145

Comparing the three cross-VNet
connectivity options   146
Hands-on exercise – clean up
resources   147
Summary   148
Further reading   148

Part 2: Design, Implement, and Manage Hybrid Networking

5

Design and Implement Hybrid Network Connectivity with VPN Gateway   151

Technical requirements   152
Understanding Azure hybrid
network connection options   152

Understanding the Azure VPN
gateway   152

Choosing the right VPN gateway SKU and generation   153

Selecting between route-based or policy-based VPN types   156

Selecting high-availability options for VPN connections   159

Understanding third-party device compatibility   163

Hands-on exercise – provision resources for chapter exercises   164

Task 1: Initialize template deployment in GitHub, complete parameters, and deploy the template to Azure   165

Hands-on exercise: implement a BGP-enabled VPN connection in Azure   168

Task 1: Create the gateway subnet   168

Task 2: Deploy the VPN gateway into the subnet (with an existing public IP)   170

Task 3: Create the local network gateway   172

Task 4: Configure the VPN connection   174

Task 5: Verify VPN connection status and BGP peering   177

Task 6: Verify connectivity between the on-premises network and the Azure VNet   178

Understanding point-to-site connections   180

Defining a connection pool for P2S VPN connectivity   181

Selecting the tunnel type(s) for P2S VPN connectivity   182

Selecting the authentication type for P2S VPN connectivity   183

Hands-on exercise – implement a P2S VPN connection with Azure certificate authentication   184

Task 1: Connect to the remote user's PC via RDP   184

Task 2: Configure the P2S VPN gateway settings   189

Task 3: Configure settings for VPN clients   192

Task 4: Verify connectivity between the remote PC and the Azure VNet   194

Troubleshoot Azure VPN Gateway using diagnostic logs   195

Hands-on exercise – clean up resources   195

Summary   196

Designing and Implementing Hybrid Network Connectivity with the ExpressRoute Gateway   197

Technical requirements   198

Understanding what ExpressRoute is and its main use cases   198

Choosing between private peering and public peering   199

Understanding ExpressRoute components   200

Deciding on an ExpressRoute connectivity model   201

Understanding the provider model   202

Understanding the ExpressRoute direct model   205

Selecting the right ExpressRoute circuit SKU   206

Selecting the right ExpressRoute
gateway SKU   211
Implementing ExpressRoute with zone
redundancy   215
Modifying a gateway SKU`   216
Implementing the gateway subnet   217

Improving data path performance
with ExpressRoute FastPath   218
Understanding FastPath unsupported
scenarios   220
Configuring FastPath for new or existing
connections   221

Designing and implementing
cross-network connectivity over
ExpressRoute   222
Enhancing cross-network connectivity using
VNet peering   223
Enhancing cross-network connectivity
using multiple ExpressRoute VNet
connections   224
Enhancing cross-network connectivity
using ExpressRoute Global Reach   225

Understanding the implementation
of encryption over
ExpressRoute   228
Understanding the implementation
of BFD   229
Hands-on exercise – implementing
an ExpressRoute gateway   231
Task 1 – create a VNet and gateway
subnet   231
Task 2 – deploy the ExpressRoute VNet
gateway service   232
Task 3 – create and provision an
ExpressRoute circuit   232
Task 4 – retrieve your service key (you need
to send this to your SP)   232
Task 5 – check
serviceProviderProvisioningState status   232
Task 6 – connect the ExpressRoute gateway
to the ExpressRoute circuit   233
Task 7 – deprovision an ExpressRoute
circuit   233
Task 8 – clean up resources   233
Summary   234

7

Design and Implement Hybrid Network Connectivity with Virtual WAN

235

Technical requirements   236
Designing a scalable network
topology in Azure   236
The standard hub-and-spoke topology   237
The Azure vWAN hub-and-spoke
topology   238

Understanding the design
considerations of a vWAN hub   241
Selecting the regions for the VWAN
hub   241

Selecting an IP address space for the
VWAN hub   242
Configuring the routing infrastructure for
the VWAN hub   244
Configuring the VWAN hub routing
preference   245
Connecting VNets together using VWAN   248

Understanding the routing and
SD-WAN configuration in a
virtual hub   249

Understanding VNet connection route table
association   249
Understanding VNet connection route
propagation   250
Implementing BGP peering between an
NVA and a virtual hub   251
Implementing a third-party SD-WAN NVA
in a virtual hub   252

**Hands-on exercise 1 – provision
resources for chapter exercises   254**
Task 1 – initialize template deployment in
GitHub   254

**Configuring Site-to-Site connectivity
using VWAN   258**
Understanding the scalability considerations
of a VWAN hub S2S VPN   259
Understanding the availability considerations
of a VWAN hub S2S VPN   260
Understanding the performance
considerations of a VWAN hub S2S VPN   261

**Hands-on exercise 2 – implement
site-to-site VPN connectivity
using VWAN   262**
Task 1 – add a site-to-site gateway to
VWAN   263

Task 2 – create a VPN site in VWAN   265
Task 3 – connect the VPN site to a VWAN
hub   268
Task 4 – obtain VPN configuration
information   271
Task 5 – configure the "on-premises"
VPN device   274
Task 6 – verify routes and connectivity to the
"on-premises" site through VWAN   277
Task 7 – clean up the resources   279

**Implementing a global transit
network architecture using
VWAN   279**

**Understanding the security
considerations of a virtual hub   280**
Approach 1 – deploy Azure Firewall in the
virtual hub   280
Approach 2 – deploy a third-party security
virtual appliance in the virtual hub   282
Approach 3 – deploy a third-party network
virtual appliance in a connected VNet and
route traffic to it for inspection   282
Comparing virtual hub NVA deployment
options   283

Summary   284
Further reading   284

8

Designing and Implementing Network Security   285

Technical requirements   285
**Securing the Azure virtual
network perimeter   285**
Implementing DDoS protection   286
Understanding Azure DDoS Protection
service tiers   287

**Hands-on exercise 1 – provisioning
resources for Chapter 8's
exercises   290**

**Hands-on exercise 2 – implementing
DDoS Protection, monitoring, and
validation   293**
Task 1 – creating a DDoS Protection
plan   294
Task 2 – enabling DDoS Protection on a
virtual network   296
Task 3 – reviewing DDoS metrics for
telemetry   298

Task 4 – configure DDoS diagnostic logs
forwarding   299
Task 5 – configuring DDoS alerts   301
Task 6 – creating a BreakingPoint Cloud
account and authorizing your Azure
subscription   303
Task 7 – running a DDoS Test   308
Task 8 – reviewing DDoS test results   309

Implementing Azure Firewall   310
Understanding Azure Firewall service
tiers   310
Understanding Azure Firewall's features   310
Understanding some considerations for an
Azure Firewall deployment   320

**Hands-on exercise 3 – deploying
Azure Firewall into a VNet and a
Virtual WAN Hub   322**
Task 1 – deploying an Azure Firewall test
environment template with the Azure CLI   323

Task 2 – reviewing the firewall service and the
firewall policy   324
Task 3 – testing connectivity through the
firewall   328

Implementing a WAF in Azure   331
Understanding managed rule sets and
WAF policies   332
Understanding custom rule sets   334
Understanding WAF policy modes and
rule actions   337
Understanding WAF policy associations   339
Understanding WAF policy limitations   341

**Implementing central management
with Firewall Manager   341**
Summary   342
Further reading   343

Part 3: Design and Implement Traffic Management and Network Monitoring

9

Designing and Implementing Application Delivery Services   347

Technical requirements   348
**Understanding Azure's load-
balancing and application delivery
services   348**
Understanding Azure load-balancing and
application delivery services categories   348

**Designing and implementing an
Azure Load Balancer service   350**
Understanding use cases for the Basic
SKU   351

Understanding use cases for the Standard
SKU   351
Hands-on exercise 1 – Provisioning resources
for this chapter's exercises   358
Hands-on exercise 2 – Creating and
configuring a global (cross-region) load
balancer   361

**Designing and implementing an
Azure Application Gateway
service   368**

Understanding Azure Application Gateway
tiers   368
Understanding the scalability and
performance of the tiers   369
Considerations for the Application Gateway
subnet   370
Understanding Azure Application Gateway
components   371

**Designing and implementing an
Azure Front Door load balancer
service   379**

Understanding Azure Front Door tiers   380
Understanding Front Door components   381
Hands-on exercise 1 – Creating and
configuring an Azure Front Door service   394

**Designing and implementing an
Azure Traffic Manager service   404**
Configuring a traffic routing method   406
Configuring Traffic Manager endpoints   407

**Choosing an optimal load-balancing
and application delivery solution   408**
Summary   410

10

Designing and Implementing Platform Service Connectivity   411

Technical requirements   411
**Implementing platform service
network security   412**
Understanding the platform service firewall
and its exceptions   412
Understanding service endpoints   416
Hands-on exercise 1 – provisioning the
resources for this chapter's exercises   419

Hands-on exercise 2 – configuring service
endpoints for a storage account   422
Designing and implementing Azure Private
Link and Azure private endpoints   437
Hands-on exercise 3 – configuring an Azure
private endpoint for an Azure WebApp   438

Summary   448
Further reading   448

11

Monitoring Networks in Azure   449

Technical requirements   449
**Introducing Azure Network Watcher
for monitoring, network diagnostics,
and logs   450**
**Understanding the network
monitoring tools of Network
Watcher   451**
Topology visualization   451
Connection monitor   452

**Understanding the Network
diagnostic tools of Network
Watcher   455**
Connection troubleshoot   455
IP flow verify   456
NSG diagnostics   457
Next hop   459
VPN troubleshoot   460
Packet capture   460

Hands-on exercise 1 – provisioning the resources for the chapter's exercises   461

Task 1 – initialize template deployment in GitHub, complete the parameters, and deploy a template to Azure   462

Hands-on exercise 2 – implementing the network monitoring tools of Network Watcher   465

Task 1 – visualize the topology of an Azure VNet   465

Task 2 – create an Azure Network Watcher connection monitor   466

Task 3 – Trigger a network issue and review Connection Monitor   474

Understanding NSG flow logs   475

NSG flow logs limitations and use cases   477

Hands-on exercise 3 – enabling NSG flow logs   478

Task 1 – enable an NSG flow log   478

Task 2 – download and review the flow log   480

Summary   481

Further reading   481

Index   483

Other Books You May Enjoy   500

Preface

In a world heavily dependent on cloud services, understanding and managing cloud network infrastructure is critical. In this book, you will gain both the knowledge and the practical skills to plan, design, implement, manage, and secure networks in the Azure cloud.

This book is also a comprehensive guide designed for those who are preparing for the Azure Network Engineer certification exam (AZ-700) and for those interested in mastering the Azure networking infrastructure. You will dive deep into concepts such as hybrid networking, routing, securing, and monitoring networks, as well as implementing private access to Azure services using native Azure capabilities.

Complete with hands-on labs, this book will take you beyond foundational knowledge to having a clear understanding of key design principles and implementation best practices. By the end of this book, you will be fully equipped and ready to architect and deploy highly scalable, performance-efficient networks in the Azure cloud.

Who this book is for

This book is aimed at new and experienced IT professionals, network engineers, cloud administrators, and architects with interests in planning, designing, implementing, managing, and securing networks in the cloud.

Technical professionals who are preparing to take the Azure Network Engineer certification exam (AZ-700) will also benefit tremendously from reading this book.

What this book covers

Chapter 1, *Azure Networking Fundamentals*, introduces core concepts of Azure networking, such as virtual networks, public and private IP addressing, network segmentation using subnets, and routing concepts.

Chapter 2, *Design and Implement Name Resolution*, covers the four DNS implementation options for virtual networks in Azure and their use cases: Azure-provided name resolution, customer-managed DNS servers, Azure DNS private zones, and Azure DNS public zones.

Chapter 3, *Design, Implement, and Manage VNet Routing*, explains Azure routing, and you will create custom routes to control traffic flow. You will learn how to redirect traffic through network virtual appliances so you can inspect the traffic before it's allowed through. You will also learn how to implement Azure Route Server – a fully managed service that simplifies dynamic routing between your **network virtual appliance (NVA)** and Azure Virtual Network.

Chapter 4, Design and Implement Cross-VNet Connectivity, covers the design and implementation of cross-VNet connectivity using VNet peering.

Chapter 5, Design and Implement Hybrid Network Connectivity with VPN Gateway, covers one of the diverse options to connect remote users and networks to networks in Azure offered by the Azure cloud – the Azure VPN Gateway service, which allows us to create a secure connection between remote networks and Azure VNets over the public internet.

Chapter 6, Design and Implement Hybrid Network Connectivity with an ExpressRoute Gateway, explores the implementation of ExpressRoute, another gateway service offered by Azure, as an alternative solution for remote network connectivity. ExpressRoute connections bypass the public internet, which means that traffic takes fewer hops and has fewer points of failure that could cause network disruption.

Chapter 7, Design and Implement an Azure Virtual WAN Architecture, explains how to design a scalable network architecture in Azure using the VWAN service.

Chapter 8, Design and Implement Network Security, looks into securing the Azure network perimeter and VNet workloads using native capabilities such as DDoS protection, Azure Firewall, and Azure Firewall Manager.

Chapter 9, Design and Implement Application Delivery Services, discusses the four main load balancing services in Azure (Load Balancer, Application Gateway, Front Door, and Traffic Manager) and aspects to consider when designing and implementing these services.

Chapter 10, Design and Implement Platform Service Connectivity, looks at the three main options to control network connections to services when deploying platform services outside of customer-managed virtual networks in Azure (a platform service firewall, a service endpoint, and a private endpoint). This chapter will provide you with a clear understanding of these three options and how to design and implement them.

Chapter 11, Monitoring Networks in Azure, covers network monitoring and diagnostics – essential components in maintaining the smooth functioning and optimal performance of a network infrastructure. In this chapter, we will cover the tools available in Azure Network Watcher that we can use to monitor and diagnose network services.

To get the most out of this book

Foundation-level knowledge of the Azure cloud platform as well as a general knowledge of networking concepts are required to get the most out of this book.

Software/hardware covered in the book	Operating system requirements
A PC with an internet connection and a web browser	Windows, macOS, or Linux
An Azure subscription	

If you are using the digital version of this book, we advise you to type the code yourself or access the code from the book's GitHub repository (a link is available in the next section). Doing so will help you avoid any potential errors related to the copying and pasting of code.

Download the example code files

You can download the example code files for this book from GitHub at `https://github.com/PacktPublishing/Designing-and-Implementing-Microsoft-Azure-Networking-Solutions`. If there's an update to the code, it will be updated in the GitHub repository.

We also have other code bundles from our rich catalog of books and videos available at `https://github.com/PacktPublishing/`. Check them out!

Conventions used

There are a number of text conventions used throughout this book.

`Code in text`: Indicates code words in text, database table names, folder names, filenames, file extensions, pathnames, dummy URLs, user input, and Twitter handles. Here is an example: "In the search box at the top of the portal, enter `Load balancer`."

Bold: Indicates a new term, an important word, or words that you see onscreen. For instance, words in menus or dialog boxes appear in **bold**. Here is an example: "Select **System info** from the **Administration** panel."

> **Tips or important notes**
> Appear like this.

Get in touch

Feedback from our readers is always welcome.

General feedback: If you have questions about any aspect of this book, email us at `customercare@packtpub.com` and mention the book title in the subject of your message.

Errata: Although we have taken every care to ensure the accuracy of our content, mistakes do happen. If you have found a mistake in this book, we would be grateful if you would report this to us. Please visit www.packtpub.com/support/errata and fill in the form.

Piracy: If you come across any illegal copies of our works in any form on the internet, we would be grateful if you would provide us with the location address or website name. Please contact us at copyright@packt.com with a link to the material.

If you are interested in becoming an author: If there is a topic that you have expertise in and you are interested in either writing or contributing to a book, please visit authors.packtpub.com.

Share your thoughts

Once you've read *Designing and Implementing Microsoft Azure Networking Solutions*, we'd love to hear your thoughts! Scan the QR code below to go straight to the Amazon review page for this book and share your feedback.

https://packt.link/r/1803242035

Your review is important to us and the tech community and will help us make sure we're delivering excellent quality content.

Download a free PDF copy of this book

Thanks for purchasing this book!

Do you like to read on the go but are unable to carry your print books everywhere?

Is your eBook purchase not compatible with the device of your choice?

Don't worry, now with every Packt book you get a DRM-free PDF version of that book at no cost.

Read anywhere, any place, on any device. Search, copy, and paste code from your favorite technical books directly into your application.

The perks don't stop there, you can get exclusive access to discounts, newsletters, and great free content in your inbox daily

Follow these simple steps to get the benefits:

1. Scan the QR code or visit the link below

https://packt.link/free-ebook/9781803242033

2. Submit your proof of purchase

3. That's it! We'll send your free PDF and other benefits to your email directly

Part 1:
Design and Implement
Core Networking Infrastructure
in Azure

Welcome to this comprehensive guide on Azure networking, where we will embark on a journey through the fundamental principles and practical implementations of networking within the Azure cloud environment. Over the course of this part, we will explore four key chapters that delve into the crucial aspects of Azure networking. Throughout this part, we will combine theoretical knowledge with practical hands-on examples, empowering you to design, implement, and manage Azure networking solutions confidently. So, let's embark on this enriching journey and unlock the true potential of networking in the Azure cloud. Let's get started!

This part comprises the following chapters:

- *Chapter 1, Azure Networking Fundamentals*
- *Chapter 2, Design and Implement Name Resolution*
- *Chapter 3, Design, Implement, and Manage VNet Routing*
- *Chapter 4, Design and Implement Cross-VNet Connectivity*

1

Azure Networking Fundamentals

As more organizations migrate business-critical workloads to the Azure cloud platform (or build new ones), they rely on applications and services being able to communicate with each other securely to provide services to their internal teams, business partners, and customers. Azure **Virtual Network** (**VNet**) is the core service for implementing secure private networking in Azure. A **VNet** is a virtual version of a physical network, implemented on the Azure cloud platform.

In this chapter, we will focus on the foundational concepts of implementing private network connectivity in Azure. We will walk through what Azure VNet is, its capabilities, the key differences between Azure VNet and a traditional on-premises network, and supported services that can be launched into Azure VNet (spoiler: as well as a **virtual machine** (**VM**), we can also deploy 20 other services into Azure VNet).

We'll then go on to discuss key implementation options such as designing/assigning IP address spaces, segmentation using subnets, and resource IP address assignments – how resources are allocated an IP address (another spoiler: you can't use self-managed DHCP!).

Lastly, we'll talk about the routing and traffic flow functionalities of Azure VNet. In other words, how does routing work and how do we control traffic flow?

In this chapter, we will cover the following topics:

- Understanding Azure VNet

- Planning VNet naming and location

- Planning VNet IP address spaces

- Planning VNet subnet segmentation

- Hands-on exercise – creating a single-stack VNet in Azure

- Hands-on exercise – creating a dual-stack VNet in Azure

- Understanding private IP address assignment for subnet workloads

- Hands-on exercise – determining the VM location and sizes for future exercises
- Hands-on exercise – exploring private IP assignments
- Cleaning up resources

Each topic has been structured to align with the recommended network connectivity best practices in Azure. Let us get into this!

Technical requirements

To follow along with the instructions in this chapter, you will need the following:

- A PC with an internet connection
- An Azure subscription

Before we proceed to cover the security best practices, let us prepare our Azure subscription for the hands-on exercises that we will complete later in the chapter.

Understanding Azure VNet

Before we get too far into Azure networking concepts, let's establish what Azure VNet is and the capabilities that it provides.

A VNet is a virtual version of a physical network, implemented on the Azure cloud platform. The main advantage that it has over a traditional network is that we don't need to implement or maintain the underlying physical hardware for this network (these responsibilities are offloaded to our cloud provider – Microsoft). But for the most part, we can achieve similar capabilities and architectures that we can achieve on-premises. We can even implement more flexible architectures with Azure VNets due to the software-defined nature.

So, what capabilities does Azure VNet provide? Here is a short list of some use cases:

- Connectivity for supported Azure services including **VM**, **virtual machine scale sets** (**VMSSs**), and 32 other services
- Native Internal TCP/UDP Load Balancing and proxy systems for Internal HTTP(S) Load Balancing
- Connects to on-premises networks using Cloud VPN tunnels and Cloud Interconnect attachments

> **Limitation**
> An Azure subscription can have up to 1,000 VNets as of the time of writing (April, 2022). An additional subscription will be needed to grow beyond this limit.

Azure VNet versus traditional networks

Even though Azure VNet is similar to a traditional on-premises network in many ways, there are still important differences, mainly due to restrictions that have been put in place by Microsoft to ensure security in a multi-tenant platform such as Azure. Here are some key ones:

- Azure VNet does not support Layer-2 semantics (Only Layer-3 and Layer-4). This means that concepts such as **virtual LANs (vLANs)** and Layer-2 broadcasts don't work in Azure VNet. *Figure 1.1* shows the output of running the `arp -a` command on a VM that is deployed in Azure VNet. You will notice that the MAC address resolution for VMs in the same subnet results in the same `12:34:56:78:9a:bc` value. This is because we are on a shared platform and the VNet is a Layer-3 overlay instead of Layer-2:

```
root@myLinuxVM0:~# arp -a
mylinuxvm2.internal.cloudapp.net (10.0.0.4) at 12:34:56:78:9a:bc [ether] on eth0
_gateway (10.0.0.1) at 12:34:56:78:9a:bc [ether] on eth0
mylinuxvm1.internal.cloudapp.net (10.0.0.6) at 12:34:56:78:9a:bc [ether] on eth0
root@myLinuxVM0:~#
```

Figure 1.1 – ARP table on an Azure VM

- Another key difference between a traditional network and Azure VNet is that some protocols and communication types are restricted from being used in Azure VNet. Protocols such as multicast, broadcast, DHCP unicast, UDP source port 65330, IP-in-IP encapsulated packets, and **Generic Routing Encapsulation (GRE)** packets are not allowed in Azure VNet. Any application or service capability that requires these protocols or communication types will need to be refactored before deployment into Azure VNet for it to work. The only protocols that are allowed are TCP, UDP, ICMP, and Unicast communication (except source port UDP/68 /, destination port UDP/67, and UDP source port 65330, which is reserved for the host).

> **Note**
>
> For more information on the differences of Azure VNet and traditional networks, refer to the document at https://docs.microsoft.com/en-us/azure/virtual-network/virtual-networks-faq.

Now that you have some fundamental information on what Azure VNet is, let's discuss how you would go about planning one, starting with considerations around naming it.

Planning Vnet naming

All Azure resources have a name that must be unique within a scope. The scope is different for each resource type. *When creating a Vnet, its name must be unique within the scope of the resource group.* This means that it is possible to have two Vnets in your Azure subscription with the same name as long as they don't belong to the same resource group! This can be useful in a design that involves having the same Vnet resource name for both development and production environments, as shown in *Figure 1.2.*

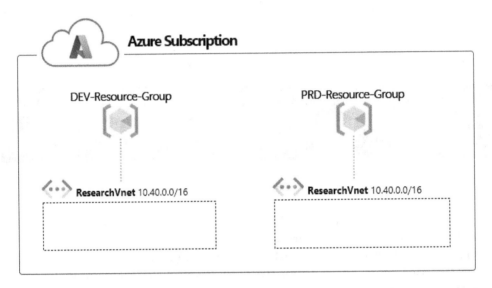

Figure 1.2 – Vnet names must be unique for the resource group scope

Even though it is possible to have duplicate names within a subscription, it is not a recommended practice as it could later lead to confusion when investigating security incidents using logging information (we will cover network logging and monitoring later in this book). When investigating security incidents, it helps to be able to quickly identify affected resources and having a **unique resource naming** strategy for your Vnets helps with this.

Regarding naming best practices, it is best to define a naming convention as early as possible. This convention should be communicated to the teams with permission to create network resources in Azure, and preferably, the naming convention should be enforced using tools such as Azure Policy. To define a good naming strategy, consider these recommendations:

- Review resource name restrictions for the Vnet and other network resources in Azure. For example, a Vnet name can have up to 64 characters made up of alphanumerics, underscores, periods, and hyphens. Your naming convention should take this into consideration. Information on Vnet naming restrictions can be found at https://docs.microsoft.com/en-us/azure/azure-resource-manager/management/resource-name-rules#microsoftnetwork.

- Consider including information about the following – resource type, resource location, deployment environment, and workload type in your naming convention. For example, a Vnet for production web services workloads in the East US region might be named `prod-eastus-webservices-Vnet` (*Figure 1.3*).

Figure 1.3 – Sample Vnet naming convention

For more thoughts on naming conventions, please refer to this document: `https://docs.microsoft.com/en-us/azure/cloud-adoption-framework/ready/azure-best-practices/resource-naming`.

Planning VNet location

Almost all Azure services are created in a regional location specified at creation time. I said *almost all* because there are some exceptions – so-called *global* or *non-regional* services that are not pinned to a region. Azure Vnet is a regional service.

As of the time of writing (April 2022), the Azure cloud has 55 active regions in which we can create Vnets (with nineteen announced regions coming soon).

So, which regions should you select when creating Vnets? Consider the following three points to guide your decision regarding this:

- **Business compliance requirements**: This is the first point that you should consider when deciding the Azure region to locate your Vnets in. If there are organizational/industry compliance requirements that require data residency or data sovereignty in a geographic area, then you must adhere to that! You don't want to end up in a situation where your organization is fined or charged for violating governmental regulations! For example, if you are providing services to a US government agency, the workloads that you are using to provide those services may be required to be in Vnets created in one of the Azure US government regions.

- **Proximity to the users**: This is the second key point to consider regarding Vnet location. You want your networks in locations close to the end users to ensure the lowest network latency. For example, if your organization is based in the UK and your network will host workloads that will provide services to your customers in the area, it will probably be best to create your Vnet(s) in either the UK South or the UK West Azure regions. You could perform your own tests to determine latency information for your end users *or* you could leverage unofficial sites such as `https://azurespeedtest.azurewebsites.net/` and `https://cloudpingtest.com/azure`.

- **Resiliency requirements**: This is another key point to consider when deciding where you should create your Vnets. Does your resiliency architecture require you to be able to distribute your network workloads in multiple data centers within the same region? If it does, then you need to select one of the regions that allow you to use **availability zones (AZs)** – distinct groups of data centers in the same region. Not all Azure regions currently support this capability. At the time of writing, only 25 of the 55 active regions support AZs. I will recommend checking this document for an up-to-date list before you create your network resources – `https://docs.microsoft.com/en-us/azure/availability-zones/az-overview`.

The following diagram shows an example of a Vnet with AZs:

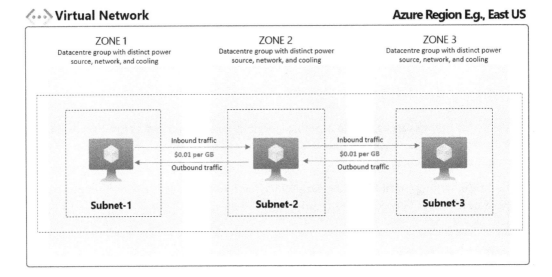

Figure 1.4 – A Vnet with AZs

Also, keep in mind that the decision to distribute your network workloads in multiple AZs in a region results in an extra cost of 0.01 USD (0.008 GBP) per gigabyte of data transferred between AZs for both inbound and outbound traffic.

Planning Vnet IP address spaces

Every Vnet must have at least one IP address space assignment. A Vnet space assignment can either be **single-stack** (IPv4 address space only) or **dual-stack** (IPv4 and IPv6 address spaces). At the time of writing, an IPv6-only Vnet is not supported! You might be able to create an IPv6-only Vnet in the portal, but you will not be able to attach a virtual **network interface card** (**NIC**) to it. Attempting it will result in the error message shown in *Figure 1.5*:

```
david@Azure:~$ az network nic create --name dsNIC0a --resource-group $group --netwo
rk-security-group dsNSG1 --vnet-name dsVNET1 --subnet dsSubNet --private-ip-address
-version IPv6 --public-ip-address dsPublicIP_v6a
(AtleastOneIpV4RequiredForIpV6NicIpConfiguration) At least one IPv4 ipConfiguration
 is required for an IPv6 ipConfiguration on the network interface '/subscriptions/0
6bb0d65-edfe-41c9-b89c-479a4b8aad72/resourceGroups/myResourceGroup/providers/Micros
oft.Network/networkInterfaces/dsNIC0a'.
Code: AtleastOneIpV4RequiredForIpV6NicIpConfiguration
Message: At least one IPv4 ipConfiguration is required for an IPv6 ipConfiguration
on the network interface '/subscriptions/06bb0d65-edfe-41c9-b89c-479a4b8aad72/resou
rceGroups/myResourceGroup/providers/Microsoft.Network/networkInterfaces/dsNIC0a'.
```

Figure 1.5 – Your Vnet must have at least one IPv4 address space to use IPv6

> **Note**
>
> Azure does not yet support an IPv6-only Vnet and subnet, but you can implement dual-stack Vnets and subnets that support both IPv4 and IPv6.

Azure VNet is not limited to one IP address space assignment. We can add more IP address spaces as needed, which is great for scalability! For example, we may want to add an additional IPv4 address space to support an unexpected workload expansion.

> **Limitation**
>
> Regardless of how many addresses are contained in the IP address spaces assigned to a Vnet, the total number of private IP addresses assigned to workloads cannot exceed 65,536.

The IP address spaces assigned to a Vnet do not have to be contiguous. *Figure 1.6* shows an example of this with a Vnet that is configured to have two IPv4 address spaces that are not contiguous – 10.1.0.0/16 and 192.168.1.0/24 and an additional IPv6 address space for a dual-stack implementation – fd00:db8:deca::/48.

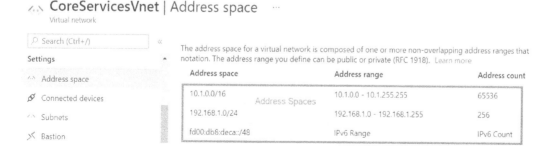

CoreServicesVnet | Address space
Virtual network

Search (Ctrl+/)	«	The address space for a virtual network is composed of one or more non-overlapping address ranges that
Settings	▲	notation. The address range you define can be public or private (RFC 1918). Learn more

Address space	Address range	Address count
10.1.0.0/16	10.1.0.0 - 10.1.255.255	65536
192.168.1.0/24	192.168.1.0 - 192.168.1.255	256
fd00:db8:deca::/48	IPv6 Range	IPv6 Count

Settings:
- Address space
- Connected devices
- Subnets
- Bastion

Figure 1.6 – A Vnet with multiple address spaces

So, which IP address spaces should we use for our Vnets in Azure? Even though it is not required, it is highly recommended to use address ranges within the private, non-internet routable address spaces! For IPv4, this will be one of the IP ranges defined in RFC 1918 and for IPv6, this will be the **Internet Engineering Task Force (IETF)** defined *Unique Local Addresses*, which use the `fc00::/7` address range.

RFC 1918 private IPv4 address ranges

Private IP address ranges defined in RFC 1918 are IP ranges that have been set aside by the IETF for private network use. They include the following:

- `10.0.0.0/8` (`10.0.0.0 – 10.255.255.255`)
- `172.16.0.0/12` (`172.16.0.0 – 172.31.255.255`)
- `192.168.0.0/16` (`192.168.0.0 – 192.168.255.255`)

Using any of the RFC 1918 private IP address ranges will require some form of address translation for internet routing and connectivity (we will cover this scenario later in this book).

Shared IPv4 address spaces reserved in RFC 6598 can also be used as they are treated as private IP address spaces in Azure. This range includes the following:

- `100.64/10` (`100.64.0.0 – 100.127.255.255`)

Other IP address spaces may work but they are not recommended as they could have undesirable routing side effects with instability! The following address ranges are not allowed to be used as Vnet IP address spaces:

- `224.0.0.0/4` (Multicast)
- `255.255.255.255/32` (Broadcast)
- `127.0.0.0/8` (Loopback)
- `169.254.0.0/16` (Link-local)
- `168.63.129.16/32` (Internal DNS)

Whatever IP address ranges you decide to use for your Vnets, it is highly recommended to plan for non-overlapping IP address spaces across Azure regions and on-premises locations in advance. You can achieve this by defining an **organization-wide** IP address scheme that ensures that each network has its own unique private IP address space if it is an Azure network or an on-premises network.

Best practice

Define an *organization-wide* IP address scheme that ensures that each *organization network* has its own unique private IP address space.

One of the reasons why this is important is that it can impact your ability to connect networks together later or leave you in a situation where you need to implement sub-optimal network address translations that add to the complexity.

For example, you cannot connect two Vnets together via **Vnet peering** if they have the same address space! *Figure 1.7* shows the error message that you will get if you attempt this:

Figure 1.7 – Vnets with overlapping address spaces cannot be peered

If you don't know what Vnet peering is, don't worry, we will cover it later in this book when we look at hybrid connectivity. You could use a VPN gateway to connect two networks with the same IP address spaces but this requires implementing address translation, which can make troubleshooting traffic flow very complex!

Planning Vnet subnet segmentation

To provide isolation within a Vnet, we can divide it into one or more subnets. Subnets are *primarily* used for workload segmentation (logical perimeters within a Vnet). *Figure 1.8* shows an example of this. In the diagram, we have a Vnet with two subnets. Web services are deployed into their own subnet (**Web tier Subnet**) and data services are deployed into their own subnet (**Data tier Subnet**).

With this approach, we can use an Azure route table to control how traffic is routed between the subnets. We can also use a **network security group** (**NSG**) or a **network virtual appliance** (**NVA**) to define allowed inbound/outbound traffic flow from/to the subnets (segments). The result of this is that if a part of our application stack is compromised, we are better placed to contain the impact of the security breach and mitigate the risk of lateral movement through the rest of our network. This is an important Zero Trust principle implementation. We will cover route tables, NSGs, and NVAs later in this book.

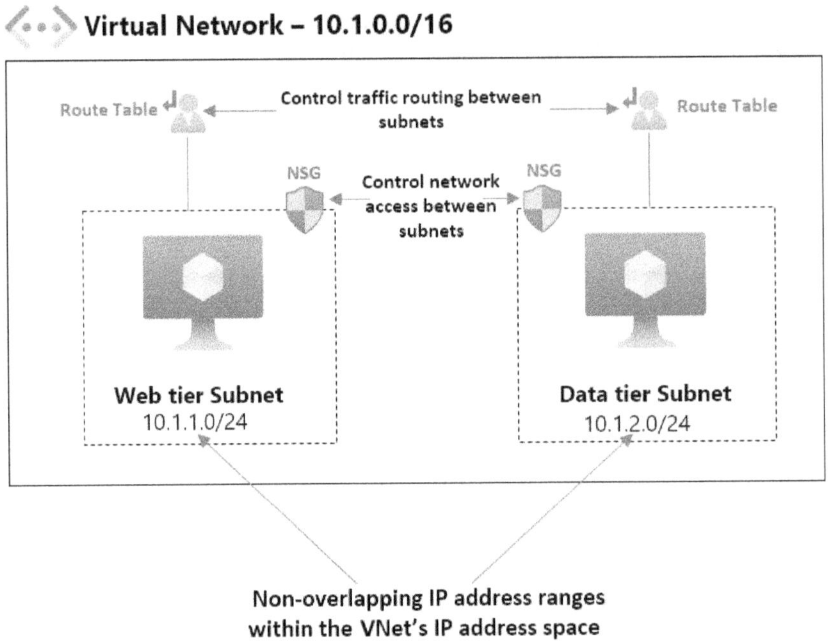

Figure 1.8 – Segmentation using subnets

How many subnets can Azure VNet have? It can have up to 3,000 subnets! Each subnet must have a unique IP address range that is within the defined IP address spaces of the Vnet (overlap is not allowed). For example, a Vnet with an IPv4 address space of 10.1.0.0/16 cannot have a subnet with an IP address range of 10.1.1.0/24 and another subnet with an address range of 10.1.1.0/25 as these ranges overlap with each other. Attempting to do so will result in the error message shown in *Figure 1.9*:

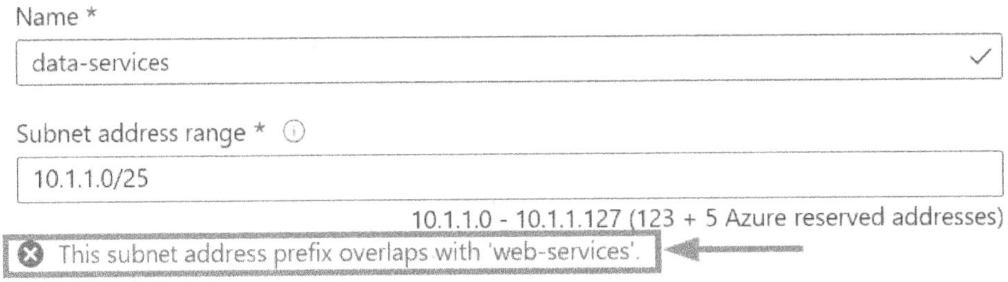

Figure 1.9 – Subnets with overlapping addresses not allowed

After defining the IP address range for a subnet, Azure reserves five IP addresses within each subnet that can't be used! The first four IP addresses and the last IP address in an Azure subnet cannot be allocated to resources for the following reasons:

- `x.x.x.<first address>`: This is reserved for protocol conformance as the network address
- `x.x.x. <second address>`: This is reserved by Azure for the default gateway of the subnet
- `x.x.x. <third address>` and `x.x.x. <fourth address>`: This is reserved by Azure to map the Azure DNS IPs to the Vnet space
- `x.x.x. <last address>`: This is reserved for protocol conformance as the broadcast address (even though Azure Vnets don't use broadcasts as we mentioned earlier)

For example, if the IP address range of your subnet is `10.1.0.0/24`, the following addresses will be reserved:

- **10.1.0.0**: Network address
- **10.1.0.1**: Default gateway address
- **10.1.0.2** and **10.1.0.3**: Used to map Azure DNS IPs to the Vnet space
- **10.1.0.255**: Broadcast address

This leaves a total of 250 addresses that can be allocated to subnet resources: `10.1.0.4 - 10.1.0.254`. Because of the required address reservation, the smallest supported IPv4 address prefix is /29, which gives five reserved addresses and three usable addresses. Specifying anything less leaves zero usable IPv4 addresses, which results in the error message shown in *Figure 1.10*:

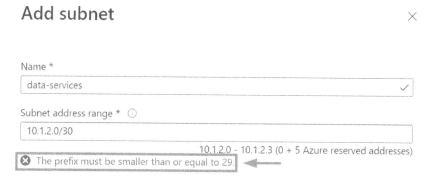

Figure 1.10 – The smallest supported IPv4 address prefix for a subnet is /29

> **Note**
> The smallest supported size for an Azure IPv4 subnet is /29. The largest is /2.

If you are implementing a dual-stack design, the standard size of the assigned IPv6 address space should be /64. This is in line with the standard defined by the IETF. A /64 space is the smallest subnet that can be used locally if auto-configuration is desired. Any attempt to add an IPv6 address space that is not a /64 will result in the error message shown in *Figure 1.11*:

Figure 1.11 – Only a /64 address space assignment allowed for a subnet

When planning your subnets, make sure that you design for scalability. Workloads in your subnets should not cover the entire address space, giving you no room to add more workloads if needed. Plan and reserve some address space for the future. Also, take into consideration that some network resources such as the VMSS may need to dynamically add more workloads based on incoming requests. Modifying the IP address range of an Azure subnet that has workloads deployed is no straightforward task. It involves you removing all existing resources! Attempting this will result in the error message shown in *Figure 1.12*:

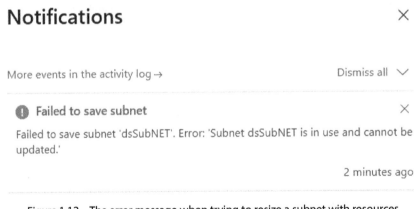

Figure 1.12 – The error message when trying to resize a subnet with resources

Working with platform services in subnets

For most organizations, the main services that they will deploy into Azure VNet subnets are **infrastructure-as-a-service (IaaS)** services such as VMs and VMSSs but there are currently about 23 more services that can be deployed into a Vnet subnet, including platform services such as Azure SQL Managed Instance, App Service, Cache for Redis, and Azure Kubernetes Service. Deploying a supported platform service into a Vnet subnet is referred to as **Vnet integration** or **Vnet injection**.

A full list of services that are supported for VNet integration can be found at `https://docs.microsoft.com/en-us/azure/virtual-network/virtual-network-for-azure-services#services-that-can-be-deployed-into-a-virtual-network`.

There are about 25 services that can be deployed into a Vnet subnet, as shown in *Figure 1.13*:

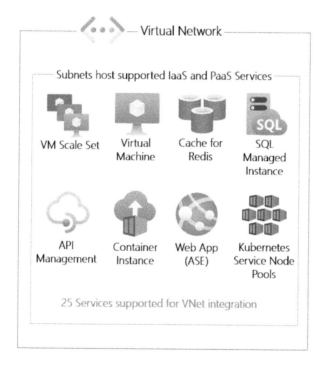

Figure 1.13 – Various types of services supported for Vnet integration

Most PaaS services that support Vnet integration impose restrictions on the subnets that they can be deployed into, and this should be considered when planning your subnets. Here are some of the restrictions to consider:

- About 14 services require a **dedicated subnet** — this means that they cannot be combined with other services in the same subnet. For example, a VPN gateway cannot be deployed together with another service in the same subnet – the subnet must be dedicated only to that service!

- Still, on dedicated subnets, some services allow multiple instances of the same service in the same dedicated subnet while some require a dedicated subnet per service instance! For example, the Azure SQL Managed Instance's service allows multiple instances of the same service to be deployed into the dedicated subnet (*Figure 1.14*), while the Azure Spring Cloud service requires dedicated subnets per service instance (*Figure 1.14*):

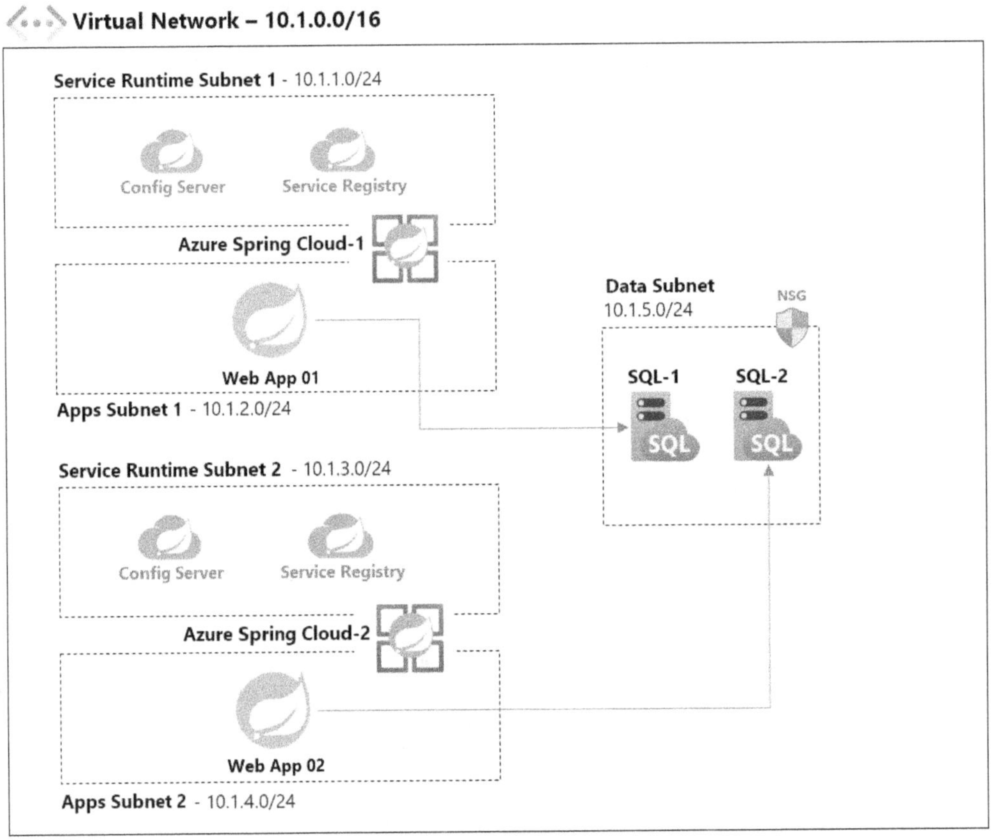

Figure 1.14 – Two SQL-managed instances in the same dedicated subnet.
Spring cloud requires dedicated subnets per instance

- Some platform services require their subnets to be called a specific name. For example, the subnet that the Azure Firewall service is deployed into must be called **AzureFirewallSubnet**, the subnet that the VPN Gateway service is deployed into must be called **GatewaySubnet**, and the subnet that the Azure Bastion service is deployed into must be called **AzureBastionSubnet**. This is required for some automation components relating to the services to work.

- Some platform services require a minimum **Classless Inter-Domain Routing (CIDR)** block for their subnets. For example, the subnet that the Azure Bastion service is deployed into must have a minimum /26 prefix.

- Some platform services require permissions to establish basic network configuration rules for the subnet that they will be deployed into. The process of assigning this permission is called **subnet delegation**. For example, when a SQL-managed instance is deployed into a subnet, it automatically creates an NSG and a route table and applies them to that subnet.

The key takeaway here is this – before deploying platform services into subnets, ensure that you follow the guidance in the service documentation regarding the aforementioned considerations to avoid inconsistencies in service functionalities. Always refer to the documentation for up-to-date information: `https://docs.microsoft.com/en-us/azure/virtual-network/virtual-network-for-azure-services#services-that-can-be-deployed-into-a-virtual-network`.

Now that you have some understanding of how to plan key aspects of Azure VNet, let us go ahead and get some implementation going!

Hands-on exercise – creating a single-stack VNet in Azure

In this exercise, we will create a single-stack IPv4 network for a fictional organization called **CharisTech**, which is in the process of migrating some on-premises applications to Azure. We will implement two VNets and subnets to support workloads that will be migrated. Here are the tasks that we will complete in this exercise:

- *Task 1*: Creating the CharisTech resource group
- *Task 2*: Creating the **CoreServicesVNet** VNet and subnets
- *Task 3*: Verifying the creation of VNets and subnets

Figure 1.15 shows the outcome that we'll get to at the end of the tasks:

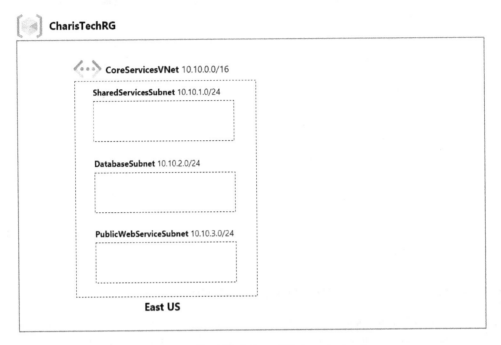

Figure 1.15 – CharisTech Azure VNets and subnets

Task 1 – creating the CharisTech resource group

A resource group is a logical container for managing related Azure resources. In this task, we will create a resource group called **CharisTechRG** that will hold the networking resources that we will create in other tasks:

1.   Open a web browser and browse to `https://portal.azure.com`.

2.   On the left-hand side, click on the portal menu icon, then click on **Create a resource**:

Figure 1.16 – Create a resource

3. In the search area, type `Resource group` and press *Enter*. Click on the **Create** button:

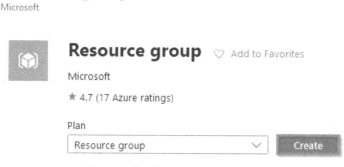

Figure 1.17 – Create a resource group

4. In the **Basics** tab, enter the following values:

    *   **Subscription**: Select your Azure subscription (*1*)

    *   **Resource group**: `CharisTechRG` (*2*)

    *   **Region**: **East US** (*3*)

    Then, select **Review + create** (*4*):

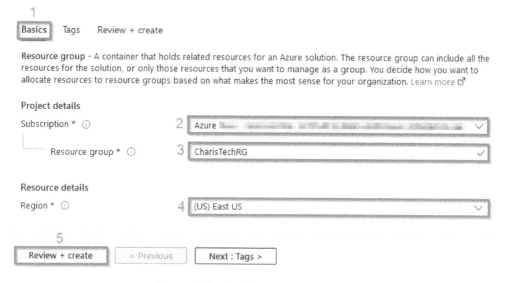

Figure 1.18 – Creating a resource group

5. Select **Create**. It should only take a few seconds to create the resource group.

6. In the top-right corner of the window, select the notification icon (the bell icon). Then, select **Go to resource group** to open the newly created resource group:

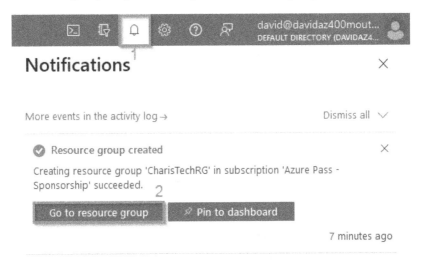

Figure 1.19 – Opening the newly created resource group

Leave this window open for the next task. Now that we have a resource group that we can use as a management container, let us proceed to create the VNets and subnets.

Task 2 – creating the CoreServicesVNet VNet and subnets

The first network that we will create is the **CoreServicesVNet** VNet (*Figure 1.15*). The network will be deployed in the East US region. It will be segmented into three subnets that will host the following workloads:

*   Public web services (**PublicWebServiceSubnet**)

*   Databases (**DatabaseSubnet**)

*   Shared services that are key to the operations of the business, such as domain controllers (**SharedServicesSubnet**)

Let's get started:

1. In the **CharisTechRG** window, select **+ Create**. In the search box, enter Virtual Network. Select **Virtual Network** in the search results:

Figure 1.20 – Creating a resource

2.   On the **Virtual Network** page, select **Create**.

3.   On the **Create virtual network** window, in the **Basics** tab, enter the following values:

- **Subscription**: Select your Azure subscription

- **Resource group**: CharisTechRG

- **Name**: CoreServicesVNet

- **Region**: East US

Then, click **Next: IP Addresses >**:

Create virtual network

Basics	IP Addresses	Security	Tags	Review + create

Azure Virtual Network (VNet) is the fundamental building block for your private network in Azure. VNet enables many types of Azure resources, such as Azure Virtual Machines (VM), to securely communicate with each other, the internet, and on-premises networks. VNet is similar to a traditional network that you'd operate in your own data center, but brings with it additional benefits of Azure's infrastructure such as scale, availability, and isolation. Learn more about virtual network

Project details

Subscription * ⓘ   2   Azure

          Resource group * ⓘ   3   CharisTechRG
                                       Create new

Instance details

Name *   4   CoreServicesVNet

Region *   5   East US

6

[Review + create]   [< Previous] [Next : IP Addresses >]   Download a template for automation

Figure 1.21 – Creating the VNet

4. In the **IP Addresses** tab, change the default IP address space to `10.10.0.0/16`. Then, select **+ Add subnet**:

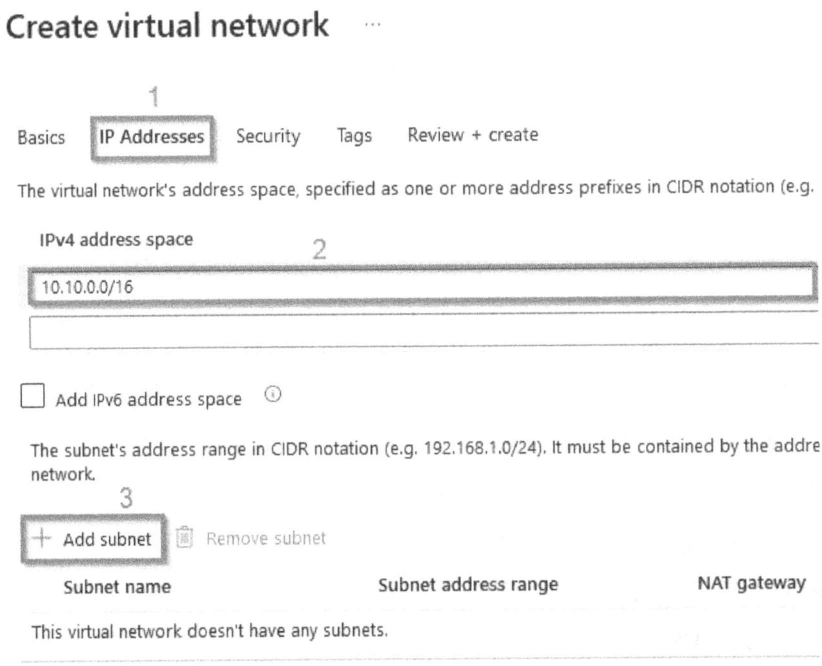

Create virtual network   ...

Figure 1.22 – Setting the IP address

5. In the **Add subnet** window, configure the following:

- **Subnet name**: `SharedServicesSubnet`

- **Subnet address range**: `10.10.1.0/24`

- **NAT gateway: None**

- **Service endpoint: 0 selected**

Then, click **Add**:

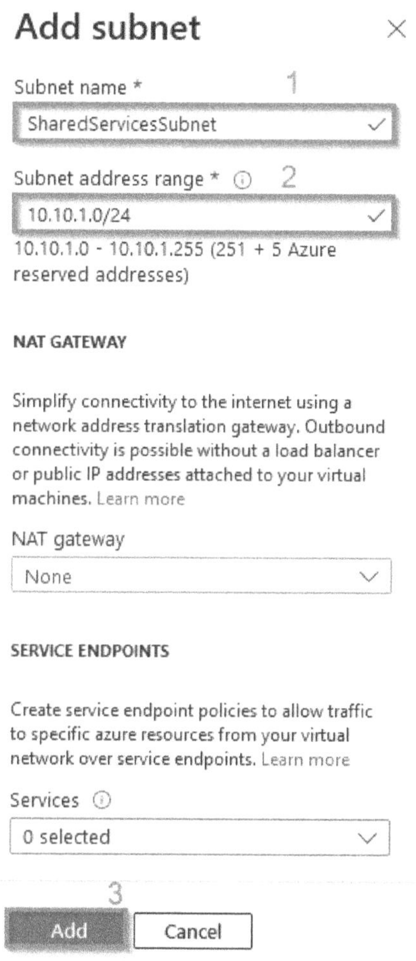

Add subnet ✕

Subnet name *   1

SharedServicesSubnet   ✓

Subnet address range * ⓘ   2

10.10.1.0/24   ✓

10.10.1.0 - 10.10.1.255 (251 + 5 Azure
reserved addresses)

NAT GATEWAY

Simplify connectivity to the internet using a
network address translation gateway. Outbound
connectivity is possible without a load balancer
or public IP addresses attached to your virtual
machines. Learn more

NAT gateway

None   ⌄

SERVICE ENDPOINTS

Create service endpoint policies to allow traffic
to specific azure resources from your virtual
network over service endpoints. Learn more

Services ⓘ

0 selected   ⌄

3

Add   Cancel

Figure 1.23 – Adding a subnet

6. Click on + **Add subnet** and repeat *Step 5* to add the following subnet configurations:

Subnet	Configuration option	Configuration value
DatabaseSubnet	Subnet name	DatabaseSubnet
	Subnet address range	10.10.2.0/24
PublicWebServiceSubnet	Subnet name	PublicWebServiceSubnet
	Subnet address range	10.10.3.0/24

Table 1.1 – Subnet configuration details

7.   The configuration should look like *Figure 1.24.* Click on **Review + create**:

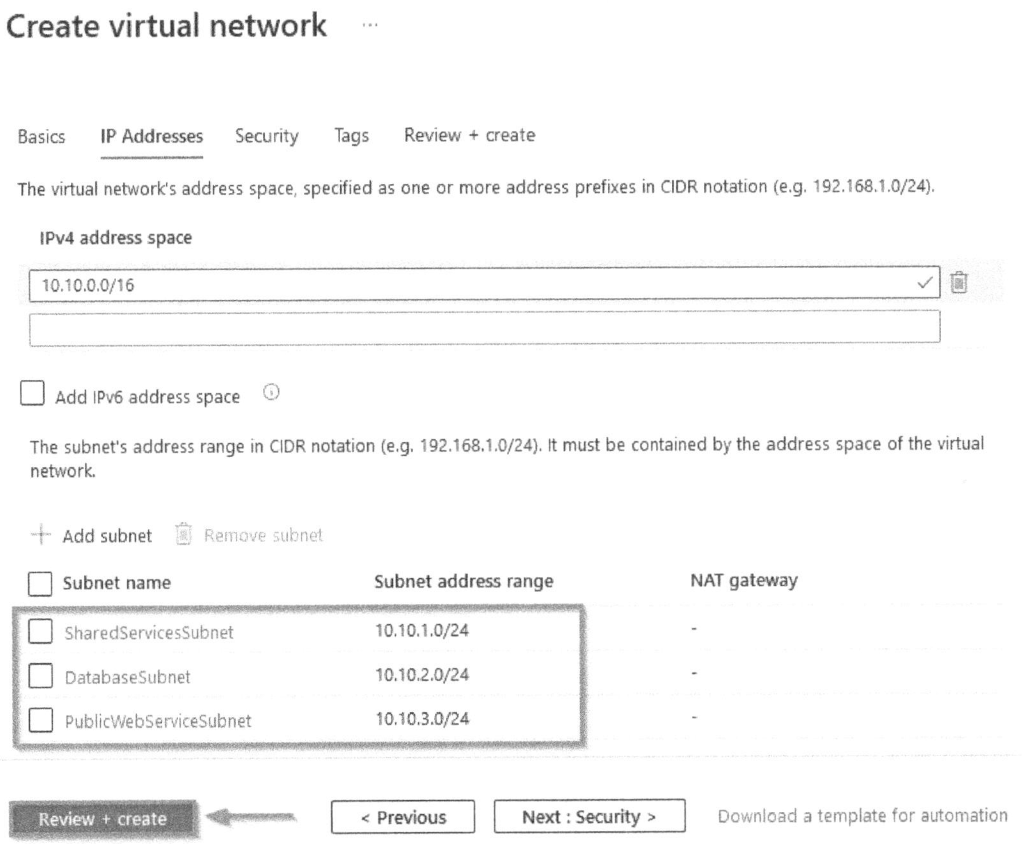

Create virtual network   ···

Basics   **IP Addresses**   Security   Tags   Review + create

The virtual network's address space, specified as one or more address prefixes in CIDR notation (e.g. 192.168.1.0/24).

IPv4 address space

| 10.10.0.0/16 | ✓ | 🗑 |

| | |

☐ Add IPv6 address space ⓘ

The subnet's address range in CIDR notation (e.g. 192.168.1.0/24). It must be contained by the address space of the virtual network.

╶┼╴ Add subnet   🗑 Remove subnet

☐ Subnet name	Subnet address range	NAT gateway
☐ SharedServicesSubnet	10.10.1.0/24	-
☐ DatabaseSubnet	10.10.2.0/24	-
☐ PublicWebServiceSubnet	10.10.3.0/24	-

| Review + create | ⟵ | < Previous | Next : Security > | Download a template for automation |

Figure 1.24 – Subnets added to the VNet configuration

8.   Select **Create**. It should only take a few seconds to create the VNet and subnets.

Awesome! After the deployment completes, let us review what has been created.

Task 3 – verifying the creation of the VNet and subnets

In this task, we will review the resources created in the last task:

1.   Click on **Go to resource** to open the newly created VNet:

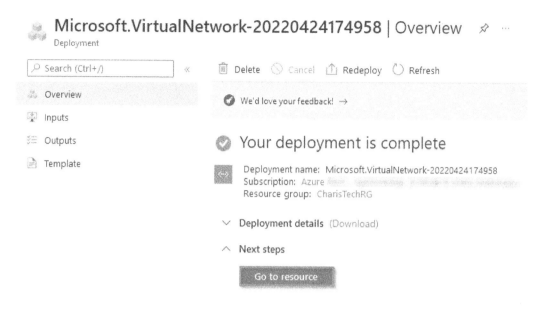

Figure 1.25 –Microsoft VNet overview

2. In the **CoreServicesVNet virtual network** blade, in the **Settings** section, click on **Subnets** to review the subnets that were created:

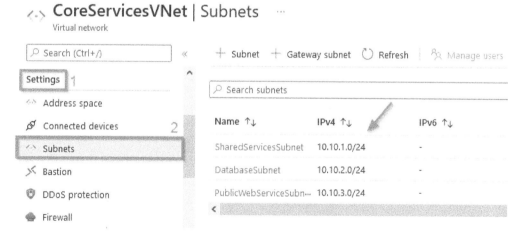

Figure 1.26 – Reviewing the subnets

You can leave this window open for the next task. Now that we have a resource group that we can use as a management container, let us proceed to create the VNets and subnets.

Hands-on exercise – creating a dual-stack VNet in Azure

In this exercise, we will create a dual-stack network in Azure that supports both IPv4 and IPv6 for the fictional organization called **CharisTech**. The activities in this task will be completed using the Azure CLI to give you familiarity with the different Azure management tools. Here are the tasks that we will complete in this exercise:

- *Task 1*: Creating the dual-stack **EngineeringVNet** VNet and subnets
- *Task 2*: Verifying the creation of the dual-stack VNet and subnets

Figure 1.27 shows the outcome that we'll get to at the end of the tasks:

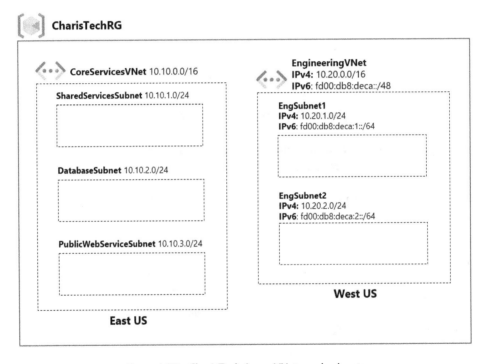

Figure 1.27 – CharisTech Azure VNets and subnets

Let's get started!

Task 1 – creating the dual-stack EngineeringVNet VNet and subnets

1. Open a web browser and go to the Azure Portal at https://portal.azure.com. Sign in with your admin user account credentials.

2. In the Azure Portal, click on the **Cloud Shell** icon in the top right corner of the Azure Portal:

Figure 1.28 – Click the icon to open Cloud Shell

3. (*Optional*) If this is your first time launching **Cloud Shell**, you will be prompted to select between the **Bash** and **PowerShell** environments. Select **Bash**. You will also be prompted to create a storage account that will be used by **Cloud Shell**. Select **Create Storage**.

4. If this is not your first launch, ensure you have **Bash** selected for your environment:

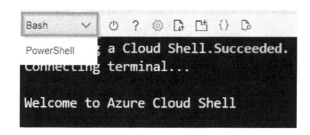

Figure 1.29 – Select the Bash shell environment

5. In **Cloud Shell**, enter the following commands to set the values that we will use for the following variables: resource group, location, and VNet:

```
group=CharisTechRG
location=westus
VNet=EngineeringVNet
```

6. Create a VNet with the az network VNet create command. The following command creates a VNet named EngineeringVNet with one subnet named EngSubnet1. Both the VNet and the subnet are dual-stack:

```
az network VNet create --name $VNet --resource-group $group
--location $location --address-prefixes "10.20.0.0/16"
"fd00:db8:deca::/48" --subnet-name EngSubnet1 --subnet-prefix
"10.20.1.0/24" "fd00:db8:deca:1::/64"
```

7. Add a second subnet with the az network VNet subnet create command. The following command adds a dual-stack subnet named EngSubnet2 to the EngineeringVNet network that we created earlier:

```
az network VNet subnet create -n EngSubnet2 --address-prefixes
"10.20.2.0/24" "fd00:db8:deca:2::/64" --resource-group $group
--VNet-name $VNet
```

Now that the dual-stack VNets and subnets are created, let us verify them.

Task 2 – verifying the creation of the dual-stack VNet and subnets

Let's get started!

1. In the **Cloud Shell** environment, enter the following command to list the VNets in the subscription and output the result in a table format:

    ```
    az network VNet list --resource-group CharisTechRG --output
    table
    ```

    The output should be like the output shown in *Figure 1.30*:

    ```
    david@Azure:~$ az network vnet list --resource-group CharisTechRG --output table
    Name                ResourceGroup    Location    NumSubnets    Prefixes
    ---------------     -------------    --------    ----------    -----------
    EngineeringVNet     CharisTechRG     westus      2             10.20.0.0/16, fd00:db8:deca::/48
    CoreServicesVNet    CharisTechRG     eastus      3             10.10.0.0/16
    david@Azure:~$
    ```

    Figure 1.30 – The VNet list output

As you can see, using command-line management tools such as the Azure CLI greatly streamlines resource management in Azure!

Understanding private IP address assignment for subnet workloads

When resources are deployed into an Azure VNet subnet, a private IP address is automatically assigned from the subnet's address range. If the subnet is a single-stack subnet (IPv4 only), Azure assigns an IPv4 address to the workload. If the subnet is a dual-stack subnet (both IPv4 and IPv6), Azure assigns both an IPv4 and an IPv6 address if the service supports IPv6 assignments. As of the time of writing, only VMs and VMSS NICs support both IPv4 and IPv6, other VNet services/resources support only IPv4 private IP assignments.

There are two methods for private IP assignments in an Azure VNet subnet (*Figure 1.31*):

- The first method is **dynamic** assignment where the next available unassigned or unreserved private IP address, from the subnet's address range, is automatically assigned to a resource. This is the equivalent of using **Dynamic Host Configuration Protocol (DHCP)** on-premises. For example, in a subnet with a 10.10.1.0/24 address range, if the 10.10.1.4 address is already assigned to another resource, the next available address – 10.10.1.5 – is automatically assigned to the next resource. This method is the default allocation method for all VNet resources, including VNet-integrated platform services. For VM and VMSS NICs, dynamic

IP addresses are released if a network interface is deleted or re-assigned to a different subnet within the same VNet.

Figure 1.31 – VNet resource private IP assignment options

- The second method is **static** assignment, where an unassigned or unreserved IP address can be reserved for a resource from the subnet's address range. This may be necessary for situations where clients or other services are hardcoded to locate an application via its IP address instead of its **Domain Name System (DNS)** record (we will cover DNS options in Azure in the second chapter of this book). *It is highly recommended to implement a static IP assignment by changing the private IP allocation method from the Azure platform instead of setting the IP statically from the operating system* (as we would do on-premises). The latter method could lead to loss of access if the resource is moved into a different subnet. This method is not supported by all VNet resources but it is supported for common ones, such as VM NIC (*Figure 1.31*) and Azure Cache for Redis (*Figure 1.32*).

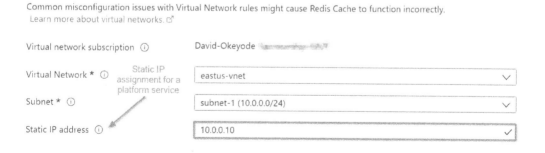

Figure 1.32 – Static IP assignment for a VNet deployed Cache for Redis resource

As a general rule, you should avoid static private IP assignments as much as possible. This is because cloud-hosted workloads are usually dynamic with capabilities such as auto-scaling that allow resources to be added/removed in response to the volume of requests being received. Using the default dynamic assignment method means that we have one less thing to worry about.

It is also important to note that VM network interfaces can have more than one private IP assignment (*Figure 1.33*). Actually, they can have up to 256 private IP assignments!

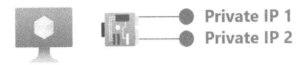

Figure 1.33 – Multiple private IP assignments for a VM NIC

Enough discussion for now; let us review this in practice. But first, we need to determine the locations and VM sizes that we will be using.

Hands-on exercise – determining the VM location and sizes for future exercises

To complete some of the hands-on exercises in this book (such as the exercise after this one), you will need to deploy VMs for testing. In Azure, not all VM sizes are available in all subscription regions! There are also CPU quota limits for VM families and subscription regions (*Figure 1.34*).

	Quota name	Region ↑		Subscription	Current Usage		
☐	Total Regional vCPUs	East US		David-Okeyode-		0%	0 of 10
☐	Virtual Machines	East US		David-Okeyode-		0%	0 of 25,000
☐	Virtual Machine Scale Sets	East US		David-Okeyode-		0%	0 of 2,500
☐	Dedicated vCPUs	East US	VM family CPU limits	David-Okeyode-		0%	0 of 3,000
☐	Total Regional Spot vCPUs	East US		David-Okeyode-		0%	0 of 10
☐	Standard LSv3 Family vCPUs	East US		David-Okeyode-		0%	0 of 10
☐	Standard LASv3 Family vCPUs	East US		David-Okeyode-		0%	0 of 10
☐	Basic A Family vCPUs ⓘ	East US		David-Okeyode-		0%	0 of 10

Figure 1.34 – Regional and VM family CPU limits per subscription

In this exercise, you will evaluate your subscription to determine the VM sizes and locations to use for the exercises in the upcoming chapters of this book. Here are the tasks that you will complete in this exercise:

- *Task 1*: Determining the CPU quota limits for recommended subscription regions

- *Task 2*: Determining the VM size availability for recommended subscription regions

For the hands-on exercise, I will be defaulting to the **East US** and **West US** Azure regions as these are the regions that I have used throughout the rest of the book. While I recommend that you also use these regions, you do not need to stick with this recommendation. There is nothing particular about them. If you decide to use other regions instead, simply replace the values as you run the specified commands. You can obtain a list of Azure locations with the `az account list-locations -o table` Azure CLI command.

Let's get into this!

Task 1 – determining the CPU quota limits for recommended subscription regions

The steps are as follows:

1. Open a web browser and go to the Azure Portal at `https://portal.azure.com`. Sign in with your admin user account credentials.

2. In the Azure Portal, click on the Cloud Shell icon in the top right corner of the screen, as shown in *Figure 1.35*.

Figure 1.35 – Click the icon to open Cloud Shell

3. Ensure you have Bash selected for your environment as we will be working with Azure CLI commands:

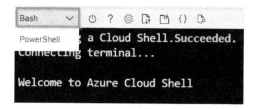

Figure 1.36 – Select the Bash shell environment

4. Use the following two commands to verify the CPU quota limit for the **East US** and **West US** Azure regions. If you plan on using different regions, remember to replace the value for the location parameter with the regions that you are planning to use:

```
az vm list-usage --location eastus --output table
az vm list-usage --location westus --output table
```

5. In the output of the commands in *step 4*, review the **Total Regional vCPUs** usage and limit to ensure that you have sufficient CPU quota available in the region. *Figure 1.37* shows a limit of **10** vCPUs for the East US region in my subscription and current usage of **4** vCPUs (by existing VM deployments). This means that I can only deploy additional 6 vCPUs in the region. The only exceptions to this are if I remove existing VM resources to free up usage or raise a Microsoft support ticket to increase the limit for that region in my subscription. *To follow the hands-on exercises, ensure that you have a minimum of 6 vCPUs available in both regions!*

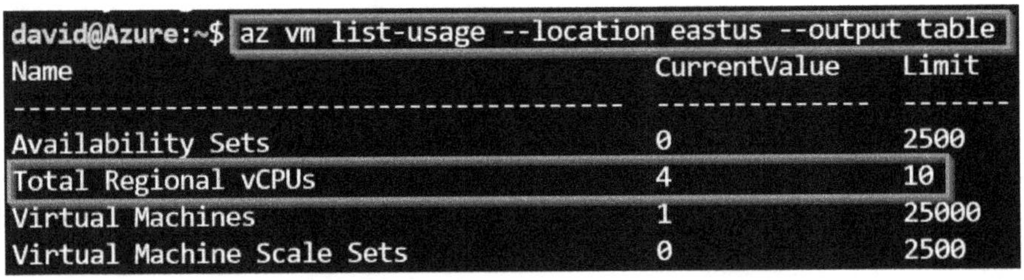

```
david@Azure:~$ az vm list-usage --location eastus --output table
Name                              CurrentValue    Limit
--------------------------------  ------------    -------
Availability Sets                 0               2500
Total Regional vCPUs              4               10
Virtual Machines                  1               25000
Virtual Machine Scale Sets        0               2500
```

Figure 1.37 – The total regional vCPU usage

6. Still in the output of the commands in *step 4*, review the **Standard BS Family vCPUs** usage and limit to ensure that you have sufficient CPU quota for the VM size family that we will be using in the hands-on exercises. *Figure 1.37* shows a limit of **10** vCPUs for the East US region in my subscription and current usage of **0** vCPUs. I will be defaulting to this VM family size in the exercise chapters. If you plan on using a different VM family, ensure that you have sufficient vCPU quota for it in the regions that you plan to use.

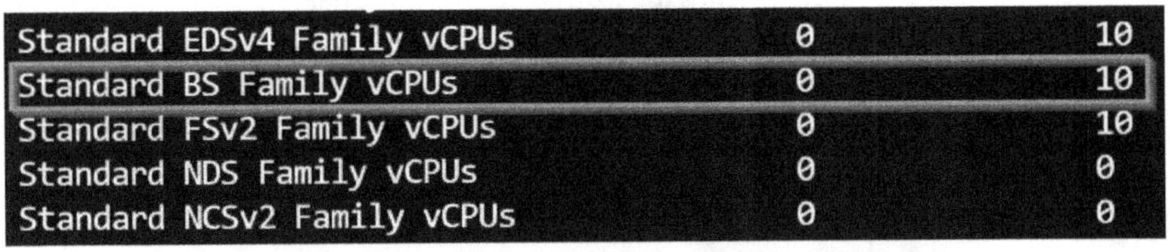

```
Standard EDSv4 Family vCPUs                  0                10
Standard BS Family vCPUs                     0                10
Standard FSv2 Family vCPUs                   0                10
Standard NDS Family vCPUs                    0                0
Standard NCSv2 Family vCPUs                  0                0
```

Figure 1.38 – Standard BS VM Family regional vCPU usage

7. In **Cloud Shell**, use the following two commands to verify available sizes for the `Standard_B` VM family in the **East US** and **West US** Azure regions. I will be defaulting to a VM size in this VM family. If you plan on using different regions, remember to replace the value for the location parameter with the regions that you are planning to use:

```
az vm list-skus --location eastus --size Standard_B
--all --query "[?restrictions[0].reasonCode !=
\`NotAvailableForSubscription\`]" --output table


az vm list-skus --location westus --size Standard_B
--all --query "[?restrictions[0].reasonCode !=
\`NotAvailableForSubscription\`]" --output table
```

8. In the output of the commands in *step 7*, review to ensure that the **Standard_B2s** VM size has no restrictions in both regions. *Figure 1.39* shows that the size is available for my subscription in the **East US** region. Leave **Cloud Shell** open for the next exercise.

```
david@Azure:~$ az vm list-skus --location eastus --size Standard_B --all --query "[?restrictions[0]
.reasonCode != \`NotAvailableForSubscription\`]" --output table
ResourceType      Name             Tier        Size    Family
----------------  ---------------  ----------  ------  ------------------
virtualMachines   Standard_B12ms   Standard    B12ms   standardBSFamily
virtualMachines   Standard_B16ms   Standard    B16ms   standardBSFamily
virtualMachines   Standard_B11s    Standard    B11s    standardBSFamily
virtualMachines   Standard_B1ms    Standard    B1ms    standardBSFamily
virtualMachines   Standard_B1s     Standard    B1s     standardBSFamily
virtualMachines   Standard_B20ms   Standard    B20ms   standardBSFamily
virtualMachines   Standard_B2ms    Standard    B2ms    standardBSFamily
virtualMachines   Standard_B2s     Standard    B2s     standardBSFamily
virtualMachines   Standard_B4ms    Standard    B4ms    standardBSFamily
virtualMachines   Standard_B8ms    Standard    B8ms    standardBSFamily
```

Figure 1.39 – The Standard_B2s VM size availability check

Now that you have verified the regions and VM size that you will be using, make a note of these as you will be needing them in the upcoming exercises in this chapter and in the rest of the chapters of this book.

Hands-on exercise – exploring private IP assignments

In this exercise, you will explore private IP assignment options for VNet resources. Here are the tasks that you will complete in this exercise:

- *Task 1* – deploying VMs with dynamic and static private IP assignments

Let's get into this!

Task 1 – deploying VMs with dynamic and static private IP assignments

The steps are as follows:

1. In the Azure Cloud Shell environment, enter the following commands to set the values that we will use for the following variables: resource group, location, VNet, subnet, and VM size. Replace the `Standard_B2s` value if you are using a different size than you verified in the previous exercise:

```
group=CharisTechRG
location=eastus
VNet=CoreServicesVNet
subnet=PublicWebServiceSubnet
size=Standard_B2s
```

2. Deploy a VM called `WebVM0` into `PublicWebServiceSubnet` of `CoreServicesVNet` with the `az vm create` command. This will default to the dynamic private IP assignment method:

```
az vm create -g $group -n WebVM0 --image UbuntuLTS --admin-
username azureuser --generate-ssh-keys --VNet-name $VNet
--subnet $subnet --size $size --public-ip-address ""
```

The following figure shows the output of this command. Ignore the warning about the public IP as the VM is created without a public IP assigned.

```
david@Azure:~$ az vm create -g $group -n WebVM0 --image UbuntuLTS --admin-username
azureuser --generate-ssh-keys --vnet-name $vnet --subnet $subnet --size $size --pub
lic-ip-address ""
It is recommended to use parameter "--public-ip-sku Standard" to create new VM with
 Standard public IP. Please note that the default public IP used for VM creation wi
ll be changed from Basic to Standard in the future.
{
  "fqdns": "",
  "id": "/subscriptions/████████ ███ ███ ███ ████████/resourceGroups/CharisT
echRG/providers/Microsoft.Compute/virtualMachines/WebVM0",
  "location": "eastus",
  "macAddress": "00-0D-3A-1F-C8-7C",
  "powerState": "VM running",
  "privateIpAddress": "10.10.3.4",◄──────
  "publicIpAddress": "",
  "resourceGroup": "CharisTechRG",
  "zones": ""
}
```

Figure 1.40 – VM creation with the default dynamic private IP assignment

3. Deploy a VM called `WebVM1` into `PublicWebServiceSubnet` of `CoreServicesVNet` with the `az vm create` command. This time around, we will specify a static private IP assignment of `10.10.3.10`:

```
az vm create -g $group -n WebVM1 --image UbuntuLTS --admin-
username azureuser --generate-ssh-keys --VNet-name $VNet
--subnet $subnet --size $size --public-ip-address "" --private-
ip-address "10.10.3.10"
```

The following figure shows the output of this command. Ignore the warning about the public IP as the VM is created without a public IP assigned.

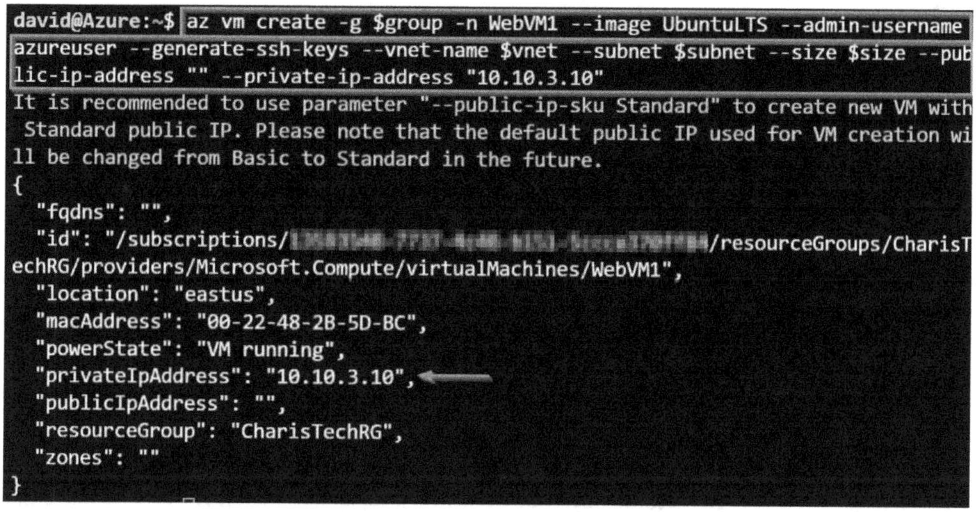

```
david@Azure:~$ az vm create -g $group -n WebVM1 --image UbuntuLTS --admin-username
azureuser --generate-ssh-keys --vnet-name $vnet --subnet $subnet --size $size --pub
lic-ip-address "" --private-ip-address "10.10.3.10"
It is recommended to use parameter "--public-ip-sku Standard" to create new VM with
 Standard public IP. Please note that the default public IP used for VM creation wi
ll be changed from Basic to Standard in the future.
{
  "fqdns": "",
  "id": "/subscriptions/1███████-████-████-████-█████████████/resourceGroups/CharisT
echRG/providers/Microsoft.Compute/virtualMachines/WebVM1",
  "location": "eastus",
  "macAddress": "00-22-48-2B-5D-BC",
  "powerState": "VM running",
  "privateIpAddress": "10.10.3.10",◄──────
  "publicIpAddress": "",
  "resourceGroup": "CharisTechRG",
  "zones": ""
}
```

Figure 1.41 – VM creation with the default dynamic private IP assignment

4.   Review the private IP assignment of the VM network interfaces using the `az network nic list` command:

```
az network nic list -g $group --query "[*].{NIC:name,
PrivateIP: ipConfigurations[0].privateIpAddress, Assignment:
ipConfigurations[0].privateIpAllocationMethod, IPVersion:
ipConfigurations[0].privateIpAddressVersion}" -o table
```

The --query parameter is used to sort through the JSON array response to select the properties that we are interested in. The following screenshot shows what the output looks like:

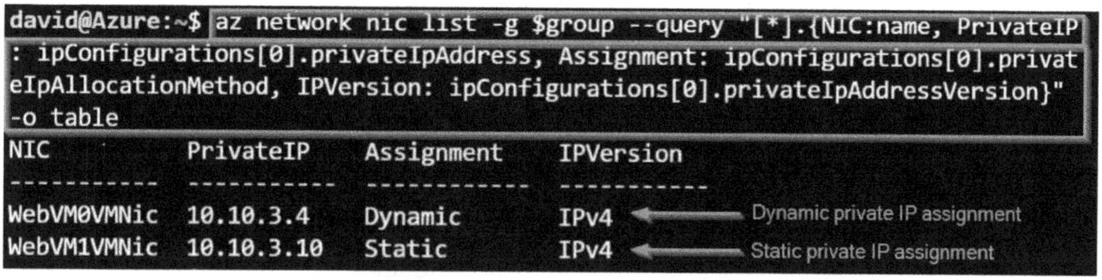

```
david@Azure:~$ az network nic list -g $group --query "[*].{NIC:name, PrivateIP
: ipConfigurations[0].privateIpAddress, Assignment: ipConfigurations[0].privat
eIpAllocationMethod, IPVersion: ipConfigurations[0].privateIpAddressVersion}"
-o table
NIC            PrivateIP      Assignment      IPVersion
-----------    -----------    -----------     -----------
WebVM0VMNic    10.10.3.4      Dynamic         IPv4   ◄────── Dynamic private IP assignment
WebVM1VMNic    10.10.3.10     Static          IPv4   ◄────── Static private IP assignment
```

Figure 1.42 – The VM NIC dynamic private IP assignment

Leave **Cloud Shell** open for the last exercise in this chapter.

Hands-on exercise – cleaning up resources

In this exercise, we will remove the resources that we created in the chapter exercises to avoid running up a large cost in Azure!

In **Cloud Shell**, run the following command to delete the `CharisTechRG` resource group. This will remove all the resources that we created for the exercises in this chapter:

```
az group delete --name CharisTechRG --yes
```

Summary

In this chapter, we covered an overview of what Azure VNet is. We discussed core VNet planning concepts such as designing a consistent naming scheme, which is critical to resource identification, especially in logging scenarios that we will cover later in this book. We discussed key considerations around selecting the right regions to deploy your networks into, specifying an IP address space that scales, and implementing private IP assignments.

We also carried out hands-on exercises on creating single-stack and dual-stack VNets, determining VM location and sizes for future exercises, and exploring private IP assignments to further solidify the concepts that you learned in this chapter.

The skills that you gained in this chapter are foundational to your being able to design reliable network architectures in Azure to host business-critical applications.

Azure network engineering is a deep and complex topic and we're only just starting to scratch the surface. In the next chapter, we will cover one of the most important aspects of designing scalable networks in Azure – DNS.

Further reading

For more information about the topics covered in this chapter, you can refer to the following:

- Explore Azure networking services – https://docs.microsoft.com/en-us/learn/modules/azure-networking-fundamentals/
- Configure and manage VNets for Azure administrators – https://docs.microsoft.com/en-us/learn/paths/azure-administrator-manage-virtual-networks/

2
Designing and Implementing Name Resolution

Domain Name System (DNS) servers are used to host records that translate human-readable domain names into machine-readable IP addresses (used by computers to communicate with each other). Traditionally, DNS servers are hosted on a customer-managed infrastructure, but Azure offers multiple options to implement name resolution without us having to manage the underlying infrastructure. This chapter covers these options for both internal and external name resolution scenarios. We will discuss what Azure DNS is, its features, and use cases. We will cover how to configure Azure DNS for private and public name resolution scenarios.

In this chapter, we will cover the following main topics:

- A hands-on exercise – provisioning resources for the chapter's exercises
- Name resolution scenarios and options
- Internal name resolution scenarios and options
- External name resolution scenarios and options
- A hands-on exercise – clean up resources

By the end of this chapter, you will have a strong understanding of the following:

- Azure name resolution options for private client scenarios
- Azure name resolution options for public client scenarios
- Using the default Azure-provided DNS for internal name resolution
- Using customer-managed DNS servers for internal name resolution
- Using Azure Private DNS for internal name resolution
- Using Azure Public DNS for external name resolution

Let's get into this!

Technical requirements

To follow along with the instructions in this chapter, you will need the following:

- A PC with an internet connection
- An Azure subscription

Before we proceed to cover the objectives of this chapter, let us prepare our Azure subscription for the hands-on exercises that we will be completing later.

A hands-on exercise – provisioning resources for the chapter's exercises

To follow along with the exercises in this chapter, we will provision some Azure resources for our fictional organization, **CharisTech**. I have prepared an Azure ARM template in the GitHub repository of this book for this purpose. The template will deploy two peered virtual networks in two Azure regions, as shown in *Figure 2.1*.

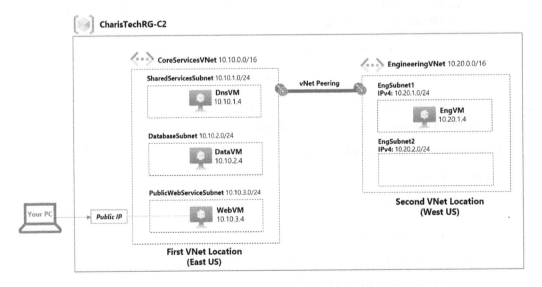

Figure 2.1 – Resources deployed via the provided ARM template

The first VNet (**CoreServicesVNet**) will have three subnets, with a virtual machine in each subnet. The second VNet (**EngineeringVNet**) will have two subnets, with a virtual machine in one subnet. One of the virtual machines (**WebVM**) will be assigned a public IP address, so you can connect to it from your PC over the internet. Here are the tasks that we will complete in this exercise:

- **Task 1**: Initialize template deployment in GitHub
- **Task 2**: Complete parameters and deploy a template to Azure

Let's get into this!

Task 1 – initializing template deployment in GitHub

The steps are as follows:

1. Open a web browser and navigate to `https://packt.link/kldEf`. This link will open the GitHub repository that has the ARM template to deploy the resources that we need.

2. In the GitHub repository that opens, click on **Deploy to Azure**, as shown in *Figure 2.2*.

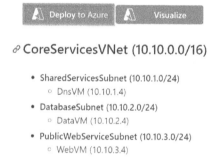

Figure 2.2 – Start the template deployment

3. If prompted to authenticate, sign in to the Azure portal with your administrative username and password.

4. In the **Custom deployment** window, configure the following:

    - **Subscription**: Select the subscription that you want to deploy the resources into.

    - **Resource group**: Click **Create new**, type `CharisTechRG-C2`, and click **OK**.

    - **Region**: **East US** (or select the region that you verified in the first chapter of this book).

    - **Admin Password**: Enter a complex password. Make a note of this, as it will be needed for later exercises.

- **Vm Size: Standard_B2s** (or select the VM size that you verified in the first chapter of this book).

- **Second Vnet Location: West US** (or select the second region that you verified in the first chapter of this book).

- Select **Review + create**.

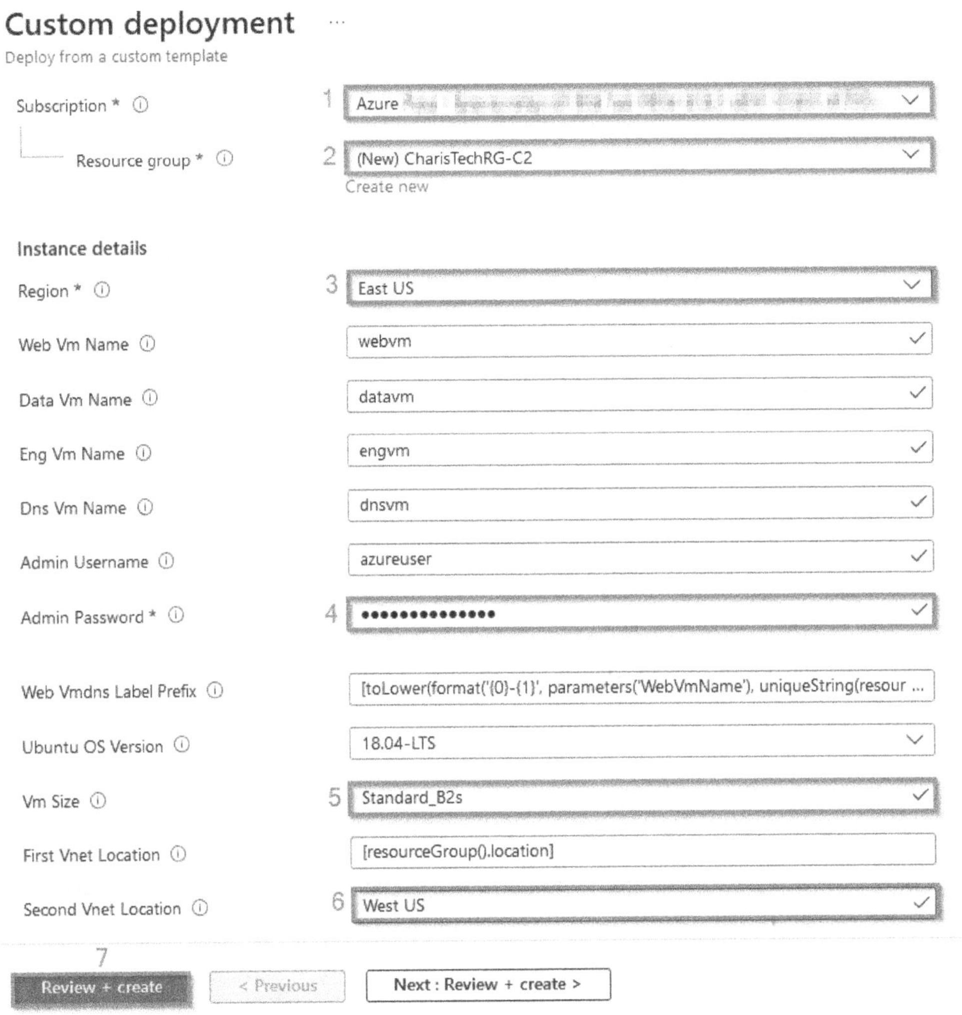

Custom deployment

Deploy from a custom template

Subscription * ⓘ	1	Azure .... ⌄
Resource group * ⓘ	2	(New) CharisTechRG-C2 ⌄
		Create new

Instance details

Region * ⓘ	3	East US ⌄
Web Vm Name ⓘ		webvm ✓
Data Vm Name ⓘ		datavm ✓
Eng Vm Name ⓘ		engvm ✓
Dns Vm Name ⓘ		dnsvm ✓
Admin Username ⓘ		azureuser ✓
Admin Password * ⓘ	4	••••••••••••• ✓
Web Vmdns Label Prefix ⓘ		[toLower(format('{0}-{1}', parameters('WebVmName'), uniqueString(resour ...
Ubuntu OS Version ⓘ		18.04-LTS ⌄
Vm Size ⓘ	5	Standard_B2s ✓
First Vnet Location ⓘ		[resourceGroup().location]
Second Vnet Location ⓘ	6	West US ✓

7
[Review + create] [< Previous] [Next : Review + create >]

Figure 2.3 – Complete the custom deployment options

5. After the validation has passed, select **Create** to proceed with the deployment. The deployment takes about 5 minutes to complete.

    After the deployment has completed, click on the **Outputs** tab (**1**), and make a note of the **sshCommand** value (**2**), which gives you the SSH command that you can use to connect to WebVM (one of the deployed virtual machines) using its public DNS name.

Microsoft.Template-20220522233927 | Outputs ⋯
Deployment

🔍 Search (Ctrl+/)	«	adminUsername

- ⚙️ Overview
- ⬆️ Inputs   1
- ☰ Outputs
- 📄 Template

adminUsername

azureuser

publicWebVM

webvm-ukdshrbbqwjbq.eastus.cloudapp.azure.com

sshCommand

2 ssh azureuser@webvm-ukdshrbbqwjbq.eastus.cloudapp.azure.com

Figure 2.4 – Obtain the SSH command to connect to WebVM's DNS name

Task 2 – connecting to Web VM using Cloud Shell

The steps are as follows:

1. In the Azure portal, click on the **Cloud Shell** icon in the top-right corner of the screen.

2. Ensure you have **Bash** selected for your environment, as we will be working with Bash commands.

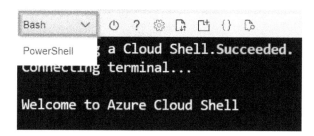

Figure 2.5 – Select the Bash shell environment

3. Paste the SSH command that you obtained in *task 1, step 6*, and then press *Enter*.

4. If you are prompted about the authenticity of the host, type `yes` and press *Enter*. When prompted to enter the password, enter the complex password that you used in *task 1, step 4*.

```
david@Azure:~$ ssh azureuser@webvm-ukdshrbbqwjbq.eastus.cloudapp.azure.com 1
The authenticity of host 'webvm-ukdshrbbqwjbq.eastus.cloudapp.azure.com (20.
228.198.185)' can't be established.
ECDSA key fingerprint is SHA256:TwM2d3dT+3ZLdlo1iDo3ctzgQrXV46No8GjIQ/6ZimQ.
Are you sure you want to continue connecting (yes/no)? yes 2
Warning: Permanently added 'webvm-ukdshrbbqwjbq.eastus.cloudapp.azure.com,20
.228.198.185' (ECDSA) to the list of known hosts.
azureuser@webvm-ukdshrbbqwjbq.eastus.cloudapp.azure.com's password:       3
Welcome to Ubuntu 18.04.6 LTS (GNU/Linux 5.4.0-1078-azure x86_64)
```

Figure 2.6 – Connecting to WebVM via SSH

5. You should now be connected to the **WebVM** virtual machine. Enter the following command
    to switch to a privileged user:

    ```
    sudo su -
    ```

Congratulations! You have now deployed the resources needed to complete the chapter exercises.

Name resolution scenarios and options

DNS servers host records that translate human-readable domain names into machine-readable IP
addresses (used by computers to communicate with each other). For example, *Figure 2.7* shows the
DNS server for the `azurecourses.xyz` domain zone, which has a single *A record* that translates
the `www.azurecourses.xyz` hostname into the IP address `1.2.3.4`. Clients that want to
communicate with the web server called `www.azurecourses.xyz` can make a DNS request to
their DNS resolver to translate the name into an IP address. The DNS resolver will then go through
an iterative process to make a record request to the DNS server (*Figure 2.7*).

Figure 2.7 – DNS server and name resolution

To facilitate network communications, there are two name resolution scenarios that we will cover:

- **Internal name resolution**: Providing name resolution for private/internal clients hosted in
  our virtual networks

- **External name resolution**: Providing name resolution for public/internet clients that need to
  access our public/internet-facing applications and services

Let's start with the internal scenario and the options that we have to implement this.

Internal name resolution scenarios and options

Azure virtual network workloads need to be able to resolve internal and external domain names to IP addresses. A comprehensive Azure internal name resolution implementation should cover the translation of domain names for the following scenarios:

- Scenario 1 – name resolution for resources within the same virtual network
- Scenario 2 – name resolution for resources in different virtual networks
- Scenario 3 – name resolution for resources in connected on-premises networks (hybrid)
- Scenario 4 – name resolution for public domain names from VNet resources

Figure 2.8 shows an example of this. By making name resolution requests to its DNS resolver (server), *VM1* (deployed into Azure *VNET-1*) should be able to resolve the private IP address for *VM2* (deployed into a separate subnet in the same Azure VNet), it should be able to resolve the private IP address for *VM3* (deployed into another Azure VNet), it should be able to resolve the private IP address for *VM4* (deployed into a connected on-premises network), and it should also be able to resolve public IP addresses for internet domain names. Of course, implementing these scenarios depends on what you are trying to achieve with your network architecture.

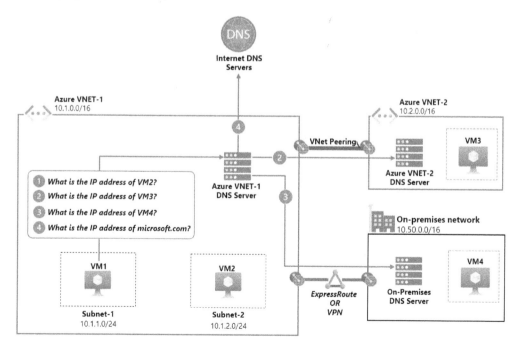

Figure 2.8 – Internal name resolution for Azure workloads

So, what options can we implement to cover these scenarios? There are four options with which we can implement Azure virtual network internal name resolution scenarios:

- **Option 1** – Azure-provided name resolution
- **Option 2** – customer-managed DNS servers
- **Option 3** – Azure Private DNS
- **Option 4** – Azure Private DNS Resolver and Azure Private DNS zones (in preview)

Let's look at these four options!

Option 1 – Azure-provided name resolution

This is the default name resolution option for virtual network workloads. Anytime we create a new virtual network in Azure, the platform configures it to use this default option (*Figure 2.9*) and assigns a unique private DNS suffix to it in the `<auto_generated_random_id>.internal.cloudapp.net` format. Azure's DHCP will also assign this DNS suffix to each VM in the virtual network to ensure that each host is resolvable within the VNet, using a **Fully Qualified Domain Name (FQDN)** of `<vm _name>.<auto_ generated_random_id>.internal.cloudapp.net`. If this does not make sense to you, don't worry too much about it, as you will explore this in an upcoming hands-on exercise.

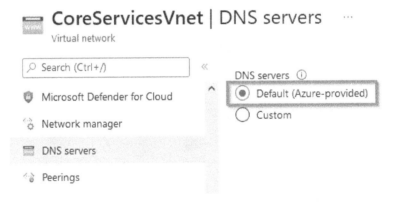

Figure 2.9 – Default VNet DNS server configuration

This default Azure-provided DNS server uses a virtual IP address of `168.63.129.16` to receive and respond to name resolution requests, as shown in *Figure 2.10*. This IP limits the number of requests from each VM to 1,000 requests per second. Anything above this gets throttled and queued.

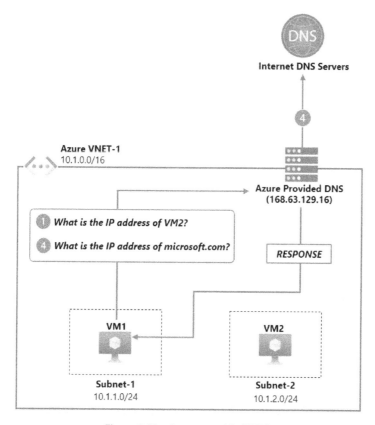

Figure 2.10 – Azure-provided DNS

The main advantage of this option is that it works out of the box, and we do not need to provision or manage our own DNS service for VMs within a VNet to resolve each other's names. However, in terms of capabilities, it is quite limited! For example, it can only cover scenario 1 (name resolution for resources within the same virtual network) and scenario 4 (name resolution for public domain names from VNet resources) out of the four scenarios that we listed earlier.

There are other limitations with this option, including the following:

- We have no ability to customize the configuration. For example, we cannot modify the auto-generated default DNS suffix assigned to our VNet (which is not very user-friendly). We cannot manually add additional DNS records to it beyond what is auto-registered. We cannot configure DNS forwarding for it so that it can resolve names using other internal DNS servers.

- We cannot enable or configure logging capabilities. DNS logs may contain insights that could be used to detect active threats.

- There is no WINS or NetBIOS support.

That's a lot of limitations! Alright, that's enough theoretical information – let's get our hands dirty and explore this option in an Azure environment.

In the next hands-on exercise, you will explore the first option for internal name resolution in Azure – Azure-provided DNS.

A hands-on exercise – exploring Azure-provided name resolution

In this exercise, you will review and test the capabilities of the Azure-provided DNS option. Here are the tasks that we will complete in this exercise:

- **Task 1**: Review and test the default name resolution option

Task 1 – reviewing and testing the default name resolution option

The steps are as follows:

1. In the Azure portal, in the search area at the top of the screen, type `CoreServicesVNet` and click on the virtual network resource that was created in the previous exercise.

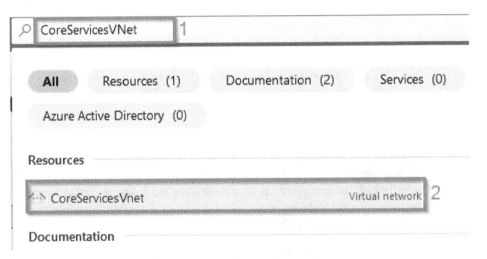

Figure 2.11 – Select the CoreServicesVnet resource

2. In the **CoreServicesVnet** blade, click on **DNS servers** (in the **Settings** section). You should see here that the virtual network is configured as **Default (Azure-provided)**. Leave the configuration as it is.

CoreServicesVnet | DNS servers
Virtual network
Search (Ctrl+/)
Microsoft Defender for Cloud
Network manager
1
DNS servers
Peerings
DNS servers
2
Default (Azure-provided)
Custom

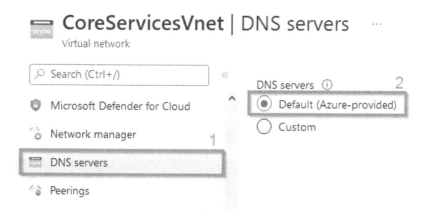

Figure 2.12 – Review the default DNS server configuration

3. Go back to the SSH session that you previously opened in **WebVM** (if the session is closed, reconnect to it again). Review the default DNS client configuration with the following command:

```
cat /run/systemd/resolve/resolv.conf
```

You should see here that the virtual machine is configured to send name resolution requests to a virtual IP address of `168.63.129.16`. You should also see the auto-generated DNS suffix here (it is not very user-friendly, is it? And remember that we cannot customize this name). Both values were provided to the client by Azure's DHCP.

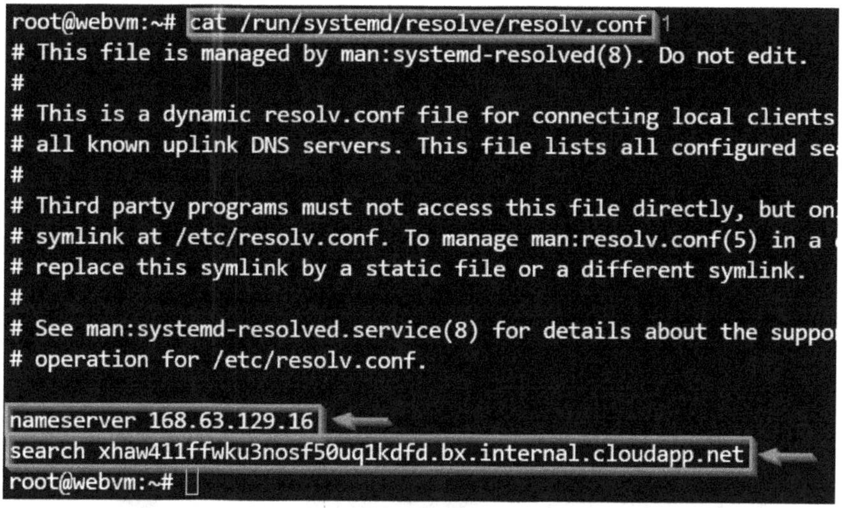

root@webvm:~# cat /run/systemd/resolve/resolv.conf
1
This file is managed by man:systemd-resolved(8). Do not edit.
#
This is a dynamic resolv.conf file for connecting local clients
all known uplink DNS servers. This file lists all configured se
#
Third party programs must not access this file directly, but on
symlink at /etc/resolv.conf. To manage man:resolv.conf(5) in a
replace this symlink by a static file or a different symlink.
#
See man:systemd-resolved.service(8) for details about the suppo
operation for /etc/resolv.conf.
nameserver 168.63.129.16
search xhaw411ffwku3nosf50uq1kdfd.bx.internal.cloudapp.net
root@webvm:~#

Figure 2.13 – Review the default DNS configuration for a VM

4. Use the following commands to resolve the hostnames of VMs in the same virtual network as WebVM:

    ```
    nslookup datavm
    nslookup dnsvm
    ```

    All the names should resolve successfully, as shown in the following screenshot. It works out of the box! Also, note that we didn't need to specify the **FQDN** with the DNS suffix. It resolves with just the hostname. This is because the DNS suffix is in the *search list* that we reviewed in the previous step.

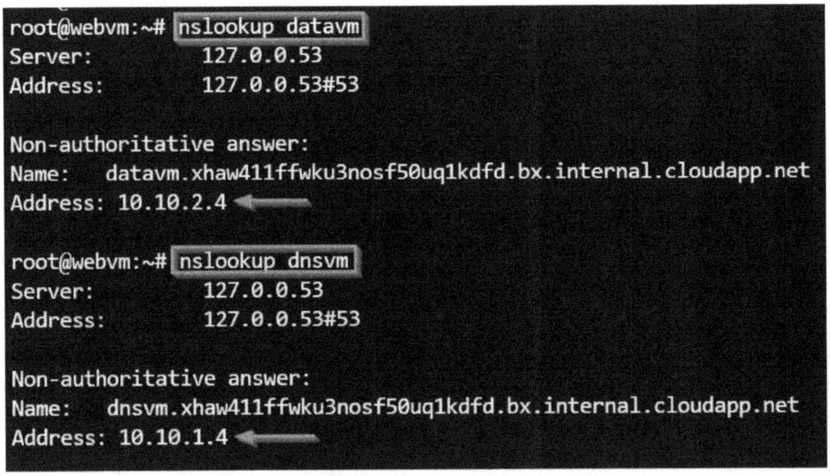

    ```
    root@webvm:~# nslookup datavm
    Server:         127.0.0.53
    Address:        127.0.0.53#53

    Non-authoritative answer:
    Name:    datavm.xhaw411ffwku3nosf50uq1kdfd.bx.internal.cloudapp.net
    Address: 10.10.2.4

    root@webvm:~# nslookup dnsvm
    Server:         127.0.0.53
    Address:        127.0.0.53#53

    Non-authoritative answer:
    Name:    dnsvm.xhaw411ffwku3nosf50uq1kdfd.bx.internal.cloudapp.net
    Address: 10.10.1.4
    ```

    Figure 2.14 – Name resolution of the same VNet workloads

5. Use the following commands to perform reverse DNS lookups for VMs in the same virtual network as **WebVM**:

    ```
    nslookup 10.10.1.4
    nslookup 10.10.2.4
    ```

    All IP addresses should resolve successfully, as shown in the following screenshot. It works out of the box!

    ```
    root@webvm:~# nslookup 10.10.1.4
    4.1.10.10.in-addr.arpa   name = dnsvm.internal.cloudapp.net.

    Authoritative answers can be found from:

    root@webvm:~# nslookup 10.10.2.4
    4.2.10.10.in-addr.arpa   name = datavm.internal.cloudapp.net.

    Authoritative answers can be found from:
    ```

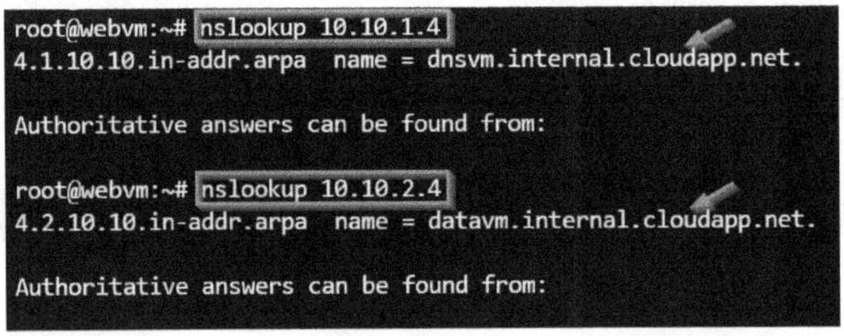

    Figure 2.15 – Reverse DNS lookup of the same VNet workloads

6. Use the following commands to perform forward and reverse DNS lookups for VMs in a different virtual network:

```
nslookup engvm
nslookup 10.20.1.4
```

Both lookups should fail, as shown in the following screenshot. The scope of the default Azure-provided DNS is limited to a virtual network! And because we don't have access to modify its configuration, this cannot be changed.

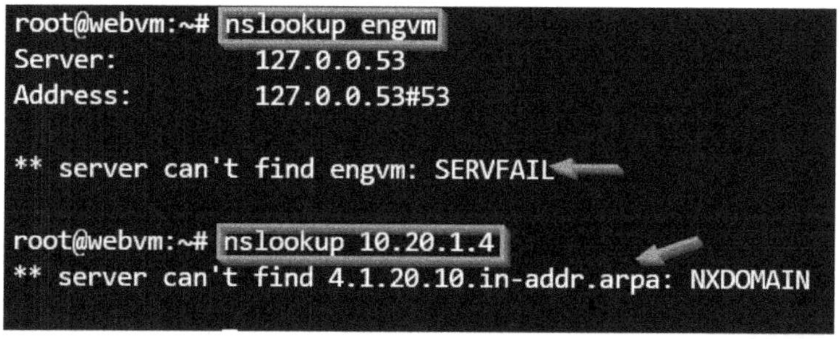

```
root@webvm:~# nslookup engvm
Server:         127.0.0.53
Address:        127.0.0.53#53

** server can't find engvm: SERVFAIL

root@webvm:~# nslookup 10.20.1.4
** server can't find 4.1.20.10.in-addr.arpa: NXDOMAIN
```

Figure 2.16 – Forward and reverse DNS lookup of workloads in a different VNet

7. Enter the following command to review how requests to the virtual IP address (168.63.129.16) are routed:

```
ip route
```

Here is the output from the preceding command. As you can see, requests are routed through the default gateway of the Azure subnet.

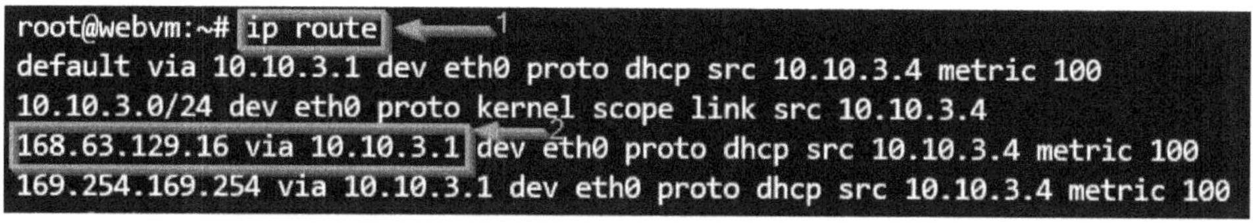

```
root@webvm:~# ip route                                    1
default via 10.10.3.1 dev eth0 proto dhcp src 10.10.3.4 metric 100
10.10.3.0/24 dev eth0 proto kernel scope link src 10.10.3.4
168.63.129.16 via 10.10.3.1 dev eth0 proto dhcp src 10.10.3.4 metric 100
169.254.169.254 via 10.10.3.1 dev eth0 proto dhcp src 10.10.3.4 metric 100
```

Figure 2.17 – Azure-provided DNS route review

Congratulations! You have now successfully explored and tested the capabilities of the default Azure-provided name resolution option. In the next section, we will cover the second option that we can use for internal name resolution – customer-managed DNS servers.

Option 2 – customer-managed DNS servers

If we need a fully featured DNS solution for our virtual networks (beyond the capabilities offered by *option 1*), we can use our own DNS servers! The server could be deployed into a virtual network subnet or any other network that is reachable, including connected on-premises networks. We then configure our virtual networks (or virtual network workloads) to use that server for name resolution.

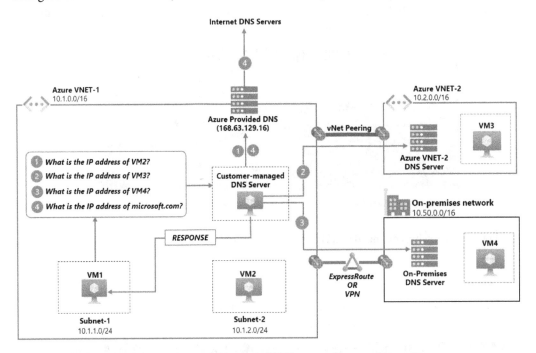

Figure 2.18 – Customer-managed DNS server-supported scenarios

Because we have full control of the DNS server, we can implement DNS forwarding however we want to! For example, our DNS servers can be configured to forward requests to the Azure-provided DNS virtual IP (168.63.129.16) for VNet and external name resolution (scenarios 1 and 4 in *Figure 2.18*). It can also be configured to forward requests to DNS servers hosted in other VNets to resolve names for resources in them (scenario 2 in *Figure 2.18*). They could also be configured to forward requests to an on-premises DNS server, to resolve names for on-premises resources (scenario 3 in *Figure 2.18*). This allows us to support all four scenarios that we listed at the beginning of this chapter!

The main downside to this option is the management overhead involved in looking after the DNS server infrastructure. Also, depending on how we implement this, we may get into scalability issues for scenario **2**. Implementing a separate DNS server for each VNet is not very scalable! Imagine having to manage this for 100 VNets! The third downside to this option is the complexity of implementing auto-registration (for example, if we want DNS records to be automatically added for newly created resources and then automatically deleted when the resources are removed). It is not that this is impossible; it just involves implementing a custom solution to manage.

Alright, that's enough discussion for now – let's explore this option in an Azure environment.

A hands-on exercise – implementing a customer-managed DNS server

In this exercise, you will implement a customer-managed DNS server for **CharisTech** in an Azure virtual network and test it. As part of the template deployment for the exercises in this chapter, a VM named **DnsVM** was deployed into the SharedServicesSubnet of the CoreServicesVNet. This VM has **Berkley Internet Naming Daemon** (**BIND**) 9 installed on it. BIND 9 is a full-featured DNS service for Linux systems. Here are the tasks that we will complete in this exercise:

- **Task 1**: Reviewing the existing DNS server configuration
- **Task 2**: Adding DNS records for a forward lookup zone
- **Task 3**: Adding DNS records for a reverse lookup zone
- **Task 4**: Configuring DNS forwarding and applying DNS server configurations
- **Task 5**: Modifying the VNet to use a custom DNS server
- **Task 6**: Testing name resolutions from WebVM

Let's get into this!

Task 1 – reviewing the existing DNS server configuration

The steps are as follows:

1. In the SSH session that you previously opened in **WebVM** (if the session is closed, reconnect to it again), use the following command to connect to the DNS server (**DnsVM**) that was deployed using the ARM template via SSH, and then press *Enter*:

    ```
    ssh azureuser@dnsvm
    ```

2. If you are prompted about the authenticity of the host, type yes and press *Enter*. When prompted to enter the password, enter the complex password that you used in the first hands-on exercise of this chapter in *task 1, step 4*.

```
azureuser@webvm:~$ ssh azureuser@dnsvm  1
The authenticity of host 'dnsvm (10.10.1.4)' can't be established.
ECDSA key fingerprint is SHA256:jAPJR1iSlnv6SxRaQRMHOwa+/R7vulqLTRPOMrjDwug.
Are you sure you want to continue connecting (yes/no)? yes  2
Warning: Permanently added 'dnsvm,10.10.1.4' (ECDSA) to the list of known hosts.
azureuser@dnsvm's password:          3
Welcome to Ubuntu 18.04.6 LTS (GNU/Linux 5.4.0-1080-azure x86_64)
```

Figure 2.19 – Connecting to WebVM via SSH

3. You should now be connected to the **DnsVM** virtual machine. Enter the following command to switch to a privileged user:

    ```
    sudo su -
    ```

4. For the DNS server implementation, we will be using **BIND**, a common Linux DNS server program. Verify the current status with the following command:

    ```
    systemctl status bind9.service
    ```

    The status should be active, as shown in the following screenshot. BIND was auto-installed as part of the template deployment process. If you are interested in reviewing the installation script, please refer to *steps 1–7* of the script at https://github.com/PacktPublishing/ Designing-and-Implementing-Microsoft-Azure-Networking-Solutions/ blob/main/Chapter02/template/bind9config.sh.

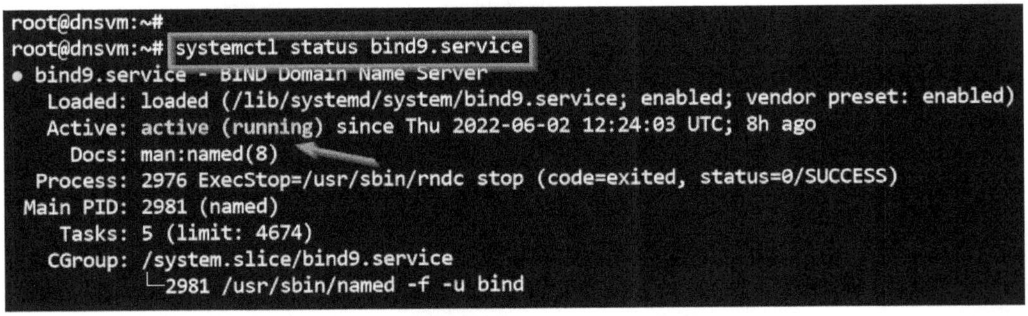

```
root@dnsvm:~#
root@dnsvm:~# systemctl status bind9.service
● bind9.service - BIND Domain Name Server
   Loaded: loaded (/lib/systemd/system/bind9.service; enabled; vendor preset: enabled)
   Active: active (running) since Thu 2022-06-02 12:24:03 UTC; 8h ago
     Docs: man:named(8)
  Process: 2976 ExecStop=/usr/sbin/rndc stop (code=exited, status=0/SUCCESS)
 Main PID: 2981 (named)
    Tasks: 5 (limit: 4674)
   CGroup: /system.slice/bind9.service
           └─2981 /usr/sbin/named -f -u bind
```

Figure 2.20 – Verifying the status

5. Review the custom DNS zone configuration for the DNS server using the following command:

    ```
    cat /etc/bind/named.conf.local
    ```

    The output shows that this DNS server is configured with a forward lookup zone of internal. charistech.xyz, with the zone file located at /etc/bind/db.internal.charistech. xyz. It is also configured with a reverse lookup zone of 10.10.in-addr.arpa, with the zone file located at /etc/bind/db.10.10.reverse.

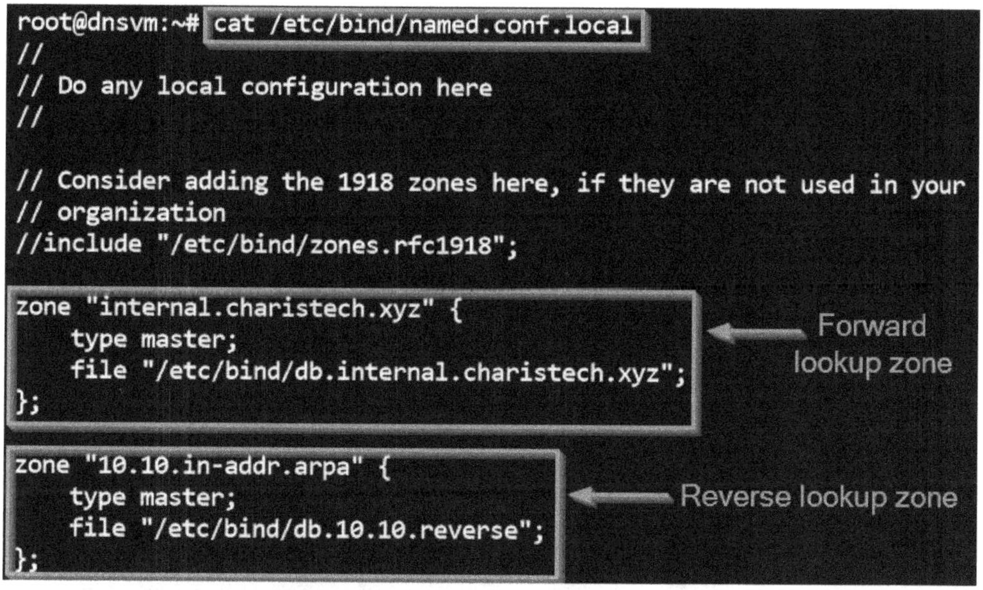

Figure 2.21 – Reviewing the custom DNS zone configuration for the DNS server

If you're interested in reviewing the script that was used for this configuration, please refer to *step 13* of the script at `https://github.com/PacktPublishing/Designing-and-Implementing-Microsoft-Azure-Networking-Solutions/blob/main/Chapter02/template/bind9config.sh`.

Task 2 – adding DNS records for a forward lookup zone

To add DNS records to the forward lookup zone, `internal.charistech.xyz`, we need to modify the zone file that the configuration file is pointing to. To avoid doing this manually, I have added a file to the GitHub repo of this book. The file contains the name records that we want to add, including *A records* for `webvm`, `datavm`, and `engvm`:

1. Download and apply the forward lookup zone file using the following command:

    ```
    curl https://raw.githubusercontent.com/PacktPublishing/
    Designing-and-Implementing-Microsoft-Azure-Networking-Solutions/
    main/Chapter02/template/zonefile -o /etc/bind/db.internal.
    charistech.xyz
    ```

2. Review the DNS records that were added to the DNS zone file for the internal.charistech.xyz zone:

```
cat /etc/bind/db.internal.charistech.xyz
```

The screenshot, for reference, is as follows:

```
root@dnsvm:~# cat /etc/bind/db.internal.charistech.xyz
;
; BIND data file for local loopback interface
; BIND data file for local the internal.charistech.xyz zone
;
$TTL    604800
@       IN      SOA     internal.charistech.xyz. root.internal.charistech.xyz. (
                              2         ; Serial
                         604800         ; Refresh
                          86400         ; Retry
                        2419200         ; Expire
                         604800 )       ; Negative Cache TTL
;
@       IN      NS      ns.internal.charistech.xyz.
@       IN      A       10.10.1.4
@       IN      AAAA    ::1
ns      IN      A       10.10.1.4
datavm  IN      A       10.10.2.4
webvm   IN      A       10.10.3.4    ◀——— A records added for the DNS zone
engvm   IN      A       10.20.1.4
```

Figure 2.22 – Reviewing the DNS records that were added to the DNS zone file

Task 3 – adding DNS records for a reverse lookup zone

To add DNS records to the reverse lookup zone, 10.10.in-addr.arpa, we need to modify the zone file that the configuration file is pointing to. To avoid doing this manually, I have added a file to the GitHub repo of this book. The file contains the name records that we want to add, including *PTR records* for webvm and datavm:

1. Download and apply the reverse lookup zone file using the following command:

```
curl https://raw.githubusercontent.com/PacktPublishing/
Designing-and-Implementing-Microsoft-Azure-Networking-Solutions/
main/Chapter02/template/reversezonefile -o /etc/bind/db.10.10.
reverse
```

2. Review the DNS records that were added to the reverse DNS zone file for the `10.10.in-addr.arpa` zone:

```
cat /etc/bind/db.10.10.reverse
```

The screenshot, for reference, is as follows:

```
azureuser@dnsvm:~$ sudo su -
root@dnsvm:~# cat /etc/bind/db.10.10.reverse
;
; BIND reverse data file for local 10.10.aaa.bbb net
;
$TTL    604800
@       IN      SOA     ns.internal.charistech.xyz. root.internal.charistech.xyz. (
                              2         ; Serial
                         604800         ; Refresh
                          86400         ; Retry
                        2419200         ; Expire
                         604800 )       ; Negative Cache TTL
;
@       IN      NS      ns.
4.1     IN      PTR     ns.internal.charistech.xyz.
4.2     IN      PTR     datavm.internal.charistech.xyz.      ← PTR records added
4.3     IN      PTR     webvm.internal.charistech.xyz.         for the DNS zone
```

Figure 2.23 – Reviewing the DNS records that were added to the reverse DNS zone file

Task 4 – configuring DNS forwarding and applying DNS server configurations

To configure the DNS server to forward other DNS queries to the Azure-provided DNS resolver, we need to modify the `/etc/bind/named.conf.options` global DNS configuration file:

1. Download and apply the global DNS configuration file with the following commands:

```
curl https://raw.githubusercontent.com/PacktPublishing/
Designing-and-Implementing-Microsoft-Azure-Networking-Solutions/
main/Chapter02/template/bindconfig-forwarder -o /etc/bind/named.
conf.options
```

2.   Review the global DNS configuration file for the forwarding configuration:

```
cat /etc/bind/named.conf.options
```

The screenshot, for reference, is as follows:

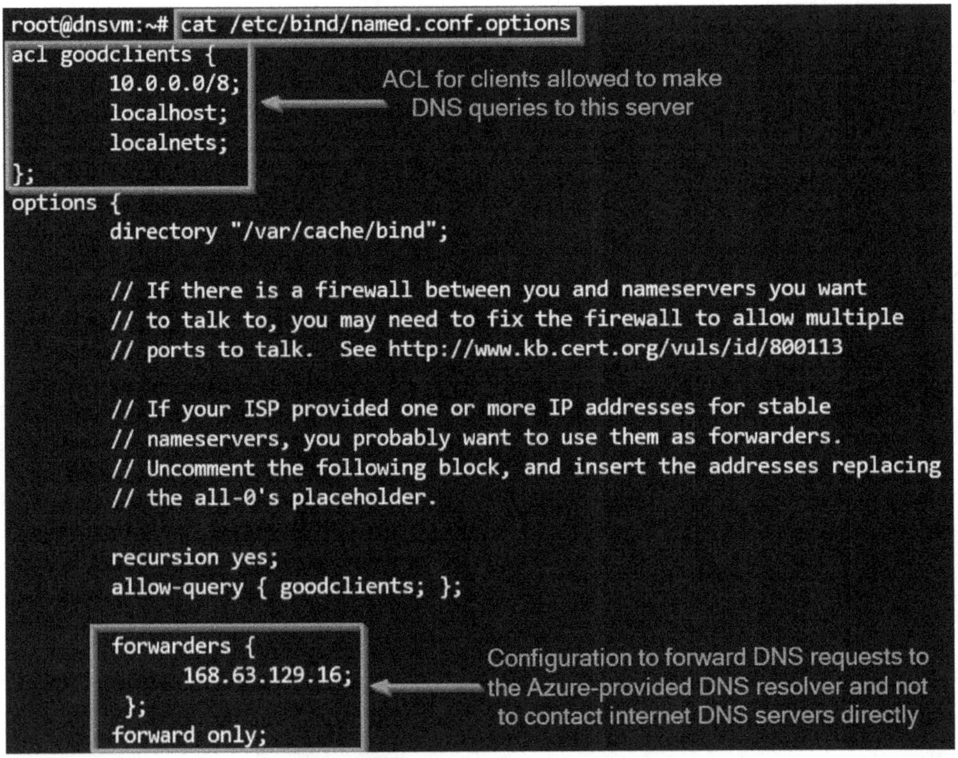

Figure 2.24 – Reviewing the global DNS configuration file for the forwarding configuration

3.   To apply the configurations that we have added, let's restart the DNS server:

```
systemctl restart bind9.service
```

Task 5 – modifying the VNet to use a custom DNS server

Now, let's modify the DNS configuration of our virtual network to use our newly configured DNS server:

1.   In the Azure portal, in the search area at the top of the screen, type `CoreServicesVNet` and click on the virtual network resource that was created in the previous exercise:

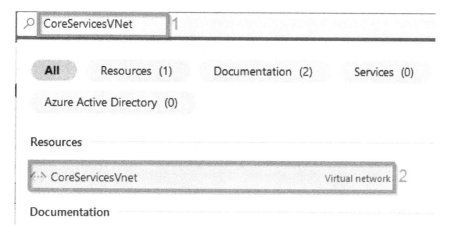

Figure 2.25 – Select the CoreServicesVnet resource

2. In the **CoreServicesVnet** blade, click on **DNS servers** (in the **Settings** section). Change the configuration to **Custom** and set the IP address to 10.10.1.4 (the IP address of the DNS server that we just configured). Note the warning about VMs needing to be restarted to utilize the updated DNS server settings. Click on **Save**.

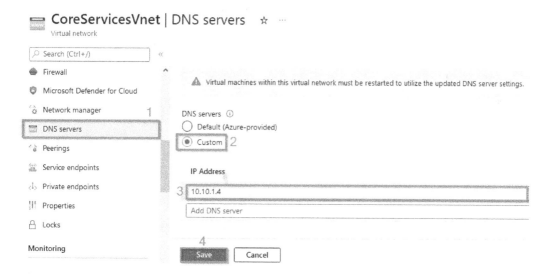

Figure 2.26 – Setting the VNet DNS configuration to use a custom DNS server

---

Note

At the time of writing, we can configure up to a maximum of 20 custom DNS servers per VNet.

Task 6 – testing name resolutions from WebVM

Now, let's test name resolutions from the **WebVM** virtual machine:

1. In the Azure portal, in the search area at the top of the screen, type webvm and click on the **webvm** virtual machine resource.

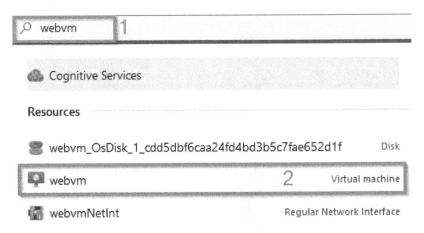

Figure 2.27 – Select the webvm virtual machine resource

2. In the **webvm** blade, click on **Restart** to restart the VM in order to apply the updated VNet DNS server setting. Wait for the restart to complete.

3. Back in the cloud shell, reconnect to **WebVM** using SSH. Enter the following command to switch to a privileged user:

    ```
    sudo su -
    ```

4. Use the following command to verify that the VNet DNS configuration has been applied to this VM:

    ```
    cat /run/systemd/resolve/resolv.conf
    ```

The screenshot, for reference, is as follows:

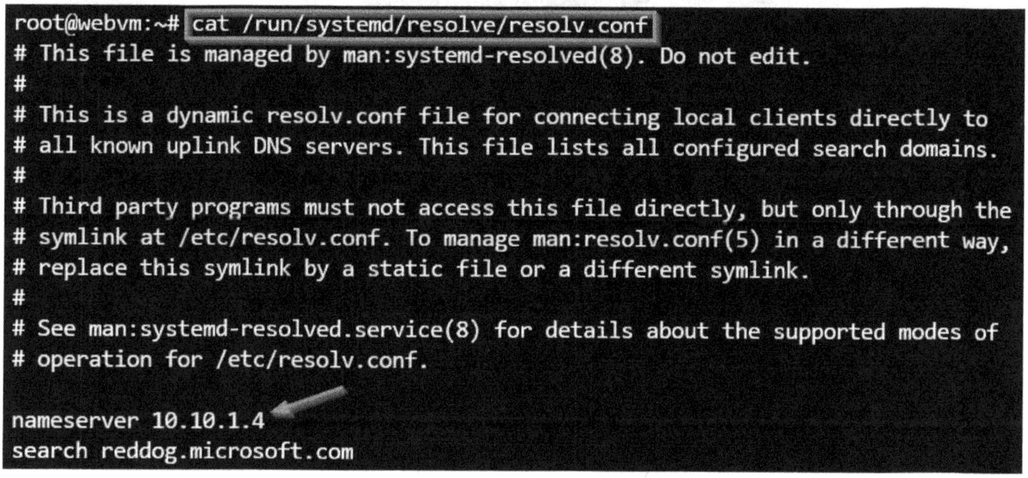

```
root@webvm:~# cat /run/systemd/resolve/resolv.conf
# This file is managed by man:systemd-resolved(8). Do not edit.
#
# This is a dynamic resolv.conf file for connecting local clients directly to
# all known uplink DNS servers. This file lists all configured search domains.
#
# Third party programs must not access this file directly, but only through the
# symlink at /etc/resolv.conf. To manage man:resolv.conf(5) in a different way,
# replace this symlink by a static file or a different symlink.
#
# See man:systemd-resolved.service(8) for details about the supported modes of
# operation for /etc/resolv.conf.

nameserver 10.10.1.4
search reddog.microsoft.com
```

Figure 2.28 – Verifying the application of the custom DNS configuration

5. Use the commands that follow to resolve the hostname of a VM in the same virtual network as WebVM. We added this record to the zone file for `internal.charistech.xyz` on our DNS server in one of the previous tasks:

    ```
    nslookup datavm.internal.charistech.xyz
    ```

    The name should resolve successfully, as shown in the following screenshot:

```
root@webvm:~# nslookup datavm.internal.charistech.xyz
Server:         127.0.0.53
Address:        127.0.0.53#53

Non-authoritative answer:
Name:   datavm.internal.charistech.xyz
Address: 10.10.2.4
```

Figure 2.29 – Verifying forward lookup

6. Use the following commands to perform reverse DNS lookups for VMs in the same virtual network as WebVM:

    ```
    nslookup 10.10.1.4
    nslookup 10.10.2.4
    ```

All IP addresses should resolve successfully, as shown in the following screenshot. We added these records to the reverse zone file on our DNS server in one of the previous tasks.

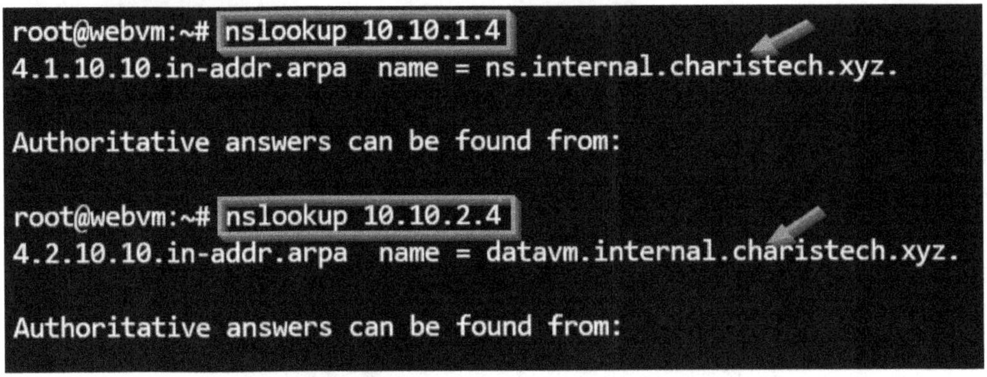

```
root@webvm:~# nslookup 10.10.1.4
4.1.10.10.in-addr.arpa   name = ns.internal.charistech.xyz.

Authoritative answers can be found from:

root@webvm:~# nslookup 10.10.2.4
4.2.10.10.in-addr.arpa   name = datavm.internal.charistech.xyz.

Authoritative answers can be found from:
```

Figure 2.30 – Verifying a reverse lookup

7. Use the following command to perform a forward lookup for a VM in a different virtual network:

    ```
    nslookup engvm.internal.charistech.xyz
    ```

    This should resolve successfully, as shown in the following screenshot. We added this record to the zone file on our DNS server in one of the previous tasks.

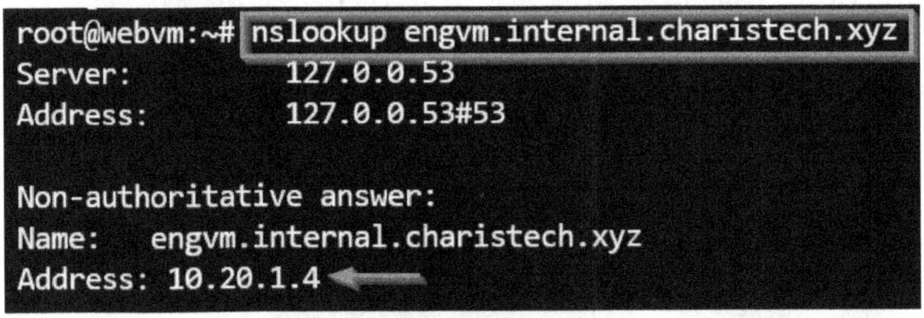

```
root@webvm:~# nslookup engvm.internal.charistech.xyz
Server:         127.0.0.53
Address:        127.0.0.53#53

Non-authoritative answer:
Name:   engvm.internal.charistech.xyz
Address: 10.20.1.4
```

Figure 2.31 – Verifying the lookup of a resource in another VNet

8. Use the following command to resolve an internet/external domain name:

    ```
    nslookup www.google.com
    ```

The name should resolve successfully, as shown in the following screenshot:

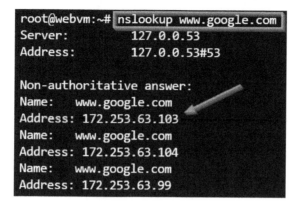

Figure 2.32 – Verifying the internet domain name lookup

You have now successfully implemented a customer-managed DNS server for **CharisTech** in an Azure virtual network and tested it. In the next section, we will cover the third option that we can use for internal name resolution – Azure Private DNS.

Option 3 – Azure Private DNS

To avoid the infrastructure management overhead and scalability concerns of implementing our own internal DNS servers, we can use an Azure service called Azure Private DNS to host and manage private DNS records! The service can be used to create forward or reverse DNS zones (up to a maximum of 1,000 per subscription). An Azure private DNS zone can contain up to 25,000 record sets, and it supports all common DNS record types: A, AAAA, CAA, CNAME, MX, NS, PTR, SOA, SRV, and TXT.

> **Note**
>
> To learn about the supported DNS record types, please refer to this document: https://learn.microsoft.com/en-us/azure/dns/dns-zones-records#dns-records.

The first step to use this option is to create a private DNS zone (**1** – *Figure 2.33*). After we create a private DNS zone in Azure, we need to *link* a virtual network to it for name resolution to work (**2** – *Figure 2.33*). When creating this link, we can choose to enable or disable *auto-registration*.

If auto-registration is enabled, Azure DNS will automatically add name records for new and existing VMs to the linked network. DNS records will also be automatically updated when the resource IP address changes, and records will be removed when resources are deleted! This significantly streamlines the life cycle management of name records, and it is implemented with just a single click.

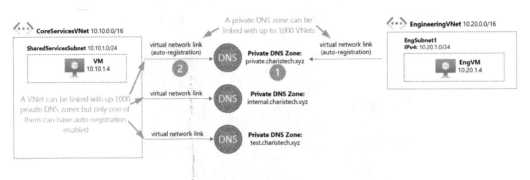

Figure 2.33 – Private DNS Zone links

As shown in *Figure 2.34*, a virtual network can be linked to multiple private DNS zones (up to 1,000), but it can only be linked with *one* zone with auto-registration enabled. Also, a private DNS zone can be linked to a maximum of 1,000 VNets (*Figure 2.34*), but only 100 of those links can have auto-registration enabled (*Figure 2.34*). A private DNS zone can contain up to 25,000 record sets (*Figure 2.34*).

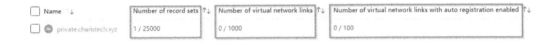

Figure 2.34 – Private DNS zone limits

Azure DNS is a cloud service that we can use to host and manage DNS records. The main advantage of the service is the ability to provide internal and external name resolution without the added overhead of managing infrastructure. The underlying infrastructure that Azure DNS is built on is highly resilient to network/infrastructure failures and offers an availability SLA of 100%. If a DNS service hosting important DNS zone data such as the records for your organization's website or email server becomes unavailable, those services will likely not function correctly. For example, a DNS server outage can not only stop people from being able to navigate to your organization's website but can also stop them from being able to email others in your organization!

A hands-on exercise – implementing Azure Private DNS

In this exercise, you will configure private DNS name resolution for **ChrisTech** using the Azure Private DNS service. You will create a private DNS zone named `private.charistech.xyz`, link the VNets that we created earlier for registration and resolution, and then test the configuration. Here are the tasks that you will complete:

- **Task 1**: Creating an Azure Private DNS zone
- **Task 2**: Linking a virtual network subnet for auto-registration

- **Task 3**: Verifying and adding DNS records to the DNS zone
- **Task 4**: Testing name resolutions from WebVM

Let's get into this!

Task 1 – creating an Azure Private DNS zone

The steps are as follows:

1. Open a web browser and navigate to the Azure portal at `https://portal.azure.com`. Sign in with your admin user account credentials.

2. On the Azure home page, in the search bar, enter DNS, and then select **Private DNS zones**.

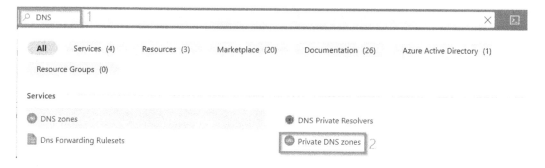

Figure 2.35 – Select Private DNS zones

3. In the **Private DNS zones** blade, select **+ Create**.

4. In the **Create Private DNS zone** window, in the **Basics** tab, enter the following values:

   - **Subscription**: Select your Azure subscription
   - **Resource group: CharisTechRG-C2**
   - **Name**: `private.charistech.xyz`
   - **Resource group location: East US**

Then, click **Review + create**.

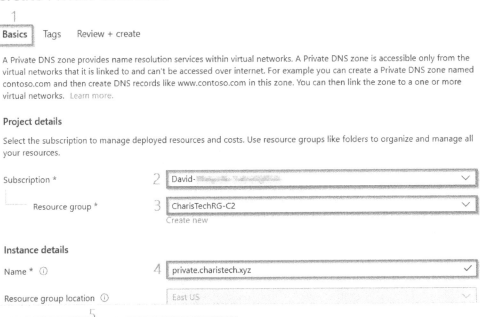

Figure 2.36 – Creating an Azure Private DNS Zone

5. Select **Create**. It should only take a few seconds to create the private DNS zone. Note that we did not have to deploy any infrastructure!

6. Wait until the deployment is complete, and then select **Go to resource**. Verify that the zone has been created.

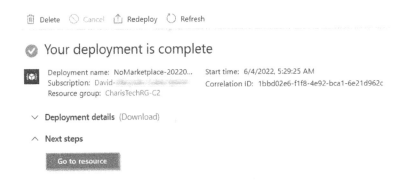

Figure 2.37 – Browsing to the created resource

Task 2 – linking a virtual network subnet for auto-registration

The steps are as follows:

1. In the **private.charistech.xyz** blade, under **Settings**, select **Virtual network links**, and then click on + **Add** to add a new link.

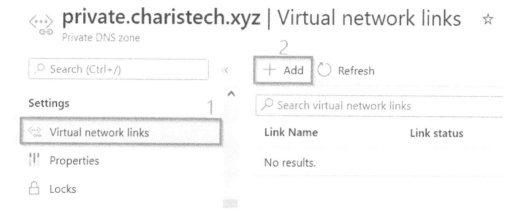

Figure 2.38 – Adding a VNet link to a private DNS zone

2. In the **Add virtual network link** blade, configure the following:

    *   **Link name**: CoreServicesVnetLink

    *   **Subscription**: Select your Azure subscription

    *   **Virtual network: CoreServicesVnet (CharisTechRG-C2)**

    *   **Enable auto registration**: Selected

Then, click **OK**.

Add virtual network link   ···   ×

private.charistech.xyz

Link name *   1

CoreServicesVnetLink   ✓

Virtual network details

ℹ️ Only virtual networks with Resource Manager deployment model are supported for linking with Private DNS zones. Virtual networks with Classic deployment model are not supported.

☐ I know the resource ID of virtual network ⓘ

Subscription * ⓘ   2

David   ⌄

Virtual network *   3

CoreServicesVnet (CharisTechRG-C2)   ⌄

Configuration 4
☑ Enable auto registration ⓘ

OK   5

Figure 2.39 – Configuring the private DNS zone VNet link

3. Select **Refresh**. Verify that the **CoreServicesVnet** link has been created and that auto-registration is enabled.

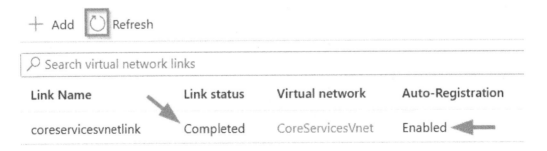

+ Add   🔄 Refresh

🔍 Search virtual network links

Link Name	Link status	Virtual network	Auto-Registration
coreservicesvnetlink	Completed	CoreServicesVnet	Enabled

Figure 2.40 – Verify the private DNS zone VNet link status

4. Repeat *steps 1–3* of this task for EngineeringVnet, using the following information:

   - **Link name**: `EngineeringVnetLink`
   - **Subscription**: Select your Azure subscription
   - **Virtual network**: **EngineeringVnet**
   - **Enable auto registration**: Selected

   Then, click **OK**.

   The virtual network link configuration should look like *Figure 2.41*.

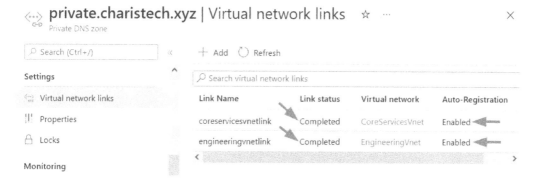

Figure 2.41 – Reviewing the private DNS zone VNet links

> **Note**
> A virtual network can be linked to multiple private DNS Zones (up to 1,000), but it can only be linked with *one* zone with auto-registration enabled.

Task 3 – verifying and adding DNS records to the DNS zone

The steps are as follows:

1. In the **private.charistech.xyz** blade, under **Overview**, review the name records that were automatically registered for existing virtual network resources.

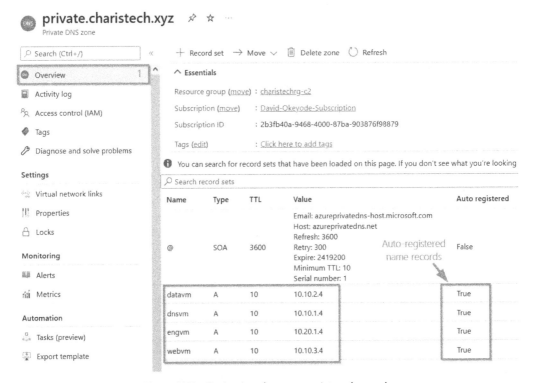

Figure 2.42 – Reviewing the auto-registered records

2. Select + **Record set** to add a record set manually.

3. In the **Add record set** blade, configure the following:

    -   **Name**: db

    -   **Type: A – Alias record to IPv4 address** (review other record types that are supported)

    -   **IP address**: 10.10.2.4

Select **OK**.

Add record set   ×

private.charistech.xyz

Name   1
db   ✓

.private.charistech.xyz

Type   2
A – Alias record to IPv4 address   ∨

TTL *   TTL unit
1   Hours   ∨

IP address   3
10.10.2.4   ✓ •••

0.0.0.0   •••

OK   4

Figure 2.43 – Adding a record set manually to a private DNS zone

Task 4 – modifying the VNet to use Azure-provided DNS

Now, let's modify the DNS configuration of our virtual network to use our newly configured DNS server:

1. In the Azure portal, in the search area at the top of the screen, type `CoreServicesVNet` and click on the virtual network resource that was created in the previous exercise.

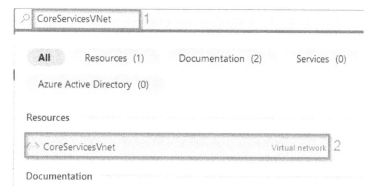

Figure 2.44 – Selecting the CoreServicesVnet virtual network

2. In the **CoreServicesVnet** blade, click on **DNS servers** (in the **Settings** section). Change the configuration to **Default (Azure-provided)**. Click on **Save**.

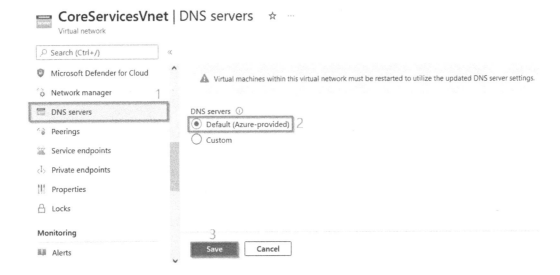

Figure 2.45 – Setting the VNet DNS configuration to use the default option

Task 5 – testing name resolutions from WebVM

Now, let's test name resolutions from the WebVM virtual machine:

1. In the Azure portal, in the search area at the top of the screen, type webvm and click on the **webvm** virtual machine resource.

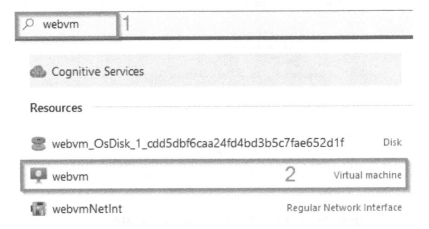

Figure 2.46 – Selecting the WebVM virtual machine resource

2. In the **webvm** blade, click on **Restart** to restart the VM in order to apply the updated VNet DNS server setting. Wait for the restart to complete.

3. Back in the cloud shell, reconnect to WebVM using SSH. Enter the following command to switch to a privileged user:

    ```
    sudo su -
    ```

4. Use the commands that follow to resolve the hostname of a VM in the same virtual network as the WebVM. The record was auto-registered when we created the virtual network link between the private DNS zone and the **CoreServicesVnet** virtual network:

    ```
    nslookup datavm.private.charistech.xyz
    ```

    The name should resolve successfully, as shown in the following screenshot:

    ```
    root@webvm:~# nslookup datavm.private.charistech.xyz
    Server:         127.0.0.53
    Address:        127.0.0.53#53

    Non-authoritative answer:
    Name:   datavm.private.charistech.xyz
    Address: 10.10.2.4 ◀──────
    ```

    Figure 2.47 – Verifying a forward lookup

5. Use the following commands to perform reverse DNS lookups for VMs in the same virtual network as WebVM:

    ```
    nslookup 10.10.1.4
    nslookup 10.10.2.4
    ```

    All IP addresses should resolve successfully, as shown in the following screenshot:

    ```
    root@webvm:~# nslookup 10.10.1.4
    4.1.10.10.in-addr.arpa   name = dnsvm.internal.cloudapp.net.
    4.1.10.10.in-addr.arpa   name = dnsvm.private.charistech.xyz. ◀──────

    Authoritative answers can be found from:
    root@webvm:~# nslookup 10.10.2.4
    4.2.10.10.in-addr.arpa   name = datavm.internal.cloudapp.net.
    4.2.10.10.in-addr.arpa   name = datavm.private.charistech.xyz. ◀──────

    Authoritative answers can be found from:
    ```

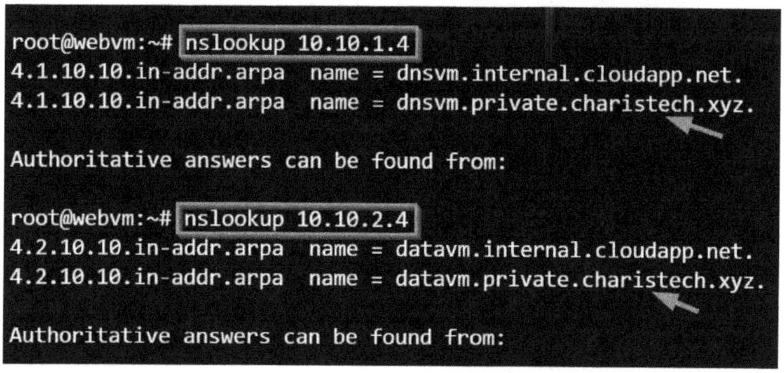

    Figure 2.48 – Verifying a reverse lookup

6. Use the following command to perform a forward lookup for a VM in a different virtual network:

    ```
    nslookup engvm.private.charistech.xyz
    ```

7. This should resolve successfully, as shown in the following screenshot. The record was auto-registered when we created the virtual network link between the private DNS zone and the **EngineeringVnet** virtual network.

```
root@webvm:~# nslookup engvm.private.charistech.xyz
Server:         127.0.0.53
Address:        127.0.0.53#53

Non-authoritative answer:
Name:   engvm.private.charistech.xyz
Address: 10.20.1.4
```

Figure 2.49 – Verifying a lookup of a resource in another VNet

8. Use the following command to resolve an internet/external domain name:

    ```
    nslookup www.google.com
    ```

    The name should resolve successfully, as shown in the following screenshot:

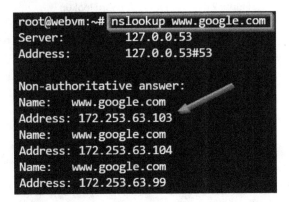

```
root@webvm:~# nslookup www.google.com
Server:          127.0.0.53
Address:         127.0.0.53#53

Non-authoritative answer:
Name:    www.google.com
Address: 172.253.63.103
Name:    www.google.com
Address: 172.253.63.104
Name:    www.google.com
Address: 172.253.63.99
```

Figure 2.50 – Verifying a internet domain name lookup

You have now successfully configured private DNS name resolution for **CharisTech** using the Azure Private DNS service. You created a private DNS zone named private.charistech.xyz, linked the VNets that we created earlier for registration and resolution, and then tested the configuration. In the next section, we will cover the fourth option that we can use for internal name resolution – Azure Private DNS.

Option 4 – Azure Private DNS Resolver and Azure Private DNS zones

While an Azure Private DNS zone is a great solution that significantly reduces the management that we need to do to implement internal name resolution, it still has some limitations – a key one being the lack of support for conditional forwarding. This means that we cannot create a custom configuration to forward certain name resolution requests to an on-premises DNS server.

External name resolution scenarios and options

To facilitate network communications, external clients (for example, clients on the internet) may need to be able to resolve domain names for our services to public IP addresses. A comprehensive Azure internal name resolution implementation should cover the translation of domain names for the following scenarios (*Figure 2.1*):

*   Scenario 1 – name resolution for internet clients

Alias recordsets are only supported for A, AAAA, and CNAME record types.

A hands-on exercise – implementing Azure Public DNS

In this exercise, you will configure public DNS name resolution for **CharisTech** using the Azure Public DNS service. You will create a public DNS zone named charistech.xyz and then test the configuration. Here are the tasks that you will complete:

*   **Task 1**: Creating an Azure Public DNS zone
*   **Task 2**: Reviewing Azure DNS name server information
*   **Task 3**: Adding a DNS record to the DNS zone
*   **Task 4**: Testing a name resolution from an internet client

Let's get into this!

Task 1 – creating an Azure Public DNS zone

The steps are as follows:

1. Open a web browser and navigate to the Azure portal: https://portal.azure.com. Sign in with your admin user account credentials.

2.   In the search area at the top of the screen, type DNS zones and click on **DNS zones**.

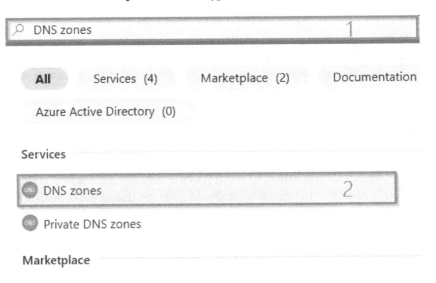

Figure 2.51 – Selecting DNS zones

3.   On the **DNS zones** page, click on + **Create**.

4.   On the **Create DNS zone** blade, in the **Basics** tab, configure the following:

- **Subscription**: Select your Azure subscription

- **Resource group**: ChsrisTechRG-C2

- **Name**: charistech.xyz

Select **Review + create**. Then, select **Create**. It may take a few minutes to create the zone.

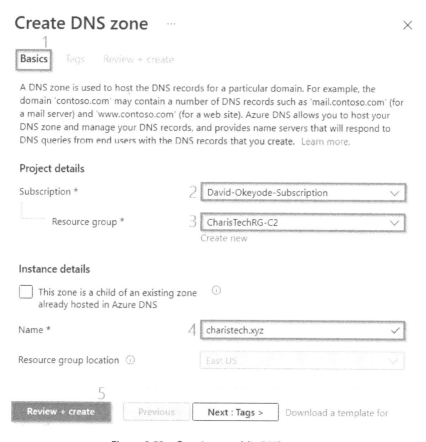

Figure 2.52 – Creating a public DNS zone

5. Wait until the deployment is complete, and then select **Go to resource**. Verify that the zone has been created.

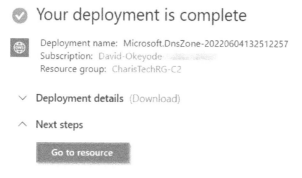

Figure 2.53 – Browse to the created resource

Task 2 – reviewing Azure DNS name server information

With a production domain name owned by your organization, you will need to visit your public domain name registrar to replace the **NS** records with the Azure DNS name servers for internet name resolution to work. This task shows you how to obtain the name servers for this, *but* since this is a test environment, there's no need to configure the Azure DNS name servers for this exercise:

1.   In the **charistech.xyz** blade, in the **Overview** section, review the four name server values and make a note of them (you will need one of these when we are testing later).

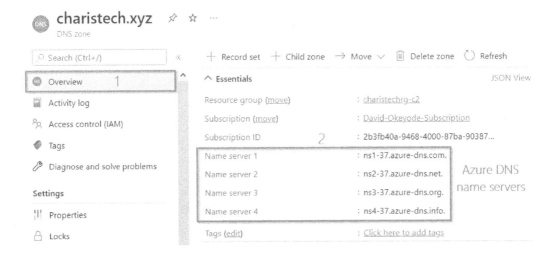

Figure 2.54 – Reviewing Azure DNS name servers

Task 3 – adding a DNS record to the DNS zone

Once we have created our DNS zone, we can add DNS entries or records to it:

1.   In the **charistech.xyz** blade, click **+ Record set**.

2.   On the **Add record set** page, configure the following:

- **Name**: www (this is the record that you want to resolve to the specified IP address)

- **Type**: A – **Alias record to IPv4 address** (review other record types that are supported, such as mail servers – MX and IPv6 addresses – AAAA)

- **Alias record set**: Select **Yes**

- **Alias type**: Select **Azure resource**

- **Choose a subscription**: Select your Azure subscription

- **Azure resource**: **webvmPublicIP**

- **TTL: 1** (this is the **time-to-live**. It specifies how long DNS servers and clients can cache a response.)

- **TTL unit: Hours**

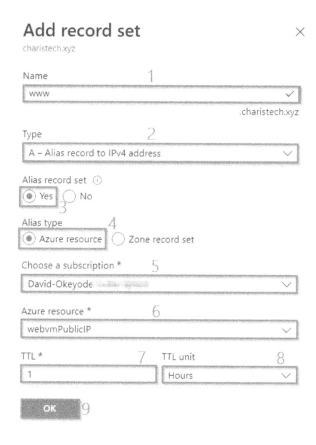

Figure 2.55 – Adding a record set to the DNS zone

Task 4 – testing a name resolution from an internet client

Now that we have a public DNS zone with an *A* record, we can test the name resolution from an internet client. For the test, we will be leveraging the cloud shell as the internet client:

1. In Cloud Shell, enter the following command to test external name resolution. Replace <NAME SERVER NAME> with one of the name server values that you made a note of in *task 2* of this exercise:

```
nslookup www.charistech.xyz <NAME SERVER NAME>
```

We have to specify the name server value to use for the name resolution because we did not update the name server with the DNS registrar.

```
david@Azure:~$ nslookup www.charistech.xyz ns1-37.azure-dns.com.
Server:         ns1-37.azure-dns.com.
Address:        150.171.10.37#53

Name:    www.charistech.xyz
Address: 20.185.191.241
```

Figure 2.56 – Public name resolution test

The www.charistech.xyz hostname resolves to the public IP of WebVM just as we configured it to. This verifies that external name resolution is working correctly.

A hands-on exercise – clean up resources

In this exercise, we will remove the resources that we created in this chapter's exercises to avoid running up a large cost in Azure!

In cloud shell, run the following command to delete the CharisTechRG-C2 resource group:

```
az group delete --name CharisTechRG-C2 --yes
```

This will remove all the resources that we created for the exercises in this chapter.

Summary

Name resolution is a critical part of any network infrastructure. In this chapter, we covered name resolution options for private and public client scenarios. We covered the default Azure-provided DNS for internal name resolution. We walked through the use of customer-managed DNS servers for internal name resolution. Finally, we covered the use of Azure Private DNS for internal name resolution and Azure Public DNS for external name resolution. All the concepts that we covered will equip you with the knowledge and skills needed to design a comprehensive name-resolution solution for Azure virtual networks.

In the next chapter, we will learn how to design, implement, and manage VNet routing.

Further reading

Refer to the following for more information about the topics covered in this chapter:

- Azure DNS FAQ: `https://aka.ms/dns-faq`
- Azure DNS documentation: `https://docs.microsoft.com/en-us/azure/dns/`
- Azure Private DNS documentation: `https://aka.ms/private-dns-overview`

3

Design, Implement, and Manage VNet Routing

The main purpose of an Azure **virtual network** (**VNet**) is to facilitate the delivery of data between point A (an Azure VNet workload) and point B (other connected systems). **Routing** defines the path that the transferred data will take between point A and point B.

There is a default routing behavior for workloads in an Azure subnet, but we also have options to customize the default behavior and control/influence the path of network traffic.

This is useful for many scenarios. For example, you may have an organizational requirement to inspect outbound network traffic with **network virtual appliances** (**NVAs**), such as third-party firewall solutions, for example, Palo Alto VM-Series firewalls. To implement this architecture, traffic must be properly routed through the NVAs for the inspection to occur. You may also have a requirement to redirect internet-bound traffic to an on-premises gateway instead of directly via Azure's internet connectivity.

In this chapter, you will learn about the default routing behavior for Azure VNets. You will learn how to customize the routing path with route tables and user-defined routes. You will also learn how to redirect traffic through NVAs so you can inspect the traffic before it's allowed through.

By the end of this chapter, you will have a strong understanding of the following:

- Identifying the routing capabilities of an Azure VNet
- Configuring routing within a VNet
- Deploying a basic NVA
- Configuring routing to send traffic through an NVA

Each topic has been structured to align with recommended routing best practices in Azure. Let us get into this!

The following topics will be covered in this chapter:

- Understanding the default routing for Azure VNet workloads
- Modifying the default routing behavior
- Hands-on exercise – cleaning up resources

Technical requirements

To follow along with the instructions in this chapter, you will need the following:

- A PC with an internet connection
- An Azure subscription

Before we proceed to cover the security best practices, let us prepare our Azure subscription for the hands-on exercises that we will be completing later in the chapter.

Understanding the default routing for Azure VNet workloads

In previous chapters of this book, we created some VNets with subnets and deployed **virtual machine** (**VM**) workloads into them. Without making any changes, the default routing behavior for Azure subnets takes effect and controls the path that traffic will follow to get to their intended destination. Let's examine what this default routing behavior looks like.

The default routing behavior for Azure subnets is controlled by **system routes**, which are automatically associated via a default route table (*Figure 3.1*). System routes are a collection of routing entries that define several *destination networks* (marked as the **Address Prefix** column in *Figure 3.1*) and the *next hop to send the traffic to* (marked as **Next Hop Type** in *Figure 3.1*) – this is the path that the traffic should follow to get to the defined destination.

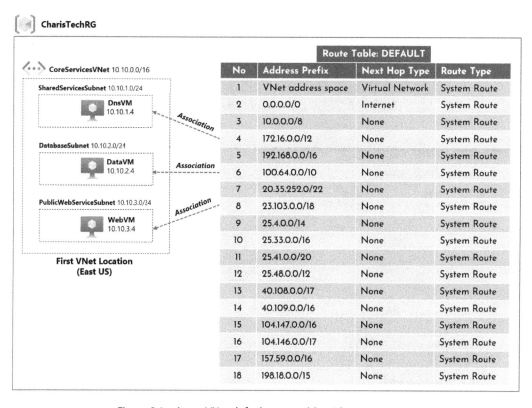

Figure 3.1 – Azure VNet default route table with system routes

As shown in *Figure 3.1*, there are 18 system route entries in the default route table. The routing entries can be divided into four main categories. The following are the explanations of the entries:

- **Entry 1** defines the default path for network traffic sent to other internal VNet addresses. The next hop type of **Virtual Network** means the traffic will be routed internally within the VNet via the subnet default gateways (*Figure 3.2*). If a VNet has multiple address spaces, an entry is added for each address space. *Figure 3.2* shows an example of the traffic path when this routing entry applies (marked as traffic path 1). In the example, traffic originating from **WebVM** and destined for the IP address of **DataVM** is first sent to the **PublicWebServiceSubnet** subnet's default gateway (the first IP address of the subnet) and then routed using the VNet's internal routing to **DatabaseSubnet**'s gateway, which then forwards the traffic to **DataVM**. Pretty straightforward!

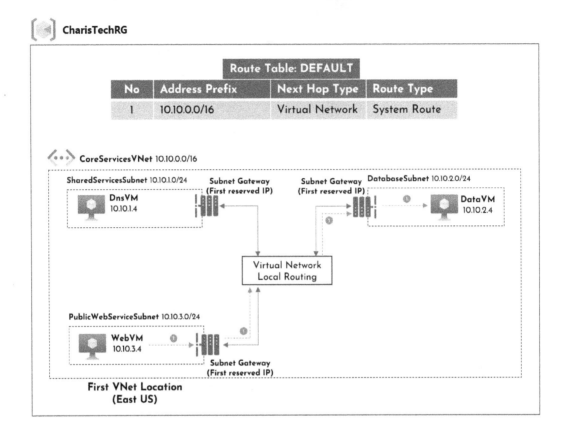

Figure 3.2 – VNet routing for a VNet subnet

- **Entry 2** defines the default path to other destinations not specified in other routing entries (also referred to as **unspecified addresses**). You can think of this as the default route in this default routing table – the route that takes effect when no other route is available for an IP destination address. The default behavior is to send the traffic directly to the internet! This is what the next hop type of **Internet** means. The only exceptions to this are traffic destined for the public IP addresses of Azure platform services – this traffic always remains on the Azure backbone network and is not routed to the internet. *Figure 3.3* shows an example of the traffic path when this routing entry applies (marked as traffic path 2). In the example, traffic originating from **WebVM** and destined for an IP address that is not matched by another routing entry is routed using Azure's internet routing and forwarded to the internet.

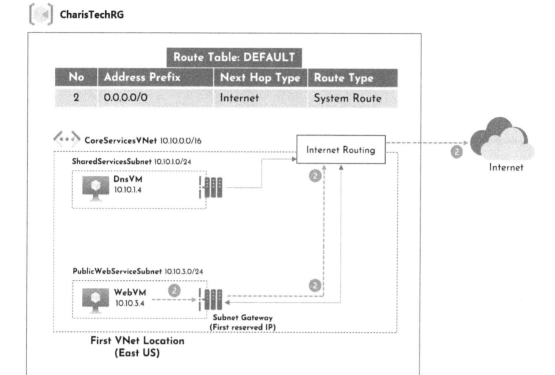

Figure 3.3 – Internet routing for a VNet subnet

- **Entries 3 to 5** are used to ensure that the RFC 1918 private IP address ranges (10.0.0.0/8, 172.16.0.0/12, and 192.168.0.0/16) are never routed to the internet. This is a standard routing requirement for all ISPs (Azure is our ISP in this case). The next hop type of **None** means the traffic will be dropped.

- **Entry 6** is used to ensure that the RFC 6598 address space (100.64.0.0/10) is not routed to the internet. This is a standard routing requirement for all ISPs. The RFC 6598 address space is used in a similar way as the RFC 1918 spaces. The next hop type of **None** means the traffic will be dropped.

- **Entries 7 to 18** are used to ensure that the Azure Management public IP address ranges are never routed to the internet. The next hop type of **None** means the traffic will be dropped.

There are additional system routes that are added to the default route table based on the implementation of networking features such as VNet peering, VNet gateways, and service endpoints. We will refer to these when we cover those features in later chapters.

Understanding default routing for dual-stack subnets

What if our subnets are configured with both IPv4 and IPv6 address spaces (dual stack) as discussed in the first chapter of this book? The system routes remain the same with the IPv6 address spaces also added for *VNet routing* and the default route of : : / 0 added for *internet routing* (*Figure 3.4*).

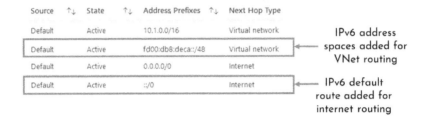

Figure 3.4 – Added system routes for dual-stack subnets

Hands-on exercise – provisioning resources for the chapter's exercises

To follow along with the exercises in this chapter, we will provision some Azure resources to work with. We have prepared an ARM template in the GitHub repository of this book for this purpose. The template will deploy two peered VNets in two Azure regions, as shown in *Figure 3.5*.

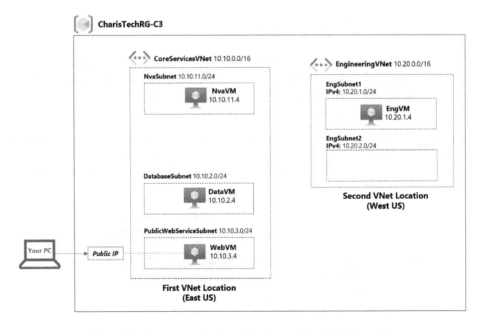

Figure 3.5 – Resources deployed via the provided ARM template

The first VNet (**CoreServicesVNet**) will have three subnets with a VM in each subnet. The second VNet (**EngineeringVNet**) will have two subnets with a VM in one subnet. One of the VMs (**WebVM**) will be assigned a public IP address so you can connect to it from your PC over the internet. Here are the tasks that we will complete in this exercise:

- **Task 1**: Initialize template deployment in GitHub
- **Task 2**: Connecting to WebVM using Cloud Shell

Let's get into this!

Task 1 – initializing template deployment in GitHub

The steps are as follows:

1. Open a web browser and browse to `https://packt.link/xUyKt`. This link will open the GitHub repository that has the ARM template to deploy the resources that we need.

2. In the GitHub repository that opens, click on **Deploy to Azure**.

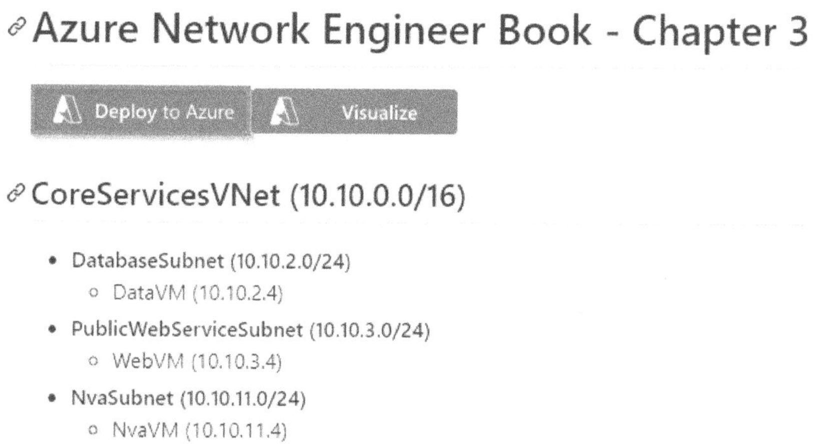

Azure Network Engineer Book - Chapter 3

CoreServicesVNet (10.10.0.0/16)

- DatabaseSubnet (10.10.2.0/24)
  - DataVM (10.10.2.4)
- PublicWebServiceSubnet (10.10.3.0/24)
  - WebVM (10.10.3.4)
- NvaSubnet (10.10.11.0/24)
  - NvaVM (10.10.11.4)

Figure 3.6 – Start the template deployment

3. If prompted to authenticate, sign in to the Azure portal with your administrative username and password.

4. In the **Custom deployment** window, configure the following:

   - **Subscription**: Select the subscription that you want to deploy the resources into.
   - **Resource group**: **Create new** | **Name**: `CharisTechRG-C3` | **OK**.
   - **Region**: **East US** (or select the region that you verified in the first chapter of this book).

- **Admin Password**: Enter a complex password. Make a note of this as it will be needed for later exercises.

- **Vm Size**: **Standard_B2s** (or select the VM size that you verified in the first chapter of this book).

- **Second Vnet Location**: **West US** (or select the second region that you verified in the first chapter of this book).

Select **Review + create**.

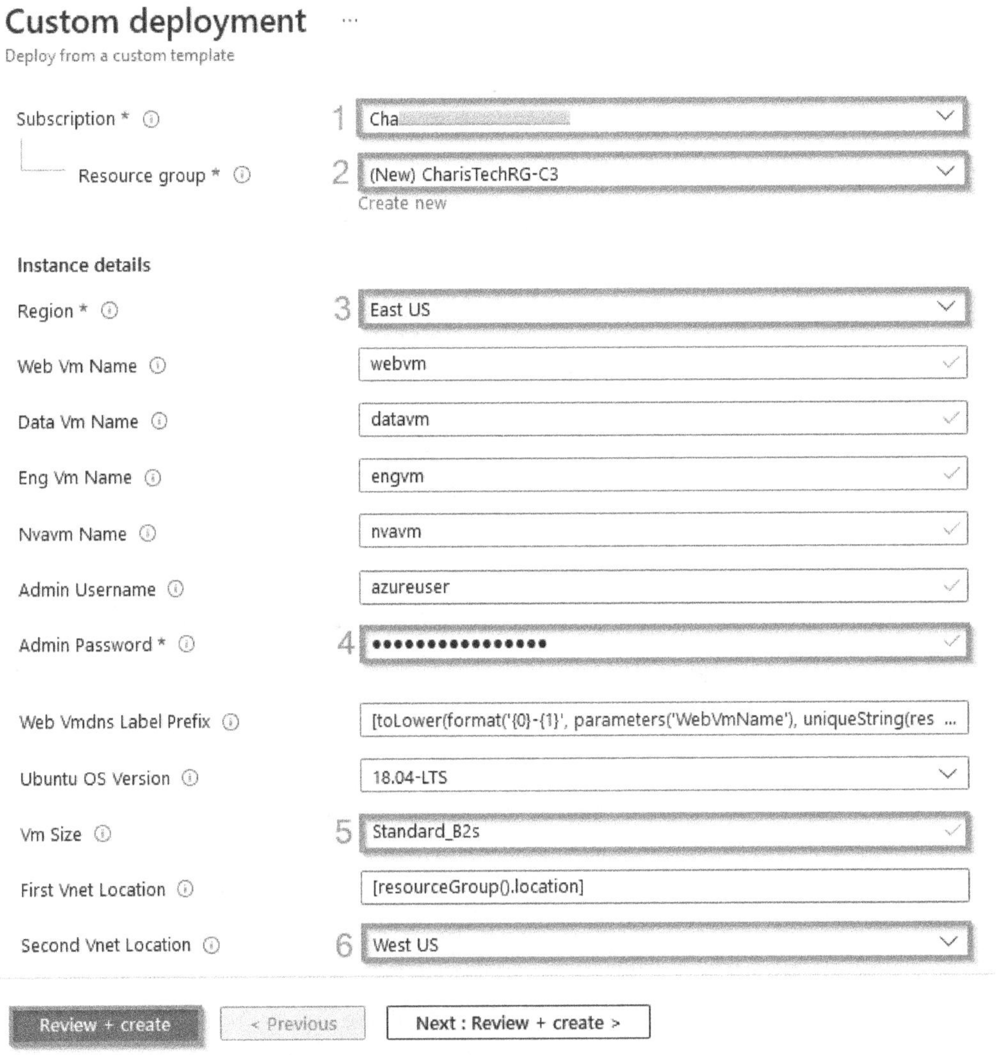

Custom deployment ···
Deploy from a custom template

Subscription * ⓘ	1	Cha▓▓▓▓▓▓▓▓▓▓▓▓▓ ⌄
Resource group * ⓘ	2	(New) CharisTechRG-C3 ⌄
		Create new

Instance details

Region * ⓘ	3	East US ⌄
Web Vm Name ⓘ		webvm ✓
Data Vm Name ⓘ		datavm ✓
Eng Vm Name ⓘ		engvm ✓
Nvavm Name ⓘ		nvavm ✓
Admin Username ⓘ		azureuser ✓
Admin Password * ⓘ	4	••••••••••••••• ✓
Web Vmdns Label Prefix ⓘ		[toLower(format('{0}-{1}', parameters('WebVmName'), uniqueString(res ...
Ubuntu OS Version ⓘ		18.04-LTS ⌄
Vm Size ⓘ	5	Standard_B2s ✓
First Vnet Location ⓘ		[resourceGroup().location]
Second Vnet Location ⓘ	6	West US ⌄

Review + create   < Previous   Next : Review + create >

Figure 3.7 – Complete the custom deployment options

5. After the validation has passed, select **Create** to proceed with the deployment. The deployment takes about 5 minutes to complete.

    After the deployment has completed, click on the **Outputs** tab (left side) and make a note of the **sshCommand** value, as this gives you the SSH command that you can use to connect to WebVM (one of the deployed VMs) using its public DNS name. We will need this in later exercises.

Microsoft.Template-20220708134042 | Outputs

Deployment

🔍 Search (Ctrl+/) «	
📊 Overview	adminUsername
📥 Inputs	azureuser
📑 Outputs 1	publicWebVM
📄 Template	webvm-7czczqegrsslc.eastus.cloudapp.azure.com
	sshCommand
	2 ssh azureuser@webvm-7czczqegrsslc.eastus.cloudapp.azure.com

Figure 3.8 – Obtain the SSH command to connect to WebVM's DNS name

Task 2 – connecting to WebVM using Cloud Shell

The steps are as follows:

1. In the Azure portal, click on the **Cloud Shell** icon in the top-right corner of the screen.

2. Ensure you have **Bash** selected for your environment as we will be working with Bash commands.

Figure 3.9 – Select the Bash shell environment

Congratulations! You have now deployed the resources needed to complete the chapter exercises. In the next hands-on exercise, you will explore the default routing of Azure subnet workloads.

Hands-on exercise – explore the default routing of Azure subnet workloads

In this exercise, you will explore the default routing behavior of Azure subnets. Here are the tasks that we will complete in this exercise:

- **Task 1**: Review default system routes for Azure subnet workloads
- **Task 2**: Review additional system routes added for networking features

Let's get into this!

Task 1 – reviewing default system routes for Azure subnet workloads

The steps are as follows:

1. In the Cloud Shell window, enter the following commands to set the values that we will use for the following variables: resource group, network interface, and VM:

    ```
    group="CharisTechRG-C3"
    nic="datavmNetInt"
    vm="datavm"
    ```

2. Examine the effective route entries applied to the network interface of the data VM using the command that follows. The --resource-group parameter specifies the name of the resource group that the network interface. The --name parameter specifies the name of the VM NIC. The --output parameter specifies the output format as a table instead of the default JSON output:

    ```
    az network nic show-effective-route-table --resource-group
    $group --name datavmNetInt --output table
    ```

You should observe the default 18 routes that we discussed earlier in this chapter:

```
david@Azure:~$
david@Azure:~$ az network nic show-effective-route-table --resource-group $group --name $nic --output table
Source    State    Address Prefix      Next Hop Type      Next Hop IP
--------  -------  ----------------    ---------------    -------------
Default   Active   10.10.0.0/16        VnetLocal
Default   Active   0.0.0.0/0           Internet
Default   Active   10.0.0.0/8          None
Default   Active   100.64.0.0/10       None
Default   Active   172.16.0.0/12       None
Default   Active   25.48.0.0/12        None
Default   Active   25.4.0.0/14         None
Default   Active   198.18.0.0/15       None
Default   Active   157.59.0.0/16       None
Default   Active   192.168.0.0/16      None
Default   Active   25.33.0.0/16        None
Default   Active   40.109.0.0/16       None
Default   Active   104.147.0.0/16      None
Default   Active   104.146.0.0/17      None
Default   Active   40.108.0.0/17       None
Default   Active   23.103.0.0/18       None
Default   Active   25.41.0.0/20        None
Default   Active   20.35.252.0/22      None
david@Azure:~$
```

Figure 3.10 – Examine the default system routes

3. Run the following two commands to verify the traffic path from **dataVM** to both **WebVM** and Google's DNS IP – 8.8.8.8. The command uses the *next-hop* feature of the Azure Network Watcher service. We will cover this service in a later chapter of this book:

```
az network watcher show-next-hop -g $group --vm dataVM
--source-ip 10.10.2.4 --dest-ip 10.10.3.4 --output table
az network watcher show-next-hop -g $group --vm dataVM
--source-ip 10.10.2.4 --dest-ip 8.8.8.8 --output table
```

You should see outputs similar to the following:

Figure 3.11 – Verify traffic path

Task 2 – reviewing additional system routes added for networking features

We previously mentioned in this chapter that more default system routes are added to subnet route tables as we configure networking features. In this task, we will explore this using two features – VNet peering and service endpoints:

1. Run the following command to verify the traffic path from the **dataVM** VM to the **WebVM** VM:

```
az network watcher show-next-hop -g $group --vm dataVM
--source-ip 10.10.2.4 --dest-ip 10.10.3.4 --output table
```

   This command should show the next hop as none (which means the traffic will be dropped). Because there is no specific route as VNet peering is not yet configured, the traffic will be dropped.

2. Configure VNet peering between the two VNets using the following commands (you can also access the commands from this URL: https://bit.ly/az700-c3-vnetpeering). This should add a new system route for the traffic path that we will verify in the next step:

```
group="CharisTechRG-C3"
vnet1="CoreServicesVnet"
vnet2="EngineeringVnet"
# Get the id for myVirtualNetwork1.
vNet1Id=$(az network vnet show --resource-group $group --name
$vnet1 --query id --out tsv)
# Get the id for myVirtualNetwork2.
vNet2Id=$(az network vnet show --resource-group $group --name
$vnet2 --query id --out tsv)
# Configure CoreServicesVnet to EngineeringVnet peering
az network vnet peering create --name $vnet1-to-$vnet2
--resource-group $group --vnet-name $vnet1 --remote-vnet
$vNet2Id --allow-vnet-access
# Configure EngineeringVnet to CoreServicesVnet peering
az network vnet peering create --name $vnet2-to-$vnet1
--resource-group $group --vnet-name $vnet2 --remote-vnet
$vNet1Id --allow-vnet-access
# Examine the VNet peering state
az network vnet peering show --name $vnet1-to-$vnet2 --resource-
group $group --vnet-name $vnet1 --query peeringState
```

3. Verify the peering state with the following command:

```
# Examine the VNet peering state
az network vnet peering show --name $vnet1-to-$vnet2 --resource-
group $group --vnet-name $vnet1 --query peeringState
```

You should get an output like the following, which confirms that the peering state is connected.

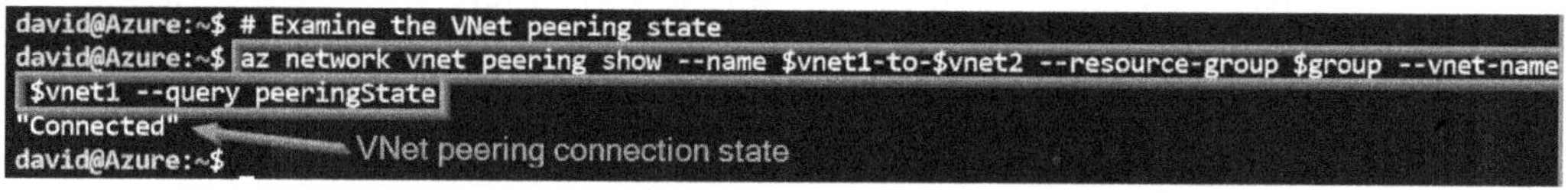

```
david@Azure:~$ # Examine the VNet peering state
david@Azure:~$ az network vnet peering show --name $vnet1-to-$vnet2 --resource-group $group --vnet-name
  $vnet1 --query peeringState
"Connected"
david@Azure:~$                    VNet peering connection state
```

Figure 3.12 – Verify the VNet peering connection state

4. Examine the effective route entries applied to the network interface of the **dataVM** VM using the following commands:

```
az network nic show-effective-route-table --resource-group
$group --name datavmNetInt --output table
```

You should observe a new default system route that was automatically added due to the VNet peering configuration:

```
david@Azure:~$
david@Azure:~$ group="CharisTechRG-C3"
david@Azure:~$ nic="webvmNetInt"
david@Azure:~$ az network nic show-effective-route-table --resource-group $group --name $nic --output table
Source    State    Address Prefix    Next Hop Type    Next Hop IP
-------   ------   ---------------   ----------------   -------------
Default   Active   10.10.0.0/16      VnetLocal
Default   Active   0.0.0.0/0         Internet
Default   Active   10.0.0.0/8        None
Default   Active   100.64.0.0/10     None
Default   Active   172.16.0.0/12     None
Default   Active   25.48.0.0/12      None
Default   Active   25.4.0.0/14       None
Default   Active   198.18.0.0/15     None
Default   Active   157.59.0.0/16     None
Default   Active   192.168.0.0/16    None
Default   Active   25.33.0.0/16      None
Default   Active   40.109.0.0/16     None
Default   Active   104.147.0.0/16    None
Default   Active   104.146.0.0/17    None
Default   Active   40.108.0.0/17     None
Default   Active   23.103.0.0/18     None
Default   Active   25.41.0.0/20      None
Default   Active   20.35.252.0/22    None                System route added as a result
Default   Active   10.20.0.0/16      VNetGlobalPeering    of VNet peering configuration
david@Azure:~$
```

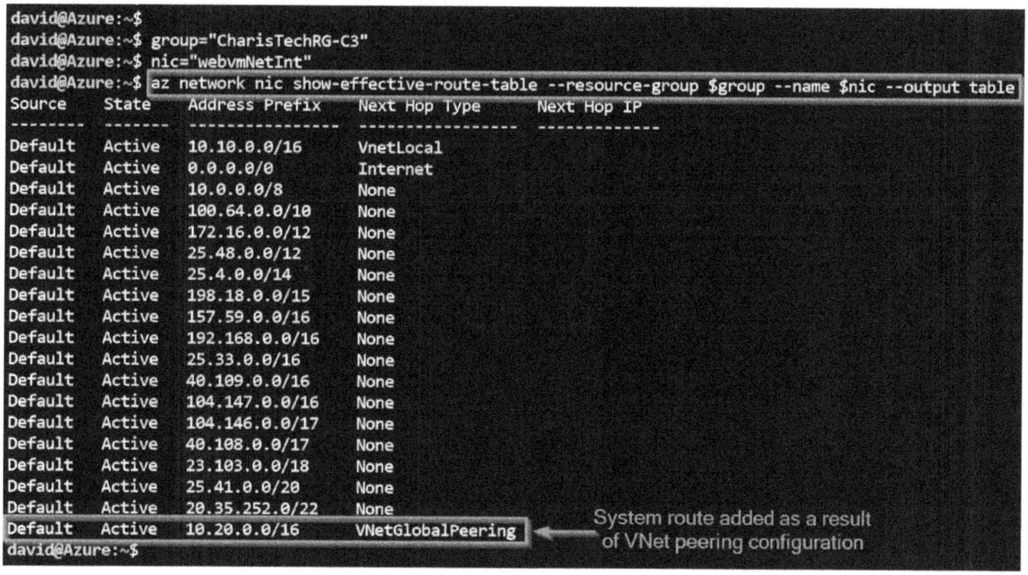

Figure 3.13 – Examine added default system routes

5. Another feature that adds system routes to subnet route tables is the service endpoint feature (which we will cover in a later chapter). Update **DatabaseSubnet** with a storage service endpoint using the following command:

```
az network vnet subnet update --resource-group $group --name
DatabaseSubnet --vnet-name CoreServicesVnet --service-endpoints
Microsoft.Storage
```

6. Run the following two commands to verify the traffic path from **dataVM** to both **EngVM** and an Azure Storage endpoint IP – 20.38.98.100. The command uses the *next-hop* feature of the Azure Network Watcher service. We will cover this service in a later chapter of this book:

```
az network watcher show-next-hop -g $group --vm dataVM
--source-ip 10.10.2.4 --dest-ip 10.20.1.4 --output table
az network watcher show-next-hop -g $group --vm dataVM
--source-ip 10.10.2.4 --dest-ip 20.38.98.100 --output table
```

You should see outputs such as the following ones, which validate that the first traffic is sent via the *VNet peering path* and the second traffic is sent via the *service endpoint path*.

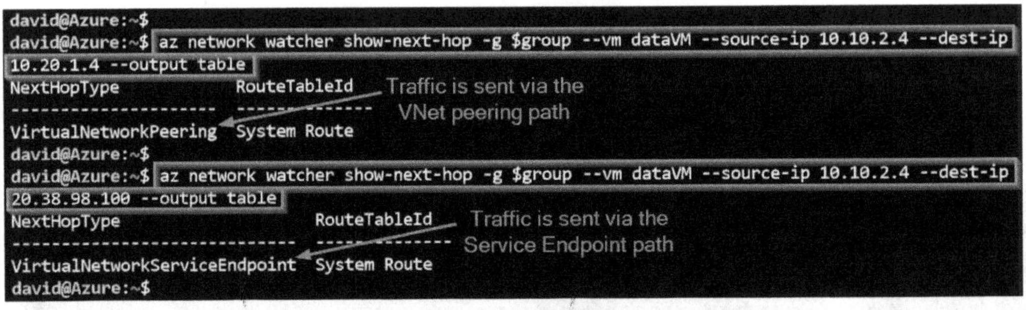

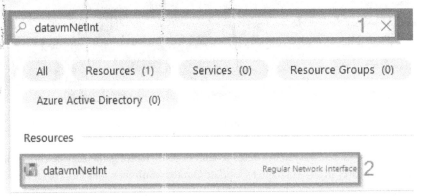

Figure 3.14 – Verify traffic path

Finally, let us examine the effective route entries using the Azure portal this time. We can do this from the VM network interface menu in the portal.

7. In the Azure portal search area, type datavmNetInt and press *Enter*. Click on the displayed network interface resource.

Figure 3.15 – Search for and select the network interface of dataVM

8. In the **datavmNetInt** blade, scroll to the **Support + troubleshooting** section in the left menu options and click on **Effective routes**.

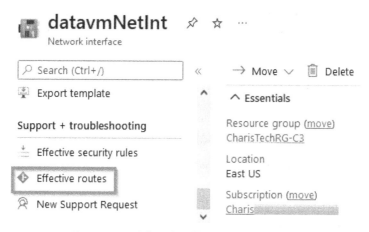

Figure 3.16 – Select the Effective routes option

9. Wait for a few seconds for the effective routes to be calculated. Observe all the system routes in the route table. You should see both the default system routes and the additional system routes that were added because of VNet peering and service endpoint configuration.

Source ↑↓	State ↑↓	Address Prefixes ↑↓	Next Hop Type ↑↓
Default	Active	10.10.0.0/16	Virtual network
Default	Active	0.0.0.0/0	Internet
Default	Active	10.0.0.0/8	None
Default	Active	100.64.0.0/10	None
Default	Active	172.16.0.0/12	None
Default	Active	25.48.0.0/12	None
Default	Active	25.4.0.0/14	None
Default	Active	25.41.0.0/20	None
Default	Active	20.35.252.0/22	None
Default	Active	191.238.0.224/28, 67 ...	VirtualNetworkServiceEndpoint
Default	Active	168.63.89.128/26, 63 ...	VirtualNetworkServiceEndpoint
Default	Active	10.20.0.0/16	VNetGlobalPeering

Figure 3.17 – Verify the system routes that were added to the effective route table

Congratulations! You have successfully explored default routing for Azure subnets and configured features that added additional system routes. In the next section, we will cover the options to modify the default routing behavior.

Modifying the default routing behavior

In some scenarios that you may have, the default flow of traffic as defined by system routes may not meet your organizational requirements. For example, you may want to implement the following scenarios:

- Forward outbound network traffic to NVAs, such as third-party firewall solutions, for inspection before being sent to the final destination.

- Direct all internet-bound traffic through your on-premises network maybe for compliance reasons. This is also referred to as forced tunneling.

- Completely isolate a VNet from the internet for compliance reasons.

For these scenarios, we have two main options for implementing custom routing. Since we cannot modify or update system routes, we can override system routes with **user-defined routes** or use the **Border Gateway Protocol (BGP)** to exchange routes.

> **What is a network virtual appliance?**
>
> An NVA is a virtual appliance that can be deployed from Azure Marketplace into Azure subnets for various use cases, such as firewalling, WAN optimization, advanced routing, load balancing, and **intrusion detection systems/intrusion prevention systems (IDS/IPS)**. Common providers of NVAs include Palo Alto Networks, Cisco, Check Point, and Sophos.

Implementing custom routing with user-defined routes

We previously covered the default route table that automatically comes with Azure subnets. It controls the routing for all subnets using the system routes that we discussed. To implement customized routing, we can create and associate a custom route table resource with our subnets. As of the time of writing (early July 2022), we can have up to 200 custom route tables per region per subscription.

A route table resource contains a set of rules, called **user-defined routes**, that specifies the path for network traffic leaving our subnets to its intended destination. Unlike the default routing table (with system routes), we can add, delete, or update user-defined routing entries as needed. We can have up to 400 routes in a custom route table.

When we associate a route table with an Azure subnet, the effective route table of the subnet is the combination of system routes in the default route table and user-defined routes in the custom route table (*Figure 3.18*).

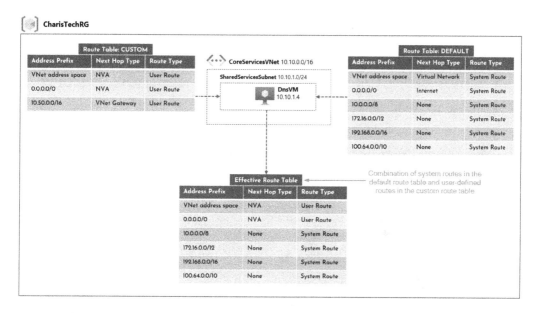

Figure 3.18 – Effective route table – a combination of the default and custom route tables

Here is some key information about using user-defined routes with custom route tables:

- A subnet can be associated with *only* one custom route table
- A route table can only be deleted if it is not currently associated with a subnet

You can use a user-defined route to override the default system routes so traffic can be routed through firewalls or NVAs. Enough discussion for now. Let's head over to Azure for implementation!

Hands-on exercise – route network traffic with a route table

In this exercise, you will implement custom routing for an Azure subnet using a route table with user-defined routes. Here are the tasks that we will complete in this exercise:

- **Task 1**: Connect to WebVM using Cloud Shell
- **Task 2**: Review the NVA that will be used to route traffic
- **Task 3**: Create a route table
- **Task 4**: Create a user-defined route in the route table
- **Task 5**: Associate a route table to a subnet
- **Task 6**: Verify traffic routing from one subnet to another through the NVA

Task 1 – connecting to WebVM using Cloud Shell

The steps are as follows:

1. In the Azure portal, click on the **Cloud Shell** icon in the top-right corner of the screen.

2. Ensure you have **Bash** selected for your environment as we will be working with Bash commands.

3. Paste the SSH command that you obtained in *Hands-on exercise 1 – Task 1 – Step 5* and press *Enter*.

4. If you are prompted about the authenticity of the host, type `yes` and press *Enter*. When prompted to enter the password, enter the complex password that you set in *Hands-on exercise 1 – Task 1 – Step 4*.

```
david@Azure:~$ ssh azureuser@webvm-7czczqegrsslc.eastus.cloudapp.azure.com  1
The authenticity of host 'webvm-7czczqegrsslc.eastus.cloudapp.azure.com (13.9
0.42.18)' can't be established.
ECDSA key fingerprint is SHA256:UUxmIvpDqP5I/ht+8TL3BpQ5j+/EPvMmj953Xvd7CNg.
Are you sure you want to continue connecting (yes/no)? yes  2
Warning: Permanently added 'webvm-7czczqegrsslc.eastus.cloudapp.azure.com,13.
90.42.18' (ECDSA) to the list of known hosts.
azureuser@webvm-7czczqegrsslc.eastus.cloudapp.azure.com's password:  3
Welcome to Ubuntu 18.04.6 LTS (GNU/Linux 5.4.0-1085-azure x86_64)
```

Figure 3.19 – Connect to WebVM via SSH

5. You should now be connected to the **WebVM** VM. Enter the following command to switch to a privileged user:

```
sudo su -
```

Task 2 – reviewing the NVA that will be used to route traffic

In the first hands-on exercise in this chapter, we deployed a template for the chapter exercises. One of the resources that was deployed was a Linux VM called **NvaVM**. This is the VM that we will be using as our NVA. As part of the deployment, Quagga was installed on it. In this task, we will review the VM and the static routing implemented on it:

> **What is Quagga?**
>
> Quagga is an open source routing software suite. It is a fork of GNU Zebra, which was developed by Kunihiro Ishiguro. It can be used to implement static and dynamic routing with the support of routing protocols such as OSPFv2, OSPFv3, and BGP-4.

1. In the Azure portal search area, type `NvavmNetInt` and press *Enter*. Click on the **NvavmNetInt** network interface resource.

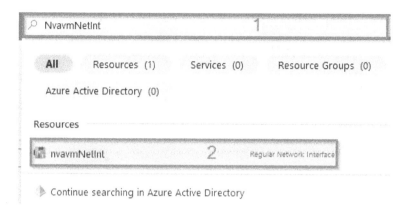

Figure 3.20 – Select NvaVM's network interface

2. On the **nvavmNetInt** page, in the **Settings** section, click on **IP configurations**.

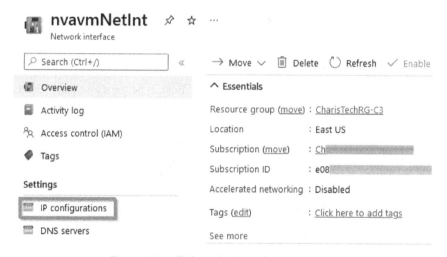

Figure 3.21 – Click on the IP configurations tab

3. In the **nvavmNetInt | IP configurations** window, verify that IP configuration is enabled.

nvavmNetInt | IP configurations
Network interface
Add
Save
Discard
Refresh
IP forwarding settings
IP forwarding
Disabled
Enabled
Virtual network
CoreServicesVnet

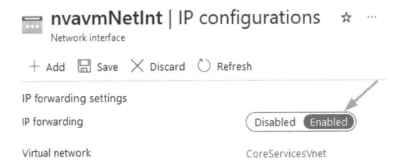

Figure 3.22 – Review the IP forwarding setting

When Azure sends network traffic to **NvaVM**, as we will configure in later tasks in this exercise, if the traffic is destined for a different IP address, IP forwarding allows the traffic to be sent to the correct location. Now that we have verified this setting, let us connect **NvaVM** via **WebVM**.

4. From the SSH session to **WebVM**, connect to **NvaVM** using the following command:

```
ssh azureuser@nvavm
```

5. If you are prompted about the authenticity of the host, type `yes` and press *Enter*. When prompted to enter the password, enter the complex password that you set in *Hands-on exercise 1 – Task 1 – Step 4*.

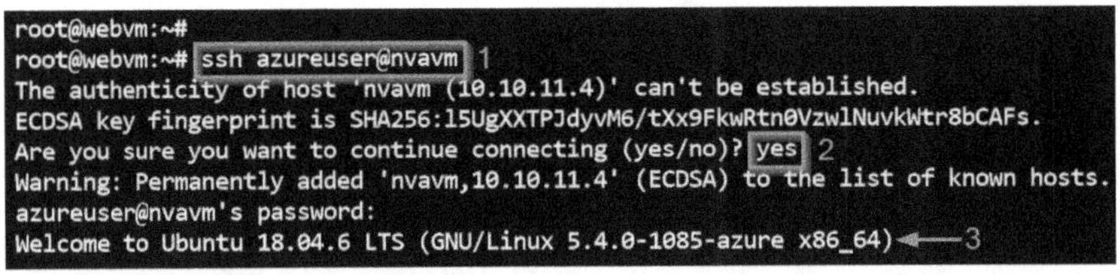

root@webvm:~#
root@webvm:~# ssh azureuser@nvavm 1
The authenticity of host 'nvavm (10.10.11.4)' can't be established.
ECDSA key fingerprint is SHA256:l5UgXXTPJdyvM6/tXx9FkwRtn0VzwlNuvkWtr8bCAFs.
Are you sure you want to continue connecting (yes/no)? yes 2
Warning: Permanently added 'nvavm,10.10.11.4' (ECDSA) to the list of known hosts.
azureuser@nvavm's password:
Welcome to Ubuntu 18.04.6 LTS (GNU/Linux 5.4.0-1085-azure x86_64) 3

Figure 3.23 – Connect to NvaVM via SSH

6. You should now be connected to the **NvaVM** VM. Enter the following command to switch to a privileged user:

```
sudo su -
```

7. Verify that Quagga is installed on this VM with the following command:

```
systemctl status zebra.service
```

The output should show that the service is active, as shown:

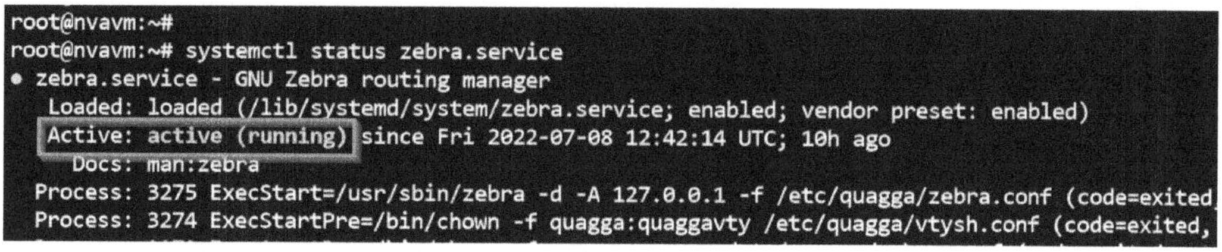

```
root@nvavm:~#
root@nvavm:~# systemctl status zebra.service
● zebra.service - GNU Zebra routing manager
   Loaded: loaded (/lib/systemd/system/zebra.service; enabled; vendor preset: enabled)
   Active: active (running) since Fri 2022-07-08 12:42:14 UTC; 10h ago
     Docs: man:zebra
  Process: 3275 ExecStart=/usr/sbin/zebra -d -A 127.0.0.1 -f /etc/quagga/zebra.conf (code=exited
  Process: 3274 ExecStartPre=/bin/chown -f quagga:quaggavty /etc/quagga/vtysh.conf (code=exited,
```

Figure 3.24 – Verify Quagga installation

8. Review the Zebra configuration file for the static routes to the **EngineeringVNet** VNet address space and the **DatabaseSubnet** address prefix:

    ```
    cat /etc/quagga/zebra.conf
    ```

    You should observe the two static routes, as shown. These routes were automatically added using a script during deployment. You can see the script at https://raw.githubusercontent. com/PacktPublishing/Designing-and-Implementing-Microsoft-Azure- Networking-Solutions/main/Chapter03/template/nvaconfig.sh.

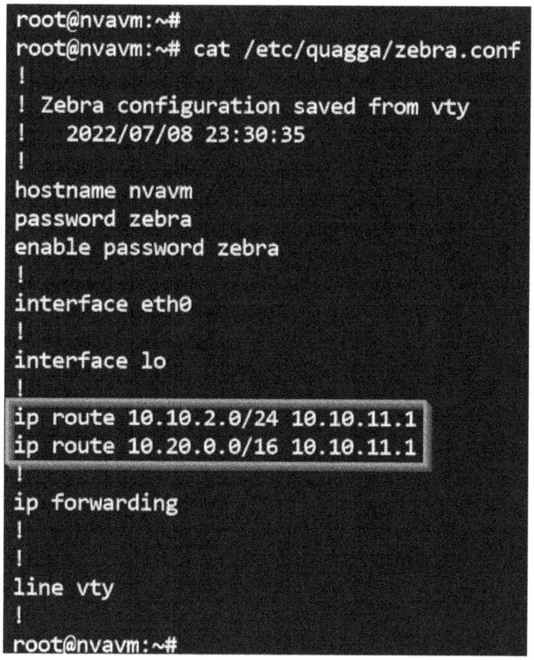

```
root@nvavm:~#
root@nvavm:~# cat /etc/quagga/zebra.conf
!
! Zebra configuration saved from vty
!    2022/07/08 23:30:35
!
hostname nvavm
password zebra
enable password zebra
!
interface eth0
!
interface lo
!
ip route 10.10.2.0/24 10.10.11.1
ip route 10.20.0.0/16 10.10.11.1
!
ip forwarding
!
!
line vty
!
root@nvavm:~#
```

Figure 3.25 – Review the Zebra configuration file

Task 3 – creating a route table

In this task, we will create a custom route table to which we will add user-defined routes:

1. In the Azure portal search area, type `route table` and press *Enter*. Click on the **Route tables** service.

Figure 3.26 – Select the Route tables service

2. On the **Route table** page, select **Create**.

3. In the **Create Route table** window, in the **Basics** tab, enter the following values:

    *   **Subscription**: Select your Azure subscription

    *   **Resource group: CharisTechRG-C3**

    *   **Region: East US**

    *   **Name**: `DatabaseSubnet-RouteTable`

    *   **Propagate gateway routes**: Yes

Then, click **Review + create**.

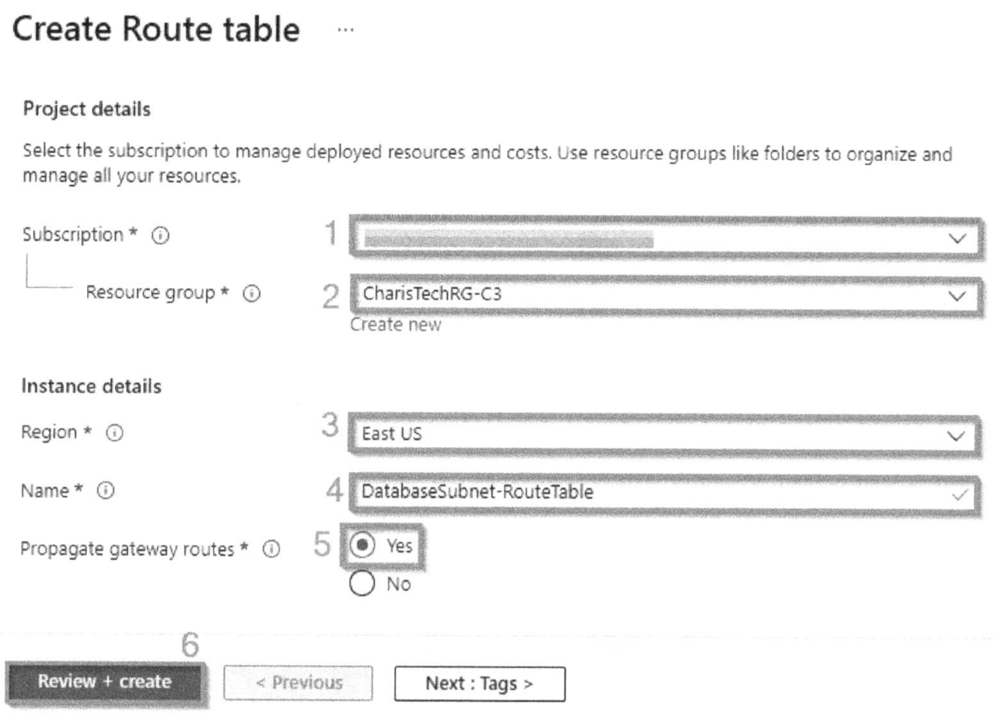

Create Route table ...

Project details

Select the subscription to manage deployed resources and costs. Use resource groups like folders to organize and manage all your resources.

Subscription * ⓘ   1 [_____] ⌄

       Resource group * ⓘ   2 [CharisTechRG-C3] ⌄
                                Create new

Instance details

Region * ⓘ   3 [East US] ⌄

Name * ⓘ   4 [DatabaseSubnet-RouteTable] ⌄

Propagate gateway routes * ⓘ   5 ◉ Yes
                                  ◯ No

6
[**Review + create**]   [< Previous]   [Next : Tags >]

Figure 3.27 – Configure route table parameters

4.   In the **Review + create** tab, select **create**.

5. Wait for the resource creation process to complete, then click on **Go to resource**.

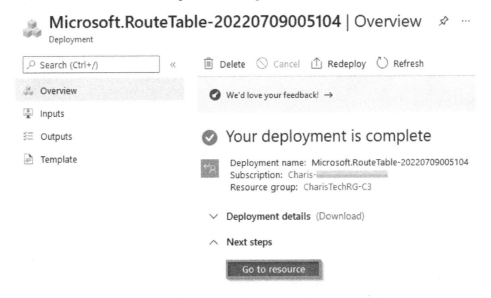

Figure 3.28 – Click to go to the resource that was created

Task 4 – creating a user-defined route in the route table

The steps are as follows:

1. On the **DatabaseSubnet-RouteTable** page, in the **Settings** section, select **Routes**.

Figure 3.29 – Click on Routes

2. In the **Routes** window, select the + **Add** button.

3. In the **Add route** window, enter the following values:

    - **Route name**: RouteToEngVNet
    - **Address prefix destination: IP Addresses**
    - **Destination IP addresses/CIDR ranges**: 10.20.0.0/16
    - **Next hop type: Virtual appliance**
    - **Next hop address**: 10.10.11.4

    Click **Add**.

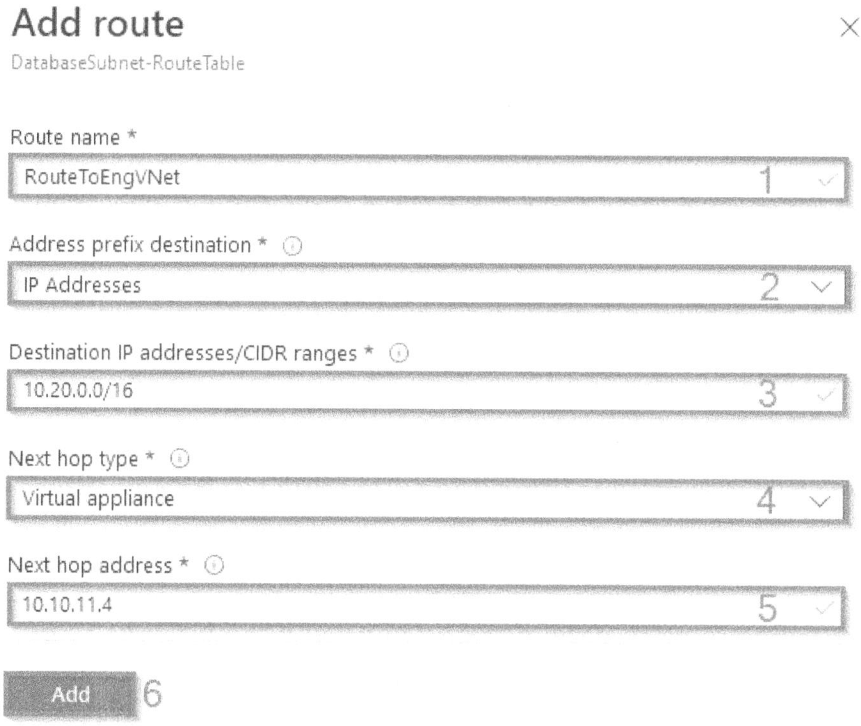

Add route   ×
DatabaseSubnet-RouteTable

Route name *

| RouteToEngVNet | 1 ⌄ |

Address prefix destination * ⓘ

| IP Addresses | 2 ⌄ |

Destination IP addresses/CIDR ranges * ⓘ

| 10.20.0.0/16 | 3 ⌄ |

Next hop type * ⓘ

| Virtual appliance | 4 ⌄ |

Next hop address * ⓘ

| 10.10.11.4 | 5 ⌄ |

[Add] 6

Figure 3.30 – Configure the user-defined route parameters

Task 5 – associating a route table to a subnet

The steps are as follows:

1. On the **DatabaseSubnet-RouteTable** page, in the **Settings** section, select **Subnets**.
2. In the **Subnets** window, select the **+ Associate** button.
3. In the **Associate subnet** window, configure the following values:

- **Virtual network: CoreServicesVnet**

- **Subnet**: **DatabaseSubnet**

Click **OK**.

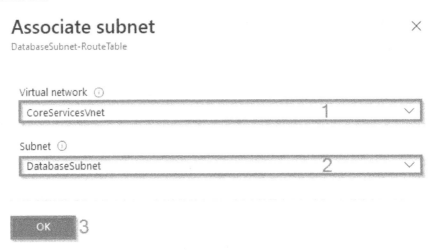

Figure 3.31 – Associate the route table to the subnet

Task 6 – verifying traffic routing from one subnet to another through the NVA

The steps are as follows:

1. In the Azure portal search area, type NvavmNetInt and click on the **NvavmNetInt** network interface resource.

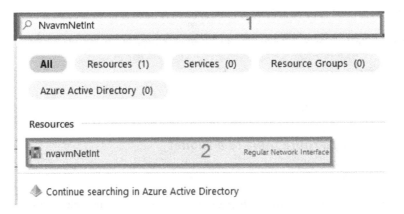

Figure 3.32 – Select NvaVM's network interface

2. On the **nvavmNetInt** page, in the **Support + troubleshooting** section, click on **Effective routes**.

3. Wait for a few seconds for the effective routes to be calculated. Observe that the user-defined route has now been applied to route traffic sent to the address prefix of `10.20.0.0/16` through NvaVM instead of directly through the VNet peering. Also note that the VNet peering system route is now marked as invalid because it has been overridden by a user-defined route.

Effective routes

Source	State	Address Prefixes	Next Hop Type	Next Hop IP Address	User Defined Route Name
Default	Active	0.0.0.0/0	Internet	-	-
Default	Active	10.0.0.0/8	None	-	-
Default	Active	10.10.0.0/16	Virtual network	-	-
User	Active	10.20.0.0/16	Virtual appliance	10.10.11.4	RouteToEngVNet
Default	Invalid	10.20.0.0/16	VNetGlobalPeering	-	-

Figure 3.33 – Validate user-defined routes in the effective route table

Now that we have validated that the route is applied, let us validate this with actual network traffic. We will first connect to the **DataVM** system via the **WebVM** system.

4. From the SSH session to **WebVM**, connect to **DataVM** using the following command:

```
ssh azureuser@datavm
```

5. If you are prompted about the authenticity of the host, type yes and press *Enter*. When prompted to enter the password, enter the complex password that you set in *Hands-on exercise 1 – Task 1 – Step 4.*

6. You should now be connected to the **DataVM** VM. Enter the following command to switch to a privileged user:

```
sudo su -
```

7. Verify that connectivity with **EngVM** using the following command:

```
ping 10.20.1.4 -c 4
```

The output should show successful connectivity, as shown:

```
root@datavm:~# ping 10.20.1.4 -c 4
PING 10.20.1.4 (10.20.1.4) 56(84) bytes of data.
64 bytes from 10.20.1.4: icmp_seq=1 ttl=64 time=64.7 ms
64 bytes from 10.20.1.4: icmp_seq=2 ttl=64 time=63.8 ms
64 bytes from 10.20.1.4: icmp_seq=3 ttl=64 time=63.5 ms
64 bytes from 10.20.1.4: icmp_seq=4 ttl=64 time=63.7 ms

--- 10.20.1.4 ping statistics ---
4 packets transmitted, 4 received, 0% packet loss, time 3004ms
rtt min/avg/max/mdev = 63.593/64.002/64.797/0.562 ms
root@datavm:~#
```

Figure 3.34 – Test connectivity using ping

8. Verify the traffic path using `traceroute`:

    ```
    traceroute 10.20.1.4
    ```

    Observe that the traffic is routed through NvaVM (`10.10.11.4`).

```
root@datavm:~#
root@datavm:~# traceroute 10.20.1.4
traceroute to 10.20.1.4 (10.20.1.4), 64 hops max
  1   10.10.11.4  0.638ms  0.346ms  0.270ms
  2   10.20.1.4  62.842ms  61.523ms  61.619ms
root@datavm:~#
```

Figure 3.35 – Validate traffic path using traceroute

Congratulations! You have now successfully configured custom routing using a custom route table and user-defined routes.

Implementing dynamic custom routing with BGP

Another option to get custom routing into Azure subnet route tables is dynamically via BGP advertisements. This option removes the burden of manually updating user-defined routes when a new network is added or when there is a change in network path due to a loss of connection.

While there are many dynamic routing protocols (OSPF, RIPv2, and EIGRP) that we use on-premises, Azure VNets supports only one – BGP. BGP is a standard routing protocol typically used to exchange routing information across the internet or between smaller networks called autonomous systems. BGP offers network stability because Azure subnet routing information can quickly adjust to changing network conditions, such as new networks being added or a connection path going down.

Implementing BGP for dynamic routing can happen in one of two ways:

- BGP advertisements through a VNet gateway and propagated directly to subnets or via a custom route table
- BGP advertisements through a route server and propagated via a custom route table

> **Note**
>
> Details of BGP and how it works are beyond the scope of this book. If you are not familiar with BGP, I highly recommend that you consider books on network routing by Packt Publishing.

Let's examine how these two options are implemented.

BGP advertisements through a VNet gateway and propagated directly to subnets or via a custom route table

If we have a VNet gateway (ExpressRoute or VPN Gateway) implemented to connect on-premises networks to our hub VNet, we can implement BGP to learn and propagate network and routing information dynamically. If you're not familiar with ExpressRoute or VPN Gateway, don't worry; we will cover them in the next chapter of this book.

We typically use BGP to advertise on-premises routes to Azure and vice versa. *Figure 3.36* breaks down the process of how this is implemented into four steps (listed after the figure):

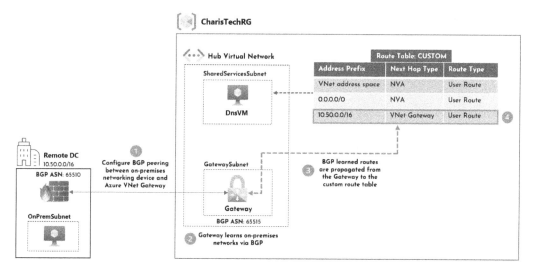

Figure 3.36 – BGP route advertisement via a VNet gateway

- *(1)* we configure BGP peering between our on-premises networking device and Azure VNet Gateway.

- *(2)* the VNet gateway learns on-premises networks and routing information via BGP. The on-premises network device also learns Azure networks and routing information via BGP.

- *(3)* BGP-learned routes are propagated from the VNet gateway to the custom route tables that are associated with the subnets. Note that this step will only happen if the option to propagate gateway routes is configured for the route table, as shown in *Figure 3.37*.

- *(4)* the learned routes are added (and removed) dynamically to the route table.

Figure 3.37 – Route table configuration to propagate gateway routes

BGP advertisements through a route server and propagated via a custom route table

If we have networking devices (NVAs) that support BGP dynamic routing in our VNets, we can implement an Azure service called Route Server to learn and propagate network and routing information dynamically. **Azure Route Server** is a managed service that simplifies dynamic routing information exchange between NVAs and our VNet subnets. The service has built-in high availability, so we don't need to worry about manually implementing this.

To implement this, we first need to create a dedicated subnet called **RouteServerSubnet**. This subnet must be a minimum of /27 or larger. The subnet should also not have an NSG or a route table associated with it – doing so will break functionality!

Once we have the subnet, we can deploy the Route Server resource into it using the Azure portal, Azure CLI, or even ARM templates. Once Route Server is deployed, we can follow the process highlighted in *Figure 3.38* to complete the rest of the implementation:

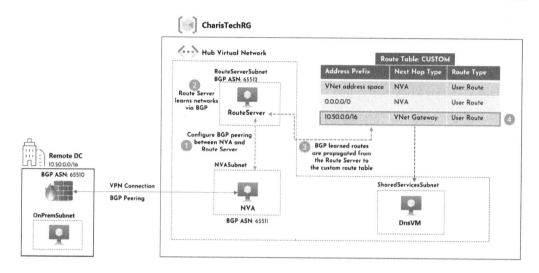

Figure 3.38 – BGP route advertisement via Route Server

- *(1)* we configure BGP peering between the NVA and Route Server.

- *(2)* Route Server learns networks and exchanges routing information with the NVA via BGP.

- *(3)* BGP-learned routes are propagated from Route Server to the custom route table. Note that this step will only happen if the option to propagate gateway routes is configured for the route table, as shown in *Figure 3.37.*

- *(4)* the learned routes are added (and removed) dynamically to the route table.

For high availability, we implement two NVAs and peer Route Server with both NVAs. We just need to ensure that we don't use conflicting BGP **autonomous system numbers** (**ASN**).

Enough discussion for now; let's head over to our Azure environment to implement BGP dynamic routing with Azure Route Server.

Hands-on exercise – implementing BGP dynamic routing with Azure Route Server

Azure routes traffic between all subnets within a VNet by default. You can create your own routes to override Azure's default routing. Custom routes are helpful when, for example, you want to route traffic between subnets through an NVA.

In this exercise, we will inject three routes into Azure subnet route tables using the Azure Route Server option: `10.100.1.0/24`, `10.100.2.0/24`, and `10.100.3.0/24`.

In this exercise, you will review and test the capabilities of the Azure-provided DNS option. Here are the tasks that we will complete in this exercise:

- **Task 1**: Add a dedicated subnet for the route server
- **Task 2**: Deploy Route Server into `RouteServerSubnet`
- **Task 3**: Configure BGP peering on NvaVM
- **Task 4**: Configure BGP peering on the route server
- **Task 5**: Validate the configuration and learned routes

Task 1 – adding a dedicated subnet for the route server

Azure Route Server requires a dedicated subnet named `RouteServerSubnet`. (Yes, it must be called exactly that.) The subnet size has to be at least `/27` or a short prefix (such as `/26` or `/25`), or you'll receive an error message when deploying Route Server.

1. Run the following command to add `RouteServerSubnet` to your VNet:

    ```
    az network vnet subnet create --name RouteServerSubnet
    --resource-group CharisTechRG-C3 --vnet-name CoreServicesVNet
    --address-prefix 10.10.10.0/24
    ```

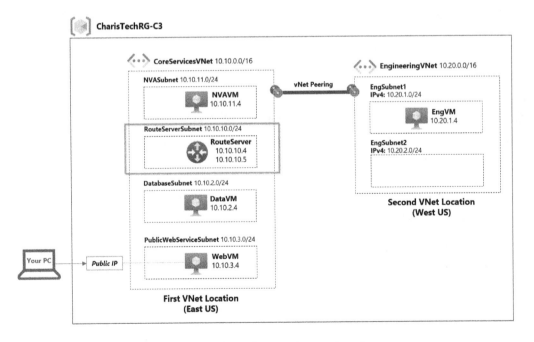

Figure 3.39 – Route Server subnet and service

2. Obtain the resource ID of the newly created `RouteServerSubnet` and store it as a variable called `subnet_id`:

    ```
    subnet_id=$(az network vnet subnet show --name RouteServerSubnet
    --resource-group CharisTechRG-C3 --vnet-name CoreServicesVNet
    --query id -o tsv)
    ```

Task 2 – deploying Route Server into RouteServerSubnet

To allow connectivity to the backend management service that manages the Route Server configuration, it needs to be assigned a public IP address:

1. Create a standard public IP resource using the following command:

    ```
    az network public-ip create --name CoreServicesRouteServerIP
    --resource-group CharisTechRG-C3 --version IPv4 --sku Standard
    ```

2. Deploy Route Server with the command that follows. The `hosted-subnet` parameter specified the resource ID of `RouteServerSubnet` that we obtained in the previous task:

    ```
    az network routeserver create --name CoreServicesRouteServer
    --resource-group CharisTechRG-C3 --hosted-subnet $subnet_id
    --public-ip-address CoreServicesRouteServerIP
    ```

    This command takes about 20 minutes to complete, so feel free to get a cup of coffee/tea and come back to this later.

Task 3 – configuring BGP peering on NvaVM

The steps are as follows:

1. From the SSH session to **WebVM**, connect to **NvaVM** using the following command:

    ```
    ssh azureuser@nvavm
    ```

2. If you are prompted about the authenticity of the host, type `yes` and press *Enter*. When prompted to enter the password, enter the complex password that you used in *Hands-on exercise 1 – Task 1 – Step 4*.

3. You should now be connected to the **NvaVM** VM. Enter the following command to switch to a privileged user:

    ```
    sudo su -
    ```

4. Verify that the BGP service is running on this VM with the following command:

    ```
    systemctl status bgpd.service
    ```

The screenshot for reference is as follows:

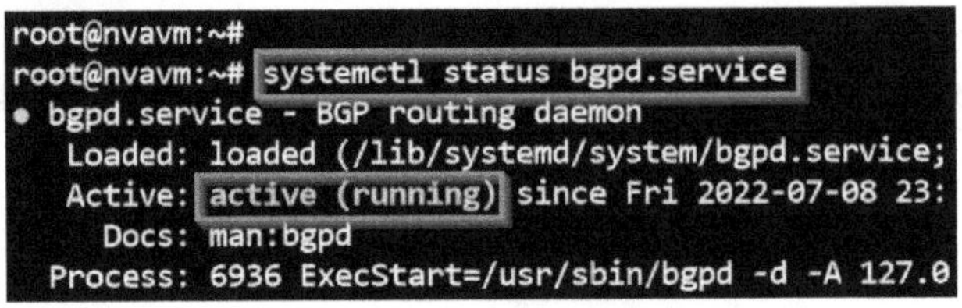

```
root@nvavm:~#
root@nvavm:~# systemctl status bgpd.service
● bgpd.service - BGP routing daemon
   Loaded: loaded (/lib/systemd/system/bgpd.service;
   Active: active (running) since Fri 2022-07-08 23:
     Docs: man:bgpd
  Process: 6936 ExecStart=/usr/sbin/bgpd -d -A 127.0
```

Figure 3.40 – Verify the status of the BGP service

5. To simplify things, I have prepared a script that we will use to configure BGP on NvaVM. Download the script using the following command:

    ```
    wget https://raw.githubusercontent.com/PacktPublishing/
    Designing-and-Implementing-Microsoft-Azure-Networking-Solutions/
    main/Chapter03/template/nvabgpconfig.sh
    ```

6. Run the script using the following commands:

    ```
    chmod +x nvabgpconfig.sh
    ./nvabgpconfig.sh
    ```

7. Review the Quagga configuration file using the following command:

    ```
    cat /etc/quagga/bgpd.conf
    ```

The configuration that will be used in the next task will match the configuration specified in this file:

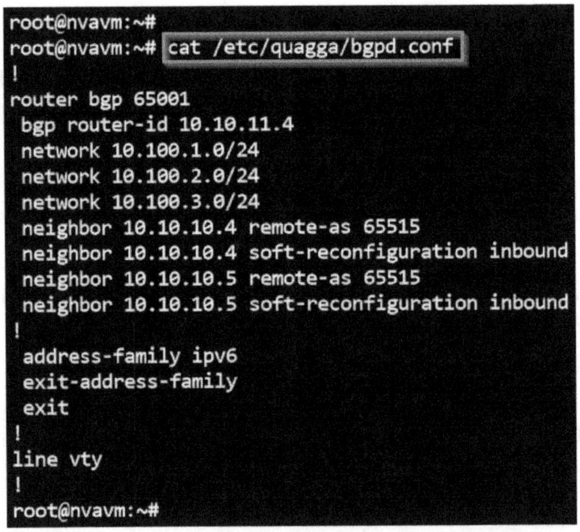

```
root@nvavm:~#
root@nvavm:~# cat /etc/quagga/bgpd.conf
!
router bgp 65001
 bgp router-id 10.10.11.4
 network 10.100.1.0/24
 network 10.100.2.0/24
 network 10.100.3.0/24
 neighbor 10.10.10.4 remote-as 65515
 neighbor 10.10.10.4 soft-reconfiguration inbound
 neighbor 10.10.10.5 remote-as 65515
 neighbor 10.10.10.5 soft-reconfiguration inbound
!
 address-family ipv6
 exit-address-family
 exit
!
line vty
!
root@nvavm:~#
```

Figure 3.41 – Review the BGP configuration file

8. The information used for the neighbor IPs and the remote **Autonomous System Numbers** (**ASNs**) can be obtained using the following commands:

```
az network routeserver show --name CoreServicesRouteServer
--resource-group CharisTechRG-C3 --query virtualRouterAsn
az network routeserver show --name CoreServicesRouteServer
--resource-group CharisTechRG-C3 --query virtualRouterIps
```

Task 4 – configuring BGP peering on the route server

In Azure Cloud Shell, run the following command to establish BGP peering between Route Server and the NVA. peer-ip is the VNet IP assigned to the NVA. peer-asn is the ASN configured in the NVA. The ASN can be any 16-bit number other than the ones in the range of 65515-65520. This range of ASNs is reserved by Microsoft:

```
az network routeserver peering create --name NvaVM-Peering --peer-
ip 10.10.11.4 --peer-asn 65001 --routeserver CoreServicesRouteServer
--resource-group CharisTechRG-C3
```

The output should show successful provisioning, as shown:

```
david@Azure:~$
david@Azure:~$ az network routeserver peering create --name NvaVM-Peering --peer-ip
10.10.11.4 --peer-asn 65001 --routeserver CoreServicesRouteServer --resource-group
CharisTechRG-C3
{
  "connectionState": null,
  "etag": "W/\"2750f893-d5cf-465f-b777-77a323d89c75\"",
  "hubVirtualNetworkConnection": null,
  "id": "/subscriptions/e08ac56b-a93c-435e-8ada-49eeabc2cc64/resourceGroups/CharisT
echRG-C3/providers/Microsoft.Network/virtualHubs/CoreServicesRouteServer/bgpConnect
ions/NvaVM-Peering",
  "name": "NvaVM-Peering",
  "peerAsn": 65001,
  "peerIp": "10.10.11.4",
  "provisioningState": "Succeeded",   ◀——————
  "resourceGroup": "CharisTechRG-C3",
  "type": "Microsoft.Network/virtualHubs/bgpConnections"
}
david@Azure:~$
```

Figure 3.42 – Output of the route server peering configuration

For redundancy, we could repeat the same process to peer the route server with a different NVA or another instance of the same NVA. We just need to use a different *peer name*, *peer IP*, and *peer ASN*.

Task 5 – validating the configuration and learned routes

Now, let us validate that the route server has learned the three networks from the NVA via BGP. We will also validate that these three networks have now been advertised to subnet route tables:

1. In Azure Cloud Shell, run the following command to list the routes that are learned by Azure Route Server from the peered NVA:

    ```
    az network routeserver peering list-learned-routes --name NvaVM-
    Peering --routeserver CoreServicesRouteServer --resource-group
    CharisTechRG-C3
    ```

    The output should be like what we have here:

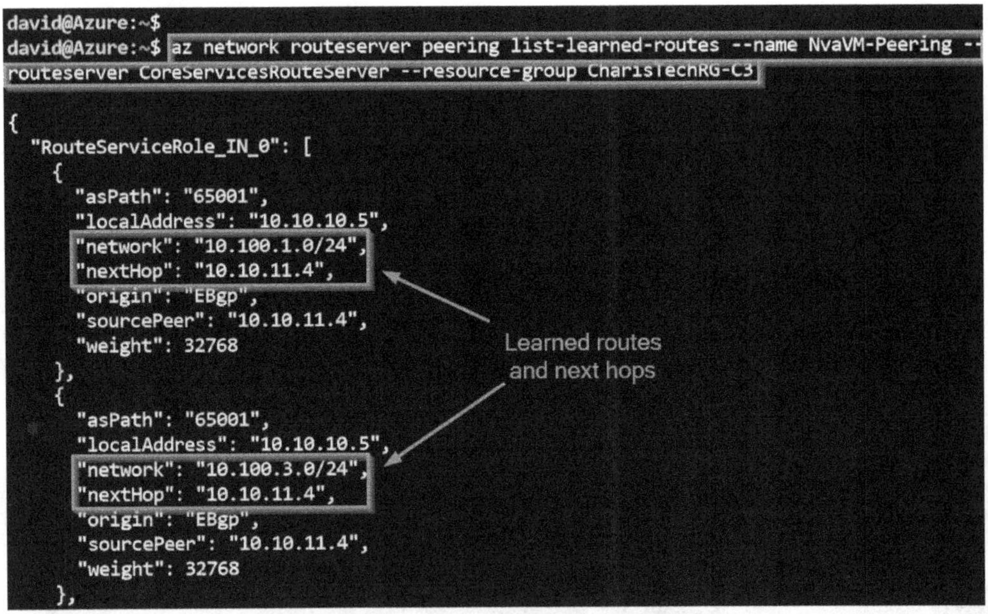

Figure 3.43 – Review the learned routes and next hops

2. In the Azure portal search area, type datavmNetInt and press *Enter*. Click on the displayed network interface resource.

3. In the **datavmNetInt** blade, scroll to the **Support + troubleshooting** section in the left menu options and click on **Effective routes**.

4. Wait for a few seconds for the effective routes to be calculated. Observe the routes that were advertised by the route server. They are marked with a source of **Virtual network gateway**, as shown in *Figure 3.44*.

Effective routes

Source	State	Address Prefixes	Next Hop Type	Next Hop IP Address
Default	Active	10.10.0.0/16	Virtual network	-
Virtual network gateway	Active	10.100.1.0/24	Virtual network gateway	10.10.11.4
Virtual network gateway	Active	10.100.2.0/24	Virtual network gateway	10.10.11.4
Virtual network gateway	Active	10.100.3.0/24	Virtual network gateway	10.10.11.4
Default	Active	0.0.0.0/0	Internet	-

Figure 3.44 – Verify the system routes that were added to the effective route table

Route selection and priority

With these manual and dynamic options to modify subnet route tables, how are routing decisions made if more than one routing entry matches for the same destination (overlapping routes)? *Figure 3.45* shows an example of this. It shows a subnet route table with two overlapping route entries: a route entry for the destination network of 10.10.0.0/24 (next hop: VNet peering) and another route entry for the destination network 10.10.0.0/16 (next hop: VNet gateway). How will traffic sent to 10.10.0.100 be routed as the IP address is matched by both route entries?

Route Table: DEFAULT	
Address Prefix	Next Hop Type
10.10.0.0/24	VNet Peering
10.10.0.0/16	VNet Gateway

Which route will be used?

Destination IP: 10.10.0.100

Figure 3.45 – Route selection when entries overlap

In scenarios like this, Azure goes through a route selection process to determine how the traffic will be routed. The following are the algorithms used for this selection:

- **Longest prefix match**: This is the first algorithm that Azure considers for route selection. When outbound traffic is sent from a subnet, Azure selects the path based on the *most specific route* that matches the traffic. In the preceding example, the route entry for the destination prefix of 10.10.0.0/24 will be used because it is more specific than the route for 10.10.0.0/24 even though 10.10.0.100 is within both address prefixes.

- **Route type match**: If there are two route entries with the same address prefix, Azure uses the route type to determine the path selection. Route type selection is based on the following priority: *static user-defined route entries | dynamically learned routes (BGP) | system routes*. *Figure 3.46* shows a similar example to the previous one, but this time, both route entries have the same prefix. In this case, the destination prefix of 10.10.0.0/24 will be used because user-defined routes have a higher priority than dynamically (BGP) learned routes.

Subnet Effective Route Table		
Source	Address Prefix	Next Hop Type
User-defined (static)	10.10.0.0/24	Network Virtual Appliance
BGP	10.10.0.0/24	VNet Gateway

Which route will be used?

Destination IP: 10.10.0.100

Figure 3.46 – Route selection with route-type match

> **Note**
> You can't configure multiple user-defined routes with the same address prefix.

Hands-on exercise – cleaning up resources

In this exercise, we will remove the resources that we created in the chapter exercises to avoid running up a large cost in Azure!

In Cloud Shell, run the following command to delete the `CharisTechRG-C3` resource group:

```
az group delete --name CharisTechRG-C3 --yes
```

This will remove all the resources that we created for the exercises in this chapter.

Summary

In this chapter, we established a good foundation of understanding routing in Azure and how we can control/influence the path that traffic takes when it leaves an Azure subnet. We discussed how to implement custom routing with route tables and user-defined routes. We implemented custom routing with user-defined routes and BGP-advertised routes via a route server.

In the next chapter, we will start to build on this foundation by covering the first aspect of connectivity – cross-VNet connectivity. See you in the next chapter!

Further reading

Refer to the following links for more information about the topics covered in this chapter:

- VNet routing: https://docs.microsoft.com/en-us/azure/virtual-network/virtual-networks-udr-overview

- Azure Route Server FAQ: https://docs.microsoft.com/en-us/azure/route-server/route-server-faq

4

Design and Implement Cross-VNet Connectivity

The main purpose of an **Azure Virtual Network** (**Azure VNet**) is to facilitate the delivery of data between point A (an Azure VNet workload) and point B (other connected systems). Sometimes, point B is a workload in another Azure VNet.

In this chapter, we will cover the options that we have to connect workloads in different Azure VNets together. By the end of this chapter, you will have a strong understanding of the following:

- Connecting VNets using VNet peering
- Connecting VNets using a VPN gateway connection
- Connecting VNets using a **virtual WAN** (**vWan**)

Each topic has been structured to align with the recommended network connectivity best practices in Azure. Let us get into this!

The following are the main topics that we will cover in this chapter:

- Understanding cross-VNet connectivity
- Connecting VNets using VNet peering
- Connecting VNets using a VPN gateway connection
- Connecting VNets using a vWAN
- Hands-on exercise – provisioning resources for the chapter
- Hands-on exercise – implementing cross-region VNet connectivity using a vWAN
- Comparing the three cross-VNet connectivity options
- Hands-on exercise – cleaning up resources

Technical requirements

To follow along with the instructions in this chapter, you will need the following:

- A PC with an internet connection
- An Azure subscription

Before we proceed to cover the security best practices, let us prepare our Azure subscription for the hands-on exercises that we complete later in the chapter.

Understanding cross-VNet connectivity options

There are three main ways to connect VNets (*Figure 4.1*):

- VNet peering
- A VPN gateway connection (VNet-to-VNet or Site-to-Site)
- A vWAN (covered in the *Connecting VNets using a vWAN* section)

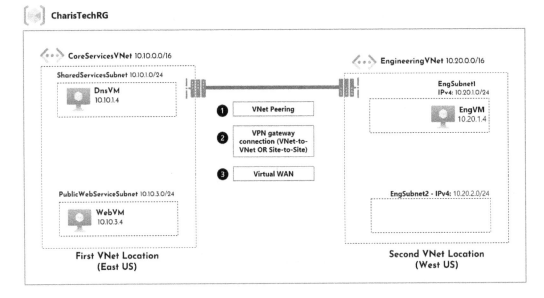

Figure 4.1 – Cross-VNet connectivity options

Let us examine these options starting from the first one – VNet peering!

Connecting VNets using VNet peering

As we have seen in previous chapters of this book, VNet peering enables us to transfer data between VNets within and across Azure subscriptions, Azure Active Directory tenants, and Azure regions. Since we have implemented VNet peering and seen it in action previously, we will focus more on use cases in this discussion.

The main advantage of this option is that the traffic flow between workloads with peered VNets will leverage the *low-latency* and *high-bandwidth* Microsoft backbone infrastructure. The traffic is not routed through a gateway or over the public internet.

Another advantage of this option is its *ease of implementation* – we don't need to deploy any extra resources such as a virtual network gateway to implement this connectivity option. We can connect two VNets in a matter of seconds!

So, which scenarios are supported for peering? VNet peering supports connecting VNets within the same Azure region (**Regional peering**) and connecting VNets across Azure regions (**Global peering**) – see *Figure 4.2*. The VNets could be in the same or different Azure subscription or Azure AD tenant! The VNets could also have IPv4 only or dual-stack address spaces – see *Figure 4.2*:

Figure 4.2 – Supported scenarios for VNet peering

Planning VNet peering implementation

As mentioned earlier, VNet peering is very easy to implement. However, there are some prerequisites to keep in mind. The first one is that *there can be no overlap between the IP address spaces of the VNets*. This would result in an error message such as the one in *Figure 4.3*.

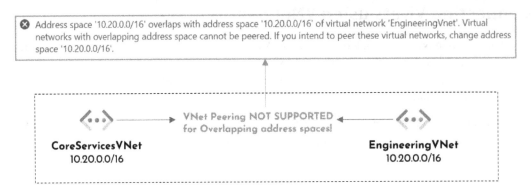

> ⊗ Address space '10.20.0.0/16' overlaps with address space '10.20.0.0/16' of virtual network 'EngineeringVnet'. Virtual networks with overlapping address space cannot be peered. If you intend to peer these virtual networks, change address space '10.20.0.0/16'.

Figure 4.3 – Peering not supported for overlapping address spaces

The other prerequisite to note is the permissions needed to configure the peering relationship. The **Network Contributor** built-in role or a custom role with the following permissions will be sufficient:

- Microsoft.Network/virtualNetworks/virtualNetworkPeerings/read

- Microsoft.Network/virtualNetworks/virtualNetworkPeerings/write

- Microsoft.Network/virtualNetworks/peer/action

Because peering needs to be established at both ends of the connection, the permissions must be assigned to both the source and target VNet.

What about downtime? Do we need to plan for downtime when implementing VNet peering? The answer is *no*. There is no connectivity downtime for resources in either VNet when creating the peering, or after the peering is created. However, keep in mind that if you implement the default configuration, the effective route table will be modified.

Understanding VNet peering architecture considerations

From a **scalability** perspective, the address spaces of the peered VNets can be modified without incurring any downtime. This is useful when we need to grow or resize the address spaces of the VNets after creating the peering connection. This wasn't always the case. In the past, we needed to disconnect and re-establish the peering relationship for any address space changes to be applied!

From a **performance** perspective, regional VNet peering does not add any extra latency between workloads in the connected VNets.

From a **security** perspective, we can implement **network security groups (NSGs)** in VNet subnets to block or allow access as needed. NSGs will be covered in a later chapter in this book.

Understanding VNet peering and transitive routing

Apart from the inability to peer VNets with overlapping address spaces, the main limitation of VNet peering is that they are not transitive. For example, *Figure 4.4* shows two peering relationships established between three VNets: a peering relationship between the **CoreServices** VNet and the **Engineering** VNet, and another peering relationship between the **Engineering** VNet and the **Research** VNet. In this setup, there is no transitive peering between the **CoreServices** VNet and the **Research** VNet!

If we want resources in the **CoreServices** VNet and the **Research** VNet to directly communicate, we can establish explicit peering between them in a full-mesh architecture. The downside to this approach is that if we have a lot of VNets in our environment, we might exceed the maximum number of possible peering connections, which is 500 at the time of writing.

Another approach is to add a **network virtual appliance** (**NVA**) with routing capabilities to the **Engineering** VNet to route between the two VNets.

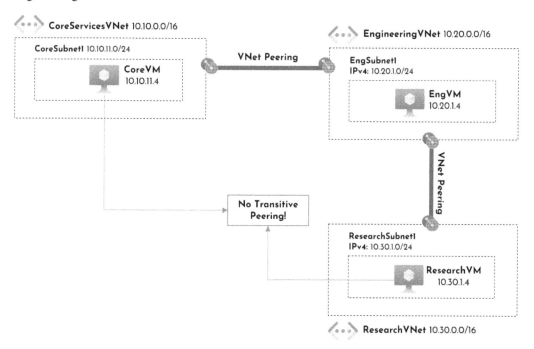

Figure 4.4 – No transitive peering support

Configuring VNet peering

Configuration of the peering relationship between two VNets can be done using any Azure management tool that you prefer – the portal, the CLI, PowerShell, ARM, or Bicep. Here are the steps involved:

1. Create two VNets.
2. Configure the peering relationship on the source network to the target network.
3. Configure the peering relationship on the target network to the source network.
4. Test the peering relationship.

If the peering relationship is between two VNets in the same Azure AD tenant and if the admin has the right level of permissions, *steps 2* and *3* can be performed at the same time for quicker implementation!

VNet peering in a hub-and-spoke architecture

VNet peering is commonly used in the implementation of the *hub-and-spoke network architecture* in which the hub VNet acts as the central point of connectivity to the internet, our on-premises networks, and other networks in Azure. Services that are shared organization-wide can also be hosted in the hub VNet. The spoke VNets host the workloads and are peered with the hub but not directly with each other. *Figure 4.5* shows an example of this architecture.

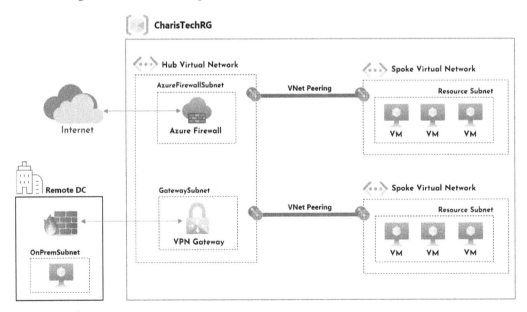

Figure 4.5 – Hub-and-spoke network architecture in Azure

In this setup, there are settings that we can enable to facilitate this architecture. For example, if we want to allow workloads in the spoke VNet to use the VPN gateway in the hub VNet to communicate with the on-premises or remote DC network, we need to implement **Setting A** in *Figure 4.6* on the peering connection on the hub VNet and the **Setting B** in *Figure 4.6* on the peering connection on the spoke VNet.

When both **Setting A (Use this virtual network's gateway or Route Server)** and **Setting B (Use the remote virtual network's gateway or Route Server)** are configured as part of the hub-and-spoke peering connection respectively, it allows the workloads in the peered spoke VNets to use the VNet gateway in the hub or the routes injected by the route server into the hub.

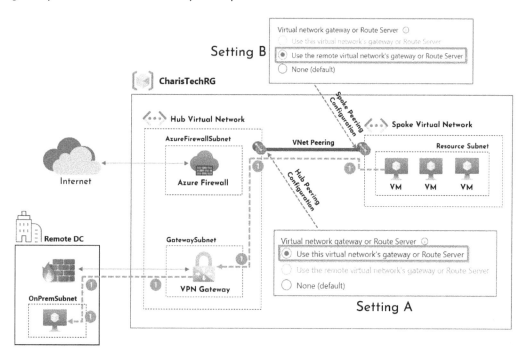

Figure 4.6 – Gateway transit and connectivity

To allow a service chaining architecture in which traffic flows through NVAs or VPN gateways in the hub VNet to the spoke VNets without network address translation, we can implement the setting in *Figure 4.7* when configuring the peering relationship. This setting allows traffic forwarding via the hub VNet:

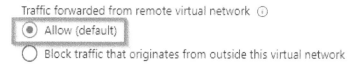

Figure 4.7 – Allow traffic forwarding

The benefits of using a hub-and-spoke architecture include cost savings because we don't need to implement a gateway or shared services across each spoke VNet, and overcoming subscription limits because services are reused.

Connecting VNets using a VPN gateway connection

The second option for connecting two VNets is to use a VPN gateway connection. This option uses Azure VPN Gateway to provide a secure IPsec/IKE tunnel to the target VNet. It is not as easy to implement, as it requires a VPN gateway with a public IP to be deployed in the VNets (*Figure 4.8*). Deploying the gateway could take around 40 minutes.

Also, unlike VNet peering, the traffic is routed over the public internet and not privately via the Microsoft backbone:

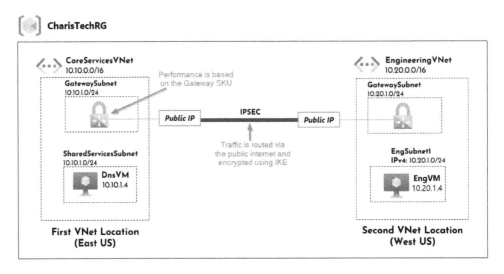

Figure 4.8 – Traffic is routed over the public internet

So why would we use this option if it is more complex to implement and if it is routed over the public internet? The main advantage of this option is that the traffic flow between the VNets is encrypted using IKE, and this may be a security or compliance requirement for specific use cases that we have.

When implementing the VPN gateway to connect two VNets, there are two connection types that we can use (see *Figure 4.9*):

- **VNet-to-VNet connection**: If the source and target VNets are in the same Azure subscription, we can use this option (marked **1** in *Figure 4.9*).

- **Site-to-Site (IPsec) connection**: If the source and target VNets are not in the same Azure subscription (for example, different Azure AD tenants), we can use this (marked **2** in *Figure 4.9*):

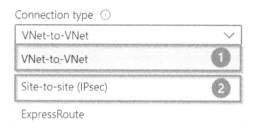

Figure 4.9 – VPN Gateway connection types

The **VNet-to-VNet connection type** is typically faster and easier to implement than the **Site-to-Site connection type**. When we use a **VNet-to-VNet connection**, the configuration for the remote gateway and networks are automatically created and populated. Also, if the address space for one of the connected VNets is populated, the other VNet automatically routes to the updated address space.

> **Note**
>
> If you're working with a complicated network configuration, you may prefer to connect your VNets by using a Site-to-Site connection instead. When you follow the Site-to-Site IPsec steps, you create and configure the local network gateways manually. The local network gateway for each VNet treats the other VNet as a local site.

Another advantage of this option is that we can use it to connect VNets with overlapping address spaces using its support for NAT rules (see *Figure 4.10*):

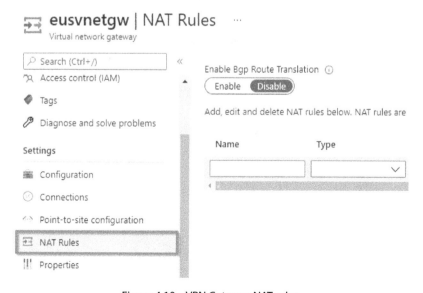

Figure 4.10 – VPN Gateway NAT rules

Understanding VPN Gateway architecture considerations

From a **performance** perspective, the bandwidth is restricted depending on the SKU of the VPN gateway that is deployed. We will cover VPN gateways in further detail in the next chapter.

From a **security** perspective, we can implement NSGs in VNet subnets to block or allow access as needed. NSGs will be covered in a later chapter in this book.

Connecting VNets using a vWAN

A **vWAN** is a networking service that optimizes network connectivity implementation in Azure. Here are some of the capabilities that it offers:

- **Cloud network connectivity**: Connecting VNets to each other and hybrid networks
- **Private WAN connectivity**: Connecting remote data centers to Azure and each other using the ExpressRoute gateway
- **Branch connectivity and remote user connectivity**: Connecting branch offices and remote users to Azure and other connected networks using Azure VPN Gateway (a Site-to-Site VPN or Point-to-Site VPN)
- **Network security integration**: Azure Firewall

As you can see, these capabilities are not unique to Azure vWAN, but it simplifies them and integrates them into a single service. The good thing is we don't have to implement all the use cases of the vWAN all at once. We can get started with just one use case, and then adjust as our requirement evolves.

We will be covering the vWAN as a service, along with other capabilities that it supports, in greater detail in *Chapter 5* of this book but we will just focus on its cross-VNet connectivity capability in this chapter!

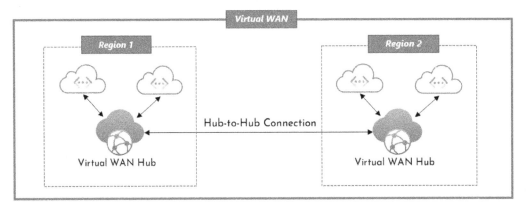

Figure 4.11 – Sample virtual WAN implementation for cross-VNet connectivity

One of the main advantages of using a vWAN to connect VNets together is transitivity. Azure Virtual WAN enables full transitivity among connected networks which is a limitation of VNet peering.

Hands-on exercise – provisioning resources for the chapter

To follow along with the exercises in this chapter, we will provision some Azure resources to work with. We have prepared an Azure ARM template in the GitHub repository of this book for this purpose. The template will deploy two peered VNets in two Azure regions as shown in *Figure 4.12*:

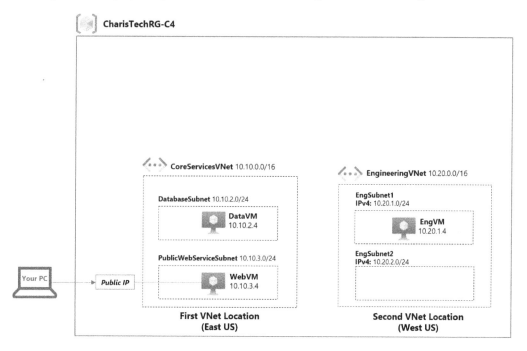

Figure 4.12 – Resources deployed via the provided ARM template

The first VNet (**CoreServicesVNet**) will have two subnets with a **virtual machine** (**VM**) in each subnet. The second VNet (**EngineeringVNet**) will have two subnets with a VM in one subnet. One of the VMs (**WebVM**) will be assigned a public IP address so you can connect to it from your PC over the internet. Here are the tasks that we will complete in this exercise:

- **Task 1**: Initialize the template deployment in GitHub

Let's get into it!

Task 1 – initializing the template deployment in GitHub

1. Open a web browser and browse to `https://packt.link/6y9nu`. This link will open the GitHub repository that has the ARM template to deploy the resources that we need.

2. In the GitHub repository that opens, click on **Deploy to Azure**.

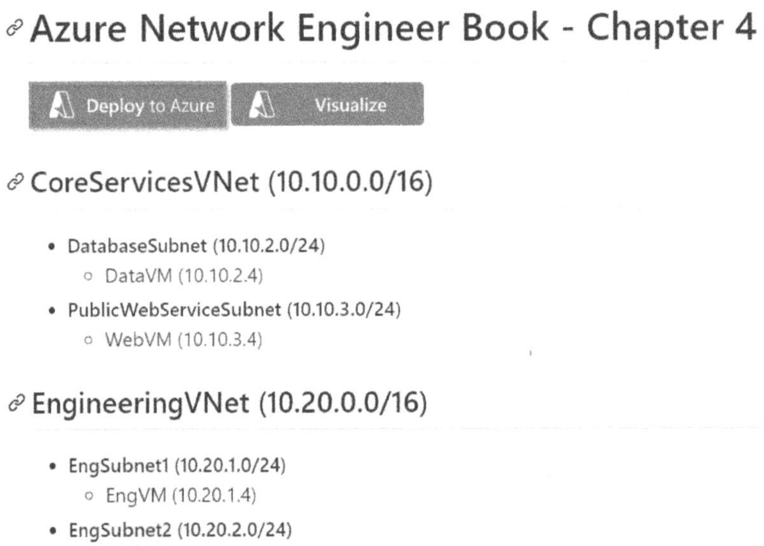

🔗 Azure Network Engineer Book - Chapter 4

🔗 CoreServicesVNet (10.10.0.0/16)

- DatabaseSubnet (10.10.2.0/24)
    - DataVM (10.10.2.4)
- PublicWebServiceSubnet (10.10.3.0/24)
    - WebVM (10.10.3.4)

🔗 EngineeringVNet (10.20.0.0/16)

- EngSubnet1 (10.20.1.0/24)
    - EngVM (10.20.1.4)
- EngSubnet2 (10.20.2.0/24)

Figure 4.13 – Starting the template deployment

3. If prompted to authenticate, sign in to the Azure portal with your administrative username and password.

4. In the **Custom Deployment** window, configure the following:

    - **Subscription**: Select the subscription that you want to deploy the resources into

    - **Resource group**: **Create New** | **Name**: `CharisTechRG-C4` | **OK**

    - **Region**: **East US** (or select the region that you verified in the first chapter of this book)

    - **Admin Password**: Enter a complex password and make a note of it, as it will be needed for later exercises

    - **Vm Size**: **Standard_B2s** (or select the VM size that you verified in the first chapter of this book)

    - **Second Vnet Location**: **West US** (or select the second region that you verified in the first chapter of this book)

Select **Review + Create**:

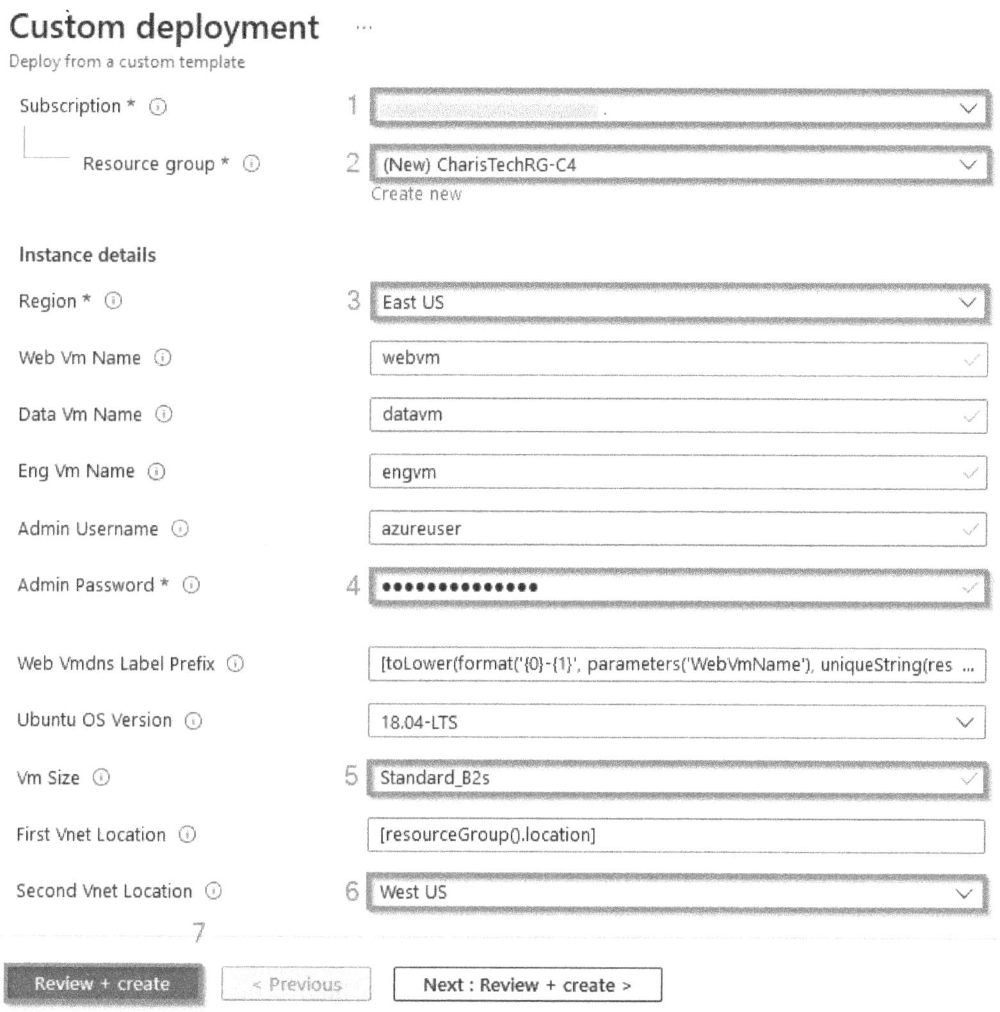

Custom deployment ...
Deploy from a custom template

Subscription * ⓘ	1 [_____] ⌄
└ Resource group * ⓘ	2 (New) CharisTechRG-C4 ⌄
	Create new

Instance details

Region * ⓘ	3 East US ⌄
Web Vm Name ⓘ	webvm ✓
Data Vm Name ⓘ	datavm ✓
Eng Vm Name ⓘ	engvm ✓
Admin Username ⓘ	azureuser ✓
Admin Password * ⓘ	4 ••••••••••••••• ✓
Web Vmdns Label Prefix ⓘ	[toLower(format('{0}-{1}', parameters('WebVmName'), uniqueString(res ...
Ubuntu OS Version ⓘ	18.04-LTS ⌄
Vm Size ⓘ	5 Standard_B2s ✓
First Vnet Location ⓘ	[resourceGroup().location]
Second Vnet Location ⓘ	6 West US ⌄

7

[Review + create]   [< Previous]   [Next : Review + create >]

Figure 4.14 – Completing the custom deployment options

5. Once it has been validated, select **Create** to proceed with the deployment. The deployment takes about 5 minutes to complete.

6. After the deployment has been completed, click on the **Outputs** tab (on the left-hand side), and make a note of the following values:

   - **sshCommand**: This gives you the SSH command that you can use to connect to **WebVM** (one of the deployed VMs) using its public DNS name. We will need this in later exercises.

Figure 4.15 – Obtaining the SSH command to connect to WebVM's DNS name

Congratulations! You have now deployed the resources needed to complete the exercises in this chapter. In the next hands-on exercise, you will explore the default routing of Azure subnet workloads.

Hands-on exercise – implementing cross-region VNet connectivity using the vWAN

Here are the tasks that we will complete in this exercise:

- **Task 1**: Create a vWAN
- **Task 2**: Create a virtual hub in each VNet location in the vWAN
- **Task 3**: Connect the VNets to the regional virtual hubs
- **Task 4**: Verify effective routes on the VNets and the virtual hubs
- **Task 5**: Verify the connectivity between the VNets

Let's get into it!

Task 1 – creating a vWAN

1.   The first thing that we will do is create a vWAN called CharisTechVirtualWAN. A vWAN is a virtual overlay that we can use to connect cloud and hybrid networks in a seamless way. *Figure 4.16* shows what our implementation will look like at the end of this task:

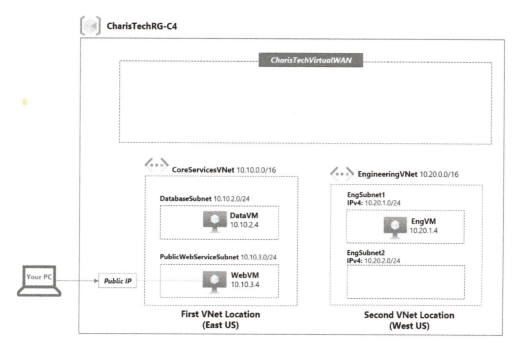

Figure 4.16 – Implementation by the end of this task

2. Open a web browser and go to the Azure portal – `https://portal.azure.com`. If prompted to authenticate, sign in with your administrative username and password.

3. In the Azure portal search area, type `Virtual WAN` and press *Enter*. Click on the vWAN service displayed.

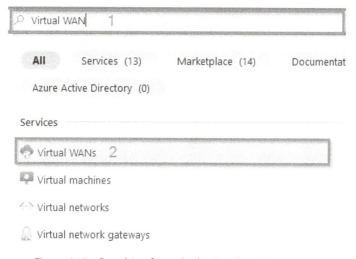

Figure 4.17 – Searching for and selecting the vWAN service

4. On the **Virtual WAN** page, select **+ Create**.

5. On the **Create WAN** page, on the **Basics** tab, set the following configurations:

    -   **Subscription**: Select the subscription that you want to deploy the resources into

    -   **Resource group**: **CharisTechRG-C4**

    -   **Region**: **East US**

    -   **Name**: CharisTechVirtualWAN

    -   **Type**: **Standard**

    Select **Review + Create**:

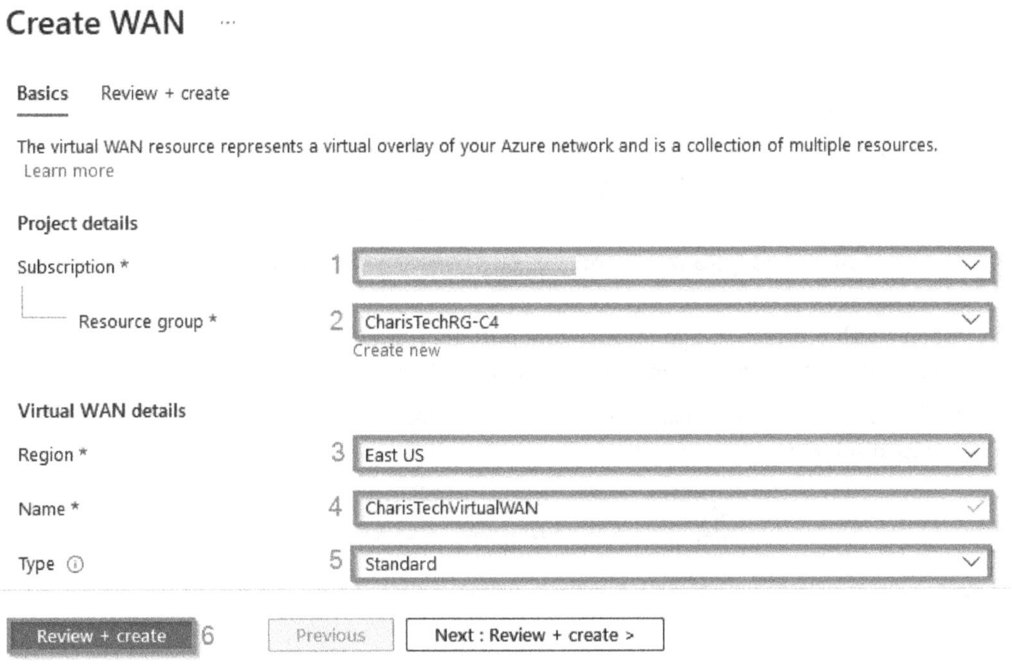

Create WAN   ···

Basics   Review + create

The virtual WAN resource represents a virtual overlay of your Azure network and is a collection of multiple resources.
Learn more

Project details

Subscription *	1	
└── Resource group *	2	CharisTechRG-C4
		Create new

Virtual WAN details

Region *	3	East US
Name *	4	CharisTechVirtualWAN
Type ⓘ	5	Standard

[Review + create] 6   [Previous]   [Next : Review + create >]

Figure 4.18 – Configuring the parameters of the virtual WAN

6. Once validation passes, select **Create** to create the vWAN.

7. Wait for the resource creation process to complete and then click on **Go to resource**.

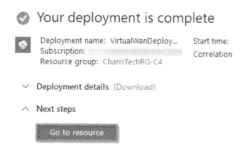

Figure 4.19 – Going to the resource that was created

Task 2 – creating a virtual hub in each VNet location in the vWAN

To connect VNets to the vWAN, we need to create at least one virtual hub. Behind the scenes, a virtual hub is a Microsoft-managed VNet that we can use for simplified connectivity.

It is a good practice to create a virtual hub in each Azure region in which you have a cluster of resources present. That is what we will be doing in this task! We will create two virtual hubs – one in the same region as the first VNet called `CharisTechVirtualWANHub-EastUS` and another in the region of the second VNet called `CharisTechVirtualWANHub-WestUS`.

By the end of this task, our implementation will look like what we can see in *Figure 4.20*:

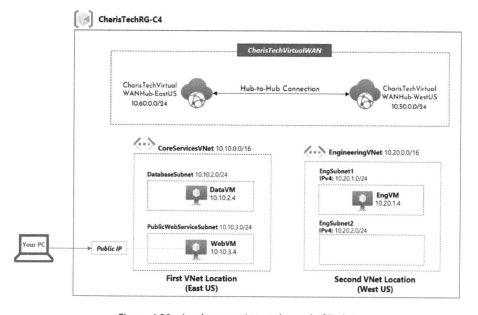

Figure 4.20 – Implementation at the end of Task 2

1. In the ** CharisTech VirtualWAN** window, in the **Connectivity** section, select **Hubs**. On the **Hubs** page, select **+New Hub** to create a new vWAN hub.

Figure 4.21 – Creating a new vWAN hub

2. In the **Create virtual hub** window, in the **Basics** tab, configure the following:

    • **Region**: **East US** (or select the region that you verified in the first chapter of this book)

    • **Name**: CharisTechVirtualWANHub-EastUS

    • **Hub private address space**: 10.60.0.0/24 (remember that this is a Microsoft-managed VNet behind the scenes, so it needs an address space)

    • **Virtual hub capacity**: **2 Routing Infrastructure Units, 3 Gbps Router, Support 2000 VMs** (this value determines the throughput of the vWAN hub router and the number of a that can be deployed in VNets connected to the vWAN hub)

    As we won't be adding a VPN or ExpressRoute to this hub, we can leave the defaults and click on **Review + create**. Remember that we will cover more aspects of the vWAN service in the next chapter.

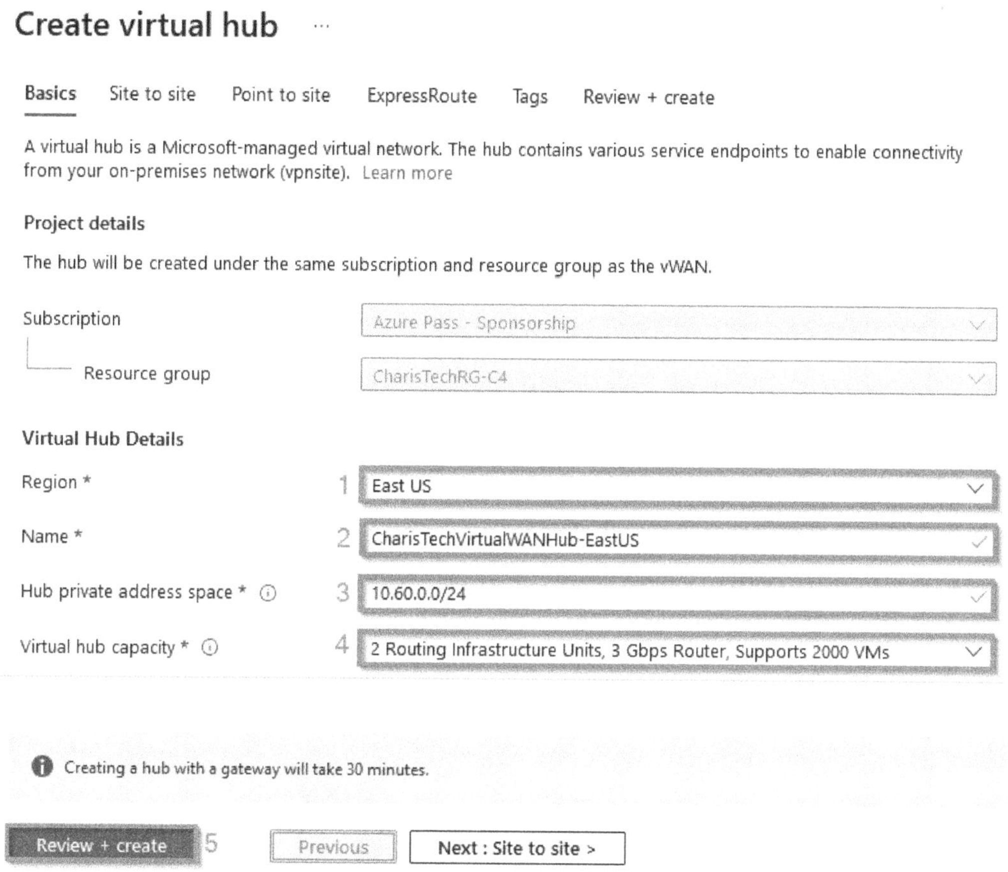

Create virtual hub ⋯

Basics   Site to site   Point to site   ExpressRoute   Tags   Review + create

A virtual hub is a Microsoft-managed virtual network. The hub contains various service endpoints to enable connectivity from your on-premises network (vpnsite). Learn more

Project details

The hub will be created under the same subscription and resource group as the vWAN.

Subscription	Azure Pass - Sponsorship ⌄
└── Resource group	CharisTechRG-C4 ⌄

Virtual Hub Details

Region *	1	East US ⌄
Name *	2	CharisTechVirtualWANHub-EastUS ✓
Hub private address space * ⓘ	3	10.60.0.0/24 ✓
Virtual hub capacity * ⓘ	4	2 Routing Infrastructure Units, 3 Gbps Router, Supports 2000 VMs ⌄

ⓘ Creating a hub with a gateway will take 30 minutes.

[Review + create] 5   [Previous]   [Next : Site to site >]

Figure 4.22 – Configuration options for the East US virtual hub

3. Select **Create** to create the hub. This could take up to 30 minutes to complete, so feel free to go to grab a glass of water or cup of tea or coffee.

4. Repeat *steps 1* to *3* of this task to create a second virtual hub in the second VNet region. Use the following configuration:

    • **Region: West US** (or select the second region that you verified in the first chapter of this book)

    • **Name**: CharisTechVirtualWANHub-WestUS

    • **Hub private address space**: 10.50.0.0/24

    • **Virtual hub capacity: 2 Routing Infrastructure Units, 3 Gbps Router, Support 2000 VMs**

    Click on **Review + create**.

Click on **Create**:

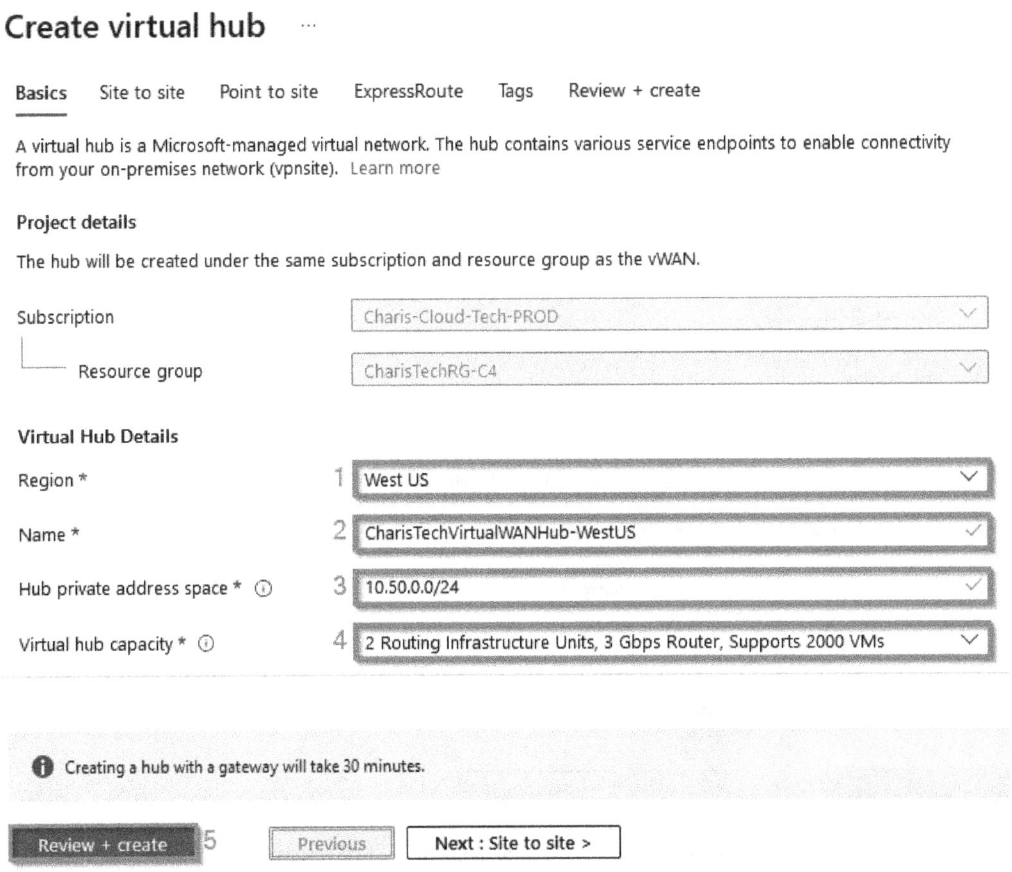

Create virtual hub   ...

Basics   Site to site   Point to site   ExpressRoute   Tags   Review + create

A virtual hub is a Microsoft-managed virtual network. The hub contains various service endpoints to enable connectivity from your on-premises network (vpnsite). Learn more

Project details

The hub will be created under the same subscription and resource group as the vWAN.

Subscription	Charis-Cloud-Tech-PROD	⌄
└─ Resource group	CharisTechRG-C4	⌄

Virtual Hub Details

Region *	1	West US	⌄
Name *	2	CharisTechVirtualWANHub-WestUS	✓
Hub private address space * ⓘ	3	10.50.0.0/24	✓
Virtual hub capacity * ⓘ	4	2 Routing Infrastructure Units, 3 Gbps Router, Supports 2000 VMs	⌄

ⓘ Creating a hub with a gateway will take 30 minutes.

Review + create	5	Previous	Next : Site to site >

Figure 4.23 – Configuration options for the West US virtual hub

After the virtual hubs are successfully created, let us review their status and their connectivity configuration.

5. To review the statuses of the virtual hubs, go to the **CharisTechVirtualWAN** resource window, and in the **Overview** section, review the hub statuses:

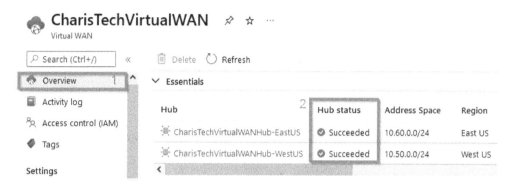

Figure 4.24 – Reviewing the virtual hub health statuses

6. Hubs in a vWAN are automatically connected. To review this, in the **CharisTechVirtualWAN** resource window, in the **Settings** section, click on **Configuration**:

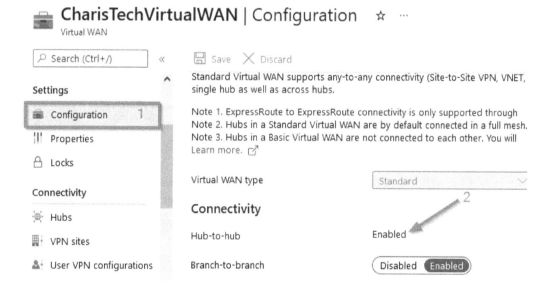

Figure 4.25 – Reviewing the hub-to-hub configuration

Task 3 – connecting the VNets to the regional virtual hubs

In this task, we will connect the VNets to the hubs in their respective regions. *Figure 4.26* shows what our implementation will look like at the end of this task:

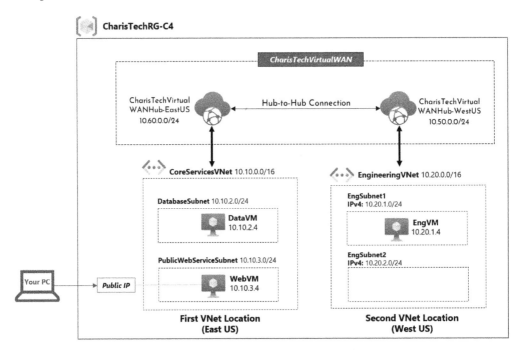

Figure 4.26 – Implementation by the end of Task 3

1. In the **CharisTechVirtualWAN** resource window, in the **Connectivity** section, select **Virtual network connections**. In the **CharisTechVirtualWAN | Virtual network connections** blade, select **+ Add connection**.

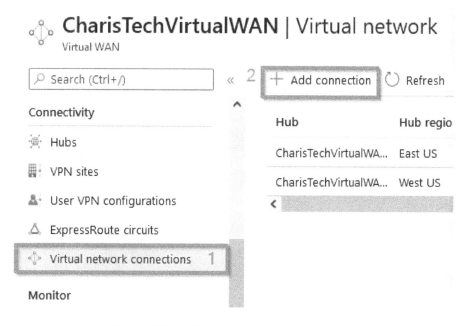

Figure 4.27 – Adding a virtual network connection

2. In the **Add connection** blade, configure the following:

    - **Connection name**: `CharisTechVirtualWAN-to-CoreServicesVNet`

    - **Hubs: CharisTechVirtualWANHub-EastUS**

    - **Subscription**: Select your Azure subscription

    - **Resource group: CharisTechRG-C4**

    - **Virtual network: CoreServicesVNet**

    - **Propagate to none: No**

    - **Associate Route Table: Default**

Select **Create**:

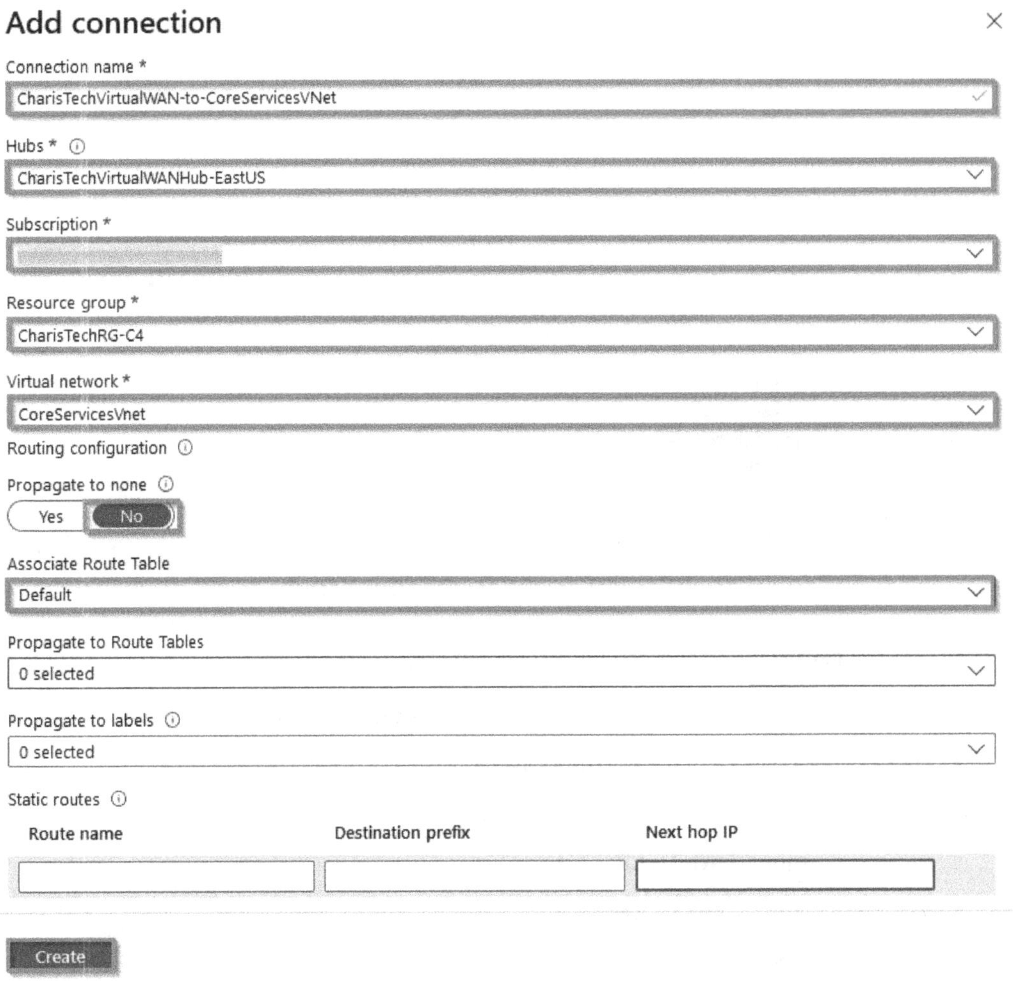

Add connection   ✕

Connection name *

CharisTechVirtualWAN-to-CoreServicesVNet   ⌄

Hubs * ⓘ

CharisTechVirtualWANHub-EastUS   ⌄

Subscription *

[_____]   ⌄

Resource group *

CharisTechRG-C4   ⌄

Virtual network *

CoreServicesVnet   ⌄

Routing configuration ⓘ

Propagate to none ⓘ

Yes [**No**]

Associate Route Table

Default   ⌄

Propagate to Route Tables

0 selected   ⌄

Propagate to labels ⓘ

0 selected   ⌄

Static routes ⓘ

Route name	Destination prefix	Next hop IP

Create

Figure 4.28 – Adding the configuration for the VNet connection

This creates a peering connection between the hub and the VNet.

3. Still in the **CharisTechVirtualWAN | Virtual network connections** blade, select + **Add connection** to create a second VNet connection. Configure the following in the **Add connection** blade:

    -   **Connection name**: `CharisTechVirtualWAN-to-EngineeringVNet`

    -   **Hubs: CharisTechVirtualWANHub-WestUS**

    -   **Subscription**: Select your Azure subscription

- **Resource group**: **CharisTechRG-C4**

- **Virtual network**: **EngineeringVNet**

- **Propagate to none**: **No**

- **Associate Route Table**: **Default**

Select **Create**.

Congratulations! You have created the necessary VNet connection to the virtual hubs.

Task 4 – verifying effective routes on the VNets and the virtual hubs

1. In the **CharisTechVirtualWAN** resource window, in the **Connectivity** section, select **Hubs**. Click on the **CharisTechVirtualWANHub-EastUS** hub:

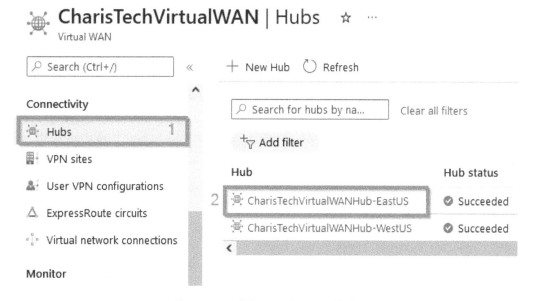

Figure 4.29 – Selecting the virtual hub

2. In the **CharisTechVirtualWANHub-EastUS** blade, in the **Routing** section, click on **Effective Routes**.

3. In the **CharisTechVirtualWANHub-EastUS | Effective Routes** blade, set the **Route Table** option to **Default**:

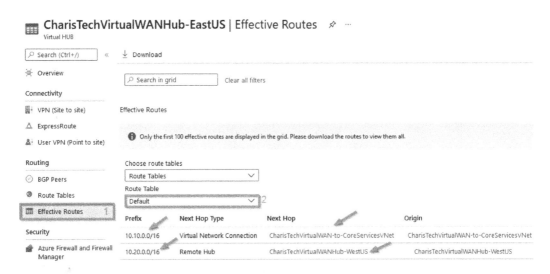

Figure 4.30 – Reviewing the virtual hub's effective routes

You should see two routes as shown in *Figure 4.30* – one for the **CoreServicesVNet** address space that routes through the virtual network connection and another for the **CharisTechVirtualWANHub-WestUS** address space that routes through the Hub-to-Hub connection.

4. You can follow *steps 1* to *3* of this task to review the effective route for the second virtual hub.

5. In the Azure portal, click on the **Cloud Shell** icon in the top-right corner of the screen. Ensure you have **Bash** selected for your environment, as we will be working with bash commands.

6. In the Cloud Shell window, enter the following commands to set the values that we will use for the resource group, network interface, and VM:

```
group="CharisTechRG-C4"
nic="webvmNetInt"
vm="webvm"
```

7. Examine the effective route entries applied to the network interface of the web VM using the following command:

```
az network nic show-effective-route-table --resource-group
$group --name webvmNetInt --output table
```

You should see that two routes were added by the configuration that we just completed. You should see two routes as shown in *Figure 4.31* – one for the remote VNet **EngineeringVNet** address space that routes through the **VNetGlobalPeering** connection, and another for the **CharisTechVirtualWANHub-EastUS** address space that routes through the Hub-to-Hub connection:

```
dave@Azure:~$
dave@Azure:~$ az network nic show-effective-route-table --resource-group
$group --name webvmNetInt --output table
Source     State     Address Prefix     Next Hop Type     Next Hop IP
--------   -------   ----------------   --------------   -------------
Default    Active    10.10.0.0/16       VnetLocal
Default    Active    10.60.0.0/24       VNetPeering
Default    Active    0.0.0.0/0          Internet
Default    Active    10.0.0.0/8         None
Default    Active    100.64.0.0/10      None
Default    Active    172.16.0.0/12      None
Default    Active    25.48.0.0/12       None
Default    Active    25.4.0.0/14        None
Default    Active    198.18.0.0/15      None
Default    Active    157.59.0.0/16      None
Default    Active    192.168.0.0/16     None
Default    Active    25.33.0.0/16       None
Default    Active    40.109.0.0/16      None
Default    Active    104.147.0.0/16     None
Default    Active    104.146.0.0/17     None
Default    Active    40.108.0.0/17      None
Default    Active    23.103.0.0/18      None
Default    Active    25.41.0.0/20       None
Default    Active    20.35.252.0/22     None
Default    Active    10.20.0.0/16       VNetGlobalPeering
dave@Azure:~$
```

Figure 4.31 – Reviewing the effective routes for WebVM

Task 5 – verifying the connectivity between the VNets

In this task, we will connect to **WebVM** and verify connectivity to **EngVM** via the vWAN:

1. In Cloud Shell, paste the SSH command that you obtained in *step 6* of *Task 1* of *Hands-on exercise – provisioning resources for the chapter* and press *Enter*.

2. If you are prompted about the authenticity of the host, type in yes and press *Enter*. When prompted to enter the password, enter the complex password that you used in *step 4* of the same provisioning exercise.

```
david@Azure:~$ ssh azureuser@webvm-7czczqegrsslc.eastus.cloudapp.azure.com    1
The authenticity of host 'webvm-7czczqegrsslc.eastus.cloudapp.azure.com (13.9
0.42.18)' can't be established.
ECDSA key fingerprint is SHA256:UUxmIvpDqP5I/ht+8TL3BpQ5j+/EPvMmj953Xvd7CNg.
Are you sure you want to continue connecting (yes/no)? yes    2
Warning: Permanently added 'webvm-7czczqegrsslc.eastus.cloudapp.azure.com,13.
90.42.18' (ECDSA) to the list of known hosts.
azureuser@webvm-7czczqegrsslc.eastus.cloudapp.azure.com's password: ◄    3
Welcome to Ubuntu 18.04.6 LTS (GNU/Linux 5.4.0-1085-azure x86_64)
```

Figure 4.32 – Connecting to WebVM via SSH

3. You should now be connected to the **WebVM** VM. Enter the following command to verify connectivity to the **EngVM** VM in the remote Vnet:

```
ping 10.20.1.4
```

The connection should be successful!

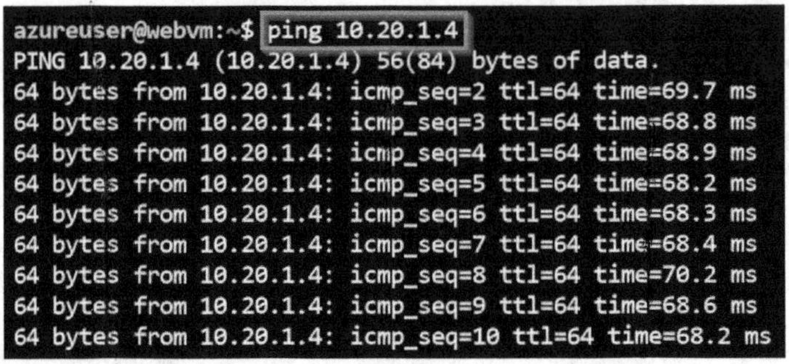

```
azureuser@webvm:~$ ping 10.20.1.4
PING 10.20.1.4 (10.20.1.4) 56(84) bytes of data.
64 bytes from 10.20.1.4: icmp_seq=2 ttl=64 time=69.7 ms
64 bytes from 10.20.1.4: icmp_seq=3 ttl=64 time=68.8 ms
64 bytes from 10.20.1.4: icmp_seq=4 ttl=64 time=68.9 ms
64 bytes from 10.20.1.4: icmp_seq=5 ttl=64 time=68.2 ms
64 bytes from 10.20.1.4: icmp_seq=6 ttl=64 time=68.3 ms
64 bytes from 10.20.1.4: icmp_seq=7 ttl=64 time=68.4 ms
64 bytes from 10.20.1.4: icmp_seq=8 ttl=64 time=70.2 ms
64 bytes from 10.20.1.4: icmp_seq=9 ttl=64 time=68.6 ms
64 bytes from 10.20.1.4: icmp_seq=10 ttl=64 time=68.2 ms
```

Figure 4.33 – Verifying connectivity using ping

Congratulations! You have successfully configured and verified cross-VNet connectivity via a vWAN. To conclude this chapter, let us summarize the key information across the three cross-VNet connectivity options that we have covered.

Comparing the three cross-VNet connectivity options

Here is a table that summarizes the key points to take away from the discussions in this chapter:

Design consideration	VNet peering	VPN Gateway: VNet-to-VNet or Site-to-Site	vWAN
Cross-region support?	Yes – supported via the Global peering option	Yes	Yes
Cross-Azure Active Directory tenant support?	Yes	Yes	Yes – through a Site-to-Site VPN connection
Cross-subscription support?	Yes	Yes	Yes
Overlapping IP address spaces	Not supported	Yes – supported via the NAT rules options	No
Maximum number of connections	500 VNets	30 VNets (based on the gateway SKU)	
Transitivity	No direct spoke-to-spoke connectivity	Supports direct spoke-to-spoke connectivity with BGP enabled	Yes – full mesh connection supported

Pricing implication	Ingress and Egress data transfer are charged	Gateway and Egress data charged	vWAN hub per deployment hour plus Ingress/ Egress data transfer charge plus hub processing charge
Ease of implementation	Very easy – can be implemented in seconds or at most a few minutes	Need to deploy the VNet VPN gateway resources and could take up to 40 minutes for the gateway to be deployed	
Latency and performance	Low latency, high bandwidth connection. Since there is no gateway in the path, there are no extra hops, ensuring low-latency connections.	Useful in scenarios where encryption is needed, but bandwidth restrictions are tolerable	
Limitations		VNets in different AAD tenants are not supported. Limited bandwidth connection.	
Traffic encryption in transit	No	Yes	
Bandwidth limitations?	No bandwidth limitations	Depends on the gateway SKU selected	
Private?	Completely private. No public IP or public internet involved. endpoints. Routed through the Microsoft backbone.	Public IP involved	
Typical use cases	Data replication, database failover, and other scenarios that require frequent backups of large data	Encryption-specific scenarios that are not latency-sensitive and do not need high throughput	

Table 4.1 – Comparing cross-VNet connectivity options

Hands-on exercise – clean up resources

In this exercise, we will remove the resources that we created in the chapter's exercises to avoid running up a large cost in Azure!

In Cloud Shell, run the following command to delete the `CharisTechRG-C3` resource group:

```
az group delete --name CharisTechRG-C4 --yes
```

This will remove all the resources that we created for the exercises in this chapter.

Summary

In this chapter, we covered the three main options that we have available to connect workloads in different VNets with each other. We started by discussing further details on the VNet peering option that we introduced in previous chapters. We also discussed the VPN gateway option and its advantages for use cases that require encryption for advanced security and compliance. Finally, we covered the vWAN option, which provides more seamless connectivity with a full mesh architecture.

In the next chapter, we will cover the connectivity options that we have for on-premises networks and remote users. We will go into further detail about the VPN gateway and the vWAN services. See you in the next chapter!

Further reading

Refer to the following for more information about the topics covered in this chapter:

- *Virtual network peering*: https://docs.microsoft.com/en-us/azure/virtual-network/virtual-network-peering-overview

- *VPN Gateway FAQ*: https://docs.microsoft.com/en-us/azure/vpn-gateway/vpn-gateway-vpn-faq

- *Virtual WAN FAQ*: https://docs.microsoft.com/en-us/azure/virtual-wan/virtual-wan-faq

Part 2:
Design, Implement, and
Manage Hybrid Networking

In this part, we will explore four essential chapters that delve into the intricacies of connecting your on-premises infrastructure with the Azure cloud while ensuring robust network security. Throughout this part, we will combine in-depth theory with hands-on implementation, empowering you to create and manage hybrid network connections while fortifying your Azure environment with robust security measures. Are you ready to enhance your networking expertise and strengthen your organization's cloud infrastructure? Let's embark on this exciting journey together! Let's get started!

This part comprises the following chapters:

- *Chapter 5, Design and Implement Hybrid Network Connectivity with VPN Gateway*
- *Chapter 6, Design and Implement Hybrid Network Connectivity with an ExpressRoute Gateway*
- *Chapter 7, Design and Implement Hybrid Network Connectivity with Virtual WAN*
- *Chapter 8, Design and Implement Network Security*

5

Design and Implement Hybrid Network Connectivity with VPN Gateway

Most organizations do not have cloud-only environments (that is, migrating all their workloads to the cloud). Instead, they maintain both on-premises networks and Azure networks, which gives them the flexibility to choose where to best host a workload according to business requirements.

By default, remote networks and remote users can't communicate with workloads in Azure VNets. We can enable access for both scenarios by implementing an Azure VPN gateway and configuring routing to pass traffic through the connection.

In this chapter, we will cover the implementation of a remote network and user connectivity using the VPN Gateway service. By the end of this chapter, you will have a strong understanding of the following:

- Choosing the right VPN Gateway SKU and generation
- Selecting between route-based and policy-based implementations
- Third-party device compatibility with VPN Gateway
- Implementing a BGP-enabled site-to-site VPN connection with VPN Gateway
- Implementing a point-to-site VPN connection with VPN Gateway

The following are the main topics to be covered in this chapter:

- Understanding Azure hybrid network connection options
- Hands-on exercise – provision resources for chapter exercises
- Hands-on exercise – implement a BGP-enabled VPN connection in Azure
- Point-to-site connections

- Hands-on exercise – implement a P2S VPN connection with Azure certificate authentication
- Troubleshoot Azure VPN Gateway using diagnostic logs
- Hands-on exercise – clean up resources

Each topic has been structured to align with recommended hybrid network connectivity best practices in Azure. Let us get into this!

Technical requirements

To follow along with the instructions in this chapter, you will need the following:

- A PC with an internet connection
- An Azure subscription

Before we proceed to cover the security best practices, let us prepare our Azure subscription for the hands-on exercises that we will be completing later in the chapter.

Understanding Azure hybrid network connection options

Hybrid networks connect on-premises networks and remote users to Azure VNet resources. Azure hybrid network connectivity is powered by the **Azure Virtual Network Gateway** service. The service supports two types of gateway – the Virtual Private Network (**VPN**) gateway and the **ExpressRoute** gateway (*Figure 5.1*).

This chapter focuses on the **VPN** gateway option. We will cover the **ExpressRoute** gateway option in the next chapter.

Create virtual network gateway   ...

Gateway type * ⓘ   ⦿ VPN   ◯ ExpressRoute

Figure 5.1 – Azure virtual network gateway types

Understanding the Azure VPN gateway

As mentioned earlier, the Azure VPN gateway is one of the gateway options supported by the Azure Virtual Network Gateway service. The VPN gateway type supports the following hybrid connection options:

- **Site-to-site (S2S) VPN connection over IPsec (IKE v1 and IKE v2)**: This option can be used to connect a remote network or multiple remote networks to an Azure VNet. This option relies on an IPsec VPN appliance (hardware device or software appliance) with a public IP address to be deployed on the remote network (*Figure 5.2*).

- **VNet-to-VNet VPN connection over IPsec (IKE v1 and IKE v2)**: This is a variation of a site-to-site configuration option. It can be used to connect an Azure VNet to another Azure VNet. We covered this option in the previous chapter of this book (*Chapter 4*).

- **Point-to-site (P2S) VPN connection over SSTP (Secure Socket Tunneling Protocol) or IKE v2**: This option can be used to connect remote users to an Azure VNet. Remote users can connect using supported client devices including Windows, Linux, and macOS systems.

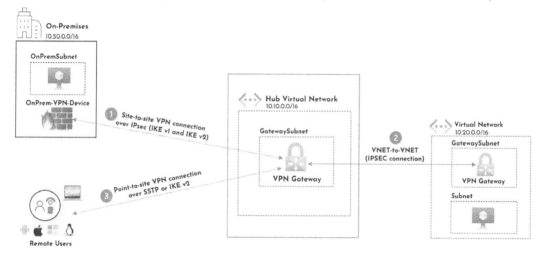

Figure 5.2 – VPN gateway hybrid connectivity options

Now, let's look at the factors you need to consider when planning your VPN gateway.

Choosing the right VPN gateway SKU and generation

When planning a VPN gateway implementation, we need to decide on the gateway SKU to use. We do this by selecting the SKU and the generation at deployment (*Figure 5.3*).

Figure 5.3 – Selecting a VPN gateway SKU and generation

This decision should be guided by the following organization requirements:

- Performance
- Scalability
- Supported features

The following table lists VPN gateway SKUs for comparison:

VPN Gateway Generation	SKU	S2S/VNet-to-Vnet Tunnels	P2S SSTP Connections	P2S IKEv2/OpenVPN Connections	Aggregate Throughput Benchmark	BGP	Zone-redundant
Generation1	Basic	Max. 10	Max. 128	Not Supported	100 Mbps	Not Supported	No
Generation1	VpnGw1	Max. 30*	Max. 128	Max. 250	650 Mbps	Supported	No
Generation1	VpnGw2	Max. 30*	Max. 128	Max. 500	1 Gbps	Supported	No
Generation1	VpnGw3	Max. 30*	Max. 128	Max. 1000	1.25 Gbps	Supported	No
Generation1	VpnGw1AZ	Max. 30*	Max. 128	Max. 250	650 Mbps	Supported	Yes
Generation1	VpnGw2AZ	Max. 30*	Max. 128	Max. 500	1 Gbps	Supported	Yes
Generation1	VpnGw3AZ	Max. 30*	Max. 128	Max. 1000	1.25 Gbps	Supported	Yes
Generation2	VpnGw2	Max. 30*	Max. 128	Max. 500	1.25 Gbps	Supported	No
Generation2	VpnGw3	Max. 30*	Max. 128	Max. 1000	2.5 Gbps	Supported	No
Generation2	VpnGw4	Max. 30*	Max. 128	Max. 5000	5 Gbps	Supported	No
Generation2	VpnGw5	Max. 30*	Max. 128	Max. 10000	10 Gbps	Supported	No
Generation2	VpnGw2AZ	Max. 30*	Max. 128	Max. 500	1.25 Gbps	Supported	Yes
Generation2	VpnGw3AZ	Max. 30*	Max. 128	Max. 1000	2.5 Gbps	Supported	Yes
Generation2	VpnGw4AZ	Max. 30*	Max. 128	Max. 5000	5 Gbps	Supported	Yes
Generation2	VpnGw5AZ	Max. 30*	Max. 128	Max. 10000	10 Gbps	Supported	Yes

Figure 5.4 – VPN gateway SKU comparison

Performance considerations

You need to ensure that you select a SKU that meets your required throughput. Generation 2 SKUs have better performance than generation 1 SKUs of the same equivalent. For example, **VpnGw2 (Gen1)** has a *1 Gbps aggregate throughput* while generation 2 of the same SKU – **VpnGw2 (Gen2)** – has a *1.25 Gbps aggregate throughput* (*Figure 5.4*). The maximum aggregate throughput is *10 Gbps*, which can be achieved on the **VpnGw5** and **VpnGw5AZ** SKUs.

Please note that the aggregate throughput benchmark shown in *Figure 5.4* is based on a measurement of multiple S2S and P2S tunnels aggregated through a single gateway! The value does not reflect the throughput for a single tunnel! This means having a lot of remote user connections (using P2S VPN) can result in a negative impact on S2S connection throughput.

Also, keep in mind that there are other conditions that can impact the aggregate throughput that you get. These include internet traffic conditions, application traffic behaviors, and remote hardware capabilities.

Scalability considerations

You also need to ensure that your selected SKU can support the number of connections that you need. The maximum number of connections is supported by the **VpnGw5 VpnGw5AZ** gateway SKUs. They can support up to 100 S2S connections, 128 P2S SSTP connections, and 10,000 P2S IKEv2/OpenVPN connections. If your requirement exceeds this limit, you can consider using the Azure Virtual WAN service for hybrid network connectivity. Please review *Figure 5.4*for the other connection limit values.

Supported feature considerations

The third consideration when deciding on your gateway SKU is feature support. For example, the basic gateway SKU does not support point-to-site IKEv2/OpenVPN connections. So, if you need support for this, you will need to select another SKU.

Also, not all gateway SKUs support zone configurations. Gateway SKUs that have AZ in their name means they can be configured to be zonal or zone-redundant (*Figure 5.5*). Other SKUs (that do not have AZ in the name) are non-zone-redundant and non-zonal gateways.

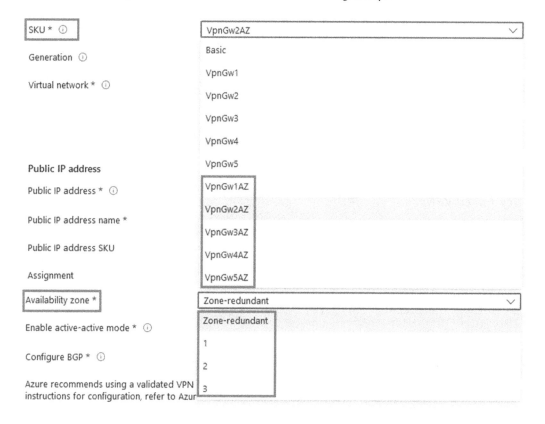

Figure 5.5 – VPN gateway zonal/zone-redundant SKUs

> **Can I change my VPN Gateway SKU after deployment?**
>
> Resizing a VPN gateway to a different SKU is only allowed within the same generation. A generation 1 SKU can be resized to another generation 1 SKU. A generation 2 SKU can be resized to another generation 2 SKU.

It is highly recommended to avoid the **Basic** SKU option (if possible) as it is a legacy option and has a lot of feature limitations (for example, its lack of support for point-to-site connections).

Selecting between route-based or policy-based VPN types

The next key decision when creating a VPN gateway is the VPN type. Azure supports two modes of VPN – route-based VPN gateways and policy-based VPN gateways (*Figure 5.6*).

Figure 5.6 – Selecting Route-based or Policy-based VPN type

The option that we select should be guided by two main considerations:

- Do we need to implement a P2S VPN connection? If the answer is *yes*, then we need to implement the **Route-based** VPN type.

- The compatibility of our on-premises VPN device. If our on-premises VPN device is legacy and does not support route-based VPN, then we need to implement the **Policy-based** VPN option.

Let us examine these two options in more detail!

Policy-based VPNs

With policy-based VPNs, the gateway sends traffic through the VPN tunnel based on a defined policy. The policy defines an access list of traffic that should be sent through the VPN tunnel between the on-premises VPN device and the Azure VPN gateway. This is done using traffic selectors. The following is an example of a traffic selector policy using Azure PowerShell:

```
New-AzIpsecTrafficSelectorPolicy -LocalAddressRange ("10.10.0.0/16",
"10.20.0.0/16") -RemoteAddressRange ("192.168.0.0/16",
"172.16.0.0/16")
```

Every line in the access list will result in a bidirectional pair of IPsec **security associations (SAs)** between the VPN endpoints. The preceding traffic selector example will result in the following pairs:

```
10.10.0.0/16 <====> 192.168.0.0/16
10.10.0.0/16 <====> 172.16.0.0/16
10.20.0.0/16 <====> 192.168.0.0/16
10.20.0.0/16 <====> 172.16.0.0/16
```

If using the **Policy-based** VPN type, it is worth noting the following limitations:

- There is no support for dynamic routing using BGP
- It can only be used to establish S2S VPN connections (no support for P2S VPN connections)
- It only supports one (1) tunnel when implemented with the basic gateway

That's a lot of limitations! With all these limitations, why would anyone consider this option? The main reason is compatibility with legacy VPN devices. If our on-premises VPN device specification supports only policy-based connections, then we can use this VPN type to establish connectivity.

It used to be that only the **Basic** gateway SKU supports policy-based VPNs, but not so anymore! We can now configure Azure route-based VPN gateways to use prefix-based traffic selectors with the **PolicyBasedTrafficSelectors** option. This allows other gateway SKUs (apart from **Basic**) to connect to on-premises policy-based VPN devices. It also removes the single tunnel limitation of the **Basic** gateway SKU by allowing connections to multiple on-premises policy-based VPN/firewall devices (*Figure 5.7*)!

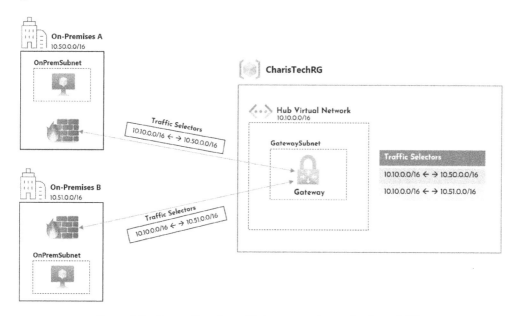

Figure 5.7 – Connections to multiple on-premises policy-based VPNs

This option can be configured using all management options (the Azure portal, Azure PowerShell, the Azure CLI, ARM templates, or BICEP templates). The following command shows an example of doing this with Azure PowerShell. The first command creates a route-based VPN gateway. The second command creates a policy-based VPN connection between the route-based VPN gateway and an on-premises policy-based VPN connection:

```
## Create a route-based VPN gateway
New-AzVirtualNetworkGateway -Name <Gateway_Name> -ResourceGroupName
```

```
<Resource_Group_Name> -Location <Location> -IpConfigurations <IP_
Configurations> -GatewayType Vpn -VpnType RouteBased -GatewaySku
HighPerformance
## Create a policy-based VPN connection
New-AzVirtualNetworkGatewayConnection -Name <Connection_Name>
-ResourceGroupName <Resource_Group_Name> -VirtualNetworkGateway1
<VPN_Gateway_Name> -LocalNetworkGateway2 <Local_Network_
Gateway_Name> -Location <Location> -ConnectionType IPsec
-UsePolicyBasedTrafficSelectors $True -IpsecPolicies <IPSEC_Policy>
-SharedKey <SharedKey>
```

When implementing multiple connections with the policy-based option, transit routing via the Azure VPN gateway does not work! *Figure 5.8* shows an example of this. In the scenario, on-premises sites *A* and *B* can each communicate with the *Hub Virtual Network* respectively but cannot communicate with each other via the gateway. This is because traffic selectors only exist for direct connections.

> **Note**
>
> This documentation covers how to connect a route-based Azure VPN gateway to multiple on-premises policy-based VPN devices using PowerShell: https://docs.microsoft.com/en-us/azure/vpn-gateway/vpn-gateway-connect-multiple-policybased-rm-ps.

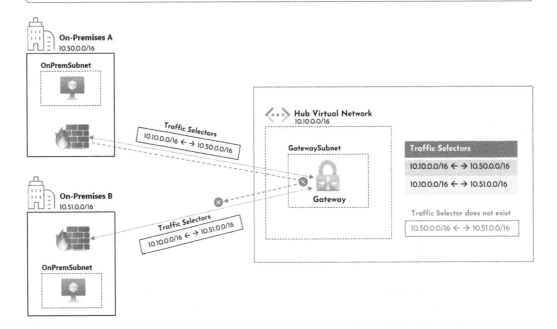

Figure 5.8 – Traffic selectors in policy-based VPN

Route-based VPNs

With route-based VPNs, the gateway uses routes in the IP forwarding or routing table to direct packets into tunnel interfaces. The policy (or traffic selector) for route-based VPNs is configured as any-to-any (or wild cards).

Figure 5.9 summarizes the key differences between the policy-based and route-based VPN types for Azure VPN Gateway.

	Policy-Based	Route-Based
Site-to-Site VPN connections	Yes	Yes
Point-to-Site VPN connections	No	Yes
BGP Support	No	Yes
Gateway SKU support	• Basic gateway SKU when configured using the Azure portal • Other Gateway SKUs with the **PolicyBasedTrafficSelectors** option	All SKUs
Maximum S2S connections	• One (1) VPN connection when implemented with the Basic gateway SKU • Multiple VPN connections when implemented with other gateway SKUs	Up to 100 based on the SKU
IKE version	IKEv1 only	IKEv1 and IKEv2
Connection-to-Connection transit routing	No	Yes
Active-active high availability mode	No	Yes

Figure 5.9 – Policy-based versus route-based VPN comparison

Selecting high-availability options for VPN connections

The next key decision when creating a VPN gateway is the availability option. Two availability modes are supported – **active-passive** mode (which is the default option) and **active-active** mode, which can be enabled at deployment time for only route-based gateway SKUs (*Figure 5.10*).

Figure 5.10 – Enabling the active-active HA option

Active-passive mode

Behind the scenes, an Azure VPN gateway deployment always consists of two instances. If we used the default configuration, the instances would be in active-passive mode (*Figure 5.11*). If there is planned maintenance or if an unplanned disruption impacts the active instance, the passive instance will take over automatically without any user involvement (marked as *1* in *Figure 5.11*)!

For S2S connections, the failover usually results in a brief interruption (marked as *2* in *Figure 5.11*). If the triggering event is planned maintenance, the connection recovery could be up to 15 seconds. If the triggering event is an unplanned disruption, the connection recovery could be up to three (3) minutes. For P2S VPN client connections, the failover will result in disconnection and users will need to reconnect their client devices (marked as *3* in *Figure 5.11*).

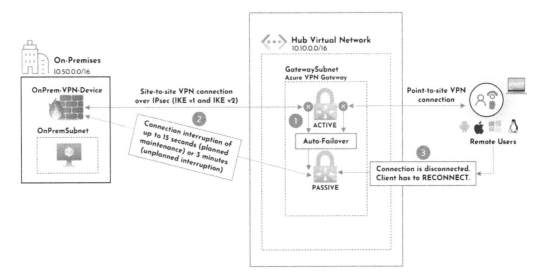

Figure 5.11 – Single Azure VPN gateway in active standby VPN configuration

For S2S VPN, we could add another layer of redundancy by implementing multiple VPN devices to our remote network (*Figure 5.12*). This provides additional protection against failures or interruptions on our on-premises network.

With this configuration, there will be an active connection from each on-premises device to the active Azure VPN gateway (*Figure 5.12*). This, however, does not improve the failover behavior on the Azure side. The failover behavior remains the same as what was described earlier.

Implementing this setup has certain requirements for it to work:

- Each on-premises VPN device must have a unique public IP address.
- BGP is a must for this configuration! Each on-premises device must be configured with a unique BGP peer IP address.

- BGP should be used to advertise the same on-premises network prefixes to the Azure VPN gateway with **equal-cost multi-path routing (ECMP)**.

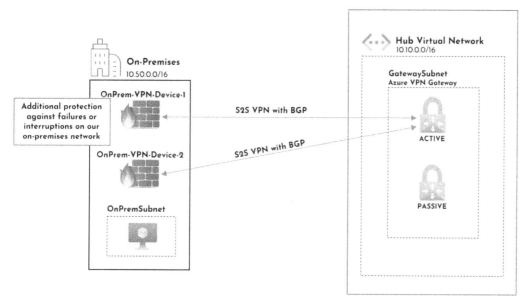

Figure 5.12 – Multiple Azure VPN gateways in active standby VPN configuration

Active-active mode

The second high-availability option is to implement the VPN gateway in active-active mode. In this configuration, each gateway instance will have its own public IP address and will establish an S2S VPN connection to the on-premises VPN device (*Figure 5.13*). Traffic from Azure VNet workloads to the on-premises network will be routed through both tunnels. Azure will attempt to use the same tunnel if the packets are part of the same TCP or UDP flow.

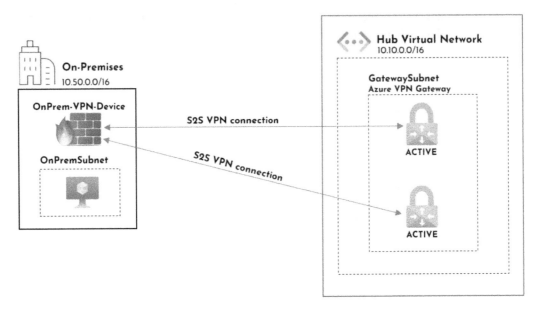

Figure 5.13 – Single Azure VPN gateway in active-active mode

If there is planned maintenance or if an unplanned disruption impacts one of the instances, the tunnel to that instance will be disconnected. This will cause associated routes for the impacted tunnel to be withdrawn so that traffic is automatically directed to the tunnel that is still active (there is no need to reestablish a connection). This switch happens automatically on the Azure side.

The most reliable option is to implement active-active redundancy on both the Azure side and the remote network side (dual-redundancy) (*Figure 5.14*). This results in full mesh connectivity of four IPsec tunnels. The advantage is that we will always have a pair of tunnels available for any planned maintenance events.

Like the on-premises redundancy scenario described in the *Active-passive mode* section, BGP is required for this configuration to allow the two connections to the same on-premises network.

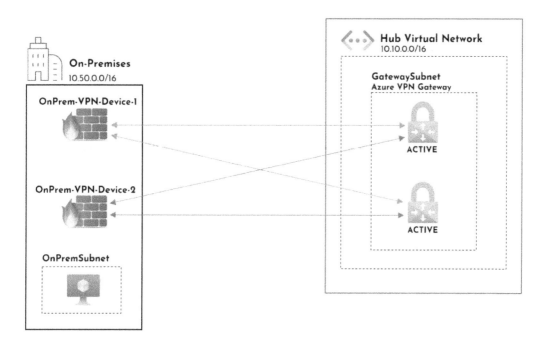

Figure 5.14 – Dual-redundancy VPN gateway configuration

Understanding third-party device compatibility

Microsoft maintains a list of third-party network devices that have been validated to work well with VPN Gateway. This list was created in conjunction with network device vendors such as Palo Alto Networks, Sophos, and so on. The list shows validated devices, supported configurations, and links to configuration guides. It can be found at `https://docs.microsoft.com/en-us/azure/vpn-gateway/vpn-gateway-about-vpn-devices#devicetable`.

Does this mean that you cannot connect a device to Azure VPN Gateway if it is not on this list? Not at all. Your device may, in fact, still work. You may need to reach out to your vendor for configuration instructions.

Depending on your device vendor, a simpler configuration option using an automated VPN device configuration script may be possible (*Figure 5.15*).

Figure 5.15 – Downloading the VPN configuration script

Well, that's enough discussion for now. Let's get hands-on with implementing a VPN connection using Azure VPN Gateway!

Hands-on exercise – provision resources for chapter exercises

To follow along with the exercises in this chapter, we will provision some Azure resources to work with. We have prepared an Azure ARM template in the GitHub repository of this book for this purpose. The template will deploy two peered virtual networks in two Azure regions as shown in *Figure 5.16*.

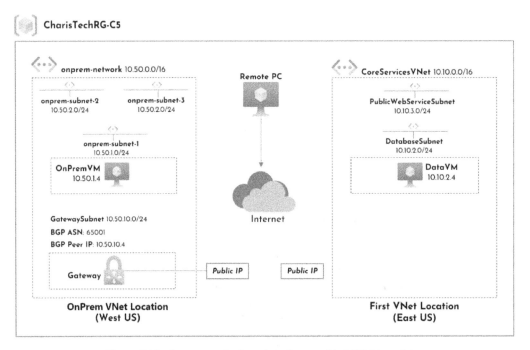

Figure 5.16 – Resources deployed via the provided ARM template

The first VNet (**CoreServicesVNet**) will have two subnets with a virtual machine in the data subnet. The second VNet (**onprem-network**) will be used to simulate an on-premises network. It has four subnets and a virtual machine (**OnPremVM**) that will be used to simulate an on-premises VM.

A VM called **Remote PC** will also be deployed to simulate a remote user's PC. Here is the task that we will complete in this exercise:

- **Task 1**: Initialize template deployment in GitHub, complete parameters, and deploy the template to Azure

Let's get into this!

Task 1: Initialize template deployment in GitHub, complete parameters, and deploy the template to Azure

1. Open a web browser and browse to `https://packt.link/iZFJd`. This link will open the GitHub repository that has the ARM template to deploy the resources that we need.

2. In the GitHub repository that opens, click on **Deploy to Azure**:

Figure 5.17 – Start the template deployment

3. If prompted to authenticate, sign into the Azure portal with your administrative username and password.

4. In the **Custom Deployment** window, configure the following:

    -   **Subscription**: Select the subscription that you want to deploy the resources to.

    -   **Resource group**: **Create new** | **Name**: `CharisTechRG-C5` **OK**.

    -   **Region**: **East US** (or select the region that you verified in the first chapter of this book).

    -   **Password**: Enter a complex password. This will be the password for all deployed VM instances. Make a note of this as it will be needed for later exercises.

    -   **VM Size**: **Standard_B2s** (or select the VM size that you verified in the first chapter of this book).

    -   **Second Vnet Location**: **West US** (or select the second region that you verified in the first chapter of this book).

Select **Review + create**.

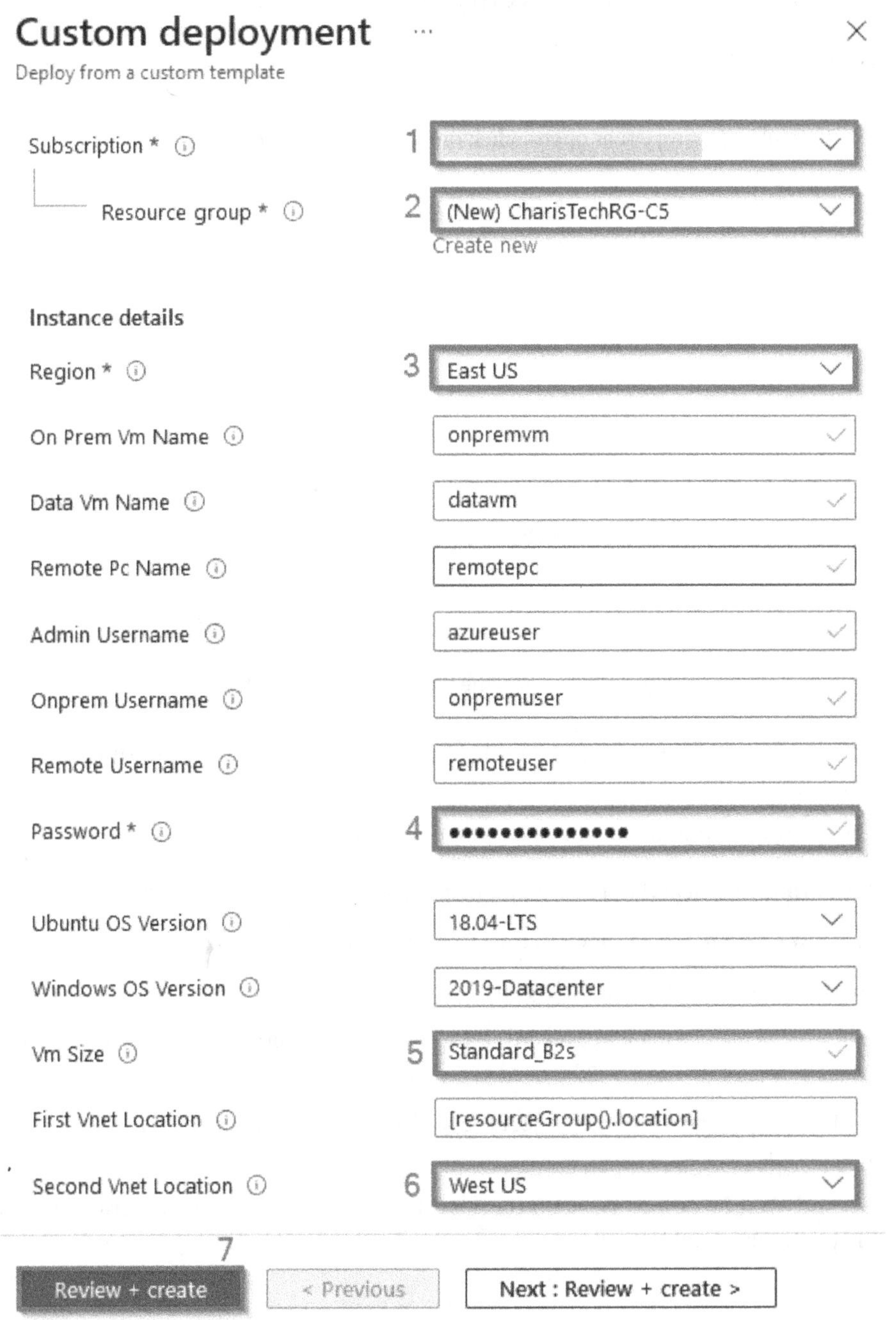

Custom deployment   ⋯   ✕
Deploy from a custom template

Subscription * ⓘ	1	[_____] ⌄
Resource group * ⓘ	2	(New) CharisTechRG-C5 ⌄
		Create new

Instance details

Region * ⓘ	3	East US ⌄
On Prem Vm Name ⓘ		onpremvm ✓
Data Vm Name ⓘ		datavm ✓
Remote Pc Name ⓘ		remotepc ✓
Admin Username ⓘ		azureuser ✓
Onprem Username ⓘ		onpremuser ✓
Remote Username ⓘ		remoteuser ✓
Password * ⓘ	4	●●●●●●●●●●●●● ✓
Ubuntu OS Version ⓘ		18.04-LTS ⌄
Windows OS Version ⓘ		2019-Datacenter ⌄
Vm Size ⓘ	5	Standard_B2s ✓
First Vnet Location ⓘ		[resourceGroup().location]
Second Vnet Location ⓘ	6	West US ⌄

7

[Review + create]   [< Previous]   [Next : Review + create >]

Figure 5.18 – Complete the custom deployment options

5. After the validation has passed, select **Create** to proceed with the deployment. The deployment takes about 50 minutes to complete! So, feel free to get a glass of water or a cup of coffee!

6. After the deployment has completed, click on the **Outputs** tab (left side), and make a note of the following values:

- **remoteUsername:** This is the username for the remote PC. We will need this in later exercises.

- **remotePC-FQDN:** This is the public FQDN of the remote PC.

- **OnPremVPNDevice-FQDN:** This is the public FQDN of the on-premises VPN device.

- **OnPremVPNDevice-BGP-ASN:** This is the autonomous system number of the on-premises VPN device.

- **OnPremVPNDevice-BGP-PeerIP:** This is the BGP peering IP of the on-premises VPN device.

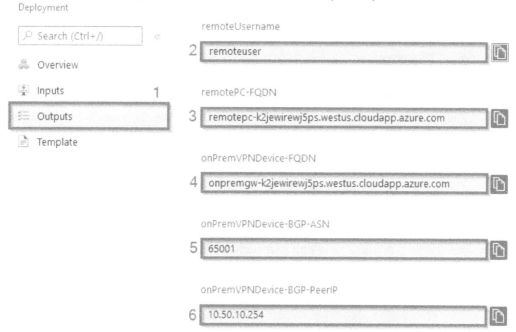

Figure 5.19 – Obtain information from the deployment output

Congratulations! You have now deployed the resources needed to complete the chapter exercises. In the next hands-on exercise, you will implement a BGP-enabled VPN connection between the on-premises network and the Azure VNet.

Hands-on exercise: implement a BGP-enabled VPN connection in Azure

Here are the tasks that we will complete in this exercise:

- **Task 1**: Create the gateway subnet
- **Task 2**: Deploy the VPN gateway into the subnet (with an existing public IP)
- **Task 3**: Create the local network gateway
- **Task 4**: Configure the VPN connection
- **Task 5**: Verify VPN connection status and BGP peering
- **Task 6**: Verify connectivity between the on-premises network and the Azure VNet

Let's get into this!

Task 1: Create the gateway subnet

To implement a VPN gateway, the first thing to do is to create a gateway subnet in our hub VNet called `GatewaySubnet` (the subnet cannot be named anything else). Also, this must be a dedicated subnet, which means no other resource should be deployed into it apart from the gateway.

During creation, we need to specify the subnet address range. This defines the number of IP addresses that will be available to the gateway service for allocation. The smallest CIDR prefix that we can specify is `/29`. However, keep in mind that configurations like active-active mode require more IP addresses. You may not currently be implementing this configuration, but it is a good idea to plan for future growth. The recommendation is to use at least a `/27` subnet – this will accommodate most configurations. In our case, we will use the `/24` range:

1. Open a web browser and browse to the Azure portal – `https://portal.azure.com`. If prompted to authenticate, sign in with your administrative username and password.

2. In the Azure portal search area, type `CoreServicesVnet`. Click on the displayed virtual network resource, **CoreServicesVnet**.

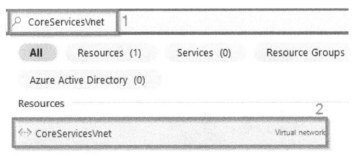

Figure 5.20 – Search for CoreServicesVnet

3. In the **CoreServicesVnet** blade, in the **Settings** section, click on **Subnets**. In the **CoreServicesVnet** | **Subnets** blade, click + **Gateway subnet**.

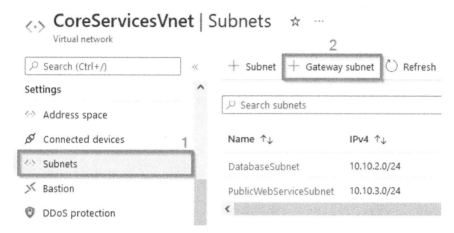

Figure 5.21 – Create the gateway subnet

4. In the **Add subnet** blade, configure the following:

    - **Subnet address range**: 10.10.10.0/24

    Click on **Save**.

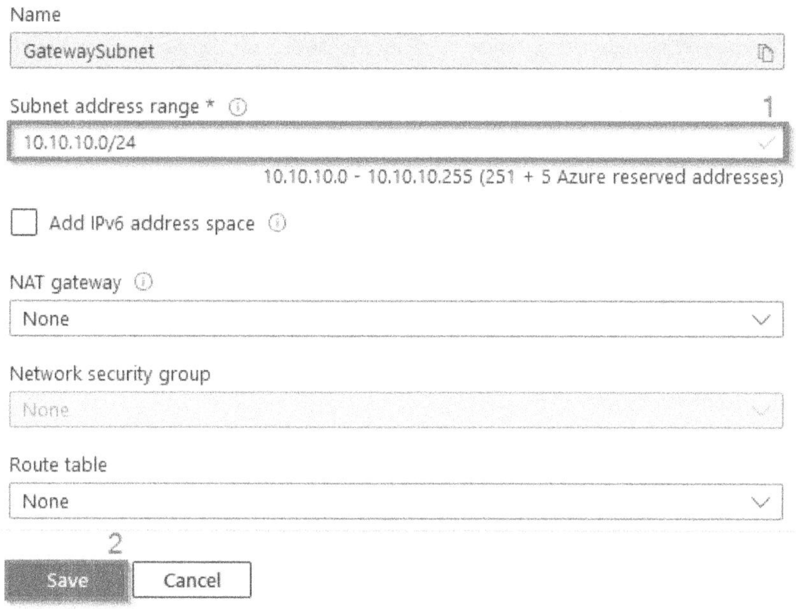

Figure 5.22 – Specify the gateway subnet address range

Task 2: Deploy the VPN gateway into the subnet (with an existing public IP)

In this task, we will deploy the virtual network gateway (VPN gateway) into the subnet that we created. Please note that creating a VPN gateway can often take 45 minutes or more, depending on the gateway SKU that we select:

1. In the Azure portal search area, type `virtual network gateway`. Click on the displayed **Virtual network gateways** service.

Figure 5.23 – Search for the virtual network gateway

2. On the **Virtual network gateways** blade, click **+ Create**.

3. On the **Create virtual network gateway** page, on the **Basics** tab, set the following configurations:

    *   **Subscription**: Select the subscription that you want to deploy the resources into.

    *   **Name**: `azurevnetgw` (or select the region that you deployed CoreServicesVNet into).

    *   **Gateway type**: **VPN**

    *   **VPN type**: **Route-based**

    *   **SKU**: **VpnGw1AZ**

    *   **Generation**: **Generation1**

    *   **Virtual network**: **CoreServicesVnet**

    *   **Public IP Address Type**: **Standard**

    *   **Public IP address**: **Use existing**

    *   **Choose public IP address**: **azuregwPublicIP**

    *   **Enabled active-active mode**: **Disabled**

    *   **Configure BGP**: **Enabled**

    *   **Autonomous system number (ASN)**: **65002**

Click **Review + create** and then click **Create**.

Create virtual network gateway ...

Basics	Tags	Review + create

Azure has provided a planning and design guide to help you configure the various VPN gateway options. Learn more.

Project details

Select the subscription to manage deployed resources and costs. Use resource groups like folders to organize and manage all your resources.

Subscription *   1 [_____ ⌄]

Resource group ⓘ   CharisTechRG-C5 (derived from virtual network's resource group)

Instance details

Name *   2 [azurevnetgw ⌄]

Region *   3 [East US ⌄]

Gateway type * ⓘ   4 (●) VPN ( ) ExpressRoute

VPN type * ⓘ   5 (●) Route-based ( ) Policy-based

SKU * ⓘ   6 [VpnGw1AZ ⌄]

Generation ⓘ   7 [Generation1 ⌄]

Virtual network * ⓘ   8 [CoreServicesVnet ⌄]
                                Create virtual network

Subnet ⓘ   [GatewaySubnet (10.10.10.0/24) ⌄]

Public IP address

Public IP address * ⓘ   ( ) Create new (●) Use existing 9

Choose public IP address *   10 [azuregwPublicIP _____ ⌄]

Enable active-active mode * ⓘ   ( ) Enabled (●) Disabled 11

Configure BGP * ⓘ   12 (●) Enabled ( ) Disabled

                                                                    13
Autonomous system number (ASN) * ⓘ   [65002   ⌄]

Custom Azure APIPA BGP IP address ⓘ

[Peer Address   ]

Azure recommends using a validated VPN device with your virtual network gateway. To view a list of validated devices and instructions for configuration, refer to Azure's documentation regarding validated VPN devices.

          14
[Review + create] [Previous] [Next : Tags >] Download a template for automation

Figure 5.24 – Configure the parameters of the VPN gateway

4. Once validation passes, select **Create** to create the Virtual WAN.

Task 3: Create the local network gateway

In this task, we will create the local network gateway. This defines the configuration needed to connect to the on-premises VPN device. You also specify the IP address prefixes that will be routed through the VPN gateway to the VPN device. The address prefixes you specify are the prefixes located in the on-premises network:

1. In the Azure portal search area, type Local network gateway. Click on the displayed **Local network gateways** service.

Figure 5.25 – Search for Local network gateway

2. On the **Local network gateways** blade, click + **Create**.

3. On the **Create local network gateway** page, on the **Basics** tab, set the following configurations:

    *   **Subscription**: Select the subscription that you want to deploy the resources into

    *   **Resource group: CharisTechRG-C5**

    *   **Region: East US** (or select the region that you deployed CoreServicesVNet into)

    *   **Name**: OnPrem-Gateway-LNG

    *   **Endpoint: FQDN**

    *   **FQDN**: Enter the value that you noted in the first exercise in this chapter for **OnPremVPNDevice-FQDN**

Click **Next: Advanced >**.

Figure 5.26 - Configure the basic parameters of the local network gateway

4. On the **Advanced** tab, set the following configurations:

    - **Configure BGP settings: Yes**

    - **Autonomous system number (ASN): 65001**

    - **BGP peer IP address**: Enter the value that you noted in the first exercise in this chapter for **onPremVPNDevice-BGP-PeerIP**

Click **Review + create** and then click **Create**.

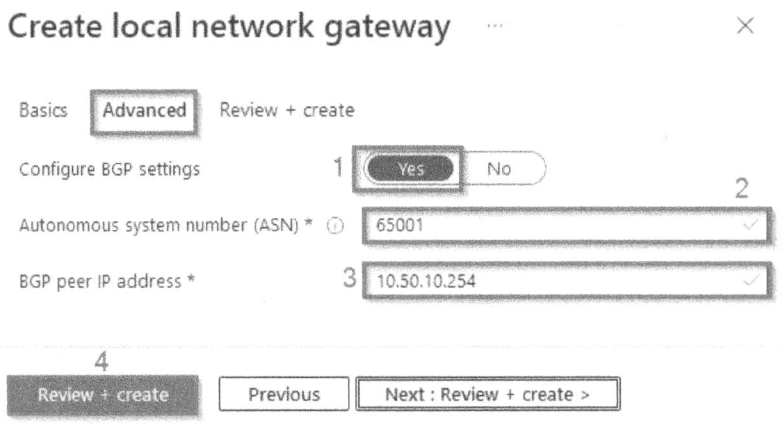

Figure 5.27 - Configure the advanced parameters of the local network gateway

Task 4: Configure the VPN connection

Once the VPN gateway and the local network gateway are created, we can create the connection between the Azure VPN gateway and the on-premises VPN device. The on-premises VPN device was auto-configured as part of the template deployment, so we only need to configure the connection from the Azure side:

1. In the Azure portal search area, type Connections. Click on the displayed **Connections** resource.

Figure 5.28 – Search for connections

2. On the **Connections** blade, click **+ Create**.

3. On the **Create connection** page, on the **Basics** tab, set the following configurations:

    -   **Subscription**: Select the subscription that you want to deploy the resources into

    -   **Resource group: CharisTechRG-C5**

- **Connection type**: **Site-to-Site (IPsec)**
- **Name**: `azure-to-onprem-vpn-connection`
- **Region**: **East US** (or select the region that you deployed CoreServicesVNet into)

Click **Next: Settings >**.

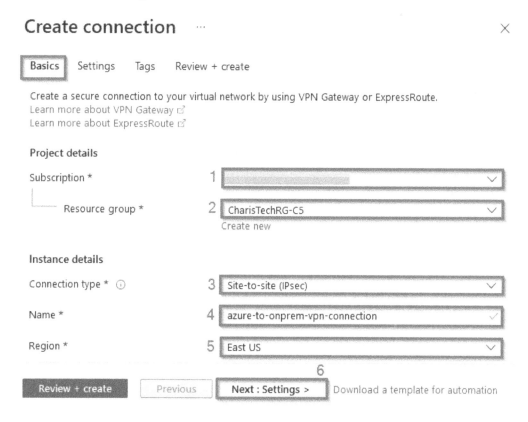

Figure 5.29 – Configure the basic parameters of the VPN connection

4. On the **Create connection** page, on the **Settings** tab, set the following configurations:

- **Virtual network gateway**: **azuregw**
- **Local network gateway**: **OnPrem-Gateway-LNG**
- **Shared key (PSK)**: **vpnPass123** (or the value that you set during deployment if you changed it)
- **IKE Protocol**: **IKEv2**
- **Enable BGP**: Selected
- **IPsec/IKE policy**: **Default**
- **Use policy based traffic selector**: **Disable**

- **DPD timeout in seconds**: 45 (This is the Dead Peer Detection timeout value of the connection. It is used to verify the availability of the peer device.)

- **Connection Mode: Default** (this option means that both Azure and on-premises VPN devices can initiate the connection)

Click **Review + create** and then click **Create**.

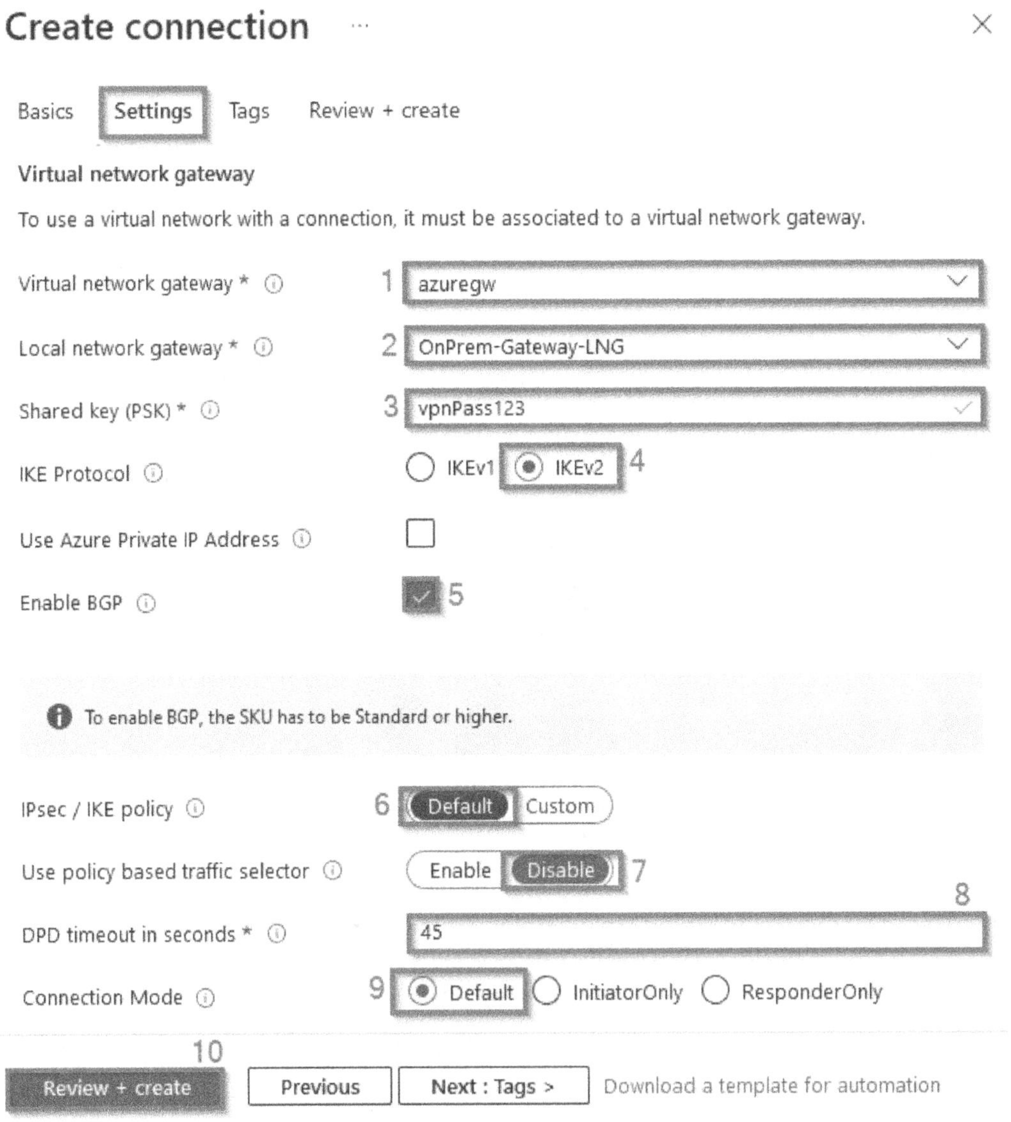

Figure 5.30 – Configure the VPN connection settings

Task 5: Verify VPN connection status and BGP peering

In this task, we will verify the VPN connection and the BGP peering status:

1. In the Azure portal search area, type `Connections`. Click on the displayed **Connections** resource.

2. In the **Connections** window, select **azure-to-onprem-vpn-connection**. In the **Overview** section of the **azure-to-onprem-vpn-connection** blade, review the status. It should display as **Connected** (*Figure 5.31*). Note that you may need to wait for a few minutes and refresh the browser window to see the updated status.

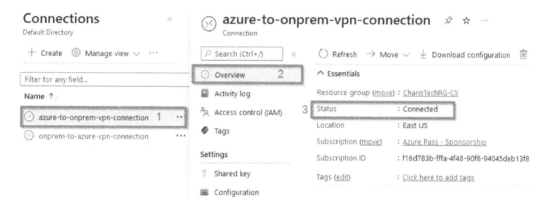

Figure 5.31 – Review the VPN connection status

3. Repeat *Steps 1* and *2* of this task for **onprem-to-azure-vpn-connection**.

4. In the Azure portal search area, type `Virtual network gateway`. Click on the displayed **Virtual network gateways** service.

5. In the **Virtual network gateways** window, select **azurevnetgw**. In the **Monitoring** section, click on **BGP peers**. It should display a connected BGP peer with the learned routes (*Figure 5.32*).

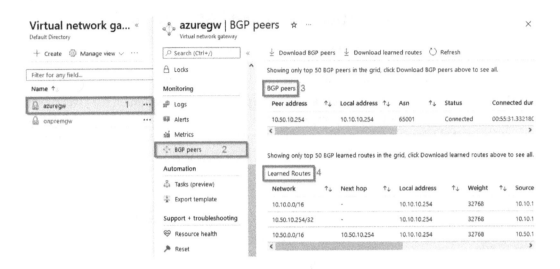

Figure 5.32 – Review the BGP peering status

6.   Repeat *Steps 4* and *5* of this task for the **onpremgw** resource.

Task 6: Verify connectivity between the on-premises network and the Azure VNet

In this task, we will verify the VPN connection and the BGP peering status:

1.   In the Azure portal search area, type `datavm`. Click on the displayed **datavm** virtual machine resource.

Figure 5.33 – Search for the datavm virtual machine

2. In the **datavm** window, in the **Operations** section, click on **Run command**, then select the **RunShellScript** option. This option allows us to run commands or scripts on the virtual machine.

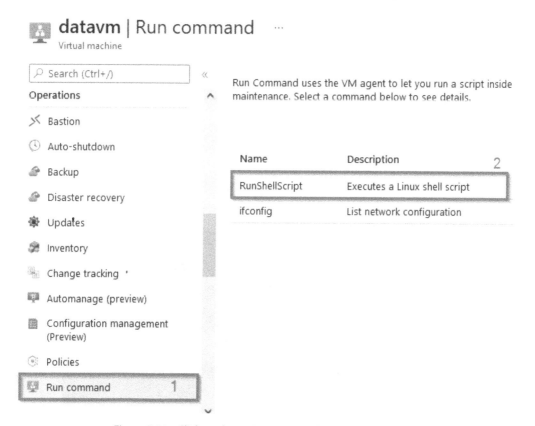

Figure 5.34 – Click on the option to run a shell script on the VM

3. In the **Linux Shell Script** section, type the following command to test connectivity to the on-premises VM (**OnPremVM**) from the Azure VM (**DataVM**). Click on **Run**:

```
ping 10.50.1.4 -c 4
```

You should see a response like the one that follows (*Figure 5.35*).

Figure 5.35 – Run a connectivity test using ping

Congratulations! You have now successfully configured and verified a BGP-enabled VPN connection between an on-premises network and an Azure VNet.

Understanding point-to-site connections

To implement a P2S VPN, we need to specify three main configuration settings: a **client address pool**, a **tunnel type**, and an **authentication type**. Let's look at considerations for selecting the right configuration for our use cases.

Defining a connection pool for P2S VPN connectivity

The client address pool defines the range of IP addresses that will be assigned to connecting clients. P2S VPN clients that connect to the gateway will automatically receive an IP address from the defined range *(Figure 5.36)*.

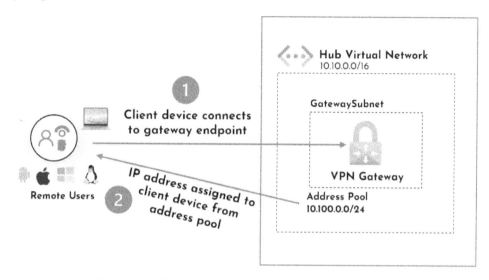

Figure 5.36 – Client address space assignment from address pool

The IP address range that you specify must not overlap with the VNet's address range or you will receive an error similar to the one shown in *Figure 5.37*. In my case, my VNet address space is **10.10.0.0/16** and when I tried to configure a point-to-site address pool of **10.10.100.0/24**, which falls within the range of the VNet's address space, I got the following error message.

Figure 5.37 – Error message due to pool address range overlap

It is recommended to use a non-overlapping address range from your other VNets. If multiple protocols are configured for the tunnel type (more on this shortly), and SSTP is one of the protocols, this address range will be split equally between both configured protocols.

It is also recommended to select an IP address range that does not conflict with that of the connecting devices to avoid routing issues. If users are mainly connecting from their home networks, it is advisable to avoid the **192.168.0/0/16** range.

For an active-passive gateway configuration, the minimum allowed address range is **/29**. For an active-active gateway configuration, the minimum allowed range is **/28**. As always, we need to include this in our scalability plan.

Selecting the tunnel type(s) for P2S VPN connectivity

The next key decision when implementing point-to-site VPN connectivity with the Azure VPN gateway is **Tunnel type**. Azure supports the three main protocols here *(Figure 5.38)*: **OpenVPN**, which is SSL-based and operates on port 443, making it firewall-friendly; **Secure Socket Tunneling Protocol (SSTP)**, which is a Microsoft proprietary SSL-based solution that also operates on port 443; and **IKEv2 VPN**, which is based on the common IPsec VPN solution that uses outbound UDP ports 500 and 4500 and IP protocol number 50.

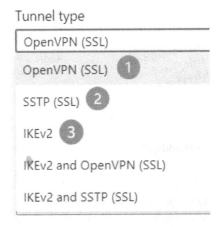

Figure 5.38 – Azure VPN gateway P2S tunnel type options

> **Note**
> Both OpenVPN and SSTP clients communicate with the gateway over TCP port 443, which is allowed by most home and public networks. IKEv2 VPN clients communicate with the gateway over ports that are not commonly allowed by most firewalls (UDP 500 and 4500).

When selecting the tunnel type, consider the following about the client devices that will be used by your users to connect:

- Android, Linux, iOS, macOS, Windows 10 (and above), and Windows Server 2016 (and above) devices come pre-installed with native clients that support IKEv2.

- Windows clients will try IKEv2 first and if that doesn't connect, they fall back to SSTP.

- OpenVPN is supported for all platforms, but a client will usually have to be downloaded and installed on the user's connecting device either manually or using a device management solution such as Microsoft Intune. Azure provides downloadable clients that can be installed on Windows 10 or later clients and macOS clients.

Selecting the authentication type for P2S VPN connectivity

The next key decision when implementing P2S VPN connectivity is the authentication type. Before a user's client device can connect to the gateway, the user must be authenticated. Azure supports the three options shown in *Figure 5.39*. All three authentication methods are supported by the three tunnel types. Let's look at these three options briefly.

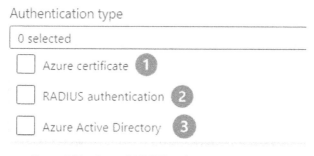

Figure 5.39 – Azure P2S VPN authentication options

Azure certificate allows authentication via a client certificate that is installed in the certificate store of the connecting device. The client certificates are usually generated from an enterprise CA issued or a self-signed trusted root certificate. In this scenario, the gateway validates the certificate, so the public key of the root certificate needs to be uploaded to the gateway. To prevent the use of some issued certificates, they could be added to a "revoke list" on the gateway. You will implement this authentication method in your next hands-on lab in this chapter!

RADIUS authentication allows user authentication via a RADIUS server that is deployed on-premises or in our Azure VNet. The RADIUS server can be implemented to integrate with an Active Directory domain or with any other external identity system. This opens up a variety of authentication options for P2S VPN, including third-party MFA authentication or an enterprise certificate service. The advantage here is we don't need to upload root certificates and revoke client certificates in Azure.

For RADIUS authentication to work, connectivity is important. The gateway needs to be able to reach the RADIUS server so that it can forward authentication messages between the client and the RADIUS server. If it is hosted on-premises, then a VPN S2S connection from Azure to the on-premises site is required for reachability.

Azure Active Directory allows users to connect to Azure using their **Azure Active Directory (Azure AD)** credentials. Native Azure AD authentication is only supported for OpenVPN connections that use the Azure VPN Client for Windows 10 or later and macOS clients. The main advantage of this method is that we can benefit from additional identity and access security capabilities of Azure AD such as MFA support, password protection, and conditional access.

Enough discussions for now, let's head back to the Azure portal to implement P2S VPN connectivity.

Hands-on exercise – implement a P2S VPN connection with Azure certificate authentication

Here are the tasks that we will complete in this exercise:

- **Task 1**: Connect to the remote user's PC via RDP
- **Task 2**: Configure the point-to-site VPN gateway settings
- **Task 3**: Configure settings for VPN clients
- **Task 4**: Verify connectivity between the remote PC and the Azure VNet

Let's get into this!

Task 1: Connect to the remote user's PC via RDP

1. On your client system, open an RDP client and enter the **remotePC-FQDN** value that you made a note of in the first exercise in this chapter. Click on **Connect**. The instructions here describe the use of a Windows RDP client. If you are using a different RDP client, the instructions may be different for you.

To open the Windows RDP client, execute `mstsc` from the Windows run dialog, or type `mstsc` in the Windows start menu.

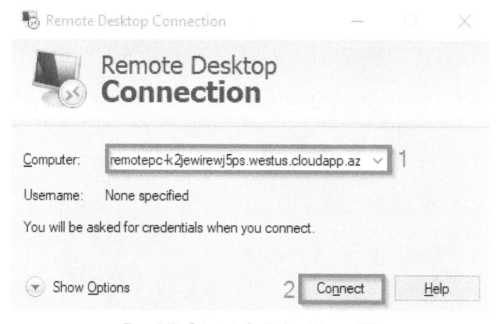

Figure 5.40 – Connect to the Windows VM using RDP

2. When prompted to sign in, click on **More choices** | **Use a different account**. Enter the following:

    • **Username**: remoteuser

    • **Password**: Enter the password that you configured during the template deployment

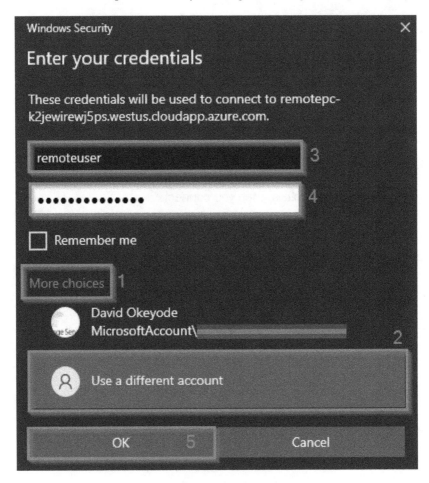

Figure 5.41 – Authenticate using the RDP client

3.   When prompted about the certificate warning, select the **Don't ask me again for connections to this computer** option, then click **Yes**.

Figure 5.42 – Skip the certificate warning

4.   You should now have an RDP session to the public Windows VM!

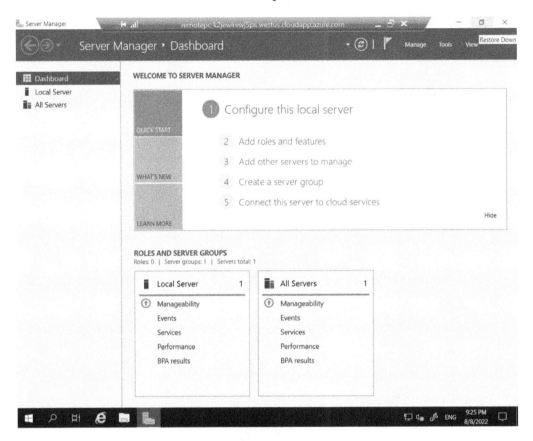

Figure 5.43 – RDP session to the public Windows VM

5.   In the RDP session, open a PowerShell or command-line session and type the following command to obtain the Base64 format of the root certificate that was auto-created at deployment time:

```
notepad C:\Users\remoteuser\Desktop\rootcert.cer
```

Make a note of the certificate data (highlighted in *Figure 5.44*) as it will be needed in the next task.

rootcert - Notepad

File   Edit   Format   View   Help

```
-----BEGIN CERTIFICATE-----
MIIC5zCCAc+gAwIBAgIQa1eyDKnFJYhNukng4geruDANBgkqhkiG9w0BAQsFADAWMRQwEgYDVQQD
DAtQMlNSb290Q2VydDAeFw0yMjA4MDgyMTE4MjhaFw0yMzA4MDgyMTM4MjhaMBYxFDASBgNVBAMM
C1AyU1Jvb3RDZXJ0MIIBIjANBgkqhkiG9w0BAQEFAAOCAQ8AMIIBCgKCAQEA3trb43B1bjkTq3+l
N/laEtvkhoXhB2IVibiQVzOjeubPPxF5lf3z/a/jkrecIIJzCTe7IS2nNQ1jB3c/N5iMX1R60IfcI
Nnq6SJXeLGO9SxWy0QEHICBke9s6OH+2hjvPDfepyvHzRoth+ks/CKfM0gOmugOsDqstFMJoVxBU
WgpFMvbaPsoh0YSoKb8VGcJq5EPb0vqI1N4Smf4/AhKk/kz9Vd13N6oze0wKIgc1vlcPC0s6uQLI
/1uml0uoSuw/QssZjHvXeOfwHblv3jS0m+OgZhaXt+EdpabfxeTcVWTGDGGYYuIWczXHIVjmHjVf
KlXv+ow1OdYrZzjRqd8wxQIDAQABozEwLzAOBgNVHQ8BAf8EBAMCAgQwHQYDVR00BBYEFCXPPCgz
oUVKafSlbj+flCToKvJNMA0GCSqGSIb3DQEBCwUAA4IBAQA2FSpz7SRGyKGqy5Kecgb8C1B1i4Gk
j/QnvNarM7u6MmhpsICNbYhcSueYyinJn4dNArjvVsWB0V470gkcyPnhN0YfgGysrMecbfQiMM1W
3ZUvcaWCk11x0nKNtUri942nnsJJ/6a3znE/ZhrMqpzQpTJ51q8bUBpaqOMgEOgDq7O/VMs671+3
sKktc/rRiyBe+MjEtUveCwUd2xBlVILsiou86bxlfkZOPRGsbkM2tgL22S3ymiVnUau5oeebHCmM
Rjr0QO5VwSGX6MIVc51Eu43PfQXT3mPneuhzUrLK/us7Gr0yaOqJu5cphnTABTxLvhf0VgBVVute
Y8TS1tqM)
-----END CERTIFICATE-----
```

Figure 5.44 – Copy the root certificate data

Keep the RDP session open as you will need it for later tasks in this exercise.

Task 2: Configure the P2S VPN gateway settings

To implement P2S VPN, we need to specify a client address pool, a tunnel type, and authentication types:

1. In the Azure portal search area, type `Virtual network gateway`. Click on the displayed **Virtual network gateways** service.

2. In the **Virtual network gateways** window, select **azuregw**. In the **Settings** section, click on **Point-to-site configuration**, then click on **Configure now** (*Figure 5.45*).

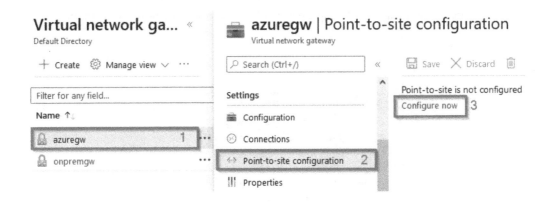

Figure 5.45 – Initiate P2S VPN configuration

3. In the **azurevnetgw | Point-to-site configuration** blade, configure the following:

- **Address pool**: **10.100.0.0/16**

- **Tunnel type**: **IKEv2 and SSTP (SSL)**

- **Authentication type**: **Azure certificate**

- **Root certificates Name**: **P2SrootCert**

- **Root certificates Public certificate data**: Paste the Base64 certificate data that you made a note of in the previous task

Click **Save**.

Figure 5.46 – Configure the connection settings

If you receive an error message about invalid certificate information, ensure that there are no spaces in the data pasted. You may need to edit in Notepad to remove any extra space.

Wait for the configuration to be successfully applied.

4. Once the configuration is applied, click on the **Download VPN client** option to download the client configuration that we will use in the next task. The configuration files will be downloaded in a compressed ZIP format.

Figure 5.47 – Download the VPN client configuration

5. Copy the downloaded VPN configuration (the downloaded ZIP file) into the RDP session of the remote PC.

Task 3: Configure settings for VPN clients

In this task, we will connect the remote user's PC to Azure VPN Gateway using the operating system's natively installed VPN client:

1. Back in the RDP session of the remote PC, extract the configuration file. In the extracted folder, open the WindowsAmd64 folder, then double-click the VpnClientSetupAmd64 file to run it.

Figure 5.48 – Initiate the installation of the VPN client configuration

2. When prompted to install the VPN client, click on **Yes**. This installs the downloaded configuration.

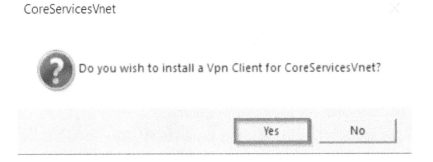

Figure 5.49 – Approve the installation of the VPN client configuration

3.   Click on the **Start** button, then type **VPN**. Click on **VPN settings**.

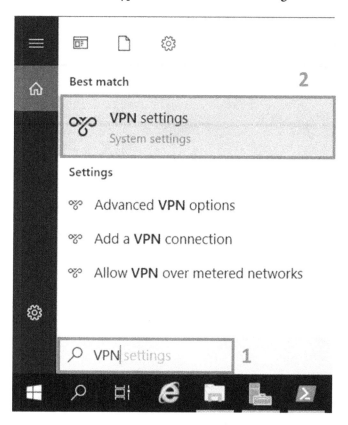

Figure 5.50 – Open the VPN settings in Windows

4.   In the VPN window, click on **CoreServicesVnet**, then **Connect**, to initiate the connection to Azure VPN Gateway.

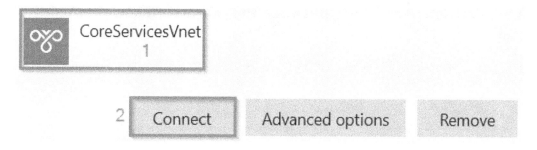

Figure 5.51 – Initiate the connection to Azure VPN Gateway

5.   In the **CoreServicesVnet** window that opens, click on **Connect**. Click on **Continue** when prompted.

Figure 5.52 – Initiate the connection to Azure VPN Gateway

Task 4: Verify connectivity between the remote PC and the Azure VNet

6.   Verify connectivity to **DataVM** in Azure by using PowerShell to test it. You can use the following command:

```
ping 10.10.2.4
```

The test should be successful, as shown:

```
PS C:\Users\remoteuser>
PS C:\Users\remoteuser> ping 10.10.2.4

Pinging 10.10.2.4 with 32 bytes of data:
Reply from 10.10.2.4: bytes=32 time=64ms TTL=64
Reply from 10.10.2.4: bytes=32 time=64ms TTL=64
Reply from 10.10.2.4: bytes=32 time=63ms TTL=64
Reply from 10.10.2.4: bytes=32 time=66ms TTL=64
```

Figure 5.53 – Validate connectivity using ping

Congratulations! You have now configured and tested a P2S VPN connection in Azure!

Troubleshoot Azure VPN Gateway using diagnostic logs

Using diagnostic logs, you can troubleshoot multiple VPN gateway-related events including configuration activity, VPN tunnel connectivity, IPsec logging, BGP route exchanges, and point-to-site advanced logging.

There are several diagnostic logs you can use to help troubleshoot a problem with your VPN gateway:

- **GatewayDiagnosticLog**: This log contains diagnostic logs for the gateway, including configuration changes and maintenance events.

- **TunnelDiagnosticLog**: This log contains tunnel state change events. This log is useful to review the historical connectivity status of the tunnels (connect/disconnect events), including the reason for the state change. Once a concerning connect/disconnect event is identified, a more detailed analysis can be done with **IKEdiagnosticLog**.

- **RouteDiagnosticLog**: This log contains routing logs, including changes to static routes and BGP events.

- **IKEDiagnosticLog**: This log contains IKE control messages and events on the gateway. This is very useful to review when troubleshooting disconnections or in failure to connect VPN scenarios.

- **P2SDiagnosticLog**: This log contains point-to-site control messages and events on the gateway.

We will cover diagnostic logs in more detail later in this book.

Hands-on exercise – clean up resources

In this exercise, we will remove the resources that we created in the chapter exercises to avoid running up large costs in Azure!

In Cloud Shell, run the following command to delete the `CharisTechRG-C5` resource group:

```
az group delete --name CharisTechRG-C5 --yes
```

This will remove all the resources that we created for the exercises in this chapter.

Summary

In this chapter, we covered both site-to-site and point-to-site VPN connection options in Azure, including how to select the right size, choose the right type, define the right availability, and implement it in practice.

In the next chapter, we will cover another critical hybrid connectivity component – ExpressRoute. See you there!

Designing and Implementing Hybrid Network Connectivity with the ExpressRoute Gateway

In the previous chapter, we introduced the **virtual private network** (**VPN**) gateway service as a way to connect on-premises networks to Azure. While this method provides a secure connection, it may not always be the best option for scenarios that require high predictability and performance. In this chapter, we will explore the implementation of ExpressRoute, another gateway service offered by Azure, as an alternative solution for remote network connectivity.

You will cover the following topics in this chapter:

- Understanding what ExpressRoute is and its main use cases

- Understanding ExpressRoute components

- Deciding on an ExpressRoute connectivity model

- Selecting the right ExpressRoute circuit **stock-keeping unit** (**SKU**)

- Selecting the right ExpressRoute gateway SKU

- Improving data path performance with ExpressRoute FastPath

- Designing and implementing cross-network connectivity over ExpressRoute

- Understanding the implementation of encryption over ExpressRoute

- Understanding the implementation of **Bidirectional Forwarding Detection** (**BFD**)

- Hands-on exercise – implementing an ExpressRoute gateway

We've organized each topic to address the crucial exam objectives and also give you practical information that will be useful in real-world situations. Let's dive in!

Technical requirements

To follow along with the instructions in this chapter, you will need the following:

- A PC with an internet connection

- An Azure subscription

Understanding what ExpressRoute is and its main use cases

In the previous chapter, we covered one of the services that we can use to establish hybrid network connectivity in Azure—the VPN gateway. We explained that it can be used to create an encrypted tunnel between remote networks or users and the Azure **virtual network** (**VNet**) over the public internet.

The VPN gateway establishes a secure connection, but network throughput is not guaranteed as traffic is sent over the public internet. Once network traffic leaves any of the connected networks, the throughput is unpredictable as we have very little control over how the traffic is routed or processed (*Figure 6.1*). This makes this option non-ideal in situations where **guaranteed low latency** is required. For example, we may have a business requirement to ensure predictable performance for mission-critical services. To achieve this, we can implement **ExpressRoute** connectivity:

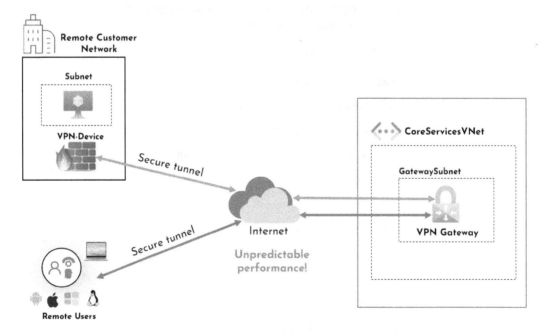

Figure 6.1 – Throughput over the VPN gateway is the best effort

Another reason why the VPN option may not be ideal is that certain organizations or government agencies may not be allowed to route sensitive traffic over the public internet for compliance reasons. This type of compliance requirement (not permitting routing over the internet) is not common! Most regulations only require data to be protected in transit using encryption standards such as *AES-256*, which the VPN gateway supports, but if the requirement is to ensure private routing only, we can implement ExpressRoute connectivity.

ExpressRoute provides a way to connect remote networks to Azure VNets and Microsoft cloud services using a dedicated private network connection (*Figure 6.2*). With ExpressRoute, all traffic stays on provider-managed private **wide area networks** (**WANs**) instead of transiting over the public internet! This way, the network throughput is more reliable and predictable as the chances of contention with other customer traffic are minimized. Performance can also reach guaranteed faster speeds with lower or more consistent latency compared to the VPN option:

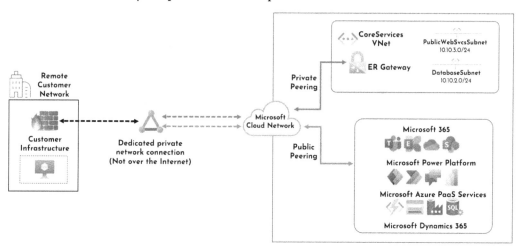

Figure 6.2 – ExpressRoute implementation

Choosing between private peering and public peering

When planning to use ExpressRoute, one important consideration is the type of peering to implement. Peering refers to the connection between two networks for traffic exchange. ExpressRoute offers two options for peering: *private* and *public* (as shown in *Figure 6.2*).

Private peering allows remote networks to access Azure VNets and resources connected to those VNets, such as infrastructure and platform services. This connection is bi-directional and can support multiple Azure VNets.

Public peering, on the other hand, enables remote networks to access Microsoft cloud services, such as Microsoft 365 and Azure platform services, through the ExpressRoute connection (as shown in *Figure 6.2*).

Connection to these services will usually be over the public internet, but with an ExpressRoute implementation, the connection will be routed over a private WAN.

> **Microsoft cloud services**
>
> Microsoft cloud services is a term that is used to refer to **Software-as-a-Service (SaaS)** offerings hosted in Microsoft **data centers (DCs)**. This includes Office 365 services such as Exchange Online, SharePoint Online, and Teams, as well as Dynamics 365 and Power Platform. These are services that are normally accessed over the internet.

Deciding which peering option to choose depends on the services that we need to access. If an organization requires access to services hosted in an Azure VNet (for example, virtual machines, VNet-integrated platform services such as Azure SQL Managed Instance, or services with a private endpoint), private peering will provide that connectivity. If secure, private access is required for services such as Microsoft 365, Power Platform, and Azure AD, the public peering option will provide that connectivity. We can also choose to implement *both* peering options if that is required.

As we go through the rest of this chapter, we will share more details on ExpressRoute and the objectives that you need to know for the exam, but before we do so, let us have a quick look at the components that makes up an end-to-end ExpressRoute connection.

Understanding ExpressRoute components

The purpose of ExpressRoute is to connect a remote customer network to a customer's Azure VNet or a customer's Microsoft cloud service tenant. But to understand how ExpressRoute works, we need to understand the components that an ExpressRoute connection is made of. Take a look at the following diagram:

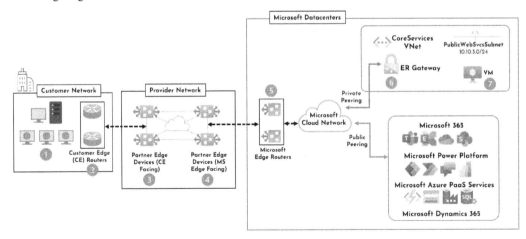

Figure 6.3 – ExpressRoute key network components

Figure 6.3 illustrates the logical connection of a customer network to the Microsoft network using ExpressRoute. The numbers in the diagram represent important network points, listed as follows:

1. **On-premises devices**: Devices located physically within an organization's premises.

2. **Customer edge (CE) routers**: Routers used by customers to connect to their ExpressRoute partner network.

3. **Provider edge devices facing CE routers**: These are routers/switches used by ExpressRoute **service providers (SPs)** to connect to CE routers.

4. **Partner edge devices facing Microsoft edge routers**: These are routers/switches used by ExpressRoute SPs to connect to Microsoft edge routers.

5. **Microsoft edge routers**: These are a redundant pair of routers on the Microsoft side of the ExpressRoute circuit. Microsoft has multiple facilities around the world where these edge devices are located. This location is the entry point to Microsoft's network. The location of the devices does not need to match the Azure region where our VNet is. For example, we can use entry points in Paris *or* Madrid to connect to VNets in UK South or UK West Azure regions. For an up-to-date mapping of ExpressRoute locations to Azure regions, please refer to this document: `https://learn.microsoft.com/en-us/azure/expressroute/expressroute-locations#locations`.

6. **ExpressRoute VNet gateway**: This is the service that connects an ExpressRoute circuit with an Azure VNet. Behind the scenes, it is a redundant pair of gateway devices that handles the sending and receiving of traffic through the ExpressRoute circuit.

7. **Azure VNet resource**: VNet infrastructure or platform resources.

Deciding on an ExpressRoute connectivity model

When architecting an ExpressRoute connection, there are different connectivity models that we can implement for a circuit—a **provider model** and an **ExpressRoute direct model**. We need to specify the option that we're using when we create our ExpressRoute gateway (*Figure 6.4*). Let's have a look at the different models:

Figure 6.4 – Selecting an ExpressRoute connectivity model

Understanding the provider model

The provider model connects a remote network to the Azure network through a third-party provider connection network. To establish this connection, we need to work with a partner that specializes in ExpressRoute connectivity (as shown in *Figure 6.3*).

Figure 6.3, which we saw earlier, actually illustrates the logical connection of a customer network to the Microsoft network using the provider model.

Depending on the service offerings of the ExpressRoute partner that we choose to work with, we have three connectivity options that we can implement, as follows:

- Cloud exchange co-location

- Point-to-point Ethernet connection

- Any-to-any IPVPN connection

Some providers offer all three options, while some only offer one. Let's have a look at these options in more detail.

> **ExpressRoute locations and partners**
>
> For a list of ExpressRoute locations and connectivity partners that support them, please refer to this document: `https://learn.microsoft.com/en-us/azure/expressroute/expressroute-locations-providers`.

The first option, **cloud exchange co-location**, involves hosting/moving our infrastructure into a co-location DC of a provider with connectivity to Microsoft. With this model, we simply host our infrastructure in the provider's facility and order virtual cross-connections to Microsoft from the facility. Our provider manages infrastructure responsibilities such as power, cooling, physical infrastructure, and connectivity to Microsoft.

Provider offerings could be either Layer 2 or managed Layer 3 cross-connections between our infrastructure in the co-location DC and the Microsoft cloud (*Figure 6.5*):

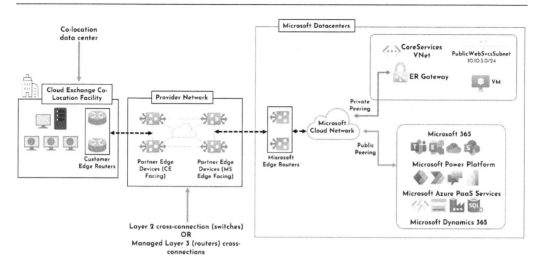

Figure 6.5 – Cloud exchange co-location provider model

The second option, **point-to-point Ethernet**, involves working with an **internet SP (ISP)** that provides single-site Layer 2 or managed Layer 3 connectivity between the remote network and the Azure VNet. The key point with this option is that connectivity is for a single customer site (*Figure 6.6*):

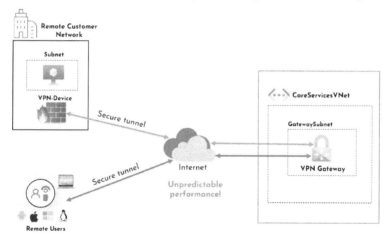

Figure 6.6 – Point-to-point provider model

In both the cloud exchange co-location and point-to-point Ethernet connectivity models, the CE routers (labeled as **2** in *Figure 6.6*) establish a connection through **Border Gateway Protocol (BGP)** with the Microsoft edge routers (labeled as **5**).

In the any-to-any connectivity model, BGP peering is established between the Microsoft-facing partner edge routers (labeled as **4**) and the Microsoft edge routers (labeled as **5**). The partner edge routers then propagate the routes received from Microsoft back to the customer network via the IPVPN SP network.

The third option, **any-to-any IPVPN connection**, leverages ISP-provided **Multiprotocol Label Switching** (**MPLS**) connectivity to connect multiple customer sites with the Microsoft cloud network. This model is recommended for organizations with existing MPLS connections. This way, the ExpressRoute circuit can be connected to their WAN architecture instead of a single site. In this scenario, the Azure VNet looks like any other branch that is connected to the WAN (*Figure 6.7*):

> **BGP peering in the ExpressRoute provider models**
>
> In the cloud exchange co-location and point-to-point Ethernet connectivity models, the CE routers (labeled as **2** in *Figure 6.7*) establish BGP peering with the Microsoft edge routers (labeled as **5**).
>
> In the any-to-any connectivity model, BGP peering is established between the Microsoft-facing partner edge routers (labeled as **4**) and the Microsoft edge routers (labeled as **5**). The partner edge routers then distribute the routes received from Microsoft to the customer network through the IPVPN SP network.

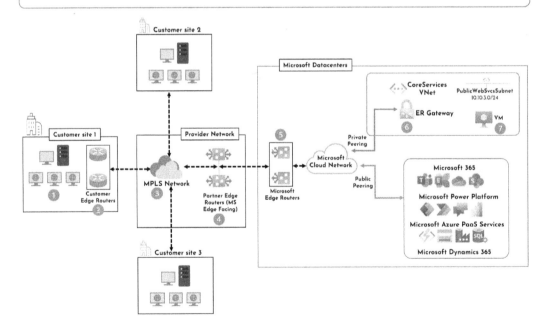

Figure 6.7 – Any-to-any IPVPN connection

Choosing the right model for your organization depends on your existing infrastructure and your requirements. For example, if your infrastructure is hosted in a co-location DC where the first option (cloud exchange) is available, it makes sense to use that. If your organization has an existing MPLS WAN, it may make sense to look to implement the third option (any-to-any IPVPN). If you're a small-to-medium organization that is looking to connect a single site to the Microsoft cloud network, it makes sense to use the second option (point-to-point Ethernet). The good news is that regardless of which provider model is implemented, ExpressRoute features are similar across all the provider connectivity models!

With regard to performance, the provider model supports bandwidth ranging from 50 **megabits per second** (**Mbps**) to 10 **gigabits per second** (**Gbps**). This type of connection is optimized for a single tenant.

Now that you have a solid understanding of the provider model and the options that it offers, let us turn our attention to the other ExpressRoute connectivity model—the direct model.

Understanding the ExpressRoute direct model

In contrast to the provider model options, the ExpressRoute direct model allows customer's remote networks to connect directly to Microsoft's globally distributed peering locations with a 10 Gbps or a 100 Gbps connection! It does not rely on a third party for ExpressRoute connectivity.

In the direct connectivity model, a provider network is not needed. Instead, the CE routers are connected directly to the Microsoft edge routers with dark fiber (*Figure 6.8*):

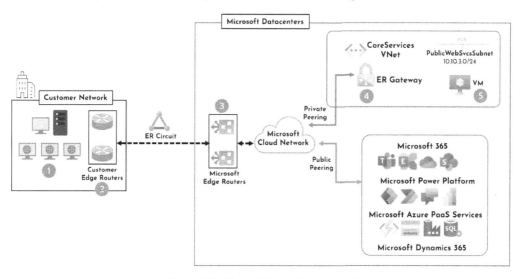

Figure 6.8 – ExpressRoute direct model

So, why might organizations choose this model instead of the provider model? The simple answer to this is high throughput for use cases such as massive data ingestion and physical isolation for regulated industries—for example, banking and government.

The ExpressRoute direct model can support organizations that require very high bandwidth connectivity beyond what the provider model options can support (up to 100 Gbps). But of course, it is not a cheap option!

The 10 Gbps ExpressRoute direct circuit option supports SKUs for 1 Gbps, 2 Gbps, 5 Gbps, or 10 Gbps ExpressRoute connections. The 100 Gbps ExpressRoute direct circuit option supports SKUs for 5 Gbps, 10 Gbps, 40 Gbps, or 100 Gbps.

ExpressRoute Direct is not yet supported for every ExpressRoute location. For an up-to-date list of ExpressRoute locations that support ExpressRoute Direct, please refer to this document: `https://learn.microsoft.com/en-us/azure/expressroute/expressroute-locations-providers#global-commercial-azure`.

To implement ExpressRoute Direct, a subscription must first be enrolled for the feature using the following Azure PowerShell command:

```
Register-AzProviderFeature -FeatureName AllowExpressRoutePorts
-ProviderNamespace Microsoft.Network
```

Selecting the right ExpressRoute circuit SKU

After deciding which ExpressRoute model we want to implement, we need to decide on an ExpressRoute circuit SKU to implement. Provisioning an ExpressRoute circuit establishes a redundant Layer 2 connection between CE/partner edge routers and the Microsoft edge routers. To do this, we need to decide on the ExpressRoute circuit SKU to implement. We have three SKU options to select from depending on our organization's requirements—**Local**, **Standard**, and **Premium** (*Figure 6.9*):

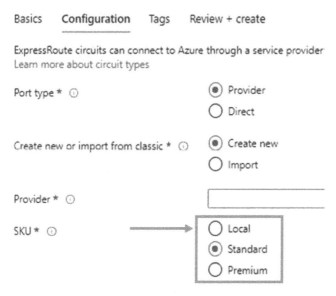

Figure 6.9 – Selecting an ExpressRoute SKU

To be able to select the right option, we need to understand the available options and how they fit within the design of an ExpressRoute implementation. Let's look at them in more detail.

The first option, **Local**, can provide connectivity to VNets in one or two Azure regions in the same metro/geographical area. For example, if we implemented an ExpressRoute **Local** circuit in the Washington DC location, the circuit could be used to access Azure services and customer networks in both the East US and the East US 2 Azure regions (labeled as **1** in *Figure 6.10*):

ER Location	Local Azure regions	Service providers
Amsterdam	West Europe	Aryaka Networks, AT&T NetBond, British Telecom, Colt, Equinix, euNetworks, GÉANT, InterCloud, Interxion, KPN, IX Reach, Level 3 Communications, Megaport, NTT Communications, Orange, Tata Communications, Telefonica, Telenor, Telia Carrier, Verizon, Zayo
Atlanta	N/A	Equinix, Megaport
Bangkok	N/A	AIS, National Telecom UIH
Los Angeles	N/A	CoreSite, Equinix, Megaport, Neutrona Networks, NTT, Zayo
Washington DC	East US, East US 2	Aryaka Networks, AT&T NetBond, British Telecom, CenturyLink Cloud Connect, Cologix, Colt, Comcast, Coresite, Cox Business Cloud Port, Equinix, Internet2, InterCloud, Iron Mountain, IX Reach, Level 3 Communications, Megaport, Neutrona Networks, NTT Communications, Orange, PacketFabric, SES, Sprint, Tata Communications, Telia Carrier, Verizon, Zayo

Figure 6.10 – Incomplete list of ExpressRoute locations to local Azure regions mapping

> **Note**
>
> For up-to-date information on ExpressRoute local mappings, please refer to this document: `https://learn.microsoft.com/en-us/azure/expressroute/expressroute-locations-providers#global-commercial-azure`.

Also, keep in mind that not all ExpressRoute locations support the ExpressRoute **Local** circuit SKU. For example, the Atlanta, Bangkok, and Los Angeles ExpressRoute locations do not support this SKU (labeled as **2** in *Figure 6.10*).

One amazing benefit of the **Local** SKU is that there is no additional cost to transferring data out of Azure through the ExpressRoute connection (egress data). This is a great benefit as other SKUs (that we will discuss) offers egress data transfer as an added cost! Ingress data transfer is free of charge for all three SKUs.

So, why would anyone want to implement this option? Well, this is a great option for organizations that are implementing a local Azure strategy (for example, they only deploy services in Azure regions within a local area such as East US, and East US 2 regions). If an organization is looking to implement a multi-region strategy in Azure with VNets created in multiple regions beyond a local area, it is recommended to implement one of the other SKUs.

The second option, **Standard**, can provide connectivity to VNets and Azure services in Azure regions in a geopolitical area.

For example, if we implemented an ExpressRoute **Standard** circuit in the Atlanta location, the circuit could be used to access Azure services and VNets in all Azure regions in North America (labeled as **1** in *Figure 6.11*) but not European regions:

ER Locations	Geopolitical Region	Azure Regions
Amsterdam, Amsterdam2, Berlin, Copenhagen, Dublin, Dublin2, Frankfurt, Frankfurt2, Geneva, London, London2, Madrid, Marseille, Milan, Munich, Newport(Wales), Oslo, Paris, Paris2, Stavanger, Stockholm, Zurich	Europe	France Central, France South, Germany North, Germany West Central, North Europe, Norway East, Norway West, Sweden Central, Switzerland North, Switzerland West, UK West, UK South, West Europe
Atlanta, Chicago, Chicago2, Dallas, Denver, Las Vegas, Los Angeles, Los Angeles2, Miami, Minneapolis, Montreal, New York, Phoenix, Quebec City, Queretaro(Mexico), Quincy, San Antonio, Seattle, Silicon Valley, Silicon Valley2, Toronto, Toronto2, Vancouver, Washington DC, Washington DC2	North America	East US, West US, East US 2, West US 2, West US 3, Central US, South Central US, North Central US, West Central US, Canada Central, Canada East
Bangkok, Hong Kong, Hong Kong2, Jakarta, Kuala Lumpur, Singapore, Singapore2, Taipei	Asia	East Asia, Southeast Asia
Cape Town, Johannesburg	South Africa	South Africa West, South Africa North

Figure 6.11 – Incomplete list of ExpressRoute locations to geopolitical region mapping

> **Note**
>
> For up-to-date information on ExpressRoute local mappings, please refer to this document: `https://learn.microsoft.com/en-us/azure/expressroute/expressroute-locations-providers#locations`.

As mentioned earlier, this SKU offers egress data transfer at an added cost. The ExpressRoute **Standard** circuit SKU has two billing models for egress data transfer charges—**Metered** and **Unlimited** (*Figure 6.12*):

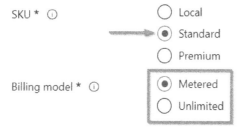

Figure 6.12 – Metered and Unlimited egress data billing models

The **Unlimited** option provides egress data transfer for a *fixed monthly fee*, while the **Metered** option provides egress data transfer for a *pre-determined rate per BG*. The **Unlimited** option is recommended for organizations that transfer a lot of data outbound as they only need to pay a single fixed rate to transfer as much data as they want. If the rate of egress data transfer is low or inconsistent, the **Metered** option may be cheaper as you only pay per gigabyte of data transferred.

So, why would anyone want to implement the ExpressRoute **Standard** circuit option? This SKU is a great choice for organizations that implement a geographic-region strategy in Azure—for example, an organization that only deploys networks and services into Azure regions within the same geographic area such as North America, Europe, and Asia.

The third option, **Premium**, can provide connectivity to VNets and services in any Azure region globally! This SKU is a great option for organizations that implement a global deployment strategy in Azure (for example, they deploy services to Azure regions in multiple geographic areas). In terms of data transfer, this option is similar to the **Standard** option. We can implement either a **Metered** or **Unlimited** egress data transfer billing model.

In summary, *Figure 6.13* shows variation in the scope of access depending on the ExpressRoute circuit SKU that is implemented using the Washington DC ExpressRoute location as an example. The following applies:

- If the **Local** SKU is implemented, the connection can be used to access Azure VNets and services in only East US and East US 2

- If the **Standard** SKU is implemented, the connection can be used to access Azure VNets and services in all Azure regions in North America

- If the **Premium** SKU is implemented, the connection can be used to access Azure VNets and services in all Azure regions globally:

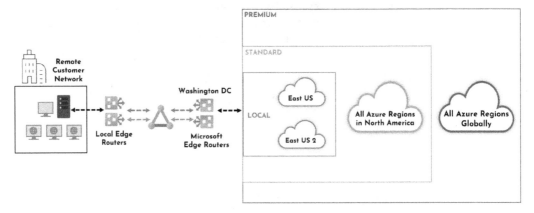

Figure 6.13 – ExpressRoute circuit SKU scope-of-access review

There are other differentiators between these SKUs beyond their scope of access and egress data charges. For example, if you're planning to access Microsoft cloud services over ExpressRoute, you will need the **Premium** SKU circuit to implement this (labeled as **1** in *Figure 6.14*). If you will be advertising over 4,000 IPv4 routes from your remote network to your Azure networks, you will also need the **Premium** SKU circuit to do this (labeled as **2**). And if you need to link your ExpressRoute connection to more than 10 VNets in Azure, you will again need the **Premium** SKU circuit (labeled as **3**):

	ExpressRoute Local	ExpressRoute Standard	ExpressRoute Premium
Azure VNet and services access	Local area region only	Geopolitical regions	All Azure regions globally
Microsoft cloud services access	Not supported	Not supported	Supported ①
Egress data charges	Unlimited at no cost	Metered or unlimited at an added cost	Metered or unlimited at an added cost
Maximum remote network IPv4 route advertisements TO private peering	4000	4000	10000 ②
Maximum remote network IPv4 route advertisements TO Microsoft peering	200	200	200
Maximum remote network IPv6 route advertisements TO private peering	100	100	100
Maximum remote network IPv6 route advertisements TO Microsoft peering	200	200	200
Maximum private peering IPv4 route advertisements TO remote network	1000	1000	1000
Maximum VNet links	10	10	100 ③
Global Reach support	No	No	Yes

Figure 6.14 – ExpressRoute circuit SKUs comparison

Please refer to *Figure 6.14* for a summary of these differentiators.

Now that we understand the available ExpressRoute circuit options and what we need to consider in selecting the right option for our implementation, let us review ExpressRoute gateway options.

Selecting the right ExpressRoute gateway SKU

After deciding which ExpressRoute circuit SKU we want to implement, we need to decide on an ExpressRoute gateway SKU to implement. An ExpressRoute gateway is a service that connects an ExpressRoute circuit with an Azure VNet (*Figure 6.15*):

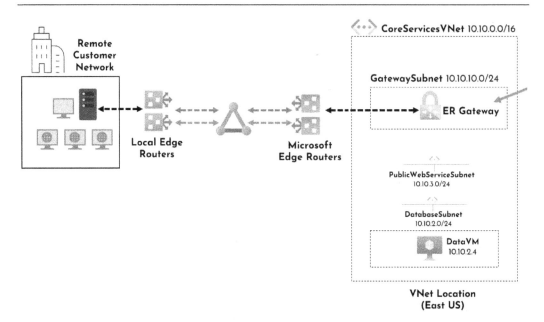

Figure 6.15 – Sample ExpressRoute implementation

When we create an ExpressRoute gateway service, we need to specify the SKU that we want to use (*Figure 6.16*) based on our organization's requirements. We have the following SKU options to choose from:

- **Standard/ErGw1AZ**
- **High performance/ErGw2AZ**
- **Ultra performance/ErGw3AZ:**

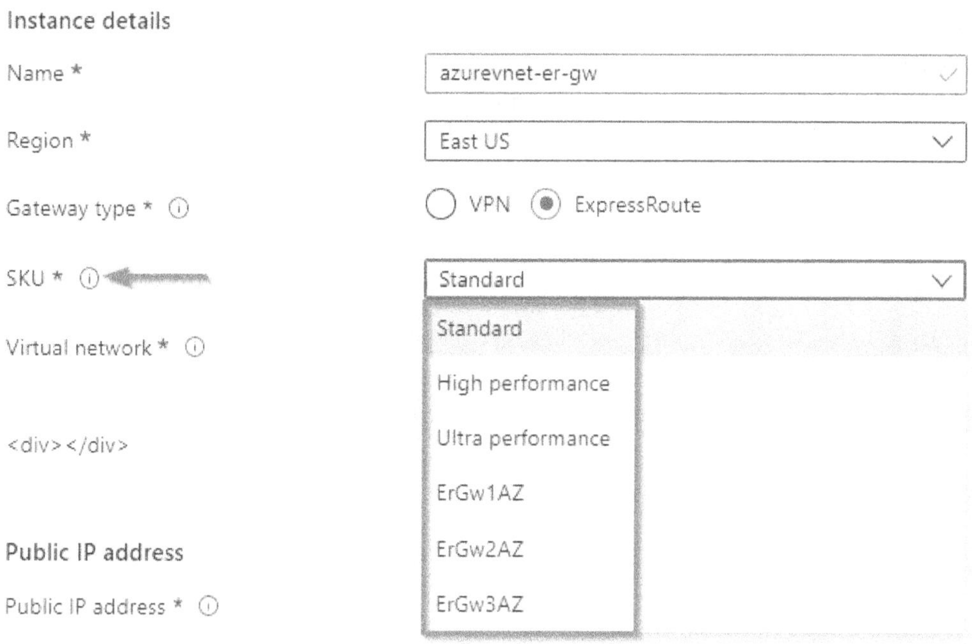

Instance details

Name *	azurevnet-er-gw

Region *	East US

Gateway type * ⓘ   ○ VPN ● ExpressRoute

SKU * ⓘ ◄━━━━━━━━━ Standard

	Standard
	High performance
	Ultra performance
	ErGw1AZ
	ErGw2AZ
	ErGw3AZ

Virtual network * ⓘ

<div></div>

Public IP address

Public IP address * ⓘ

Figure 6.16 – ExpressRoute gateway SKU options

The **Standard** and **ErGw1AZ** options support a maximum of four ExpressRoute circuit connections and up to 1 Gbps bandwidth.

The **High performance** and **ErGw2AZ** options support a maximum of eight ExpressRoute circuit connections. The gateway instances that they use come with more CPU and memory than the **Standard/ErGw1AZ** SKUs, so they support a higher network throughout—up to 2 Gbps bandwidth.

The **Ultra performance** and **ErGw3AZ** options support a maximum of 16 ExpressRoute circuit connections and up to 10 Gbps bandwidth.

> **Note**
>
> For additional information on the test conditions for the gateway network throughput numbers, please refer to this document: `https://learn.microsoft.com/en-us/azure/expressroute/expressroute-about-virtual-network-gateways#testing-conditions`. Keep in mind that actual performance may vary!

So, how do we select the right gateway SKU for our implementation? First, we want to ensure that the bandwidth of the SKU is sized to match the bandwidth of the circuit. For example, if we are provisioning an ExpressRoute circuit of 5 Gbps, selecting the **Standard** ExpressRoute gateway SKU will result in a bandwidth mismatch and a performance bottleneck (*Figure 6.17*) as it can only go up to 1 Gbps:

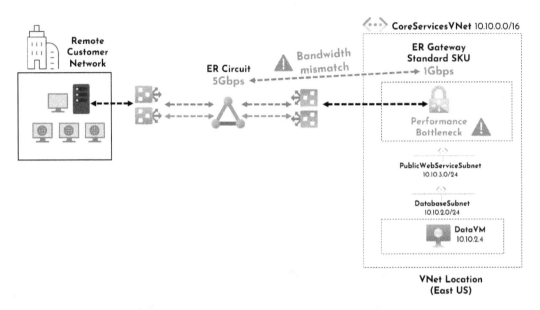

Figure 6.17 – ExpressRoute circuit-gateway SKU bandwidth mismatch

Figure 6.18 shows a summary of ExpressRoute circuit bandwidths and recommended ExpressRoute gateway SKUs to use:

ER Circuit Bandwidth	ER Gateway SKU
50 Mbps	Any SKU
100 Mbps	Any SKU
200 Mbps	Any SKU
500 Mbps	Any SKU
1 Gbps	Any SKU
2 Gbps	High performance (2Gbps) Ultra-performance (10Gbps) ErGw2AZ (2Gbps) ErGw3AZ (10Gbps)
5 Gbps	Ultra-performance (10Gbps) ErGw2AZ (2Gbps) ErGw3AZ (10Gbps)
10 Gbps	Ultra-performance (10Gbps) ErGw2AZ (2Gbps) ErGw3AZ (10Gbps)

Figure 6.18 – Matching ExpressRoute circuit to gateway SKUs

Another consideration in selecting the right gateway SKU is the features that we want to implement. For example, if we need to implement the **FastPath** feature, we need to implement the **Ultra performance** or the **ErGw3AZ** SKU. If you are wondering what the **FastPath** feature is, hold on tight—we will cover it very soon in this chapter!

Implementing ExpressRoute with zone redundancy

Another consideration in selecting the right gateway is whether we want to implement **availability zone** (**AZ**) redundancy (that is, the ability to survive the failure of a DC in an Azure region). The gateway SKU options with "AZ" in their names (ErGw1AZ/ErGw2AZ/ErGw3AZ) have AZ support, while the options with no "AZ" in their names (**Standard/High performance/Ultra performance**) have no AZ support. When we implement any of the SKUs with AZ support, we have the option to deploy our ExpressRoute gateway in a single zone or to implement zone redundancy for DC failure resiliency (*Figure 6.19*):

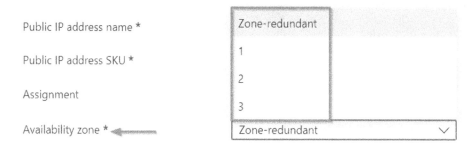

Figure 6.19 – ExpressRoute gateway AZ configuration

Implementing the zone redundancy option provides added resiliency and higher availability as the gateway instances will be distributed into different DC groups in the same region (*Figure 6.20*):

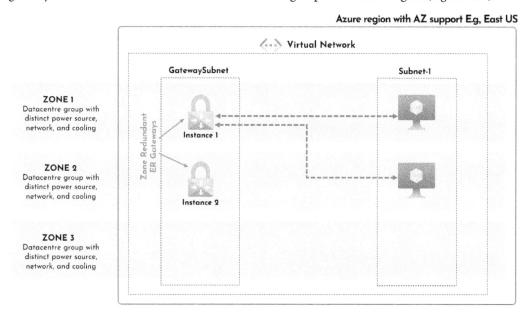

Figure 6.20 – ExpressRoute gateway redundancy

Modifying a gateway SKU

So, what about upgrading or downgrading a gateway SKU after it has been implemented? Is this possible? The good news is that it is! This can be done using the Azure portal or any of the command-line tools.

Here is the command that we can use for this in Azure PowerShell:

```
Resize-AzVirtualNetworkGateway -VirtualNetworkGateway <Gateway>
-GatewaySku <SKU>
```

And here is the same command, this time with the Azure CLI:

```
az network vnet-gateway update -g <ResourceGroup> -n <Gateway> --sku
<SKU>
```

Just keep in mind that not all upgrade/downgrade scenarios are possible. These are the supported upgrade scenarios:

- **Standard** to **High performance** *or* **Ultra performance**
- **High performance** to **Ultra performance**
- **ErGw1Az** to **ErGw2Az** *or* **ErGw3Az**
- **ErGw2Az** to **ErGw3Az**

These are the supported downgrade scenarios:

- **High performance** to **Standard**
- **ErGw2Az** to **ErGw1Az**

Other downgrade scenarios will require us to remove the existing gateway and recreate it with the SKU that we want. This *could* result in downtime if the existing gateway is active!

Implementing the gateway subnet

Similar to the VPN gateway that we discussed in the previous chapter, an ExpressRoute gateway must also be deployed in a **GatewaySubnet** (the subnet cannot be named anything else). This subnet must be a dedicated subnet, which means no other resource should be deployed into it apart from a VPN gateway if we are implementing a co-existence scenario.

During creation, we need to specify the subnet address range. This defines the number of IP addresses that will be available to the gateway service for allocation. The more gateway devices and ExpressRoute circuits that you implement, the more IP addresses will be needed.

The smallest **Classless Inter-Domain Routing** (**CIDR**) prefix that we can specify is /29 (*Figure 6.21*). However, keep in mind that configurations such as an ExpressRoute/VPN gateway co-existence scenario require more IP addresses for allocation. You may not have current plans to implement this configuration, but it is a good idea to architect it for future growth. You may even want to add more ExpressRoute circuit connections to your gateway (remember that the **Ultra performance** SKU can support up to 16 ExpressRoute circuit connections). The recommendation is to use at least a /26 subnet—this will accommodate most configurations. In our case, we will use a /24 range when we go through the hands-on lab:

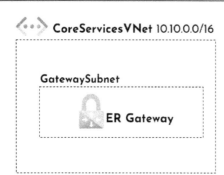

CoreServicesVNet 10.10.0.0/16

GatewaySubnet

ER Gateway

GatewaySubnet Considerations
- **Minimum CIDR:** /29
- **Recommended CIDR:** /26
- **Gateway number (ER/VPN)**
- **ER circuit number**

Unsupported GatewaySubnet configurations
- **UDR route with a 0.0.0.0/0 destination**
- **Disabling BGP route propagation**
- **Applying a NSG**

Figure 6.21 – ExpressRoute GatewaySubnet considerations

If you are implementing a dual-stack ExpressRoute gateway, a /64 IPv6 subnet range is recommended.

> **Note**
>
> Some configurations are not supported for the GatewaySubnet. For example, applying a **user-defined route** (**UDR**) with a 0.0.0.0/0 destination, applying a **network security group** (**NSG**), and disabling BGP route propagation are unsupported configurations for the GatewaySubnet. Implementing any of these will result in the gateway not being created or loss of functionality if it is!
>
> UDRs are still supported—for example, to direct traffic to a **network virtual appliance** (**NVA**) for inspection before being forwarded to the destination resource—but the UDR needs to define specific prefixes and not a default route (0.0.0.0/0).

Improving data path performance with ExpressRoute FastPath

The **FastPath** feature of ExpressRoute is designed to improve data path performance between connected remote networks and Azure VNets. To understand how the **FastPath** feature works, we need to understand the default behavior without it.

By default, the ExpressRoute gateway performs two main tasks—exchanging network routes with our remote networks *AND* routing network traffic to Azure VNet resources (*Figure 6.22*). Routing the network traffic adds a little processing overhead, which impacts performance metrics such as **packets per second** (**PPS**) and **connections per second** (**CPS**):

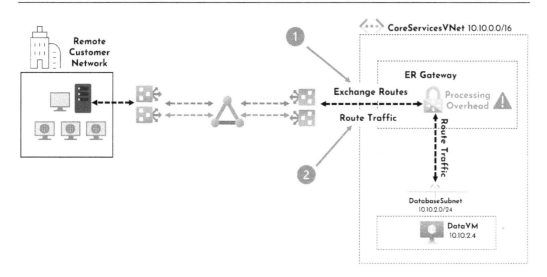

Figure 6.22 – Traffic routing without FastPath

When enabled, **FastPath** sends network traffic directly to VNet resources, bypassing the gateway (*Figure 6.23*). This results in higher throughput and overall better performance!

FastPath is available for all ExpressRoute circuits, but *the ExpressRoute gateway must be either the Ultra performance or ErGw3AZ ExpressRoute gateway SKU*:

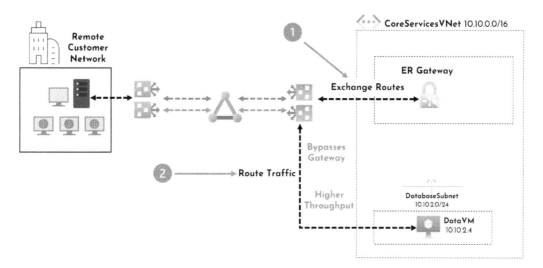

Figure 6.23 – Traffic routing with FastPath

Understanding FastPath unsupported scenarios

While **FastPath** supports most configurations, it has some limitations where traffic will still be routed through the ExpressRoute gateway. For example, if you deploy a VNet resource behind a **Basic** internal load balancer, the network traffic from remote networks will still be routed through the gateway even with **FastPath** implemented (*Figure 6.24*). The workaround for this is to upgrade the load balancer from the **Basic** SKU to the **Standard** SKU.

Also, if *a VNet has previously been peered with an ExpressRoute-connected VNet* or *a platform service is connected via a private link* (we will cover private links in a later chapter in this book), the network traffic from remote networks will still be routed through the gateway even with **FastPath** implemented. However, Microsoft recently announced a preview feature to support both scenarios: `https://azure.microsoft.com/en-us/updates/public-preview-expressroute-fastpath-improvements/`. Once the feature is generally available, peered VNet and private link traffic sent over ExpressRoute with **FastPath** configured will also bypass the gateway in the data path. The feature will support both IPv4 and IPv6 scenarios:

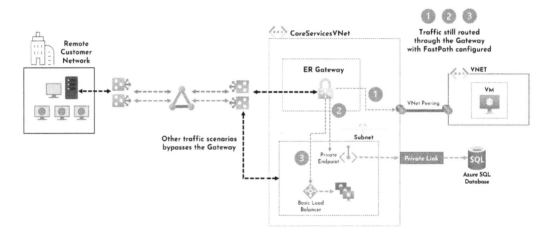

Figure 6.24 – FastPath unsupported scenarios

Also, if you are implementing UDRs on the **GatewaySubnet** to direct traffic to an NVA before sending it to the destination VNet resource (as we covered in *Chapter 3* of this book), there is a preview feature for **FastPath** to still honor this traffic-flow behavior: `https://learn.microsoft.com/en-us/azure/expressroute/about-fastpath#user-defined-routes-udrs`.

Configuring FastPath for new or existing connections

FastPath can be configured for an ExpressRoute connection via the portal, the Azure CLI, or Azure PowerShell. To configure via the portal, we can select the **FastPath** option when creating the ExpressRoute connection (*Figure 6.25*).

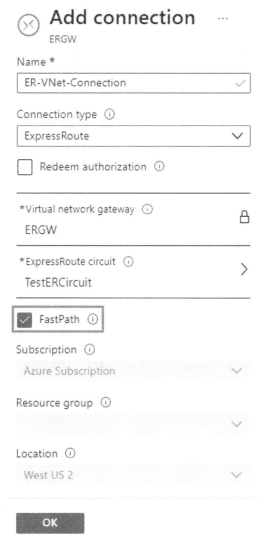

Figure 6.25 – Enabling ExpressRoute FastPath for a connection

To configure via the Azure CLI, we can use the commands shown next. The key parameter that enables **FastPath** is the `--express-route-gateway-bypass` parameter. The value of this parameter must be set to `true`.

Here is the command to do this with the Azure CLI for a new connection:

```
az network vpn-connection create --name ERConnection --resource-group
<resource-group-name> --vnet-gateway1 <vnet-gateway-name> --express-
route-circuit2 <express-route-circuit-name> --express-route-gateway-
bypass true
```

Here is the command to do this with the Azure CLI for an existing connection:

```
az network vpn-connection update --name <express-route-connection-
name> --resource-group <resource-group-name> --express-route-gateway-
bypass true
```

Now that we understand the options available for ExpressRoute circuits and gateways, let's talk a little more about architecture—cross-network connection architecture.

Designing and implementing cross-network connectivity over ExpressRoute

By default, ExpressRoute connections route network traffic only between connected remote networks and Azure VNets. For example, an organization has two branch offices connected to Azure networks (as shown in *Figure 6.26*), as follows:

- A *remote network in London* that connects to an *Azure network in "UK South"* via an *ExpressRoute circuit in London*

- A *remote network in New York* that connects to an *Azure network in "East US"* via an *ExpressRoute circuit in New York*

The result of this connectivity is that the 10.30.0.0/16 network can communicate with the 10.10.0.0/16 network, and the 10.40.0.0/16 network can communicate with the 10.20.0.0/16 network. However, no other cross-network communication will be possible:

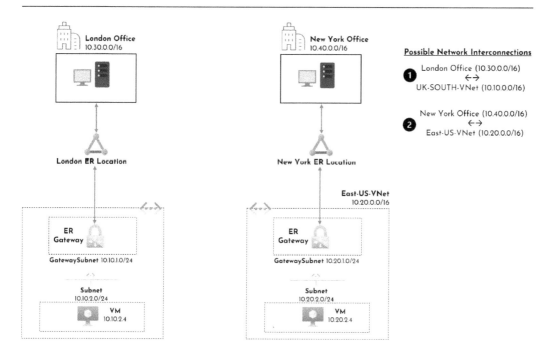

Figure 6.26 – Single-region ExpressRoute connection scenario

Enhancing cross-network connectivity using VNet peering

To enhance network interconnections in our design, we can add VNet peering between the two Azure VNets (*Figure 6.27*). VNet peering (discussed in *Chapter 4* of this book) supports peering two VNets within the same Azure region or across different Azure regions (global VNet peering).

The VNets will be able to communicate with each other once they are peered, and this enables a third network interconnection scenario—**UK-SOUTH-VNet** (10.10.0.0/16) will now be able to communicate with **East-US-VNet** (10.20.0.0/16), as illustrated in the next diagram.

VNet peering does not support default transitive routing but we could implement an NVA to support it, as discussed in *Chapter 4* of this book. This will enable additional network interconnections, but since the focus of this chapter is on ExpressRoute, let us look at another way to enhance the design:

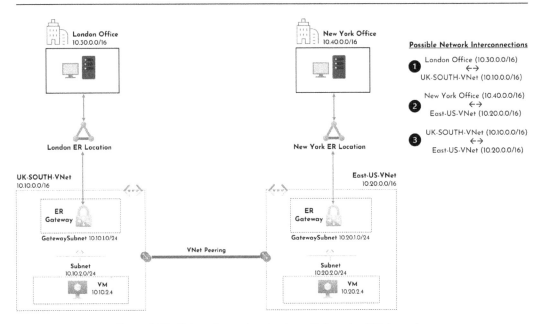

Figure 6.27 – Enhancing network connectivity using VNet peering

Enhancing cross-network connectivity using multiple ExpressRoute VNet connections

To enhance network interconnections in our design, we can add multiple ExpressRoute VNet connections (*Figure 6.28*). As discussed earlier in this chapter, an ExpressRoute circuit can be connected to multiple VNets. The possible connections depend on the SKU of our ExpressRoute circuit—**Local**, **Standard**, or **Premium**. Let's explore these a little more:

- **Local** can provide connectivity to a maximum of 10 VNets in one or two Azure regions in the same metro/geographical area

- **Standard** can provide connectivity to a maximum of 10 VNets in Azure regions in a geopolitical area

- **Premium** can provide connectivity to a maximum of 100 VNets in any Azure region, depending on the circuit capacity that we've implemented

So, which network interconnection scenarios does this design enable? It adds support for two additional scenarios—**London Office** (10.30.0.0/16) will be able to communicate with **East-US-VNet** (10.20.0.0/16). **New York Office** (10.40.0.0/16) will also be able to communicate with **UK-SOUTH-VNet** (10.10.0.0/16), as illustrated in the following diagram:

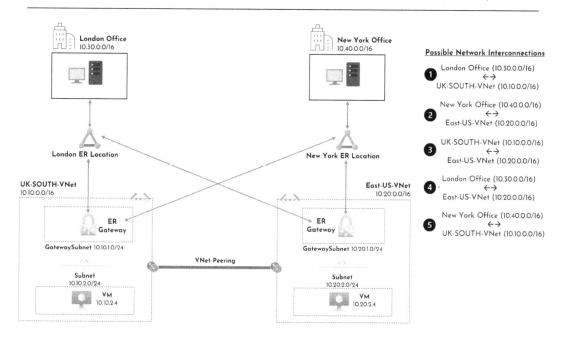

Figure 6.28 – Enhancing network connectivity with multi-region ExpressRoute connections

Enhancing cross-network connectivity using ExpressRoute Global Reach

To further enhance network interconnections in our design, we can implement a capability called **ExpressRoute Global Reach**. **ExpressRoute Global Reach** is an add-on service that allows us to link ExpressRoute circuits (*Figure 6.29*):

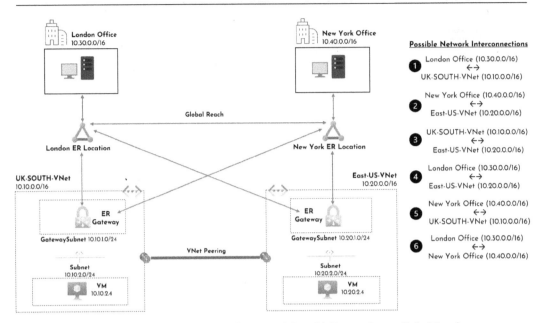

Figure 6.29 – Enhancing network connectivity with ExpressRoute Global Reach

Its main use case is to enable a remote network to connect remotely over the Microsoft global backbone network. This can be very useful as a backup WAN or if we are designing for **disaster recovery (DR)**.

To implement **ExpressRoute Global Reach**, our ExpressRoute circuits must be created at the peering locations where the feature is supported. For an up-to-date list of supported Azure regions, please refer to this documentation: https://learn.microsoft.com/en-us/azure/expressroute/expressroute-global-reach#availability.

To implement **ExpressRoute Global Reach** between different geopolitical regions (that is, connect circuits in different geo-political regions with each other), our circuits must have the **Premium** SKU. For ExpressRoute circuits in the same geopolitical region, we don't need ExpressRoute **Premium** to connect them.

Another key point to note is that there is no transitive routing between **ExpressRoute Global Reach**-connected circuits. For example, if network **A** is connected to networks **B** and **C** via **Global Reach** (*Figure 6.30*), network **B** will still not be able to communicate with network **C** over ExpressRoute except if their circuits are directly connected:

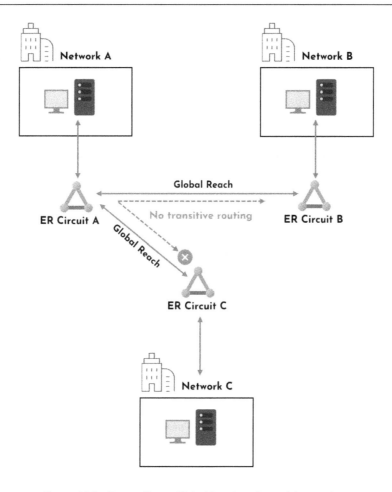

Figure 6.30 – ExpressRoute Global Reach and transitive routing

With regard to throughput, *remote network-to-Azure VNet traffic* and *remote network-to-remote network traffic* share the same circuit bandwidth that was provisioned.

With regard to pricing, we pay for three things—*the cost of the add-on service paid monthly*, *per GB of egress traffic* at the source, and *per GB of ingress traffic* at the destination.

With regard to scale, the maximum number of advertised routes to Microsoft on Azure private peering remains at 4,000 routes on a **Standard** circuit and 10,000 routes on a **Premium** circuit.

Understanding the implementation of encryption over ExpressRoute

Securing data in transit is important to mitigate security threats such as eavesdropping attacks and data theft. By default, ExpressRoute provides private connectivity but not secure (or encrypted) connectivity. For highly regulated organizations in areas such as banking and government, this may not be sufficient to meet their data security requirements, which is why Microsoft offers two *optional* solutions for encrypting data in transit on an ExpressRoute circuit—**point-to-point encryption with MACsec** and **end-to-end encryption with IPsec**.

Let's start with **MACsec**, which is only supported for the ExpressRoute Direct implementation. **MACsec** stands for **Media Access Control Security**. It is a Layer 2 encryption implementation that can be used to encrypt physical links. Once we configure it, the BGP data traffic and customer data traffic is encrypted in hardware on the routers between our network devices and Microsoft's network devices (*Figure 6.31*). It is important to note that this is not end-to-end encryption!

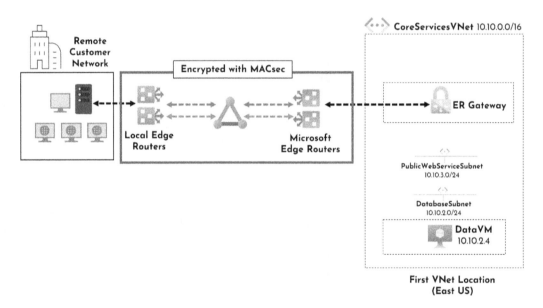

Figure 6.31 – MACsec is NOT end-to-end encryption

To implement MACsec, we need a key vault resource to store the pre-shared key that will be used for the encryption. The key is referred to as the **connectivity association key** (**CAK**). To learn more about implementing MACsec, please refer to this document: `https://learn.microsoft.com/en-us/azure/expressroute/expressroute-about-encryption`.

The second encryption option is **IPsec**, which is a standard network-level encryption protocol. This option simply layers an IPsec VPN tunnel over an ExpressRoute connection. It is supported for both

ExpressRoute models—Provider and Direct. It can be implemented alongside MACsec for ExpressRoute Direct. Unlike MACsec, this option provides end-to-end encryption between our remote networks and Azure VNets.

There are two main models that we can use to implement IPsec over ExpressRoute. The first option is to implement a site-to-site VPN over ExpressRoute private peering. This option uses a private IP address at each endpoint of the tunnel, making the full communication private.

The second option is to create an IPsec tunnel over ExpressRoute public peering. This option creates a VPN between public IPs over ExpressRoute with Microsoft peering.

Understanding the implementation of BFD

No network is completely fault-proof! Hardware issues or incorrect configurations can happen. To mitigate the effects of these failures, it is essential to have a well-designed network that includes mechanisms to minimize their impact.

Every ExpressRoute circuit is established with a primary and secondary connection between a redundant pair of CE/partner edge routers and Microsoft edge routers (as shown in *Figure 6.32*). The routing between these two sides is managed by BGP, which also detects any downlinks and automatically switches to the other available link:

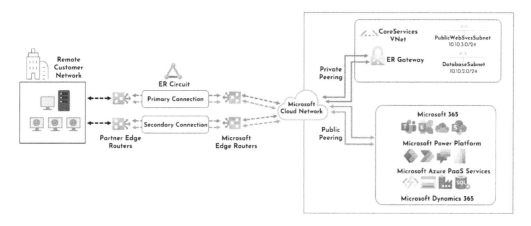

Figure 6.32 – ExpressRoute redundancy

BGP uses two key parameters to detect link failures and initiate failover—the **keep-alive time** and the **holdtime**. Keep-alive messages are sent between the routers to confirm that the connection is still active. The frequency of these messages is determined by the configured keep-alive time. On Microsoft edge routers, the BGP keep-alive time is set to 60 seconds.

The holdtime, on the other hand, is the amount of time that a router will wait for a keep-alive message before determining that the connection is down. On Microsoft edge routers, the BGP holdtime is set to 180 seconds. This means that it may take up to 3 minutes for a link failure to be detected and for traffic to be routed to an alternate link.

To implement faster detection of connection failures, we can decrease the keep-alive time and holdtime on our CE devices. When the BGP timers on the Microsoft edge routers differ from those on the CE routers, the BGP session will be established using the lower time value. It is possible to set the BGP keep-alive time as low as 3 seconds and the holdtime as low as 10 seconds, but this is not recommended as it can put a strain on the routers—the BGP protocol is process intensive.

The recommended approach to detect failed links faster is to implement BFD. BFD can greatly reduce the time for a link failover to happen, from the default of 3 minutes to less than a second! It is also not as process intensive as BGP:

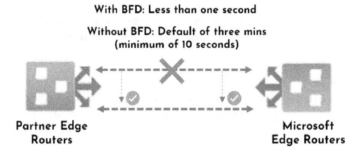

Figure 6.33 – Implementing BFD to reduce link failover time

BFD is enabled on Microsoft edge peering interfaces by default, but we will need to enable it on our CE or partner edge routers as well. The steps for doing this will vary depending on our hardware manufacturer, but at a high level, BFD needs to be configured on the interface first and then linked to the BGP session. *Figure 6.34* shows an example of this for a Cisco IOS router:

```
interface TenGigabitEthernet2/0/0.150
   description private peering to Azure
   encapsulation dot1Q 15 second-dot1q 150
   ip vrf forwarding 15
   ip address 192.168.15.17 255.255.255.252
   bfd interval 300 min_rx 300 multiplier 3 1


router bgp 65020
   address-family ipv4 vrf 15
      network 10.1.15.0 mask 255.255.255.128
      neighbor 192.168.15.18 remote-as 12076
      neighbor 192.168.15.18 fall-over bfd 2
      neighbor 192.168.15.18 activate
      neighbor 192.168.15.18 soft-reconfiguration inbound
   exit-address-family
```

Figure 6.34 – BFD configuration on a Cisco IOS router

After BFD is configured, it establishes a low-overhead connection with the BGP neighbors. When BFD peers communicate, the slower of the two determines the transmission rate. The BFD transmission/receive intervals for Microsoft edge routers are set to 300 milliseconds, but in certain situations, they may be increased to 750 milliseconds. It is possible to make the intervals longer by adjusting the configuration, but they cannot be made shorter.

Hands-on exercise – implementing an ExpressRoute gateway

Here are the tasks that we will complete in this exercise:

- *Task 1* – create a VNet and gateway subnet
- *Task 2* – deploy the ExpressRoute VNet gateway service
- *Task 3* – create and provision an ExpressRoute circuit
- *Task 4* – retrieve your service key (you need to send this to your SP)
- *Task 5* – check serviceProviderProvisioningState status
- *Task 6* – connect the ExpressRoute gateway to the ExpressRoute circuit
- *Task 7* – deprovision an ExpressRoute circuit
- *Task 8* – clean up resources

Let's get into this!

Task 1 – create a VNet and gateway subnet

To implement an ExpressRoute gateway, the first thing to do is to create a VNet with a gateway subnet called **GatewaySubnet** (the subnet cannot be named anything else). Also, this must be a dedicated subnet, which means no other resource should be deployed into it apart from the gateway.

Follow these steps:

1. Open a web browser and browse to Azure Cloud Shell at https://shell.azure.com. If prompted to authenticate, sign in with your administrative username and password.

2. Run the following commands to create a resource group, a VNet with a gateway subnet:

```
group=CharisTechRG-C6
location=eastus
vnet=CoreServicesVnet
az group create --name $group --location $location
az network vnet create -n $vnet -g $group --address-prefix
10.20.0.0/16 --subnet-name GatewaySubnet --subnet-prefix
10.20.0.0/27
```

Task 2 – deploy the ExpressRoute VNet gateway service

In the Cloud Shell window, run the following commands to create an ExpressRoute gateway in the VNet that we created earlier:

```
az network public-ip create -n CoreServicesVnetGateway-ip -g $group
--sku Basic -l eastus
az network vnet-gateway create -n CoreServicesVnetGateway -l eastus
--public-ip-address CoreServicesVnetGateway-ip -g $group --vnet $vnet
--gateway-type ExpressRoute --sku Standard --no-wait
```

Task 3 – create and provision an ExpressRoute circuit

In the Cloud Shell window, run the following commands to create an ExpressRoute circuit:

```
ername=CharisTechEastUsERCircuit
az network express-route create --bandwidth 50 -n $ername --peering-
location "Seattle" -g $group --provider "Equinix" -l $location --sku-
family UnlimitedData --sku-tier Premium --allow-classic-operations
false
```

Task 4 – retrieve your service key (you need to send this to your SP)

An ExpressRoute circuit is uniquely identified by a standard GUID called a **service key (s-key)**. The s-key is the only piece of information exchanged between Microsoft, the ExpressRoute connectivity provider, and you. The s-key isn't a secret for security purposes. There is a 1:1 mapping between an ExpressRoute circuit and the s-key.

In the Cloud Shell window, run the following commands to retrieve the s-key that you will give to your ExpressRoute connectivity provider:

```
az network express-route show --resource-group $group --name $ername
--query serviceKey
```

Task 5 – check serviceProviderProvisioningState status

We need to periodically check the status and the state of the circuit key. Checking the status and the state of the s-key will let you know when your provider has provisioned your circuit. After the circuit has been configured, **ServiceProviderProvisioningState** appears as **Provisioned**.

In the Cloud Shell window, run the following commands to check the state of the ExpressRoute circuit:

```
az network express-route show --resource-group $group --name $ername
--query provisioningState
```

```
az network express-route show --resource-group $group --name $ername
--query serviceProviderProvisioningState
az network express-route show --resource-
group $group --name $ername --query "{name:name,
location:location, provisioningState:provisioningState,
serviceProviderProvisioningState:serviceProviderProvisioningState}" -o
table
```

Task 6 – connect the ExpressRoute gateway to the ExpressRoute circuit

To connect to a circuit, the service state needs to be enabled and provisioned and have private peering enabled. *We expect this next task to fail because we do not currently have an actual provisioned ExpressRoute circuit!*

In the Cloud Shell window, run the following commands to connect an ExpressRoute gateway to an ExpressRoute circuit:

```
ername=CharisTechEastUsERCircuit
vnetgw=CoreServicesVnetGateway
az network vpn-connection create --name ERConnection --resource-group
$group --vnet-gateway1 $vnetgw --express-route-circuit2 $ername
```

Task 7 – deprovision an ExpressRoute circuit

In the Cloud Shell window, run the following commands to deprovision the ExpressRoute circuit that we created:

```
ername=ContosoEastUsERCircuit
az network express-route delete -n $ername -g $group
```

Task 8 – clean up resources

In the Cloud Shell window, run the following commands to clean up the resources that we created in this hands-on exercise:

```
group=CharisTechRG-C6
az group delete -n $group
```

This may take a while to complete, but it will delete the resource group that we created and the resources in it.

Summary

In this chapter, we delved into the topic of ExpressRoute and its various use cases. We began by discussing the components of an ExpressRoute connection, including the connectivity model, circuit SKU, and gateway SKU. We then explored ways to improve data path performance with ExpressRoute **FastPath**, as well as how to design and implement cross-network connectivity over ExpressRoute. We concluded by providing guidance on the implementation of encryption, BFD, and a hands-on exercise for implementing an ExpressRoute gateway.f

This chapter equips you with the knowledge and skills necessary to excel on the ExpressRoute objectives of the certification exam and effectively work with ExpressRoute in real-world scenarios.

In the next chapter, we will learn about designing and implementing the Azure virtual WAN service. See you there!

7

Design and Implement Hybrid Network Connectivity with Virtual WAN

The Azure Well-Architected Framework is a set of guidelines for designing efficient and effective systems in the cloud. One important aspect of this framework is designing for scalability, or the ability to handle increasing amounts of work or traffic. To make sure network connectivity and security continue to work well as we add more users or data, it is recommended to use the hub-and-spoke design. This can be achieved with the **virtual WAN (vWAN)** service in Azure. In this chapter, we will learn about the different ways we can use the vWAN service and how to set it up. By the end, you will have a good understanding of the following:

- Designing a scalable network topology in Azure

- Understanding the design considerations of a virtual hub

- Understanding the routing and SD-WAN configuration in a virtual hub

- Configuring site-to-site connectivity using vWAN

- Implementing a global transit network architecture using vWAN

- Understanding the security considerations of a virtual hub

Each topic is organized to align with the exam objectives. Let's begin!

Technical requirements

To follow along with the instructions in this chapter, you will need the following:

- A PC with an internet connection

- An Azure subscription

Before we proceed to cover the security best practices, let us prepare our Azure subscription for the hands-on exercises that we will be completing later in the chapter.

Designing a scalable network topology in Azure

If a company wants to grow in its use of Azure, it needs to make it easier for VNet resources to communicate with other VNets, on-premises networks (networks not in the cloud), and the internet. The recommended approach is to use a **hub-and-spoke topology**. In this design, we have a *hub virtual network* acting as a central point for connecting spoke networks, on-premises networks, and the internet (*Figure 7.1*).

The *spoke virtual networks* connect to the hub to access the internet and other networks. This design is helpful because it centralizes connectivity and security rules, rather than having each spoke VNet handle these things separately. Imagine having to maintain routing and security rules for 100 VNets separately! It also allows for the isolation of network communication if needed, such as creating separate VNets for production and development for traffic isolation at the network level.

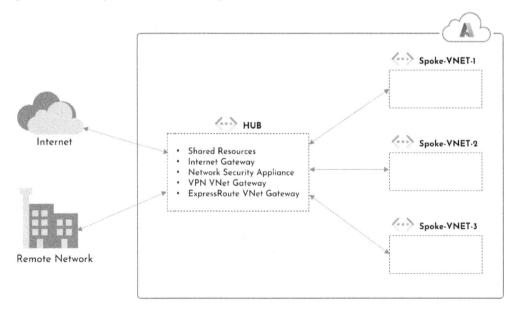

Figure 7.1 – Hub and spoke architecture

There are two ways to create a hub-and-spoke network design in Azure. One is called **standard hub-and-spoke** and the other is called **Azure vWAN hub-and-spoke**. Let's look at these two approaches and why we may want to use one over the other.

The standard hub-and-spoke topology

This approach uses a **customer-managed virtual network** to create a hub network (*Figure 7.2*). The spoke networks are connected to the hub using *VNet peering* (covered in *Chapter 4*). Traffic flow between the remote/on-premises networks and the hub/spoke networks is achieved through an *ExpressRoute or VPN gateway* deployed into the hub VNet (covered in *Chapters 5* and *6*). Routing between the spoke networks can be implemented with *Azure Route Server or a network virtual appliance* (covered in *Chapter 3*). Network security inspection can be implemented with *Azure Firewall or a network virtual appliance* (we will cover this in *Chapter 8*).

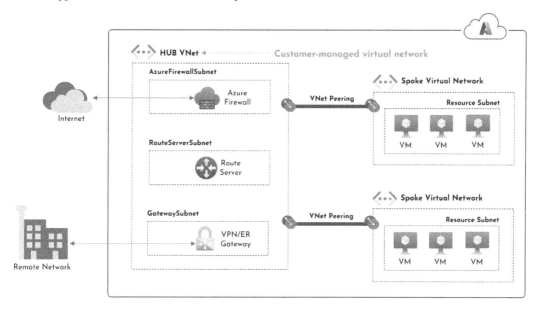

Figure 7.2 – Hub-and-spoke network topology using a customer-managed VNet

While this approach works well, it has some limitations around scalability and performance that we need to be aware of:

- There is a limit of 500 spoke networks due to VNet peering quota limitations. Some organizations may need to exceed this limit, especially if each service/application is deployed into its own separate VNet for isolation.

- The maximum number of site-to-site VPN tunnels supported by the VPN gateway is 100. So, if we need more than 100 remote networks to connect to the hub, this approach does not meet the requirement. Also, keep in mind that a single connection can be more than one tunnel. It is common for a single connection to be implemented with two tunnels for redundancy and high availability.

- There is a limit of 128 P2S SSTP connections and 10,000 P2S IKEv2/OpenVPN connections.

Apart from the above limits, there is also a management overhead associated with this approach. For example, organizations are responsible for deploying components such as ExpressRoute/VPN gateways, Route Server, and Azure Firewall into the subnets (*Figure 7.2*). There is also no default routing and connectivity between the networks, which means we need to spend some time implementing routing either by using a route server or a network virtual appliance.

This is where the second implementation option for a hub-and-spoke network topology comes in – **Azure Virtual WAN (vWAN)**!

The Azure vWAN hub-and-spoke topology

Azure vWAN is a networking service that simplifies network connectivity by using a **Microsoft-managed virtual network** to implement the hub network (*Figure 7.3*). This approach removes a lot of the management overhead that we have to deal with in the first approach, while also providing better scalability and performance. It is now the recommended way, and we will cover how to design and implement it the right way in this chapter.

Understanding vWAN components and connectivity capabilities

Azure VWAN is made up of multiple components to establish simplified connectivity. *Figure 7.3* illustrates these components:

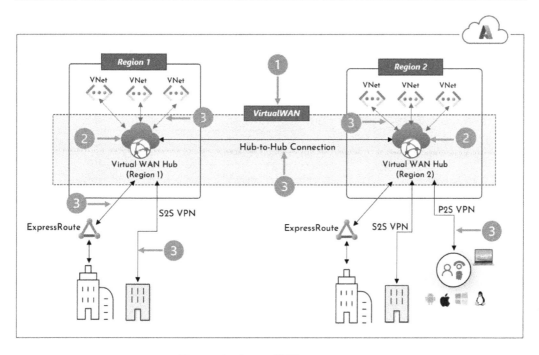

Figure 7.3 – Azure vWAN components

The components are described in further detail as follows:

1) **Virtual WAN**: This is essentially a management service that we can use to deploy, manage, and monitor resources for connecting networks together. As shown in *Figure 7.3*, it is a global resource and does not live in a particular region. We will come back to this shortly in this chapter.

2) **Virtual WAN hub**: This is a Microsoft-managed virtual network behind the scenes. It acts as the central point of connectivity in an Azure region. It is possible to have more than one hub in a region if our requirements exceed the limitations of a single hub. We will cover these limitations later in this chapter.

3) **VWAN hub connections**: These are the various connection types that the VWAN hub supports (marked as **3** in *Figure 7.3*). This includes branch connectivity using ExpressRoute or a Site-to-Site VPN; user connectivity using a Point-to-Site VPN; and virtual network connectivity and hub connectivity.

Choosing the right virtual VWAN type

When planning a VWAN implementation, we need to decide the type to use. There are two types of VWANs: **Basic** and **Standard** (*Figure 7.4*).

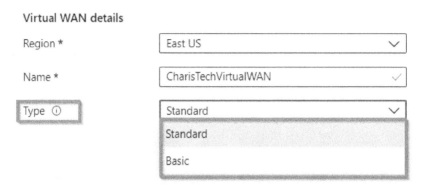

Figure 7.4 – Selecting a VWAN type

Our choice should primarily be guided by the connectivity options that we want to implement and pricing.

The Basic VWAN type only supports Site-to-site VPN connections in a single hub. So, this option cannot be used to meet the following connectivity requirements: fully meshed hubs, ExpressRoute connectivity, user VPN/Point-to-Site VPN connectivity, vNet-to-vNet transitive connectivity, VPN and ExpressRoute transit connectivity, or Azure Firewall. This is a lot of limitations! If you are not too sure what these capabilities mean, do not worry too much as we will cover them in this chapter.

The Basic VWAN does have a cost advantage as we do not have to pay the base hourly fee and data processing fee for the VWAN hubs that we implement.

The Standard VWAN type supports all connectivity options and capabilities across multiple hubs, but there is an hourly base fee for every hub that we implement (at the time of writing, this is priced at $0.25 per hour). There is also a charge for data processing in the virtual hub router for VNet-to-VNet transit connectivity.

The recommendation is to use the Standard VWAN for production scenarios, but you are free to implement the Basic VWAN if it meets your requirements. The decision is purely a cost-capability trade-off. *Figure 7.5* shows a table that summarizes the differences between the two options:

Capability	Basic VWAN	Standard VWAN
Site-to-site VPN connectivity	✓	✓
ExpressRoute connectivity	✕	✓
User VPN/Point-to-site VPN connectivity	✕	✓
VNet-to-VNet transitive connectivity	✕	✓
VPN and ExpressRoute transit connectivity	✕	✓
Azure Firewall or NVA hub implementation	✕	✓
Fully meshed hubs	✕	✓
Hub base fee	FREE	Per Hour
VNet-to-VNet data processing fee	FREE	Per GB

Figure 7.5 – Basic VWAN and Standard VWAN comparison

> **Can I change my VWAN type after deployment?**
>
> Yes – you can upgrade a **Basic** VWAN to **Standard**, but you cannot downgrade a **Standard** VWAN to **Basic**. Refer to this documentation on how to perform an upgrade: https://learn.microsoft.com/en-us/azure/virtual-wan/upgrade-virtual-wan.

Understanding the design considerations of a vWAN hub

When implementing a vWAN hub, there are certain design decisions that we need to make. Let us review some of these.

Selecting the regions for the VWAN hub

The first design decision that we need to make is the region where we want to deploy our hub, as shown in *Figure 7.6*. An Azure VWAN hub can be deployed into almost all available Azure regions except for a small number of newer regions.

Virtual Hub Details

Figure 7.6 – Selecting a region for the VWAN hub

For an updated list of supported regions, please refer to this documentation: `https://learn.microsoft.com/en-us/azure/virtual-wan/virtual-wan-locations-partners#locations`

It is a good practice to only create virtual hubs in regions where you have a cluster of virtual networks present *or* regions that are close to your branch offices/remote networks. Following this principle helps to ensure reduced latency between the connecting network and the VWAN hub.

Another point to consider here is pricing. There is an hourly cost for a standard VWAN hub even if it is not processing any traffic, so we want to ensure that we deploy VWAN hubs only in the regions where we need them. You will be implementing this in a later hands-on lab.

Selecting an IP address space for the VWAN hub

Another design decision that we need to make is the address space to assign to the VWAN hub. Azure deploys resources into a VWAN hub based on the connection capabilities that we implement. This IP address space that we specify will be used to carve out subnets for the components (*Figure 7.7*). For example, every VWAN hub deployment has virtual hub routers that are used for VNet-to-VNet routing. A subnet will be carved out for the hub routers from the address space specified.

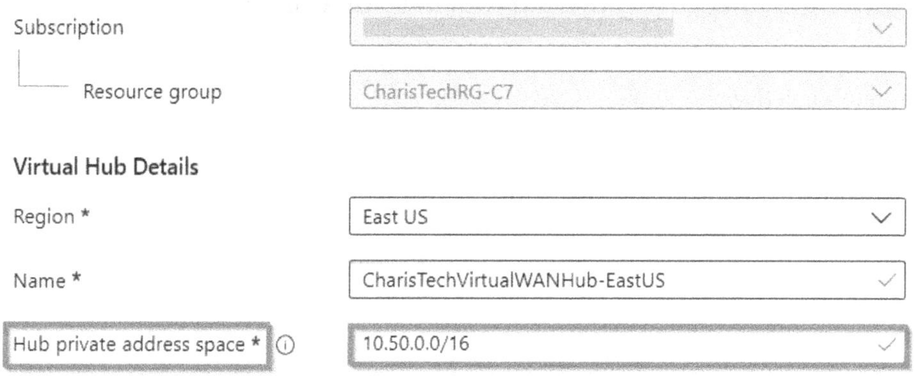

Subscription

[   ] ▽

|
└──── Resource group   CharisTechRG-C7   ▽

Virtual Hub Details

Region *   East US   ▽

Name *   CharisTechVirtualWANHub-EastUS   ✓

Hub private address space * ⓘ   10.50.0.0/16   ✓

Figure 7.7 – VWAN Hub IP address space configuration

The minimum address space that we can specify is /24 but the recommendation is to use at least /23. Our choice should be guided by the connectivity capabilities that we want to implement, but as a rule, it is better to err on the side of future scalability. For example, if we deploy an **Network Virtual Appliance** (**NVA**) inside a VWAN hub, a /28 subnet will be carved out for the NVA instances, but if we provision multiple NVAs, a /27 subnet will be carved out instead and this requires more addresses (*Figure 7.8*).

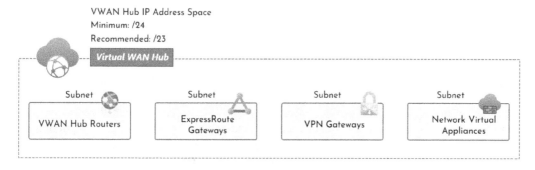

Figure 7.8 – VWAN hub components and subnets

Can I change my VWAN hub IP address space after deployment?

No. At the time of writing, this is a design limitation. The workaround is to create a new hub with your preferred IP address space and move your network connections to it.

Configuring the routing infrastructure for the VWAN hub

Another design decision that we need to make is the scale of the routing infrastructure that we want to deploy into a hub (*Figure 7.9*).

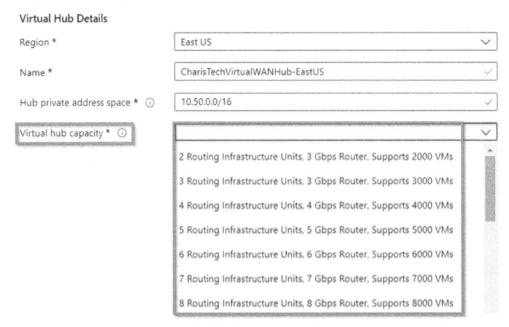

Figure 7.9 – Selecting the virtual hub routing capability

When a new VWAN hub is created, virtual hub routers are deployed into it. The virtual hub router is the central component that manages all routing between connected VNets and gateways (*Figure 7.10*).

A **routing infrastructure unit** is the unit of scale that defines both the aggregate throughput of the virtual hub router and the aggregate number of virtual machines that can be deployed in all connected VNets. By default, the virtual hub router will deploy two routing infrastructure units *at no extra cost*! The two units support 3 Gbps aggregate throughput, and 2,000 connections across all connected VNets.

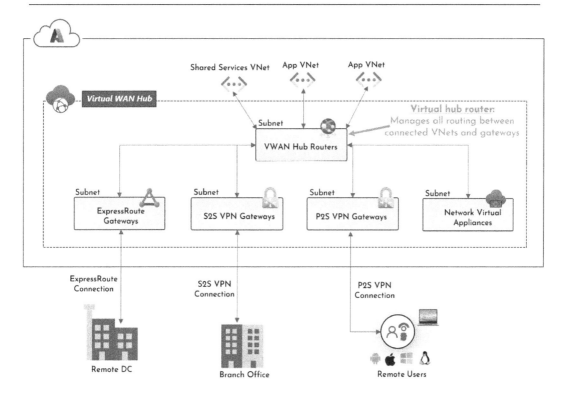

Figure 7.10 – The virtual hub router VWAN hub component

We can also specify additional routing infrastructure units to increase the default virtual hub capacity in increments of 1 Gbps and 1,000 VMs. For example, 5 routing infrastructure units will support 5 Gbps throughput and 5,000 connected VMs while 6 routing infrastructure units will support 6 Gbps throughput and 6,000 connected VMs (*Figure 7.9*). There is an additional hourly cost of $0.10 USD per routing infrastructure unit above the two free units.

> **Can I change my VWAN hub routing capacity after deployment?**
>
> Yes. This can be done by editing the hub's configuration.

Configuring the VWAN hub routing preference

Another key design decision when implementing a VWAN hub is **Hub routing preference** (*Figure 7.11*). This is a recently released configuration that allows us to influence routing decisions in the virtual hub router for traffic flow to on-premises sites. But why would we need this?

As discussed in the previous section of this chapter, the virtual hub router manages all routing between connected VNets and connection gateways (ExpressRoute, S2S VPN, and P2S VPN). Part of its role is also to make routing decisions in scenarios where on-premises sites are advertising multiple routes to the same destination prefixes!

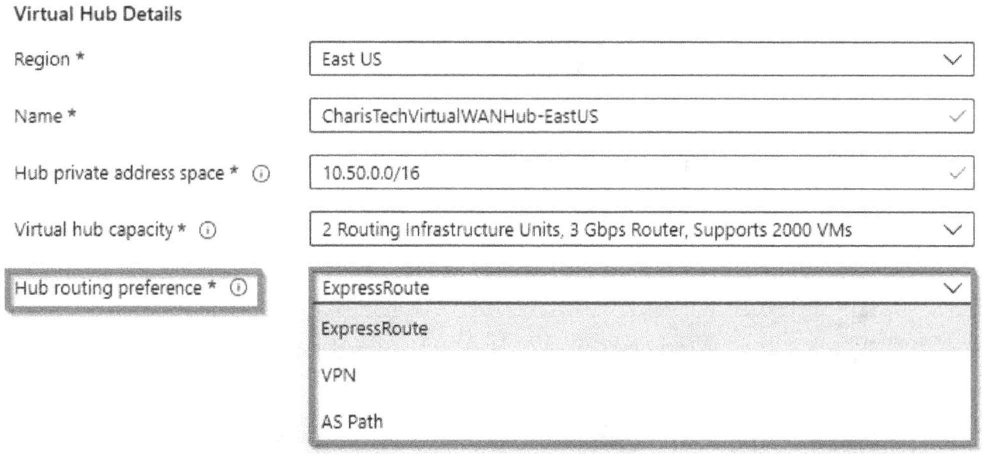

Virtual Hub Details

Region *	East US
Name *	CharisTechVirtualWANHub-EastUS
Hub private address space * ⓘ	10.50.0.0/16
Virtual hub capacity * ⓘ	2 Routing Infrastructure Units, 3 Gbps Router, Supports 2000 VMs
Hub routing preference * ⓘ	ExpressRoute
	ExpressRoute
	VPN
	AS Path

Figure 7.11 – Selecting the hub routing preference

For example, *Figure 7.12* shows a scenario where the **Remote Office 1** on-premises site is connected to **Virtual WAN Hub 1** using **ExpressRoute Connection 1** as the primary connection and **S2S VPN Connection 1** as the backup (this is a typical implementation for high availability). In case of a disaster, **Remote Office 1** is also connected via a private WAN to **Remote Office 2**, which is connected to **Virtual WAN Hub 2**, which has a hub-to-hub connection back to **Virtual WAN Hub 1**.

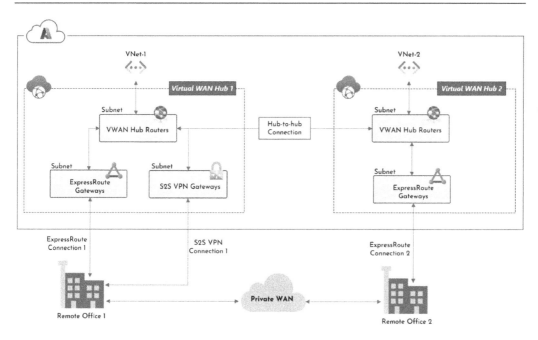

Figure 7.12 – Sample redundant connection to an on-premises site

If dynamic routing is implemented with full routing propagation, traffic leaving **Virtual Net 1** with the destination of the **Remote Office 1** on-premises site, has *three* paths that the virtual hub router in **Virtual WAN Hub 1** could use to deliver the traffic. The paths are highlighted in *Figure 7.13*:

- **1**: **VNet-1** to **Virtual WAN Hub 1** to **ExpressRoute Connection 1** to **Remote Office 1**

- **2**: **VNet-1** to **Virtual WAN Hub 1** to **S2S VPN Connection 1** to **Remote Office 1**

- **3**: **VNet-1** to **Virtual WAN Hub 1** to **Virtual WAN Hub 2** to **S2S VPN Connection 1** to **ExpressRoute Connection 2** to **Private WAN** to **Remote Office 1**

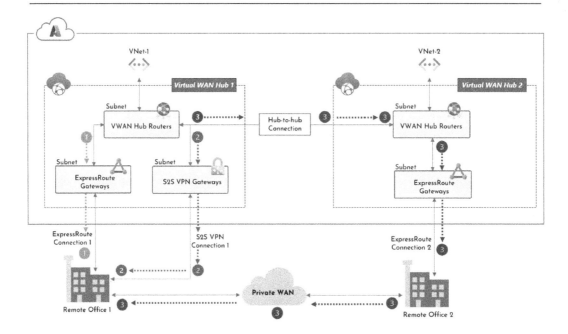

Figure 7.13 – Traffic path options from Vnet-1 to Remote Office 1

In situations like this, the virtual hub router makes routing decisions based on the following order of preference:

- Routes with the longest prefix match are always preferred

- Static routes are preferred over **Border Gateway Protocol** (**BGP**)-learned routes

- The best path is selected based on the route preference configured (ExpressRoute-learned route, VPN-learned route, or the route with the shortest BGP AS-Path Length)

If we have selected either ExpressRoute or VPN for our route preference, routes learned from local hub connections are preferred over routes learned from remote hub connections.

> **Can I change my VWAN hub routing preference after deployment?**
>
> Yes. This can be done by editing the hub's configuration.

Connecting VNets together using VWAN

One of the main advantages of using VWAN to connect VNets together is transitivity. Azure VWAN enables full transitivity among connected networks, which is a limitation of VNet peering.

Understanding the routing and SD-WAN configuration in a virtual hub

A virtual hub is a place where different networks can connect and communicate with each other. A router that lives in the routing infrastructure units that we discussed earlier is responsible for managing the routing between these networks, using BGP.

Each virtual hub has two default route tables, called **Default** and **None** and we can also create additional route tables. By default, all connections to the virtual hub are associated with the **Default** route table, but we can change this to a custom route table. We can also add static routes to both default and custom route tables, which take precedence over routes that are learned automatically.

When we connect a network (virtual network, ExpressRoute, S2S VPN, or user VPN) to a virtual hub, we can choose which route table to use for that connection (association – marked *1* in *Figure 7.14*), and we can also propagate learned routes (marked *2* in *Figure 7.14*).

The routing capabilities in a virtual hub are provided by a router that manages all routing between gateways using BGP.

Figure 7.14 – Configuring VNet connection routing options

Understanding VNet connection route table association

A virtual hub connection can only be associated with one route table. Associating a connection to a route table tells the connection to route traffic using routes defined in the route table. For example, in *Figure 7.15*, **CoreServicesVNet-To-EastUS-Hub VNet Connection** is associated with the **DEFAULT** route table in **CharisTechVirtualWANHub-EastUS**. This means that traffic flowing through the connection will be routed using the routes defined in the route table.

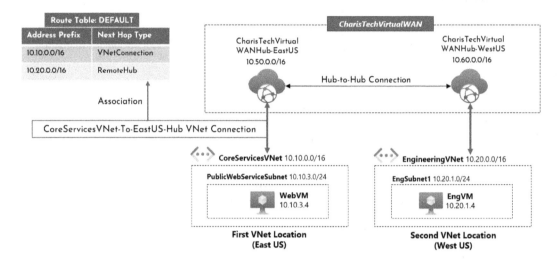

Figure 7.15 – Route table association for a VNet connection

Understanding VNet connection route propagation

If we want routes learned from a connection to be shared with other route tables in Azure VWAN, we can configure the **Propagate to Route Tables** option. This helps traffic to be sent efficiently between connected networks and locations, even if they are not directly connected to the same hub. For example, if we configure **CoreServicesVNet-To-EastUS-Hub VNet Connection** to propagate its routes to the **DEFAULT** route table in **CharisTechVirtualWANHub-WestUS**, the route for **CoreServicesVNet** (10.10.0.0/16) will be added to the route table (marked *1* in *Figure 7.16*).

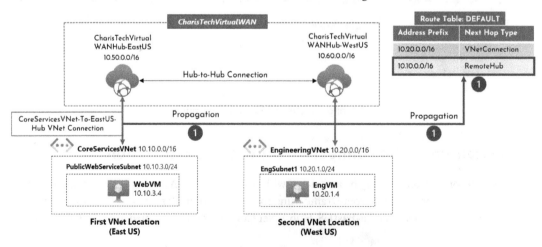

Figure 7.16 – Route propagation for a VNet connection

We can use labels to group route tables in a virtual hub and make it easier to propagate routes. Labels work like tags and can be added to multiple route tables in VWAN. By adding a label such as **critical** to several route tables, we can quickly propagate routes from a connection to all the route tables with that label (*Figure 7.17*)!

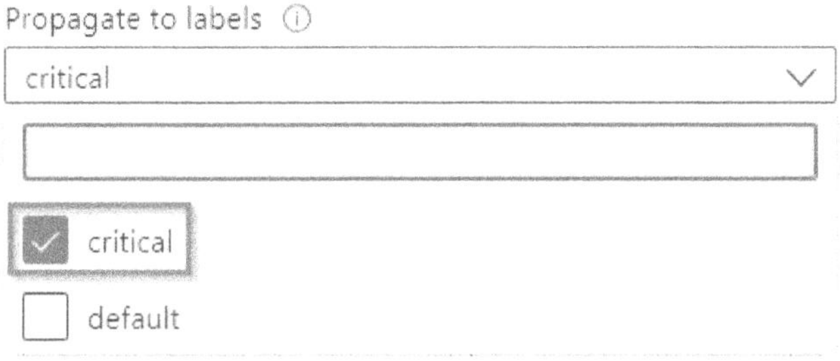

Propagate to labels ⓘ

| critical   ∨ |

| |

☑ critical

☐ default

Figure 7.17 – Propagating routes to route tables using labels

Implementing BGP peering between an NVA and a virtual hub

Sometimes we want to share routes between a NVA in an Azure VNet and a virtual hub. For example, *Figure 7.18* shows a scenario where **CoreServicesVNet** is a spoke VNet peered to **VNet1** and **VNet2**. In this scenario, we may want to configure the virtual hub router to dynamically learn routes to both VNets from the NVA. The virtual hub router could also share its routes with the NVA.

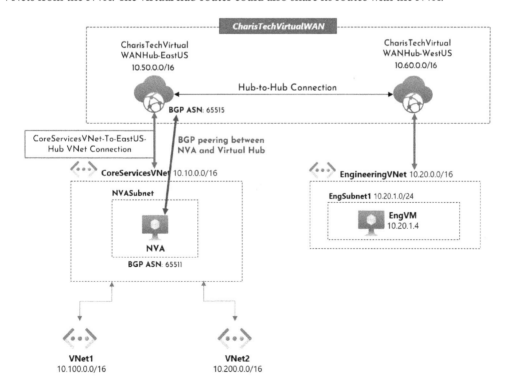

Figure 7.18 – BGP peering between virtual hub and NVA

We can make this work by configuring a direct BGP peering between the virtual hub and the NVA (*Figure 7.19*). We can do this either through the portal or using the PowerShell command line.

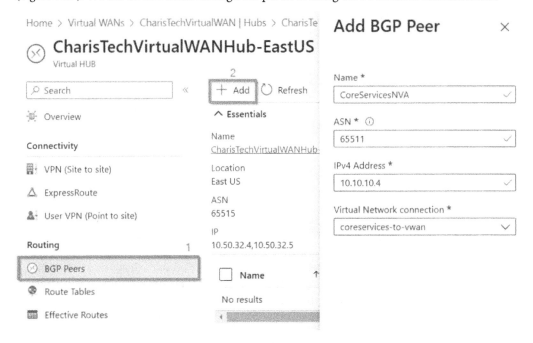

Figure 7.19 – Configure BGP peering to an NVA in a virtual hub

> **Note**
>
> To learn more about implementing this scenario, please refer to this documentation: `https://learn.microsoft.com/en-us/azure/virtual-wan/create-bgp-peering-hub-portal`

Implementing a third-party SD-WAN NVA in a virtual hub

The Azure virtual hub supports the deployment of an NVA from a third-party SD-WAN provider to the hub. This lets customers connect their branch offices to Virtual WAN using the same SD-WAN provider that they use on-premises. This is helpful if a company wants to use vendor-proprietary features from the third-party SD-WAN provider, such as traffic optimization and path selection. Right now, six SD-WAN providers are supported: Barracuda CloudGen WAN, Cisco SD-WAN, VMware SD-WAN, Versa Networks, Fortinet SD-WAN, and Aruba EdgeConnect SD-WAN (*Figure 7.20*).

Network Virtual Appliance

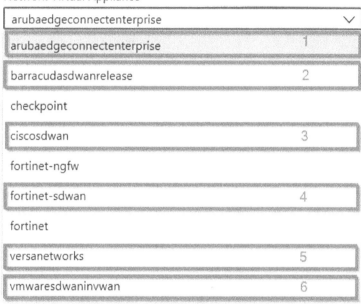

Figure 7.20 – Supported SD-WAN NVA providers

SD-WAN NVAs can be deployed in the virtual hub using the Azure portal, but once they are set up, they are usually configured using a different portal provided by the SD-WAN provider. We cannot directly access the NVA! For more information on how to set up third-party SD-WAN NVAs in a virtual hub, please refer to the guides that there are links to on this page: https://learn.microsoft.com/en-us/azure/virtual-wan/virtual-wan-locations-partners#partners-with-integrated-virtual-hub-offerings.

> **Azure Virtual WAN SD-WAN architecture options**
>
> Please refer to this documentation https://learn.microsoft.com/en-us/azure/virtual-wan/sd-wan-connectivity-architecture

Hands-on exercise 1 – provision resources for chapter exercises

To follow along with the exercises in this chapter, we will provision some Azure resources to work with. We have prepared an Azure ARM template in the GitHub repository of this book for this purpose. The template will deploy two virtual networks in two Azure regions, as shown in *Figure 7.21*.

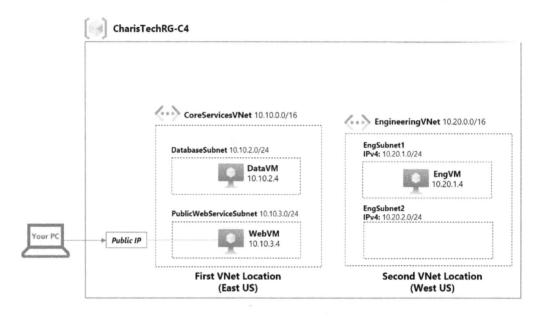

Figure 7.21 – Resources deployed via the provided ARM template

The first VNet (**CoreServicesVNet**) will have two subnets with a virtual machine in each subnet. The second VNet (**EngineeringVNet**) will have two subnets with a virtual machine in one subnet. One of the virtual machines (**WebVM**) will be assigned a public IP address so you can connect to it from your PC over the internet. Here is the task that we will complete in this exercise:

- **Task 1** – initialize template deployment in GitHub

Let's get into this!

Task 1 – initialize template deployment in GitHub

The steps are as follows:

1. Open a web browser and browse to `https://packt.link/w0VSN`. This link will open the GitHub repository that has the ARM template to deploy the resources that we need.

2.   In the GitHub repository that opens, click on **Deploy to Azure**.

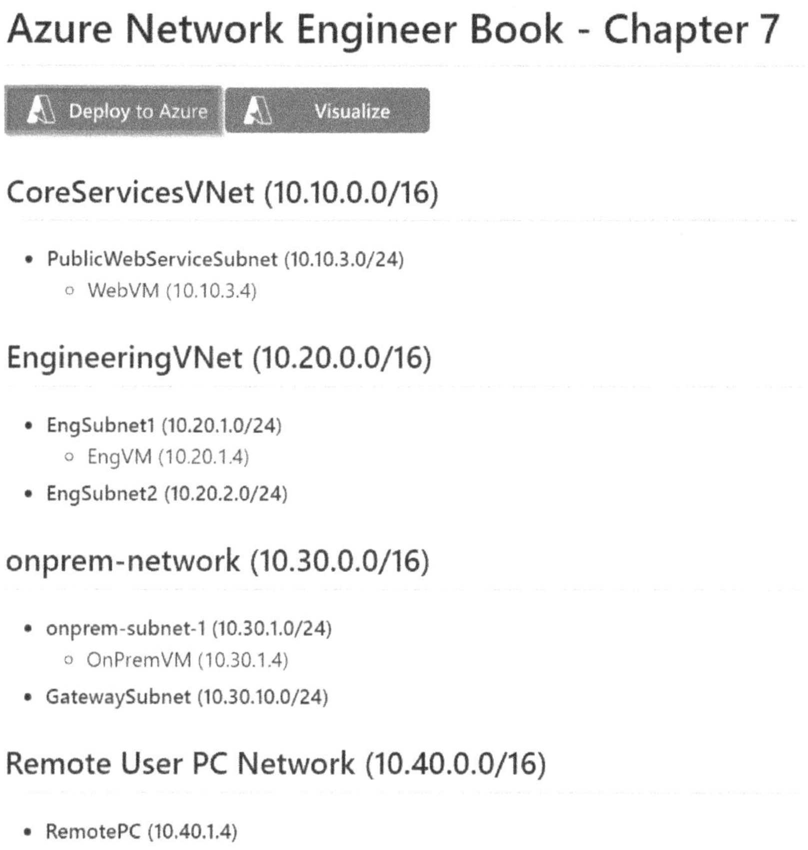

Azure Network Engineer Book - Chapter 7

CoreServicesVNet (10.10.0.0/16)

-   PublicWebServiceSubnet (10.10.3.0/24)
    -   WebVM (10.10.3.4)

EngineeringVNet (10.20.0.0/16)

-   EngSubnet1 (10.20.1.0/24)
    -   EngVM (10.20.1.4)
-   EngSubnet2 (10.20.2.0/24)

onprem-network (10.30.0.0/16)

-   onprem-subnet-1 (10.30.1.0/24)
    -   OnPremVM (10.30.1.4)
-   GatewaySubnet (10.30.10.0/24)

Remote User PC Network (10.40.0.0/16)

-   RemotePC (10.40.1.4)

Figure 7.22 – Start the template deployment

3.   If prompted to authenticate, sign in to the Azure portal with your administrative username and password.

4.   In the **Custom Deployment** window, configure the following:

-   **Subscription**: Select the subscription that you want to deploy the resources into.

-   **Resource group**: **Create New** | **Name**: **CharisTechRG-C7** | **OK**.

-   **Region**: **(US) East US** (or select the region that you verified in the first chapter of this book).

-   **Admin Password**: Enter a complex password. Make a note of this as it will be needed for later exercises. This will be the password to authenticate to all virtual machines that will be deployed.

-   **Vm Size**: **Standard_B2s** (or select the VM size that you verified in the first chapter of this book).

- **Second Vnet Location**: **West US** (or select the second region that you verified in the first chapter of this book).

Select **Review + create**.

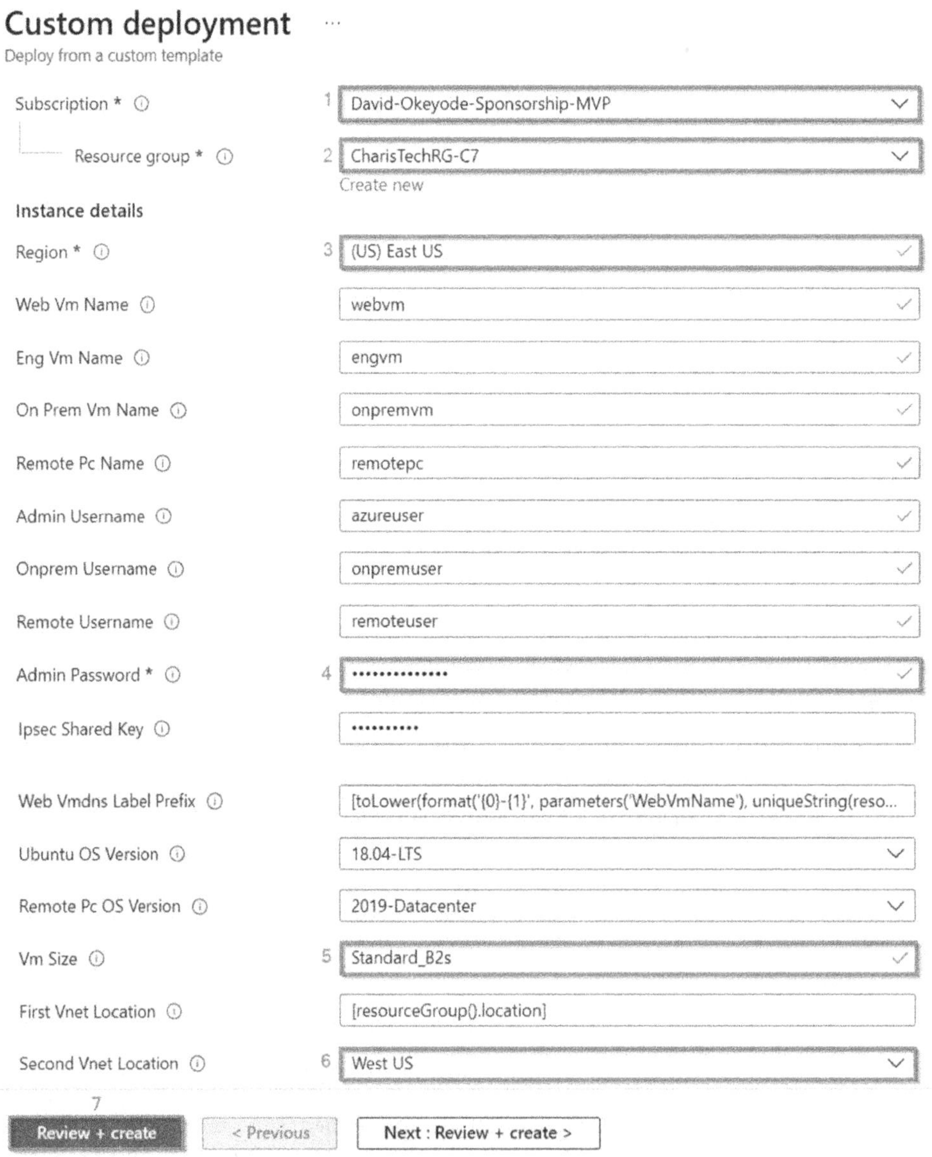

Custom deployment ...
Deploy from a custom template

Subscription * ⓘ	1	David-Okeyode-Sponsorship-MVP ⌄
⌐ Resource group * ⓘ	2	CharisTechRG-C7 ⌄
		Create new

Instance details

Region * ⓘ	3	(US) East US ✓
Web Vm Name ⓘ		webvm ✓
Eng Vm Name ⓘ		engvm ✓
On Prem Vm Name ⓘ		onpremvm ✓
Remote Pc Name ⓘ		remotepc ✓
Admin Username ⓘ		azureuser ✓
Onprem Username ⓘ		onpremuser ✓
Remote Username ⓘ		remoteuser ✓
Admin Password * ⓘ	4	•••••••••••••• ✓
Ipsec Shared Key ⓘ		••••••••••
Web Vmdns Label Prefix ⓘ		[toLower(format('{0}-{1}', parameters('WebVmName'), uniqueString(reso...
Ubuntu OS Version ⓘ		18.04-LTS ⌄
Remote Pc OS Version ⓘ		2019-Datacenter ⌄
Vm Size ⓘ	5	Standard_B2s ✓
First Vnet Location ⓘ		[resourceGroup().location]
Second Vnet Location ⓘ	6	West US ⌄

7

[Review + create]   [< Previous]   [Next : Review + create >]

Figure 7.23 – Complete the custom deployment options

5. After the validation has passed, select **Create** to proceed with the deployment. The deployment takes about 40 minutes to complete as it deploys resources such as a VNet gateway to simulate an on-premises network.

6. After the deployment has been completed, click on the **Outputs** tab (left side), and make a note of the following values:

- **sshCommand**: This gives you the SSH command that you can use to connect to WebVM (one of the deployed virtual machines) using its public DNS name. We will need this in later exercises.

- **remotePC-FQDN**: This is the FQDN of the PC that we will use to simulate a remote user PC later in this chapter.

- **remotePC-Username**: This is the username of the PC that we will use to simulate a remote user PC later in this chapter.

- **OnPremVPNDevice-FQDN**: This is the FQDN of the VPN device that we will use to simulate an on-premises location later in this chapter.

- **OnPremVPNDevice-BGP-ASN**: This is the BGP ASN that was configured for the VPN device.

- **OnPremVPNDevice-BGP-PeerIP**: This BGP Peer IP will be needed later in this chapter.

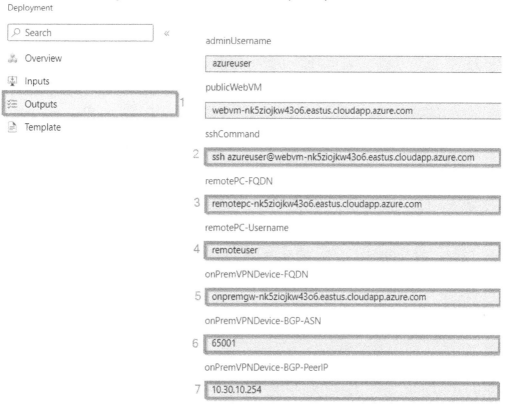

Figure 7.24 – Obtain the SSH command to connect to WebVM's DNS name

Congratulations! You have now deployed the resources needed to complete the chapter exercises. In the next hands-on exercise, you will explore the default routing of Azure subnet workloads.

Below are the resources that were deployed:

- A virtual network in a primary Azure region with a virtual machine deployed into a public subnet. This is the entry point that we will use to validate the connectivity of a lot of the hands-on labs.

- A virtual network in a secondary Azure region with a virtual machine deployed into a private subnet.

- An on-premises network with a VPN device and virtual machine deployed.

- An internet-connected VM that we will use to simulate a user's PC.

Configuring Site-to-Site connectivity using VWAN

Another key design decision is how we are going to connect remote/on-premises networks to our VWAN hub. We can either do this via ExpressRoute or **Site-to-Site VPN (S2S VPN)** connections.

To implement S2S VPN connections, we need to deploy S2S VPN gateway instances into our VWAN hub by specifying the number of gateway scale units that we want. This can be done during the creation of the hub or added after. The number that we specify for **Gateway scale units** defines the aggregate maximum throughput that will be available for S2S VPN connections (*Figure 7.25*).

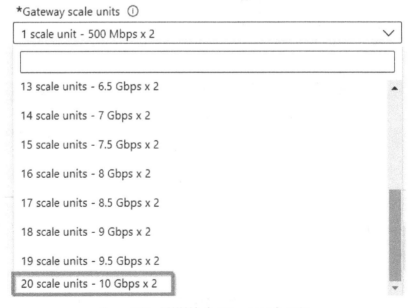

Figure 7.25 – VWAN hub gateway scale units

S2S VPN gateway instances in a VWAN hub are always deployed in an active-active setup (*Figure 7.26*). The *maximum supported number of gateway scale units* is 20 scale units (*Figure 7.25*), which deploys two active instances, with each instance supporting 10 Gbps (*Figure 7.25*). This requires an implementation of 20 scale units.

VPN gateways in a VWAN hub are always deployed in a highly available configuration (active-active setup).

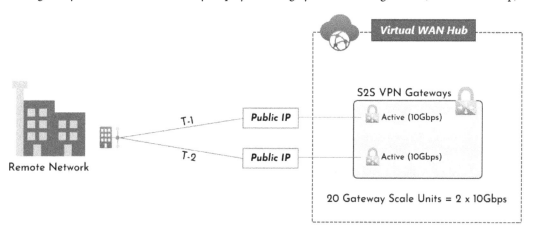

Figure 7.26 – VWAN hub gateway scale units are active-active

Understanding the scalability considerations of a VWAN hub S2S VPN

We mentioned earlier that one of the advantages of implementing a hub-and-spoke topology with VWAN instead of a traditional VNet and VPN gateway is scalability.

A VPN gateway in a user-managed VNet is limited to 30 tunnels while 20 gateway scale units in a VWAN hub can support up to 1,000 connections! A connection is an active-active IPsec tunnel from the on-premises VPN device to the virtual hub (*Figure 7.27*). The maximum total number of tunnels that can terminate in a single active instance is 1,000 and since we always have two instances, it means we can have up to 2,000 tunnels! That is a lot more than 30 tunnels.

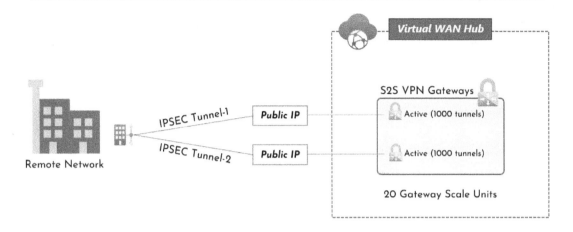

Figure 7.27 – Active-active tunnel from a remote network to the virtual hub

What if we need more than 1,000 connections (2,000 tunnels)? Remember that we can have multiple virtual hubs deployed in a region, so we can leverage this approach to support more connections, which means you can connect more than 1,000 branches to a single Azure Region by deploying multiple VWAN hubs in that Azure Region, each with its own site-to-site VPN gateway.

Understanding the availability considerations of a VWAN hub S2S VPN

As mentioned earlier, the VWAN hub always deploys two active S2S VPN gateway instances. During planned maintenance operations, each instance is upgraded one at a time, so it is highly recommended to always implement a tunnel to each instance from our on-premises VPN device (*Figure 7.28*).

If we choose to implement only one tunnel (again, this is not recommended), that tunnel would be moved to the online instance during planned maintenance, which may result in a tunnel reconnect. BGP sessions won't move across instances.

To further improve resiliency, we could implement additional redundancy on the remote side by also having two active devices, as shown in *Figure 7.28*, and connecting through different ISPs.

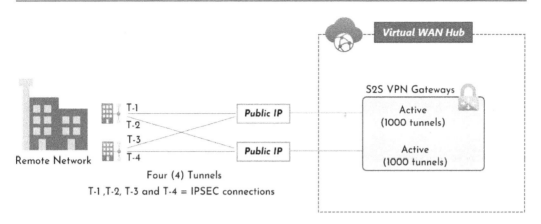

Figure 7.28 – Active-active tunnel from a remote network to the virtual hub

Understanding the performance considerations of a VWAN hub S2S VPN

As discussed earlier, during a planned maintenance operation, an instance of the S2S VPN gateway is upgraded at a time. When this is happening, there will be a brief decrease in the aggregate throughput of the S2S VPN gateway (*Figure 7.29*).

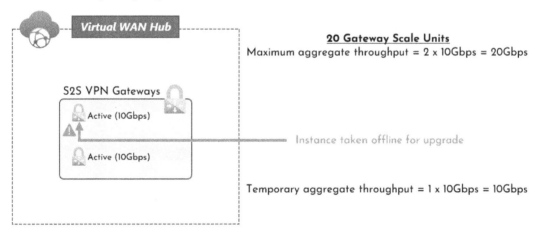

Figure 7.29 – Temporary aggregate throughput during planned maintenance

Another aspect to consider regarding performance is the IPSEC algorithm used to establish the VPN connection to the hub. The recommendation is **GCMAES256** for both IPSEC encryption and integrity. This algorithm results in a better performance than AES256 and SHA256! Implementing AES256 and SHA256 could result in latency and packet drops!

Another point to note is that the throughput specified for the gateway scale units is an aggregate value and not for individual tunnels! A single tunnel implementing the GCM algorithm can support up to a maximum of 1.25 Gbps.

In cases of multiple tunnels connected to a lower-value scale unit gateway, it's best to evaluate the need per tunnel and plan for a VPN gateway that is an aggregate value for throughput across all tunnels terminating in the VPN instance.

Hands-on exercise 2 – implement site-to-site VPN connectivity using VWAN

Here are the tasks that we will complete in this exercise:

- **Task 1** – add a site-to-site gateway to VWAN

- **Task 2** – create a VPN site in VWAN

- **Task 3** – connect the VPN site to a VWAN hub

- **Task 4** – obtain VPN configuration information

- **Task 5** – configure the "on-premises" VPN device

- **Task 6** – verify routes and connectivity to the "on-premises" site through VWAN

By the end of this exercise, our implementation will be like what is shown in *Figure 7.30*. Let's get into this!

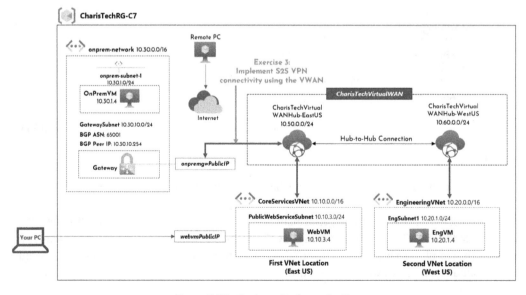

Figure 7.30 – End result of exercise 2

Task 1 – add a site-to-site gateway to VWAN

The first thing that we will do is to add a site-to-site gateway to one of our existing VWAN hubs. To do this, we need to edit its configuration:

1. In the **CharisTechVirtualWAN** window, in the **Connectivity** section, select **Hubs**, then select **CharisTechVirtualWANHub-EastUS** (or the virtual hub in the first region).

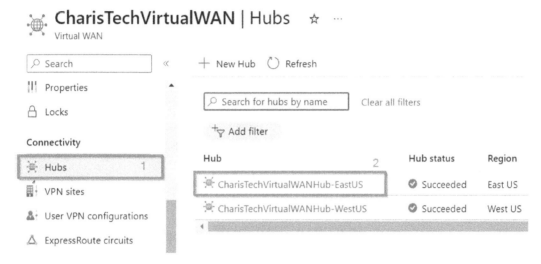

Figure 7.31 – Select the VWAN hub

2. In the **CharisTechVirtualWANHub-EastUS** window, in the **Overview** section, click on **Edit virtual hub**.

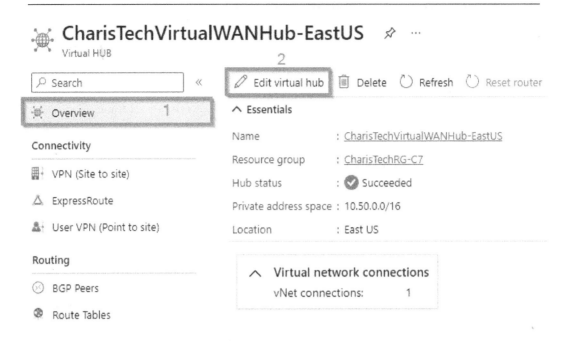

Figure 7.32 – Edit the virtual hub in the first region

3. In the **Edit virtual hub** blade, select the **Include vpn gateway for vpn sites** option and configure the following:

    - **AS Number**: This cannot be modified so leave it as the default

    - **Gateway scale units**: **1 scale unit - 500 Mbps x 2**

- Select **Confirm**.

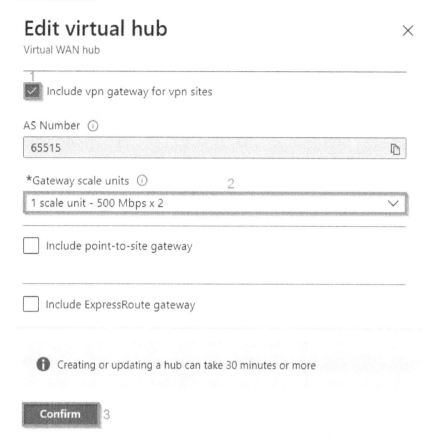

Figure 7.33 – Add S2S VPN gateway scale units to the VWAN hub

This can take about 30 minutes to complete. You do not need to wait for this to be completed before proceeding to *Task 2*, but it will need to be completed before *Task 3*.

Task 2 – create a VPN site in VWAN

The next thing that we will do is add a VPN site to VWAN. A site is meant to represent our on-premises physical locations where our VPN devices are located. For example, if we had two branch offices in Boston and London, we'd create two sites to represent them. We can create up to 1,000 sites per virtual hub in VWAN:

1.   In the **CharisTechVirtualWAN** window, in the **Connectivity** section, select **VPN sites**, then select + **Create site**.

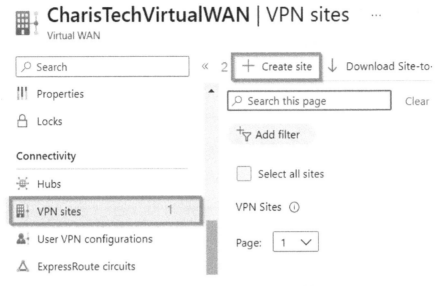

Figure 7.34 – Create a new VPN site in VWAN

2. On the **Create VPN site** page, on the **Basics** tab, configure the following:

    • **Subscription**: Your Azure subscription should be automatically selected.

    • **Resource group**: **CharisTechRG-C7** (should be automatically selected).

    • **Region**: **East US** (or your first VNet region).

    • **Name: on-premises-site**

    • **Device vendor**: **Microsoft** (Because we are simulating our Azure on-premises environment using an Azure VNet with a VPN gateway, we will enter **Microsoft** here. Ideally, this should be the name of the VPN device vendor, e.g., Palo Alto Networks.)

    • **Private address space**: Leave blank (this is because we will be implementing BGP instead of static routing).

- Select **Next : Links >**.

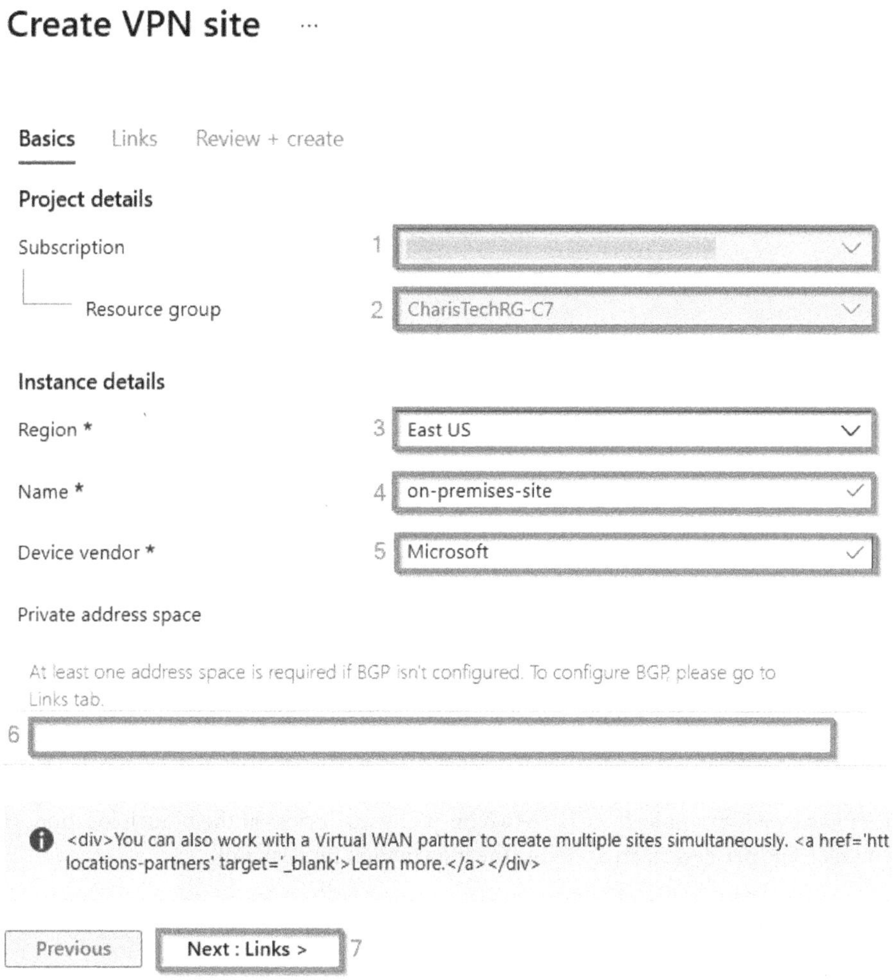

Create VPN site   ...

Basics   Links   Review + create

Project details

Subscription   1 [⌄]

└────── Resource group   2 [CharisTechRG-C7   ⌄]

Instance details

Region *   3 [East US   ⌄]

Name *   4 [on-premises-site   ✓]

Device vendor *   5 [Microsoft   ✓]

Private address space

At least one address space is required if BGP isn't configured. To configure BGP, please go to
Links tab.

6 [   ]

   ℹ <div>You can also work with a Virtual WAN partner to create multiple sites simultaneously. <a href='htt
     locations-partners' target='_blank'>Learn more.</a> </div>

[Previous]   [**Next : Links >**]   7

Figure 7.35 – Configure VPN site basic configurations

3. On the **Links** tab, configure the following:

    - **Link Name**: Link1

    - **Link speed**: 650 (this is the speed of the VPN device at the branch location)

    - **Link provider name**: **Microsoft** (the name of the physical link at the VPN site, for example,
      ATT or Verizon).

- **Link IP address / FQDN**: Enter the `onPremVPNDevice-FQDN` value that you made a note of in *Exercise 1 – Task 1 – Step 6*.

- **Link BGP address**: Enter the `onPremVPNDevice-BGP-PeerIP` value that you made a note of in *Exercise 1 – Task 1 – Step 6*.

- **Link ASN**: Enter the `onPremVPNDevice-BGP-ASN` value that you made a note of in *Exercise 1 – Task 1 – Step 6*.

- Select **Next : Review + create >**.

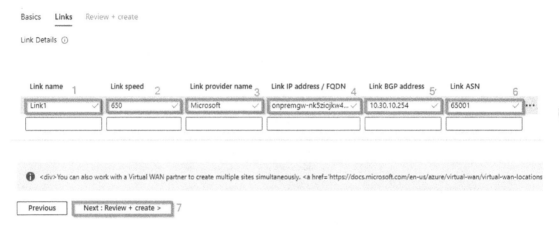

Figure 7.36 – Configure a VPN site link

Well done! We have now successfully provisioned a VPN site in Azure VWAN! We can add up to four links per VPN site. For example, if we have two on-premises devices at the branch location, we can create two links, one per device, and provide the information for each link.

Task 3 – connect the VPN site to a VWAN hub

In this next task, we will connect the on-premises site to our virtual hub:

1. In the **CharisTechVirtualWAN** window, in the **Connectivity** section, select **Hubs**, then select **CharisTechVirtualWANHub-EastUS** (or the virtual hub in the first region).

2. In the **Connectivity** section, select **VPN (Site to site)**, then click the **Clear all filters** option.

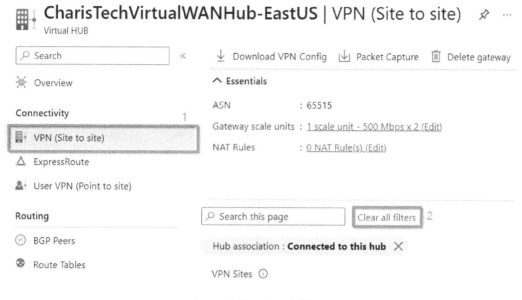

Figure 7.37 – Clear all filters

3. Select the checkbox next to **on-premises-site** (don't click the site name directly), then click **Connect VPN sites**.

Figure 7.38 – Select the VPN site

4. On the **Connect sites** blade, configure the following:

   • **Pre-shared key (PSK):** vpnPass123 (This is the pre-shared key configured for our on-premises VPN device. If we do not specify one, Azure will autogenerate one for us.)

   • **Protocol: IKEv2**

   • **IPsec: Default** (We can also configure custom settings.)

- **Propagate Default Route: Disable** (The **Enable** option allows the virtual hub to propagate a learned default route to this connection. We can modify this setting later if we want.)

- **Use policy based traffic selector: Disable**

- **Configure traffic selector?: No**

- **Connection Mode: Default** (This setting is used to decide which gateway can initiate the connection. **Default** means both the VWAN S2S VPN gateway and on-premises VPN gateways can initiate the connection. **Responder Only** means the VWAN S2S VPN gateway will never initiate the connection. **Initiator Only** means the VWAN S2S VPN gateway will initiate the connection and reject any connection attempts from the on-premises VPN gateway.)

- Select **Connect**.

Figure 7.39 – Configure VPN site connection

The connectivity status shows **Updating**. You can click **Refresh** to update the view. Leave this page open for the next task.

Figure 7.40 – Review the connection status

> **Note**
>
> **Connection Provisioning status** is the status of the Azure resource responsible for connecting the VPN site to the VWAN S2S VPN gateway. The following are the details of each of the statuses:
>
> a) **Connectivity status** is the actual data path connectivity status between the VWAN S2S VPN gateway and the VPN site.
>
> b) **Unknown**: This state is typically seen if the backend systems are working to transition to another status.
>
> c) **Connecting**: The VPN gateway is trying to reach out to the actual on-premises VPN site.
>
> d) **Connected**: Connectivity is established between the VPN gateway and the on-premises VPN site.
>
> e) **Not connected**: Connectivity is not established.
>
> f) **Disconnected**: This status is seen if, for any reason (on-premises or in Azure), the connection was disconnected.

Task 4 – obtain VPN configuration information

In this task, we will obtain the configuration information needed to configure our on-premises VPN device:

1. In the **CharisTechVirtualWANHub-EastUS | VPN (Site to site)** window, in the **Gateway configuration** section, click on **View/Configure**.

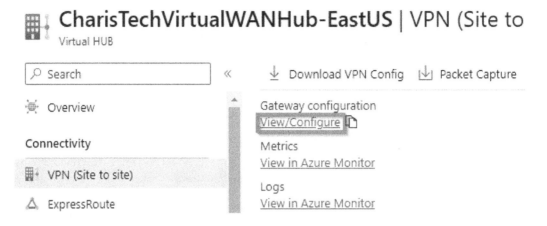

Figure 7.41 – Obtain the BGP ASN information

2.   In the **Edit VPN Gateway** blade, make a note of the following information as it will be needed in the next task:

   • **AS Number**

   • **VPN Gateway Instance 0** (**Public IP Address** and **Default BGP IP Address**)

   • **VPN Gateway Instance 1** (**Public IP Address** and **Default BGP IP Address**)

- Click to close the blade.

Edit VPN Gateway

A Site to site (VPN gateway) enables you to connect VPN sites to a hub.

AS Number ⓘ

65515

Gateway scale units ⓘ

1 scale unit - 500 Mbps x 2

Routing preference ⓘ

◉ Microsoft network   ◯ Internet

VPN Gateway Instance 0

Public IP Address ⓘ   20.62.181.27

Private IP Address ⓘ   10.50.0.4

Default BGP IP Address ⓘ   10.50.0.13

Custom BGP IP Address ⓘ

Peer Address

VPN Gateway Instance 1

Public IP Address ⓘ   20.62.180.222

Private IP Address ⓘ   10.50.0.5

Default BGP IP Address ⓘ   10.50.0.12

ⓘ <div>Updating a hub can take 30 minutes or more. <a href='https://aka.ms/virtualwan' target='_blank'>Learn more.</a></div>

Figure 7.42 – Obtain the information necessary for the on-premises VPN device configuration

Task 5 – configure the "on-premises" VPN device

In this task, we will configure the VPN connection between the on-premises VPN device and the VWAN Hub S2S VPN gateway. We will accomplish this with an ARM template as we already went through this configuration in *Chapter 5*:

1. Open a web browser and browse to `https://packt.link/JO12F`. This link will open the GitHub repository that has the ARM template to deploy the resources that we need.

2. In the GitHub repository that opens, in the *Azure Network Engineer Book - Chapter 7 - Exercise 3* section, click on **Deploy to Azure**.

⬿ Azure Network Engineer Book - Chapter 7 - Exercise 3

Figure 7.43 – Start the template deployment

3. If prompted to authenticate, sign in to the Azure portal with your administrative username and password.

4. In the **Custom Deployment** window, configure the following:

    *   **Subscription**: Select the subscription that you want to deploy the resources into.

    *   **Resource group: CharisTechRG-C7**

    *   **Region: (US) East US** (should be automatically selected).

    *   **Local Gateway0Pip Address**: Enter the public IP Address for **VPN Gateway Instance 0** that you made a note of in the previous task.

    *   **Local Gateway1Pip Address**: Enter the public IP Address for **VPN Gateway Instance 1** that you made a note of in the previous task.

    *   **Local Gateway Bgp ASN**: Enter the **VPN gateway AS** number that you made a note of in the previous task.

    *   **Local Gateway0Bgp Peering Ip**: Enter the default BGP IP address for **VPN Gateway Instance 0** that you made a note of in the previous task.

    *   **Local Gateway1Bgp Peering Ip**: Enter the default BGP IP address for **VPN Gateway Instance 1** that you made a note of in the previous task.

- Select **Review + create**.

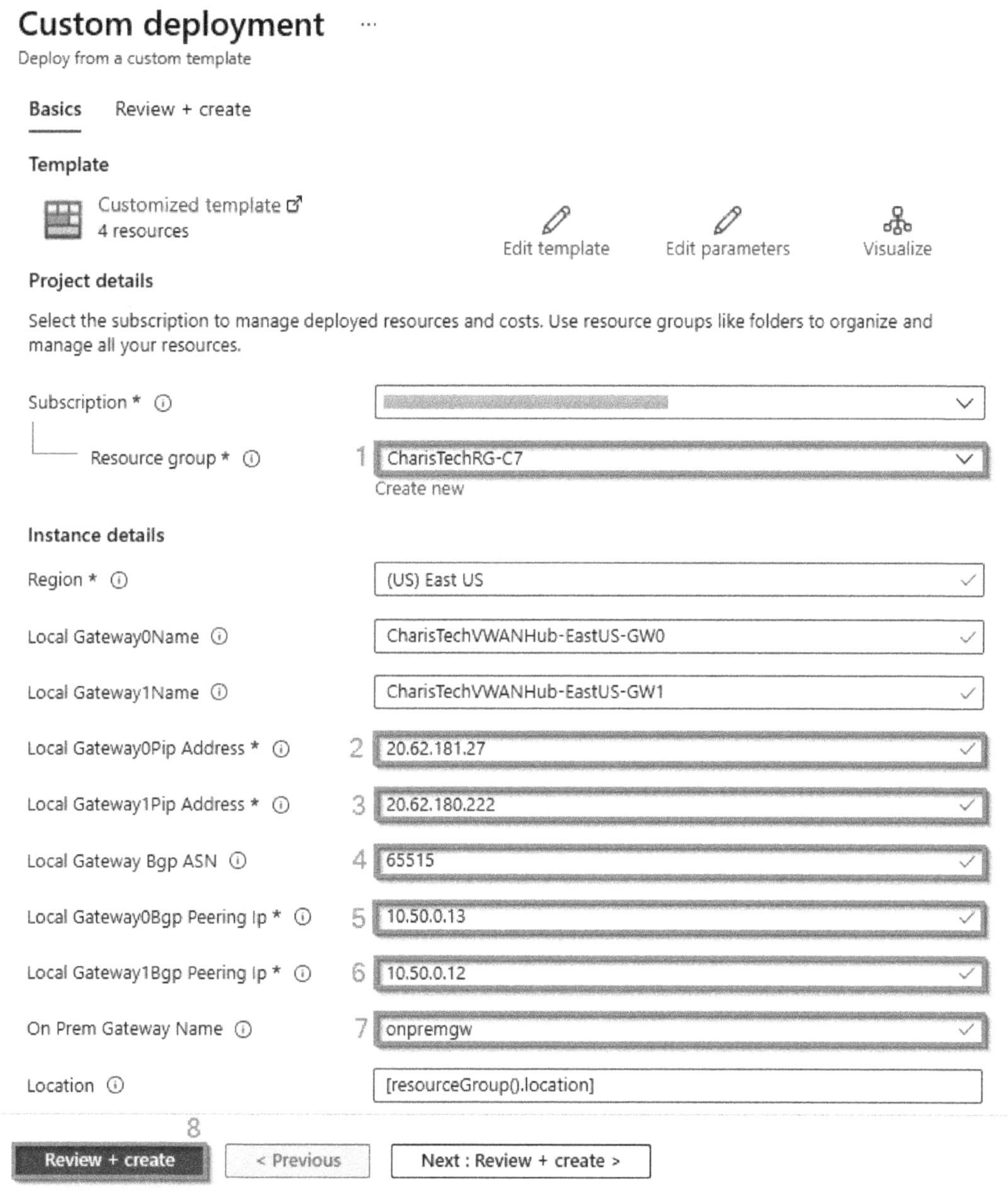

Custom deployment   ...
Deploy from a custom template

Basics   Review + create

Template

Customized template ☐'
4 resources

Edit template   Edit parameters   Visualize

Project details

Select the subscription to manage deployed resources and costs. Use resource groups like folders to organize and manage all your resources.

Subscription * ⓘ	▓▓▓▓▓▓▓▓▓▓▓▓▓▓▓▓▓▓▓▓▓▓▓ ∨
└─ Resource group * ⓘ	1 CharisTechRG-C7 ∨
	Create new

Instance details

Region * ⓘ	(US) East US ✓
Local Gateway0Name ⓘ	CharisTechVWANHub-EastUS-GW0 ✓
Local Gateway1Name ⓘ	CharisTechVWANHub-EastUS-GW1 ✓
Local Gateway0Pip Address * ⓘ	2 20.62.181.27 ✓
Local Gateway1Pip Address * ⓘ	3 20.62.180.222 ✓
Local Gateway Bgp ASN ⓘ	4 65515 ✓
Local Gateway0Bgp Peering Ip * ⓘ	5 10.50.0.13 ✓
Local Gateway1Bgp Peering Ip * ⓘ	6 10.50.0.12 ✓
On Prem Gateway Name ⓘ	7 onpremgw ✓
Location ⓘ	[resourceGroup().location]

8

[Review + create]   [< Previous]   [Next : Review + create >]

Figure 7.44 – Complete the custom deployment options

5. After the validation has passed, select **Create** to proceed with the deployment. The deployment can take up to 2 minutes to complete.

6. After the deployment has been completed, click on the **Go to resource group** option.

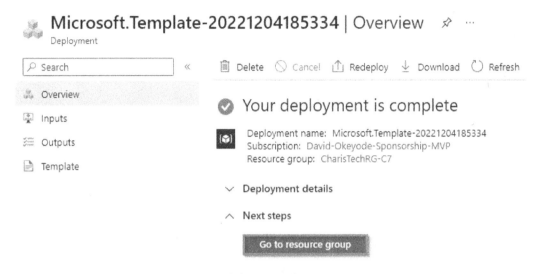

Figure 7.45 – Click to go to the resource group

7. In the **Filter for any field...** box, enter on-prem to filter for the connections that we just created. Select one of the connections.

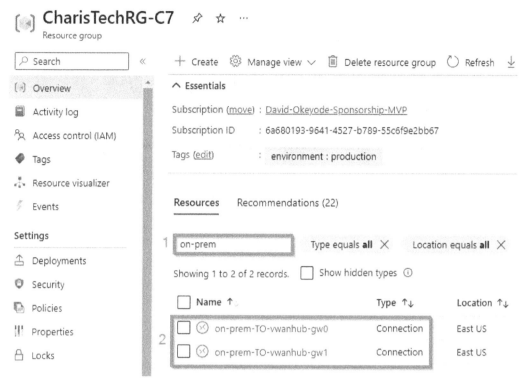

Figure 7.46 – Select one of the VPN connections

Task 6 – verify routes and connectivity to the "on-premises" site through VWAN

In this task, we will obtain test connectivity to our on-premises site through the S2S VPN connection between the VWAN hub and the on-premises VPN device. We will do this by connecting to **WebVM** and testing connectivity to **OnPremVM** via vWAN:

1. In the Cloud Shell window, enter the following commands to set the values that we will use for the resource group, network interface, and virtual machine variables:

    ```
    group="CharisTechRG-C7"
    nic="webvmNetInt"
    vm="webvm"
    ```

2. Examine the effective route entries applied to the network interface of the web VM using the following command:

    ```
    az network nic show-effective-route-table --resource-group
    $group --name webvmNetInt --output table
    ```

3. You should observe two additional routes to the on-premises network address range –
    10.30.0.0/16. Both routes were propagated via BGP and the S2S VPN connections in the
    VWAN hub, as shown in *Figure 7.47*.

```
david@Azure:~$
david@Azure:~$ az network nic show-effective-route-table --resource-group $group --name webvmNetInt
--output table  1
 \ Running ..
Source                         State     Address Prefix      Next Hop Type            Next Hop IP
----------------------------   -------   ----------------    ---------------------    ---------------
Default                        Active    10.10.0.0/16        VnetLocal
Default                        Active    10.50.0.0/16        VNetPeering
VirtualNetworkGateway          Active    10.20.0.0/16        VirtualNetworkGateway    20.231.251.106
VirtualNetworkGateway          Active    10.30.0.0/16        VirtualNetworkGateway    10.50.0.12
VirtualNetworkGateway          Active    10.30.0.0/16        VirtualNetworkGateway    10.50.0.13
Default                        Active    0.0.0.0/0           Internet
Default                        Active    10.0.0.0/8          None
```

Figure 7.47 – Verify routes to the on-premises network

4. Still in Cloud Shell, paste the SSH command that you obtained in *Hands-On Exercise 1 –
    Task 1 – Step 6* and press *Enter*.

5. If you are prompted about the authenticity of the host, type yes and press *Enter*. When
    prompted to enter the password, enter the complex password that you used in *Hands-On
    Exercise 1 – Task 1 – Step 4*.

6. You should now be connected to the **WebVM** virtual machine. Enter the following command
    to verify connectivity to the **EngVM** virtual machine in the remote VNet:

    ```
    ping 10.30.1.4
    ```

    The connection should be successful!

```
azureuser@webvm:~$ ping 10.30.1.4
PING 10.30.1.4 (10.30.1.4) 56(84) bytes of data.
64 bytes from 10.30.1.4: icmp_seq=1 ttl=64 time=10.4 ms
64 bytes from 10.30.1.4: icmp_seq=2 ttl=64 time=15.6 ms
64 bytes from 10.30.1.4: icmp_seq=3 ttl=64 time=9.00 ms
64 bytes from 10.30.1.4: icmp_seq=4 ttl=64 time=4.75 ms
64 bytes from 10.30.1.4: icmp_seq=5 ttl=64 time=4.80 ms
64 bytes from 10.30.1.4: icmp_seq=6 ttl=64 time=4.90 ms
64 bytes from 10.30.1.4: icmp_seq=7 ttl=64 time=4.90 ms
64 bytes from 10.30.1.4: icmp_seq=8 ttl=64 time=4.70 ms
64 bytes from 10.30.1.4: icmp_seq=9 ttl=64 time=4.51 ms
```

Figure 7.48 – Verify connectivity using ping

Task 7 – clean up the resources

In the Cloud Shell window, run the following commands to clean up the resources that we created in this hands-on exercise:

```
group=CharisTechRG-C7
az network express-route delete -n $ername -g $group
```

Congratulations! You have successfully configured and verified cross-VNet connectivity via vWAN.

Implementing a global transit network architecture using VWAN

One of the advantages of implementing Azure VWAN for connectivity is its support for an "out-of-the-box" global transit network architecture. This is because it allows any-to-any connectivity between all connections to VWAN (branches, VNets, and users)! This removes or reduces the need for full mesh or partial mesh connectivity between multiple networks.

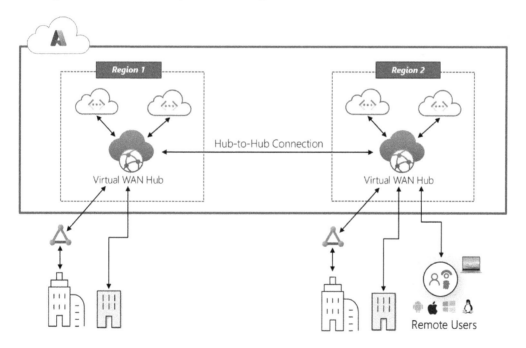

Figure 7.49 – Azure VWAN supports any-to-any connectivity

For example, in the scenario highlighted in *Figure 7.49*, VWAN supports the following global transit connectivity paths without the need for any additional routing configuration:

- Branch to VNet

- Branch to branch

- Remote user to VNet

- Remote user to branch

- VNet to VNet

- Branch-to-hub-to-hub-to-Branch

- Branch-to-hub-to-hub-to-VNet

- VNet-to-hub-to-hub-to-VNet

Understanding the security considerations of a virtual hub

So far, we have talked about how the virtual WAN makes connecting networks and routing easier. But what if we need to control and inspect the traffic between connected networks? Can we do this? The answer is yes, there are different ways we can do this, depending on what we need it for. In the next sections, we will quickly look at three common ways of doing this.

Approach 1 – deploy Azure Firewall in the virtual hub

The virtual hub (Standard tier only) supports the deployment of Azure Firewall within the hub. This creates a **secured hub** that can filter and inspect network traffic between virtual networks, branch offices or remote users, and the internet (*Figure 7.50*).

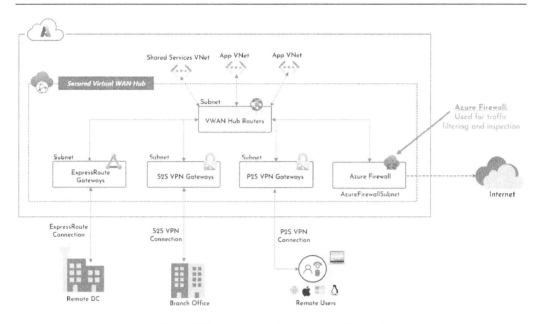

Figure 7.50 – Secured hub using Azure Firewall

Traffic inspection is supported for the following scenarios:

- Between connected virtual networks
- Between virtual networks and branch offices (ExpressRoute, S2S VPN, and P2S VPN)
- Between virtual networks and the internet
- Between branch offices and the internet

At the time of writing (December 2022), a secured hub does not have the ability to filter/inspect traffic between two branches or across different hubs. For example, the scenarios below are *not* yet supported:

- Virtual network | Virtual hub (Region 1) | Azure Firewall | Virtual hub (Region 2) | Virtual network
- Branch 1 | Virtual hub | Azure Firewall | Branch 2

Because of this limitation, it is a good idea to put a firewall in every virtual hub where there is a need to inspect traffic.

So, how do we route traffic to Azure Firewall so it can be inspected? If virtual networks are connected to the same secure virtual hub, routing to the firewall is automatically handled for traffic between virtual networks or between virtual networks and branch office destinations. There is no need for us to set up any additional routing.

To inspect internet-bound traffic, we need to configure routing to send traffic to the destination prefix of 0.0.0.0/0 to Azure Firewall.

If you want to learn more about implementing this approach, there is a lab in *Chapter 8* of this book that covers the topic of network security design and implementation in more detail.

Approach 2 – deploy a third-party security virtual appliance in the virtual hub

The virtual hub also allows companies to use their own security provider to filter and inspect network traffic. This is useful if the company wants extra security options that Azure's own firewall does not have. For example, vendor-proprietary intrusion protection capabilities. Currently, two security providers are supported: Check Point CloudGuard and Fortinet Next-Generation Firewall (*Figure 7.51*).

To use this approach, we need to buy a license directly from our preferred security NVA vendor. We can only use the "bring your own license" option right now, not the "pay as you go" option.

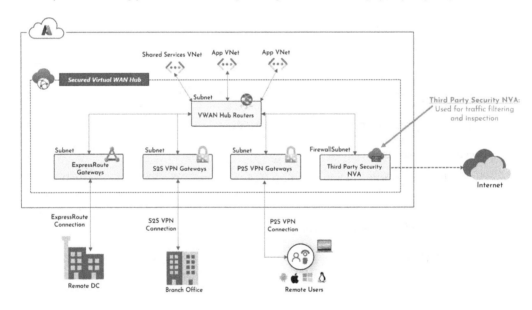

Figure 7.51 – Secured virtual WAN hub with third-party security NVA

Approach 3 – deploy a third-party network virtual appliance in a connected VNet and route traffic to it for inspection

Another option is to use a third-party NVA deployed into a connected VNet to filter and inspect network traffic (*Figure 7.52*). This allows us to use any security provider with an NVA in Azure Marketplace.

This approach is especially useful if we have different security needs for different parts of our network. For example, *Figure 7.52* shows a scenario where inspection is needed for traffic to and from **VNet1** and **VNet2** but not for traffic transiting the virtual hub.

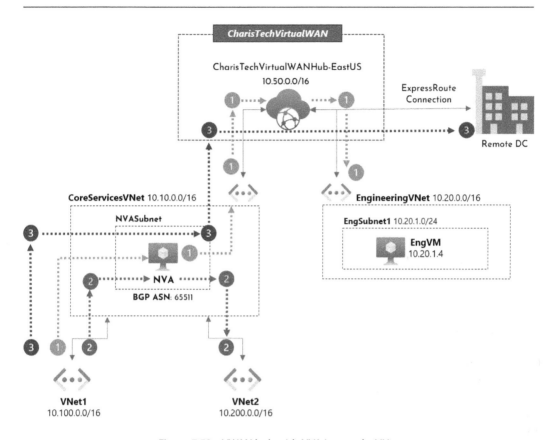

Figure 7.52 – VWAN hub with NVA in a spoke VNet

Comparing virtual hub NVA deployment options

As discussed earlier, we have two options for implementing a third-party security NVA in our VWAN architecture: using approach two, where the NVA is placed in the virtual hub, or approach three, where the NVA is placed in a connected VNet.

Using the NVA in the virtual hub (approach two) has several benefits, such as built-in availability, less management overhead (as the appliances are managed by Microsoft), and easier routing. It also has special support from Microsoft and the NVA provider to help with any customer problems. On the other hand, if we use approach three and place the NVA in a connected VNet, we will have to manage and upgrade it ourselves, but we have more flexibility with the security provider we can use. *Figure 7.53* shows a summary of this comparison.

Capability	NVA in VWAN Hub	NVA in VNet
Built-in availability	✓	✗
Reduced management overhead	✓	✗
Simplified routing	✓	✗
Special support agreement	✓	✗
Pay-as-you-go (PAYG) pricing	✗	✓
Bring your own license (BYOL) pricing	✓	✗
Supported vendors	Check Point and Fortinet ONLY	Any security vendor NVA available in Azure Marketplace

Figure 7.53 – Comparing virtual hub NVA deployment options

Well done! You have completed this chapter. Let's quickly go over what we learned in this chapter.

Summary

This chapter discussed the process of designing and implementing a scalable network topology in Azure, including understanding the design considerations of a virtual hub and configuring Site-to-Site connectivity using VWAN. It also covered routing and SD-WAN configuration in a virtual hub and the implementation of a global transit network architecture using VWAN. Finally, the chapter covered important security considerations when working with a virtual hub.

In the next chapter, we will learn more about how to keep our networks secure in Azure. This topic is important for the exam.

Further reading

For more information on the topics covered in this chapter, please refer to the following:

- https://learn.microsoft.com/en-us/azure/virtual-wan/migrate-from-hub-spoke-topology

- https://learn.microsoft.com/en-us/azure/virtual-wan/scenario-route-through-nva

- https://learn.microsoft.com/en-us/azure/virtual-wan/scenario-route-through-nvas-custom

- https://learn.microsoft.com/en-us/azure/architecture/example-scenario/infrastructure/performance-security-optimized-vwan

Designing and Implementing Network Security

Security is very important for any network design. If we don't make sure our Azure network workloads are secure, someone could use our resources for illegal activities, access sensitive customer data, or damage our reputation. To avoid these risks, we need to consider security when we set up our Azure virtual networks. This helps to keep our data and resources safe from unauthorized access or attacks. By the end of this chapter, you will have a good understanding of the following:

- Securing the Azure virtual network perimeter
- Implementing Azure **Distributed Denial-of-Service (DDoS)** Protection
- Implementing Azure Firewall
- Implementing a **Web Application Firewall (WAF)** in Azure
- Implementing central management with Firewall Manager

We have arranged the topics to match the exam objectives. Let's get started!

Technical requirements

To follow along with the instructions in this chapter, you will need the following:

- A PC with internet connection
- An Azure subscription

Securing the Azure virtual network perimeter

A network perimeter is a boundary that separates the public internet and our private virtual networks in Azure (see *Figure 8.1*). The objectives of securing the network perimeter are to keep out bad traffic, such as DDoS attacks, and to protect our network from unauthorized access and threats coming from an external network.

Azure offers several services to help with this, including the **DDoS Protection** service, **Azure Firewall**, **Azure Web Application Firewall**, and third-party security **Network Virtual Appliance** options.

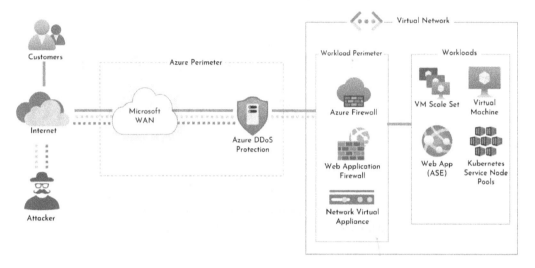

Figure 8.1 – Azure network perimeter security

Figure 8.1 shows the main perimeter security services that we will talk about in this chapter and how they fit into an Azure network architecture. We will begin by discussing the Azure DDoS protection service in the next section.

Implementing DDoS protection

A **DDoS** attack is a collection of attack types aimed at disrupting the availability of a target by overwhelming it with malicious traffic. They are usually targeted at virtual network workloads that are accessible via the internet.

The Azure DDoS Protection service helps protect **internet-facing** virtual network workloads from these attacks by identifying and blocking the malicious attempts to overwhelm our network before they can reach our resources. This service uses the scale and elasticity of Microsoft's global network to stop the attack at the edge of the Azure network (see *Figure 8.1*). There are three main types of DDoS attacks:

- **Volumetric DDoS attacks** such as amplification floods and UDP floods, which overload the network bandwidth capabilities of a target to make it inaccessible. This is the equivalent of what happens in a **traffic jam** – when vehicles cannot move forward because there is too much traffic. Mitigating this category of DDoS attack usually involves having a large enough bandwidth to absorb and scrub the traffic with a network that scales on demand.

- **Protocol DDoS attacks** such as reflection attacks and SYN flood attacks, which abuse weaknesses in OSI Layer 3 and OSI Layer 4 network protocols to render a target inaccessible. Mitigating this type of attack usually involves the use of client probing techniques to differentiate between legitimate clients and malicious clients.

- **Application DDoS attacks** such as Slowloris and low/slow attacks, which exploit weaknesses in application protocols such as HTTP (Layer 7). Mitigation usually involves deep behavioral analysis of application network traffic.

The Azure DDoS Protection service can protect against volumetric and protocol attacks, but it does not defend against application attacks. To safeguard against application DDoS attacks, we can use a **WAF** in Azure services such as Application Gateway and Front Door, or implement third-party providers from the Azure marketplace. Azure WAF will be covered later in the chapter.

Now that we have some understanding of what the Azure DDoS Protection service can do and what it cannot do, let us review the service tiers that it offers.

Understanding Azure DDoS Protection service tiers

Azure DDoS protection offers two tiers of service: **IP Protection** and **Network Protection**.

DDoS IP Protection offers a pricing model in which you pay per protected public IP address. This is suitable for small to medium organizations that only have a few public IP addresses to protect. The service continuously monitors traffic patterns to the protected IP to identify any potential DDoS attacks. If an attack is detected, the service immediately and automatically takes steps to mitigate it.

Figure 8.2 illustrates an example of **DDoS IP Protection** enabled for the public IP address of an internet-facing load balancer in an N-tier architecture. In this illustration, DDoS protection is only applied to the public IP address of the load balancer, and *not* to the public IP of the **Jumpbox** VM.

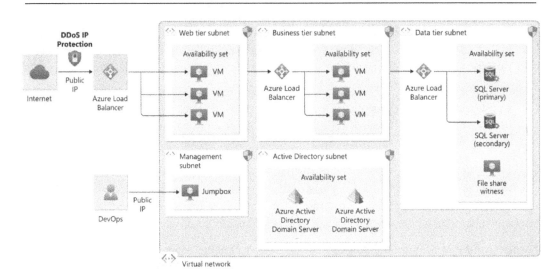

Figure 8.2 – DDoS IP Protection in an N-tier architecture

DDoS Network Protection, on the other hand, is applied to the entire virtual network and provides DDoS protection for all public IP addresses that are associated with resources in the virtual network. *Figure 8.3* illustrates an example of **DDoS Network Protection** enabled for a virtual network in an N-tier architecture. In this illustration, DDoS protection will be applied to *both* the public IP address of the load balancer and the public IP of the **Jumpbox** VM.

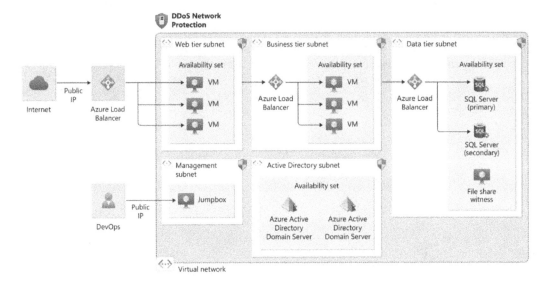

Figure 8.3 – DDoS Network Protection in an N-tier architecture

DDoS Network Protection offers a bundle pricing model that can protect up to 100 public IP addresses across multiple virtual networks. This means that the same DDoS Network Protection plan can be linked to virtual networks in different regions, subscriptions, or tenants, and it will provide protection for up to 100 public IP addresses across all networks. This pricing model can result in savings of up to 85% when compared to paying for protection on a per-IP basis!

> **Note**
>
> There is a per-resource cost if the IP address total exceeds the included 100 public IP addresses. For up-to-date information on what this is, please refer to this documentation – `https://azure.microsoft.com/en-us/pricing/details/ddos-protection/`.

DDoS Network Protection provides additional features that are not available with the IP Protection option (see *Figure 8.4*). These include **DDoS rapid response support**, which gives you access to a team of DDoS response specialists who can assist with investigations during and after an attack; **Cost protection**, which provides Azure credits back to us in the event of a successful DDoS attack that results in extra costs due to infrastructure scaling out; and **WAF discount**, which offers a pricing discount for Azure WAF. Both options include all other capabilities.

Capability	DDoS IP Protection	DDoS Network Protection
DDoS rapid response support	✗	✓
Cost protection	✗	✓
WAF discount	✗	✓
Pricing model	Per protected public IP address	Per 100 protected public IP addresses

Figure 8.4 – DDoS IP Protection versus DDoS Network Protection

> **Default DDoS protection**
>
> Azure automatically protects its own underlying infrastructure (e.g., Azure DNS) from DDoS attacks. This protection does not need to be set up and is always on, but it does not cover customer resources that are visible on the internet.

Now that you have some understanding of how the Azure DDoS Protection service can help to protect against DDoS attacks at the perimeter of our virtual networks, let us go ahead and implement it. However, before we can do this, we need to set up resources that we can use to follow along with the exercises in this chapter and the next one.

Hands-on exercise 1 – provisioning resources for Chapter 8's exercises

To follow along with the exercises in this chapter and the next one, we will provision some Azure resources to work with. We have prepared an Azure ARM template in the GitHub repository for this book for this purpose. The template will deploy an Azure virtual network with three subnets. The public subnet will have an Ubuntu Linux VM with NGINX installed as shown in *Figure 8.5*. The VM has a public IP, and it is reachable directly from the internet. The other two subnets are empty. Here are the tasks that we will complete in this exercise:

- **Task 1**: Initialize template deployment in GitHub

- **Task 2**: Complete the parameters and deploy the template to Azure

Figure 8.5 – Chapter 8 exercises scenario

Let us begin deploying our template deployment:

1. Open a web browser and browse to `https://packt.link/WJxvK`. This link will open the GitHub repository with an ARM template to deploy the resources that we need.

2. In the GitHub repository that opens, click on **Deploy to Azure**:

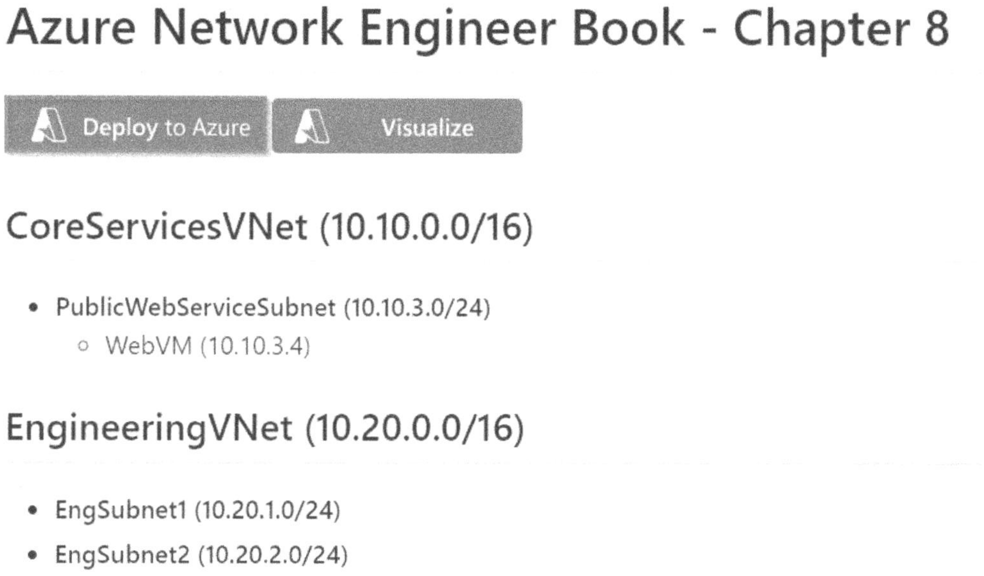
Azure Network Engineer Book - Chapter 8
Deploy to Azure
Visualize
CoreServicesVNet (10.10.0.0/16)
PublicWebServiceSubnet (10.10.3.0/24)
WebVM (10.10.3.4)
EngineeringVNet (10.20.0.0/16)
EngSubnet1 (10.20.1.0/24)
EngSubnet2 (10.20.2.0/24)

Figure 8.6 – Clicking on the Deploy to Azure option

3. If prompted, sign in with your Azure administrative credentials.
4. In the **Custom deployment** window, configure the following:
   - **Subscription**: Select the subscription that you want to deploy the resources into.
   - **Resource Group**: **Create New** | **Name**: `CharisTechRG-C8` | **OK**.
   - **Region**: Select an Azure region close to your location.
   - **Web Vm Name**: Leave the default value.
   - **Admin Username**: Leave the default value.
   - **Admin Password**: Enter a complex password. Make a note of the password that you use.
   - **Web Vmdns Label Prefix**: Leave the default value.
   - **Ubuntu OS Version**: Leave the default value.
   - **Vm Size**: Leave the default value.

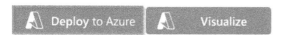

Click on **Review + Create**.

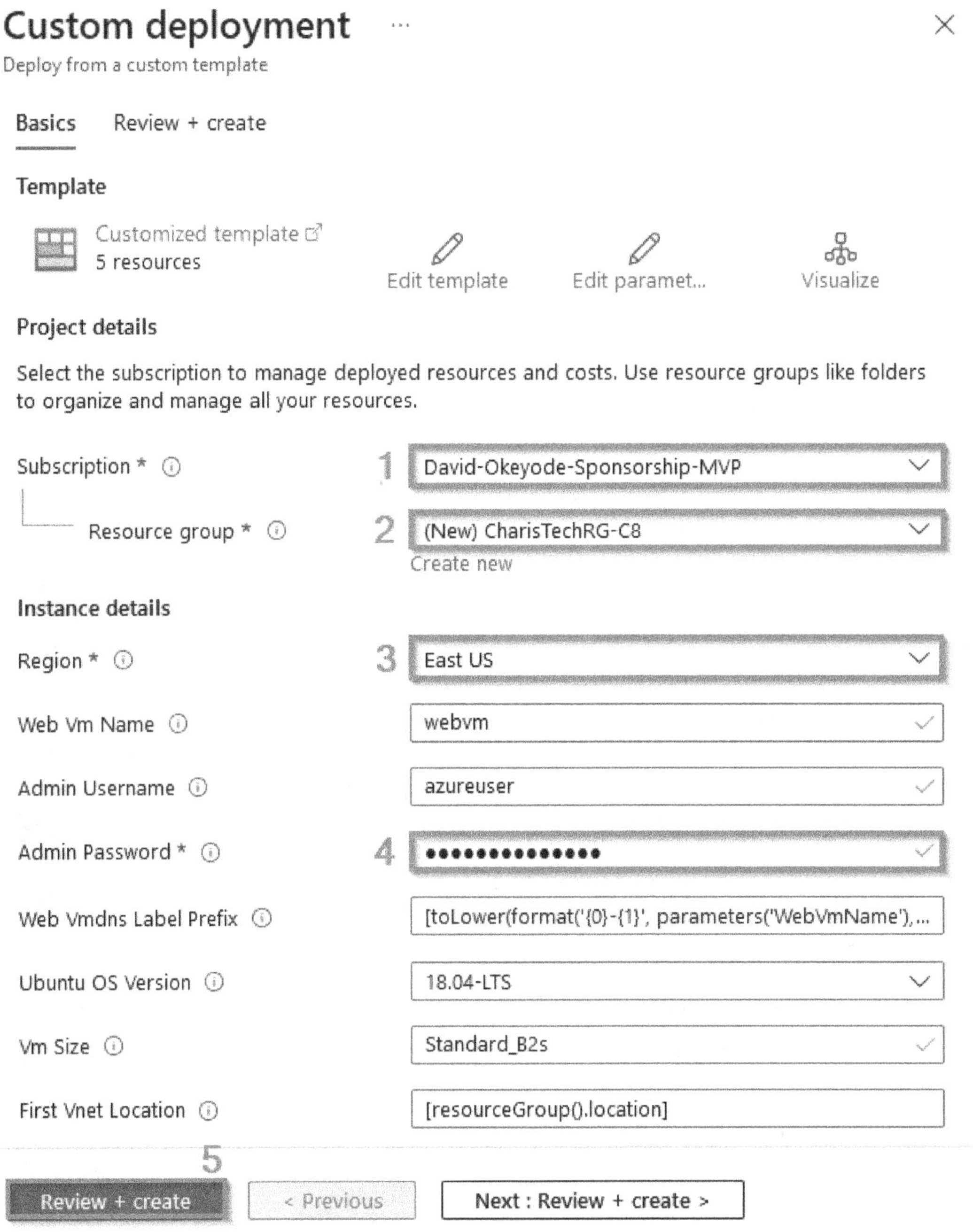

Custom deployment　···

Deploy from a custom template

Basics　Review + create

Template

Customized template ☐
5 resources

Edit template　　Edit paramet...　　Visualize

Project details

Select the subscription to manage deployed resources and costs. Use resource groups like folders to organize and manage all your resources.

Subscription * ⓘ　　　1　David-Okeyode-Sponsorship-MVP ⌄

└─ Resource group * ⓘ　2　(New) CharisTechRG-C8 ⌄
Create new

Instance details

Region * ⓘ　　　　　3　East US ⌄

Web Vm Name ⓘ　　　webvm ✓

Admin Username ⓘ　　azureuser ✓

Admin Password * ⓘ　4　•••••••••••••• ⌄

Web Vmdns Label Prefix ⓘ　[toLower(format('{0}-{1}', parameters('WebVmName'),...

Ubuntu OS Version ⓘ　　18.04-LTS ⌄

Vm Size ⓘ　　　　　Standard_B2s ✓

First Vnet Location ⓘ　　[resourceGroup().location]

5

[Review + create]　[< Previous]　[Next : Review + create >]

Figure 8.7 – Configuring template parameters

5.   After the template validation has passed, click on **Create**. This will begin the deployment process, which takes about 7 to 10 minutes to complete. Grab yourself a cup of water, tea, or coffee, and wait for the deployment to complete.

6.   After the deployment has been completed, click on the **Outputs** tab. Make a note of the **publicWebVM** and **subscriptionId** values. Both values will be needed in later exercises in this chapter. The **publicWebVM** value is the public IP address of the internet-facing web server that was deployed.

Figure 8.8 – Obtaining the needed output values

Hands-on exercise 2 – implementing DDoS Protection, monitoring, and validation

Here are the tasks that we will complete in this exercise:

- **Task 1**: Create a DDoS Protection plan

- **Task 2**: Enable DDoS Protection on a virtual network

- **Task 3**: Review DDoS metrics for telemetry

- **Task 4**: Configure DDoS diagnostic logs forwarding

- **Task 5**: Configure DDoS alerts

- **Task 6**: Create a BreakingPoint Cloud account and authorize your Azure subscription

- **Task 7**: Run a DDoS test

- **Task 8**: Review DDoS test results

By the end of this exercise, our implementation will be like what is shown in *Figure 8.9*. Let's get into this!

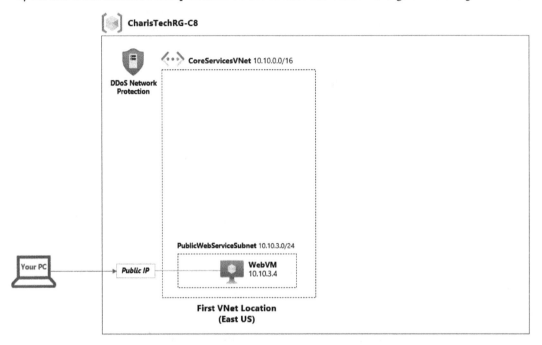

Figure 8.9 – End result of Exercise 2

Task 1 – creating a DDoS Protection plan

The first thing that we will do is to create a DDoS Network Protection plan, which we will apply to virtual networks that we want to protect:

1. On the Azure portal home page, in the search box, type DDoS and select **DDoS protection plans** when it appears.

Figure 8.10 – Selecting DDoS protection plans

2. In the **DDoS protection plans** window, select **+ Create** to create a new plan.

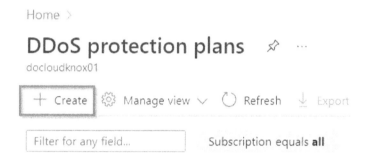

Figure 8.11 – Creating a new DDoS protection plan

3. In **Create a DDoS protection plan**, on the **Basics** tab, configure the following:

    - **Subscription**: Select the subscription that you want to deploy the resource into

    - **Resource Group**: **CharisTechRG-C8**

    - **Name**: **CharisTechDdoSProtectionPlan**

    - **Region**: **East US** (should be automatically selected)

    - Select **Review + create**

- Select **Create**

Create a DDoS protection plan   ···   ✕

Basics   Tags   Review + create

Azure DDoS protection can help defend against DDoS (distributed denial of service) attacks directed at your resources. Your resources automatically receive a basic level of protection at no additional charge. Create a DDoS protection plan to enable DDoS standard protection for an advanced level of protection. Learn more about DDoS protection plans

Project details

Subscription * ⓘ   David-Okeyode-Sponsorship-MVP   ⌄

      Resource group * ⓘ   1   CharisTechRG-C8   ⌄
                                    Create new

Instance details

Name *   2   CharisTechDdoSProtectionPlan   ✓

Region *   3   East US   ⌄

    Review + create   4   < Previous   Next : Tags >
Download a template for automation

Figure 8.12 – Configuring the parameters for a new DDoS plan

Task 2 – enabling DDoS Protection on a virtual network

Next, we will enable DDoS Network Protection on an existing virtual network:

1. At the top of the Azure portal, in the search box, enter `CoreServicesVnet` (the name of the virtual network that was created earlier). Select the **CoreServicesVnet** resource.

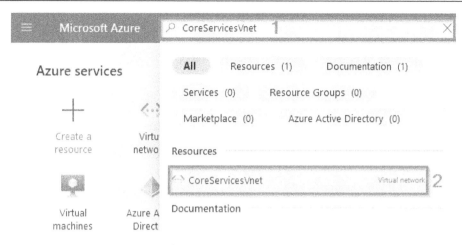

Figure 8.13 – Searching for and selecting the CoreServices virtual network

2. In the **Settings** section, select **DDoS protection**, then select **Enable**. Under **DDoS protection plan**, select **CharisTechDdoSProtectionPlan**, then click **Save**.

Figure 8.14 – Enabling and configuring the DDoS protection plan for a VNet

We can select any DDoS protection plan in the same subscription or a different subscription from the virtual network, but both subscriptions must be associated with the same Azure Active Directory tenant.

Task 3 – reviewing DDoS metrics for telemetry

Next, we will review some useful DDoS metrics that we can use to gain insights in the event of an attack:

1. At the top of the Azure portal, in the search box, enter `CharisTechDdoSProtectionPlan`. Select the **CharisTechDdoSProtectionPlan** resource.

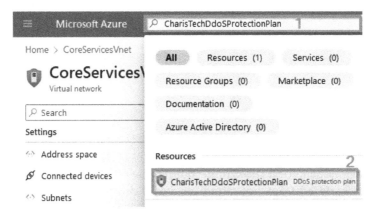

Figure 8.15 – Searching for and selecting the DDoS protection plan

2. In the **Monitoring** section, select **Metrics**. Configure the following:

    *   **Scope**: `webvmPublicIP`

    *   **Metric Namespace**: Leave default value

    *   **Metric: Inbound packets dropped DDoS**

    *   **Aggregation: Max**

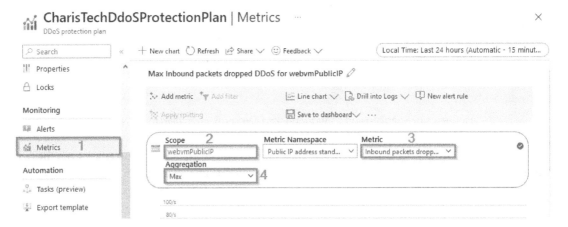

Figure 8.16 – Reviewing metrics for the DDoS protection plan

Task 4 – configure DDoS diagnostic logs forwarding

Next, we will configure DDoS diagnostic logs to be forwarded to a blob storage container. These logs can give us further insights in the event of a DDoS attack against the target (public IP address):

1. At the top of the Azure portal, in the search box, enter `webvmPublicIP`. Select the **webvmPublicIP** resource.

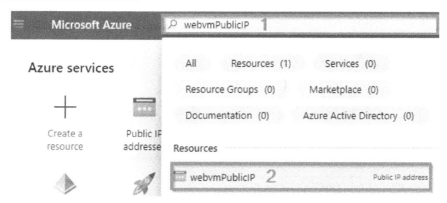

Figure 8.17 – Searching for and selecting the public IP resource

2. In the **Monitoring** section, select **Diagnostic settings**. Click **+ Add diagnostic setting**.

Figure 8.18 – Adding a new diagnostic setting

3. On the **Diagnostic setting** page, configure the following:

- **Diagnostic setting name**: `DDoSLogsDiagnosticSetting`
- **Categories**: Select **DDoS protection notifications**, **Flow logs of DDoS mitigation decisions**, and **Reports of DDoS mitigations**
- **Destination details**: Select **Archive to a storage account**
- **Storage account**: Select the storage account the name of which starts with **logstore**
- Leave the other settings as their defaults
- Click **Save**

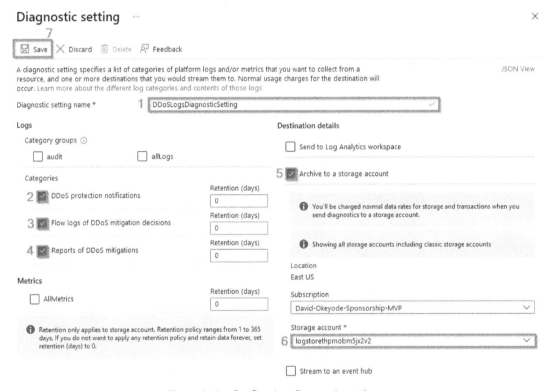

Figure 8.19 – Configuring diagnostic settings

4. Close the **Diagnostic setting** window.

Task 5 – configuring DDoS alerts

Next, we will configure an alert rule to generate an alert if the target resource (public IP address) is under a DDoS attack:

1. In the **Monitoring** section of the **webvmPublicIP** resource, select **Alerts**, then click on **Create alert rule**.

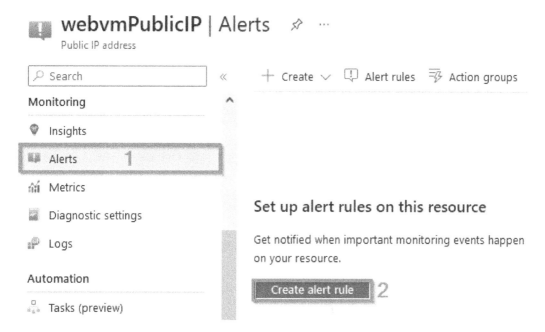

Figure 8.20 – Creating an alert rule

2.   In the **Select a signal** blade, click on **Under DDoS attack or not**.

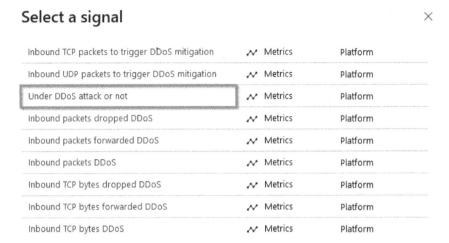

Figure 8.21 – Selecting a metric signal

3.   In the **Condition** blade, configure the following:

- **Threshold value:** 1 (this will generate an alert if the public IP is experiencing a DDoS attack)

- Leave other settings at their default values

- Click **Next: Actions >**

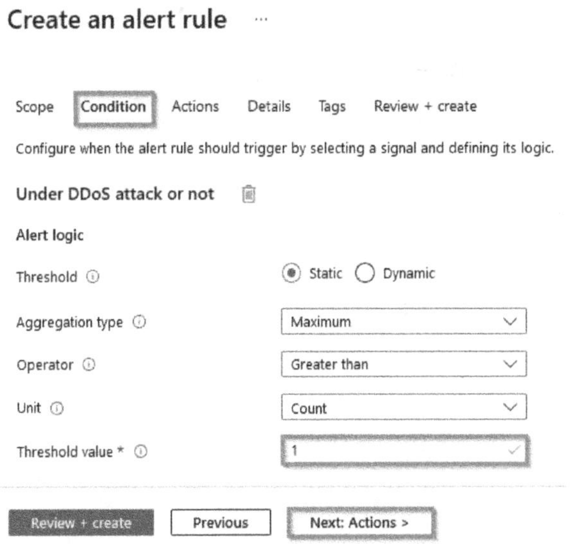

Figure 8.22 – Configuring the alert rule condition

4.   In the **Actions** blade, click **Next: Details >**.

5.   In the **Details** blade, configure the following:

- **Alert rule name**: `public-web-vm-ddos-attack-alert`

- Click **Next: Tags >**

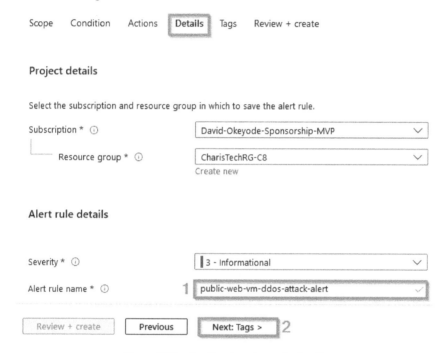

Figure 8.23 – Configuring alert rule details

6.   In the **Tags** blade, click **Next: Review + create >**, then click **Create**.

Task 6 – creating a BreakingPoint Cloud account and authorizing your Azure subscription

Next, we will create a BreakingPoint Cloud account and authorize the account to perform DDoS tests against targets in our Azure subscription:

1.   Open a web browser tab and browse to `https://breakingpoint.cloud/trial`.

2.   In the **Sign up for a free trial** window, configure the following:

- **First Name**: Enter your first name

- **Last Name**: Enter your last name

- **Email Address**: Enter your email address

- **Choose a password**: Enter a complex password

- **Re-type password**: Re-enter the complex password

- **I'm not a robot**: Selected

- **I agree with the Terms of Service**: Selected

- Click **SIGNUP**

> **Note**
>
> BreakingPoint is one of the three approved third-party testing partners for Azure DDoS Protection. The other two options are Red Button and RedWolf. You can read more about this here: `https://learn.microsoft.com/en-us/azure/ddos-protection/test-through-simulations`.

Figure 8.24 – Signing up for a BreakingPoint trial

3. It may take a few minutes to set up the identity; once completed, click on **START TRIAL**. If you do not get a response, refresh the web page.

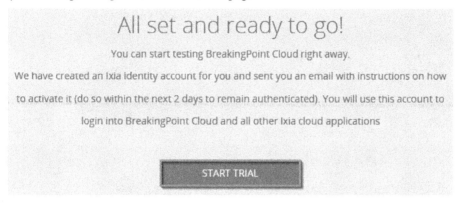

Figure 8.25 – Clicking to start the trial

4. In the **STEPS TO GET STARTED** window, click on **Add Azure Subscription**.

STEPS TO GET STARTED

1. Authorize access to your Azure Subscription for validating DDoS target IP ownership.

* View Azure Subscriptions

* Learn More

2. Identify the public IP address of your Azure resource protected from DDoS threats.

3. Configure and run DDoS validation test.

4. Use Microsoft Azure Portal to view DDoS Protection service analytics and insights.

* Learn More

Figure 8.26 – Clicking to add an Azure account to BreakingPoint

5. In the **AZURE SUBSCRIPTIONS** blade, enter the subscription ID value that you made a note of earlier and click on **ADD SUBSCRIPTION**. This should automatically redirect to Azure you for authorization but if that does not happen, click on the **Re-authorize** option.

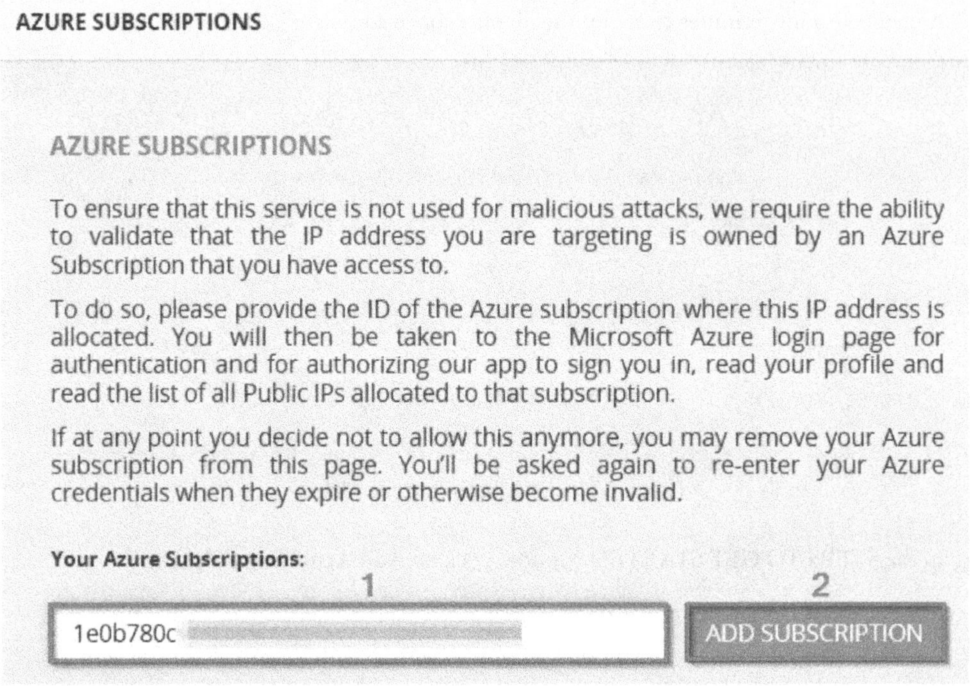

AZURE SUBSCRIPTIONS

AZURE SUBSCRIPTIONS

To ensure that this service is not used for malicious attacks, we require the ability to validate that the IP address you are targeting is owned by an Azure Subscription that you have access to.

To do so, please provide the ID of the Azure subscription where this IP address is allocated. You will then be taken to the Microsoft Azure login page for authentication and for authorizing our app to sign you in, read your profile and read the list of all Public IPs allocated to that subscription.

If at any point you decide not to allow this anymore, you may remove your Azure subscription from this page. You'll be asked again to re-enter your Azure credentials when they expire or otherwise become invalid.

Your Azure Subscriptions:

1

2

| 1e0b780c | ADD SUBSCRIPTION |

Figure 8.27 – Adding an Azure account subscription ID to BreakingPoint

6. Authenticate with your Azure admin credentials when prompted and accept the requested permissions.

 Microsoft

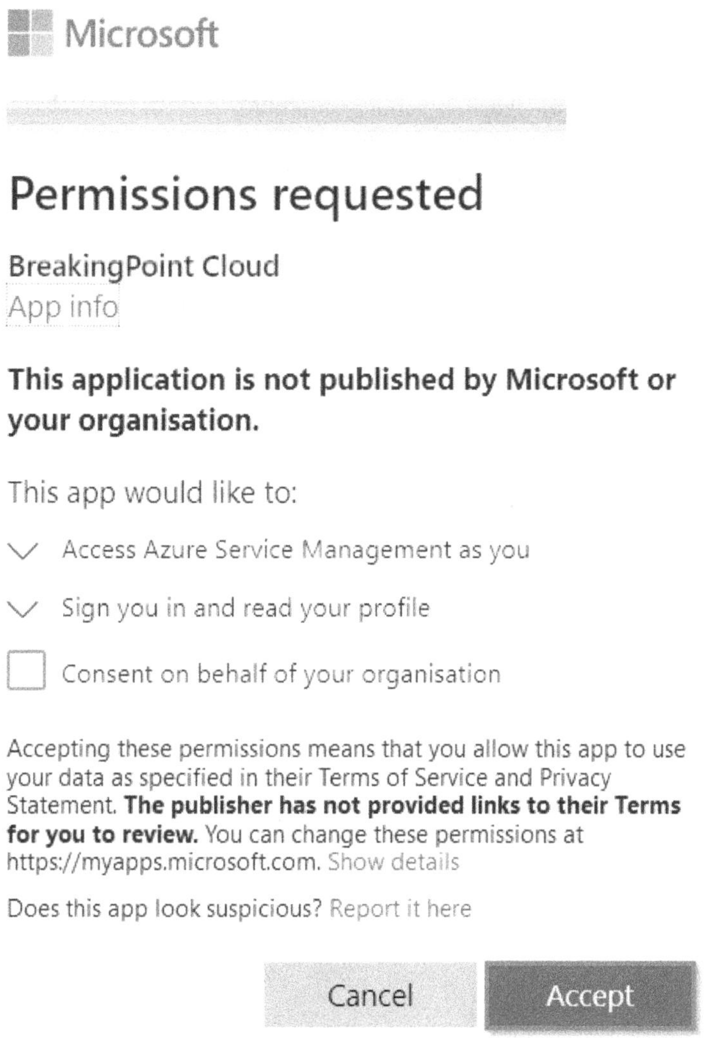

Permissions requested

BreakingPoint Cloud
App info

This application is not published by Microsoft or your organisation.

This app would like to:

∨   Access Azure Service Management as you

∨   Sign you in and read your profile

☐   Consent on behalf of your organisation

Accepting these permissions means that you allow this app to use your data as specified in their Terms of Service and Privacy Statement. **The publisher has not provided links to their Terms for you to review.** You can change these permissions at https://myapps.microsoft.com. Show details

Does this app look suspicious? Report it here

Figure 8.28 – Accepting the required permissions

7.   This should automatically redirect you to BreakingPoint with the subscription now listed as an authorized subscription. Click **Close**.

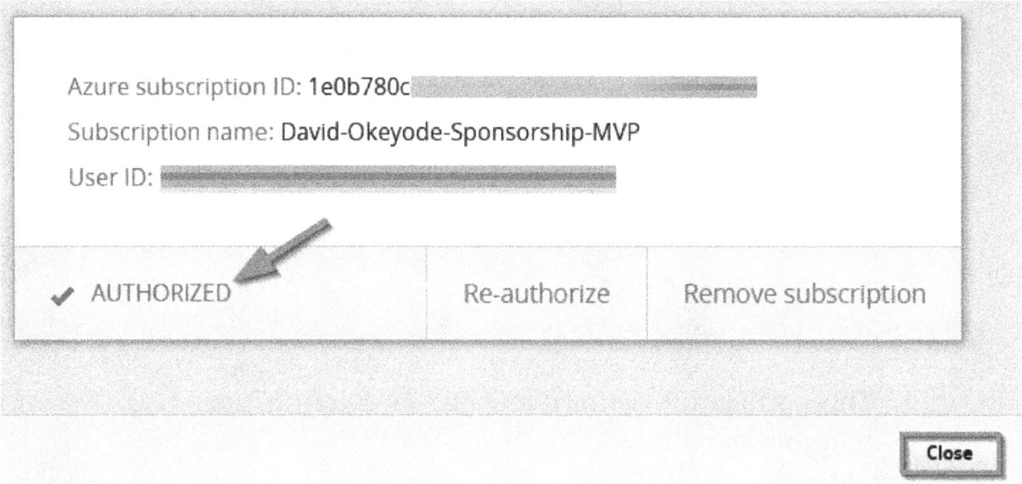

Figure 8.29 – Closing the window

Task 7 – running a DDoS Test

Next, we will run a DDoS test against the public IP address of our internet-facing web server:

1. Set up the DDoS test as per the settings in the following screenshot:

   - **Target IP Address**: Enter the value of the public IP address that you made a note of earlier

   - **Port Number**: 8 0

   - **DDoS Profile**: TCP SYN Flood

   - **Test Duration**: 10 minutes

- Click **START TEST**

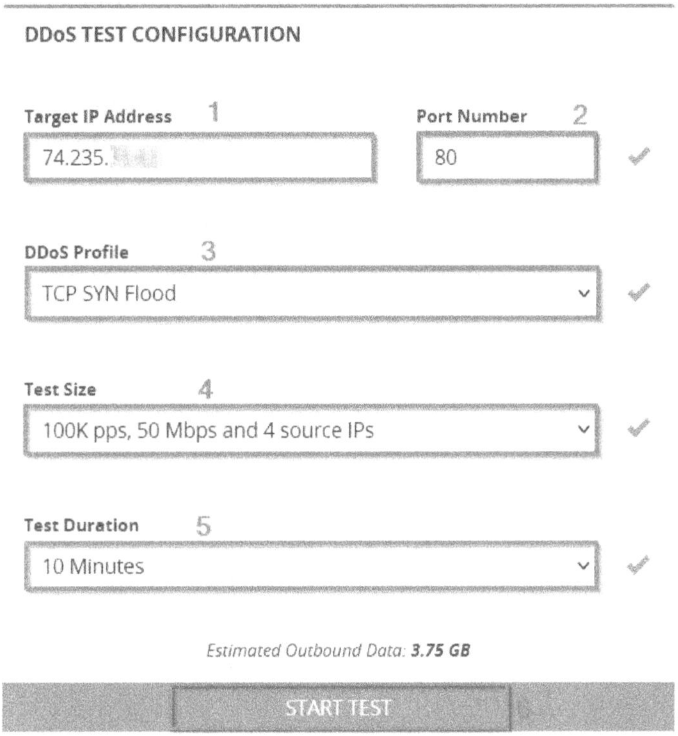

DDoS TEST CONFIGURATION

Target IP Address   1

74.235.

Port Number   2

80

DDoS Profile   3

TCP SYN Flood

Test Size   4

100K pps, 50 Mbps and 4 source IPs

Test Duration   5

10 Minutes

Estimated Outbound Data: **3.75 GB**

START TEST

Figure 8.30 – Configuring DDoS test settings

2. Wait for the test to complete.

Task 8 – reviewing DDoS test results

Next, we will run a DDoS test against the public IP address of our internet-facing web server:

1. At the top of the Azure portal, in the search box, enter `webvmPublicIP`. Select the **webvmPublicIP** resource.

2. In the **Monitoring** section, click **Metrics**. In the **Metric** box, select **Under DDoS attack or not** from the list. And here you can see the test DDoS attack as it happened. Note it may take the full 10 minutes before you see the results.

Great job! You have effectively implemented and verified DDoS defense to secure your network boundary. Now, let's explore another security service for our Azure virtual network boundary – Azure Firewall!

Implementing Azure Firewall

Azure Firewall is a perimeter network security service in Azure. It can be used to inspect both incoming and outgoing virtual network connections to keep workloads safe from malicious traffic. Unlike a third-party firewall appliance that is deployed as a **Network Virtual Appliance** (**NVA**) in Azure, Azure Firewall is a managed service, meaning we don't have to worry about maintaining its underlying operating system, updating its services, implementing high availability, or scaling it, as all these tasks are taken care of by Microsoft. All we need to do is deploy the service, configure it, use it, and pay for usage!

Understanding Azure Firewall service tiers

When implementing Azure Firewall, one of the first decisions that we need to make is the service tier that we want to implement. Azure Firewall offers three service tier options: **Basic**, **Standard**, and **Premium** (see *Figure 8.31*).

Figure 8.31 – Azure Firewall service tiers

The **Basic** tier is designed for **small and medium-sized business** (**SMB**) customers who require basic network traffic protection at an affordable cost. Its threat protection, scaling, and throughput capabilities are limited compared to the other options. For a detailed comparison of features, please refer to *Figure 8.32*. At the time of writing, the **Basic** SKU is still in public preview so we will mainly focus on the **Standard** and **Premium** offerings, even though we will make references to the **Basic** tier for awareness.

The **Standard** tier is designed for organizations that require basic network security with high scalability at a moderate price.

The **Premium** tier is designed for organizations in highly regulated industries, such as payments and healthcare, that handle sensitive information and require a higher level of network security. These organizations require advanced security features such as the ability to decrypt and inspect web traffic passing through the network (**Transport Layer Security** (**TLS**) inspection) and **Intrusion Detection and Prevention Service** (**IDPS**).

Understanding Azure Firewall's features

The features provided by Azure Firewall differ based on the chosen SKU, encompassing capabilities such as network traffic filtering, advanced threat protection, management, reliability, and performance.

Figure 8.32 presents an overview of these features and their availability across different firewall service tiers. However, for the exam, it is sufficient to have knowledge of the fundamental features. Therefore, we will focus on reviewing these features.

Feature Category	Feature	Firewall Basic	Firewall Standard	Firewall Premium
Network Filtering	Network level filtering (Source/Destination IP, port and protocol)	✓	✓	✓
	FQDN filtering (DNS based and SNI based for HTTPS/SQL)	✓	✓	✓
	URL filtering (full path - including SSL termination)	✗	✗	✓
	Web categorization filtering	✗	✓	✓
	Threat intelligence-based filtering (known malicious IP/domains)	✓	✓	✓
	Network Address Translation (SNAT + DNAT)	✓	✓	✓
Reliability & Performance	Built-in HA with autoscaling	✓	✓	✓
	Availability Zones (AZ) support	✓	✓	✓
	Maximum network throughput	250-500 Mbps	30 Gbps	100 Gbps
	Fat Flow support	✗	1 Gbps	10 Gbps
Enterprise Integration	Full logging including SIEM integration	✓	✓	✓
	DNS Proxy + Custom DNS	✗	✓	✓
Management	Central management via Firewall Manager	✓	✓	✓
	Service tags and FQDN tags for easy policy management	✓	✓	✓
	Policy Analytics (Rule management over time)	✓	✓	✓
	DevOps integration (REST/PS/CLI/Templates/Terraform)	✓	✓	✓
Advanced Threat Protection	Inbound TLS termination (TLS reverse proxy)	✗	✗	✓
	Outbound TLS termination (TLS forward proxy)	✗	✗	✓
	Intrusion Detection and Prevention Service (IDPS)	✗	✗	✓

Figure 8.32 – Azure Firewall SKU comparison

Understanding the filtering capabilities of Azure Firewall

The primary and most relevant application of a firewall is to regulate network traffic by blocking unauthorized access, malicious attacks, and other security risks. Azure Firewall provides various features for filtering network traffic, such as **Network-level filtering**, **Fully Qualified Domain Name (FQDN) filtering**, **URL filtering**, **Web categorization filtering**, and **Threat intelligence-based filtering**. This section will delve into each of these to provide a detailed understanding of their functionalities. We will also describe the address translation capability of Azure Firewall, which, although not a direct filtering feature, is a fundamental feature that holds significant importance for both the exam and practical implementation. Let's get started!

Network-level filtering can be used to allow or deny **outgoing** network connections based on the five tuples of the *source IP address*, *destination IP address*, *source port*, *destination port*, and *protocol*. For example, we can use this feature to allow access to network traffic with a source IP of 10.10.1.4 to the internet on TCP port 443, while blocking access to the same IP address on TCP port 80. This is a basic form of network filtering that does not include any in-depth packet inspection. We can define the network filtering rules using four protocol types (**TCP**, **UDP**, **ICMP**, and **Any**), and the stateful nature of the firewall means that only outgoing rules need to be defined as return traffic will automatically be approved.

To simplify the definition of rules for network filtering, we can specify *user-defined groups of IP addresses* (with **IP Group**) or *Microsoft-managed groups of IP addresses* (with **Service Tag**) for well-known services such as Microsoft and Azure services, as shown in *Figure 8.33*. This feature is supported by all firewall tiers.

Figure 8.33 – Using Service Tag or IP Group to simplify network filtering rule definitions

> **Note**
>
> A user-defined IP group can contain a maximum of 5,000 individual IP addresses or IP prefixes per each IP group.

Fully Qualified Domain Name (FQDN) filtering is simple URL filtering without TLS termination or deep packet inspection. For example, this feature can be used to allow access to `github.com` while denying access to `gambling.com`.

FQDN filtering can be configured at the *network level* or the *application level*. If configured at the *network level*, it works with DNS resolution to allow outbound FQDN filtering for any TCP/UDP protocol (including NTP, SSH, RDP, and more). However, this approach is easy to bypass by initiating requests using IP addresses, which do not require DNS resolution.

If configured at the *application level*, it uses the information in the HTTP header to allow or block **outgoing** web traffic (HTTP/HTTPS) or Azure SQL traffic. Application-level FQDN filtering rules can be defined with simple domain names such as `microsoft.com` or wildcards such as `*.microsoft.com`. This feature is supported by all firewall tiers.

> **FQDN filtering and Azure SQL Proxy mode**
>
> If application-level FQDN filtering is used to filter SQL connections to an Azure SQL database, then the database needs to be configured in Proxy mode. Further conversations about Azure SQL Proxy mode go beyond the scope of this book, but you can read more about it here: `https://learn.microsoft.com/en-us/azure/azure-sql/database/connectivity-architecture?view=azuresql#connection-policy`.

To allow or block access to a group of FQDNs used by well-known services, we can use the **FQDN Tag** option. This capability simplifies the process of allowing or blocking network traffic to well-known services such as Windows Update, Windows Diagnostics, and Azure Backup (see *Figure 8.34*).

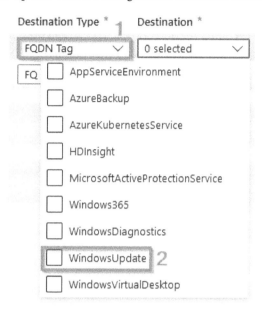

Figure 8.34 – Using an FQDN tag to simplify the FQDN filtering rule implementation

For example, instead of manually defining and maintaining the domain names linked to Windows Update, we can use the **WindowsUpdate** FQDN tag within our application rule, as shown in *Figure 8.34*. Microsoft maintains and updates the FQDN tags as needed.

URL filtering expands the FQDN filtering of Azure Firewall to evaluate entire URL paths, rather than just domain names. For example, URL filtering can be used to block a single URL such as `www.website.com/path_a/path_b`, rather than blocking the entire domain name, `www.website.com`. This feature is only available with the **Premium** SKU.

URL filtering can be applied to both HTTP and HTTPS traffic. When examining HTTPS traffic on a firewall with TLS inspection configured, the firewall can decrypt the traffic and extract the targeted URL for validation purposes. If you are unsure about what TLS inspection is, don't worry – we will discuss it later in this chapter.

Web categorization filtering can be used to allow or block **outgoing** web traffic (HTTP/HTTPS) based on website categories, such as social media and gambling sites. At the time of writing, Azure Firewall supports 64 categories, organized into 6 groups: *Liability, High-Bandwidth, Business Use, Productivity Loss, General Surfing*, and *Uncategorized*. Both the **Standard** and **Premium** firewall tiers support this feature, with the **Premium** SKU offering more accurate categorization. The **Standard** firewall matches the category to the FQDN, while the **Premium** version takes a more detailed approach by examining the entire URL path. For example, when an HTTPS request for www.google.com/news is intercepted, the **Standard** firewall will categorize it as a *search engine* based solely on the FQDN, while the **Premium** firewall will categorize it as *news*, considering the full URL.

Threat intelligence-based filtering can be activated to alert and block traffic from/to known malicious IP addresses, FQDNs, and URLs. The IP addresses, domains, and URLs come from the Microsoft Threat Intelligence feed powered by the Intelligent Security Graph.

By default, threat intelligence-based filtering is enabled in *alert mode*, but it can be changed to *alert and deny mode* or even *disabled* (refer to *Figure 8.35*). We can also create allowlists to exclude IP addresses and FQDNs from threat intelligence filtering (see *Figure 8.36*). This feature is supported by both the **Standard** and **Premium** firewall tiers.

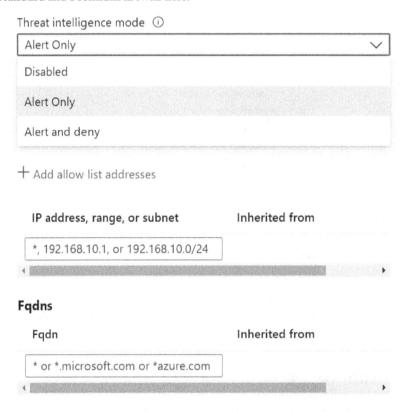

Figure 8.35 – Threat intelligence filtering configuration

Network Address Translation (SNAT + DNAT) is not a direct filtering capability but is a core functionality that is important to know for the exam and the real world. Azure Firewall requires at least one public static IP address to be configured but we can associate up to 250 public IP addresses with the firewall! This IP address (or set of addresses) acts as the external connection point for traffic entering and leaving the firewall.

By default, all outbound network traffic routed through Azure Firewall will be translated to one of the firewall's public IP addresses, except for traffic destined for private RFC 1918 IP addresses such as `10.0.0.0/8`, `172.16.0.0/12`, or `192.168.0.0/16`. This is known as **Source Network Address Translation (SNAT)**. This default behavior of SNAT can be altered in several ways. We can choose to always perform SNAT, never perform it, or exclude a specific list of IP addresses from SNAT (see *Figure 8.36*). It is important to note that these modifications only affect traffic processed through network-level filtering, not application-level filtering.

Figure 8.36 – SNAT configuration

Inbound internet traffic can also be directed to the firewall's public IP addresses and translated to the private IP addresses of resources within our virtual networks. This is known as **Destination Network Address Translation (DNAT)**. Both SNAT and DNAT are supported by all firewall tiers.

Understanding the reliability and performance capabilities of Azure Firewall

In addition to its filtering capabilities, Azure Firewall also comes equipped with some built-in features that facilitate high availability, scalability, and performance. Let's take a brief look at these capabilities.

Built-in high availability and auto-scaling: As mentioned earlier, Azure Firewall is a managed service with built-in high availability and auto-scaling. It offers an SLA of 99.95% availability. When the service is deployed, a scale set unit with a few virtual machine nodes is created. The number of the node expands when the average throughput or CPU utilization reaches 60%. Conversely, when the average throughput or CPU utilization drops below 20%, the number of nodes is gradually reduced. The scaling process can take five to seven minutes, so ensure you factor this in when performing tests.

Availability zones support: For even greater availability, Azure Firewall can be set up to cover multiple **Availability Zones (AZs)** during deployment (as shown in *Figure 8.37*). This configuration results in an increased availability SLA of 99.99% uptime. If we choose to deploy the firewall in a single AZ, the availability SLA remains at 99.95%.

Figure 8.37 – AZ configuration

While deploying the firewall in multiple AZs doesn't incur any additional cost, there are expenses related to inbound and outbound data transfers associated with AZs that we need to factor in.

Performance: In terms of performance, the size of the virtual machine utilized in the backend affects the firewall's performance. The **Premium** SKU uses a more powerful virtual machine compared to the **Standard** and **Basic** tiers, resulting in better performance.

The **Standard** Azure Firewall can handle up to 1.5 Gbps for a single TCP connection and an aggregate throughput of 30 Gbps across multiple connections. On the other hand, the **Premium** firewall can support a maximum of 9 Gbps for a single TCP connection and an aggregate throughput of 100 Gbps across multiple connections (see *Figure 8.38*).

The firewall's performance can also be affected by the security features that we enable. For example, implementing the IDPS feature in deny mode or implementing TLS inspection will increase the CPU consumption of the backend virtual machines, thereby reducing its maximum throughput. For this reason, Microsoft recommends replicating your production environment as accurately as possible and conducting performance tests to ensure that the firewall meets your throughput requirements. *Figure 8.38* provides a summary of the performance capabilities of Azure Firewall in various configuration modes.

Firewall use case	Bandwidth
Standard Firewall Max bandwidth for a single TCP connection	1.5 Gbps
Standard Firewall Max aggregated bandwidth (TCP/UDP/HTTP)	30 Gbps
Premium Firewall Max bandwidth for a single TCP connection	9 Gbps
Premium Firewall Max aggregated bandwidth (TCP/UDP/HTTP) with no TLS inspection or IDPS	100 Gbps
Premium Firewall Max aggregated bandwidth (HTTP) with TLS inspection	100 Gbps
Premium Firewall Max aggregated bandwidth (TCP/UDP/HTTP) with both TLS inspection and IDPS (alert mode)	100 Gbps
Premium Firewall Max aggregated bandwidth (TCP/UDP/HTTP) with both TLS inspection and IDPS (deny mode)	10 Gbps

Figure 8.38 – Azure Firewall use cases and bandwidth

> **Basic SKU reliability and performance**
>
> The **Basic** Firewall SKU has a fixed scale unit of two virtual machines with a maximum aggregated throughput of 250 Mbps.

Understanding the advanced threat protection capabilities of Azure Firewall

Outbound TLS inspection: The **TLS** protocol is a widely used cryptography method that provides privacy, integrity, and authenticity between communicating applications using certificates. It operates in the application layer and is commonly used to encrypt HTTP communications.

However, attackers can conceal malicious or prohibited traffic in encrypted TLS traffic, making it difficult for Azure Firewall to detect such traffic without TLS inspection. When TLS is used for end-to-end communication, Azure Firewall can only filter the traffic and cannot inspect it.

To enable TLS inspection, the certificate that Azure Firewall will use to sign requests must be stored in Azure Key Vault and referenced in the configuration (as shown in *Figure 8.39*). The CA certificate must also be installed on internal client systems as a trusted CA certificate to prevent being flagged as a man-in-the-middle attack.

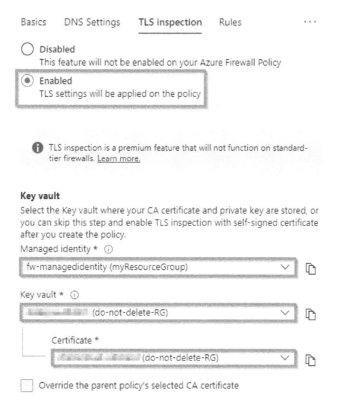

Figure 8.39 – TLS inspection configuration

Please note that this feature is only available in the **Premium** offering. Azure Firewall's TLS inspection can be implemented for outbound web traffic to protect against malicious traffic sent from internal clients to the internet or other internal servers. At present, Azure Firewall does not support inbound TLS inspection, but implementing a **WAF** in services such as Application Gateway can provide this protection. This topic will be covered in more detail later in this chapter.

IDPS can be activated to alert and block traffic from/to known malicious IP addresses, FQDNs, and URLs. The IP addresses, domains, and URLs come from the Microsoft Threat Intelligence feed powered by the Intelligent Security Graph.

By default, threat intelligence-based filtering is enabled in *alert mode*, but it can be changed to *alert and deny mode* or even *disabled* (refer to *Figure 8.40*). We can also create allowlists to exclude IP addresses and FQDNs from threat intelligence filtering (see *Figure 8.40*). This feature is supported by both the **Standard** and **Premium** firewall tiers.

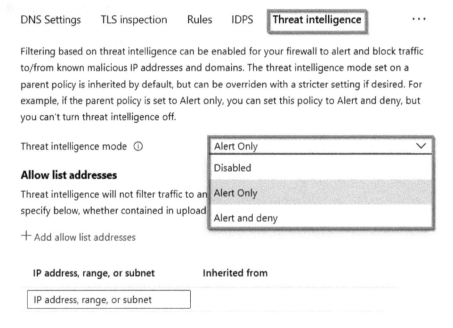

Figure 8.40 – Threat intelligence configuration

Understanding the enterprise integration capabilities of Azure Firewall

DNS Proxy + Custom DNS: Azure Firewall can be configured to function as a DNS proxy (an intermediary for DNS requests between the clients and the DNS server). This is marked as **1** in *Figure 8.41*. This is mainly useful when defining FQDN filtering rules at the network level (we discussed earlier that FQDN filtering can be applied at the network level or the application level). Enabling this feature will allow the associated Azure Firewall to listen on port 53 and forward DNS requests to the DNS server specified.

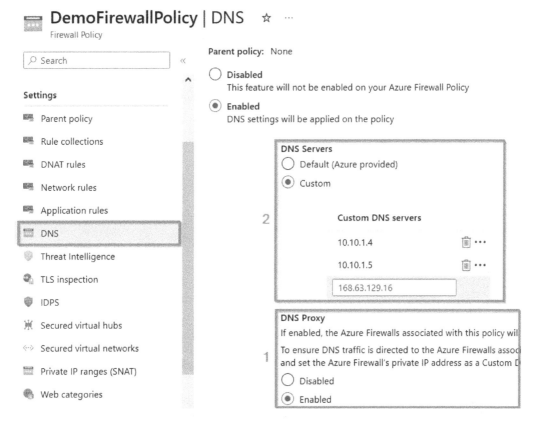

Figure 8.41 – Configuring a DNS proxy and custom DNS servers in a firewall policy

For consistent DNS resolution, it is recommended to use the firewall as the resolver if FQDNs are used in network rules. Avoid configuring the clients to use a different DNS server for primary resolution and Azure Firewall for secondary resolution as it can result in unpredictable scenarios that may be difficult to troubleshoot.

By default, Azure Firewall will forward DNS requests to the default Azure-provided name resolution service (168.63.129.16), as we thoroughly covered in *Chapter 2* of this book. However, it is possible to specify a custom DNS server for the firewall to use for name resolution, which will override the default setting (marked as **2** in *Figure 8.41*).

Understanding some considerations for an Azure Firewall deployment

To implement the Firewall, two components are required: a **Firewall** service, which is deployed within a virtual network or a virtual WAN hub, and a **Firewall Policy** option (as shown in *Figure 8.42*).

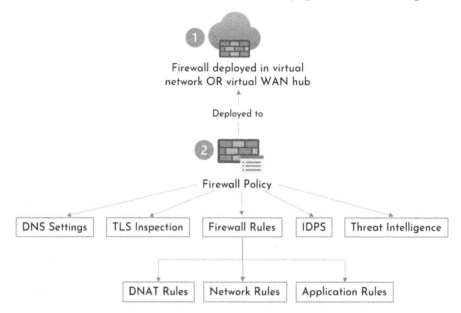

Figure 8.42 – Components of an Azure Firewall implementation

The **Firewall** component is responsible for processing traffic and can be deployed in either a customer-managed hub virtual network or a virtual WAN hub. It is required to be deployed in a dedicated subnet named **AzureFirewallSubnet**, with a minimum subnet size of **/26** to accommodate scaling. This provides the Firewall service with 59 usable IP addresses to assign to virtual machine instances as it scales out.

The **Firewall Policy** option is used to configure settings for the firewall, such as DNS settings, TLS inspection, firewall rules, IDPS, and threat intelligence, as shown in *Figure 8.43*.

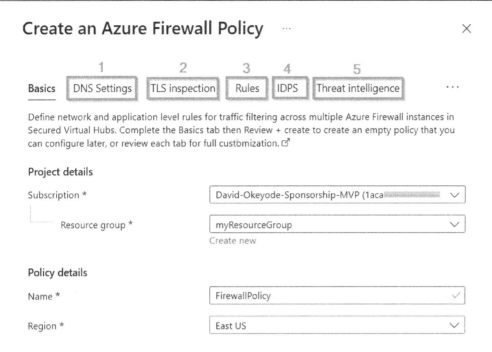

Figure 8.43 – Configuration and settings in Firewall Policy

A firewall policy can be **Basic**, **Standard**, or **Premium** (see *Figure 8.44*). The available firewall policies are tailored to specific firewall tiers. A **Basic** firewall policy can only be used to set up features for a **Basic** firewall, a **Standard** firewall policy is limited to a **Standard** firewall, and a **Premium** firewall policy is designed for a **Premium** firewall and its applicable features. For example, a **Standard** firewall policy cannot be used to configure premium features such as IDPS, TLS inspection, and URL filtering.

Policy tier   ◯ Basic (preview)

                                           ◯ Standard

                                           ⦿ Premium

Figure 8.44 – Firewall policy tiers

> **Note**
> There is a legacy way to define the firewall policy for a **Standard** firewall using **Classic** rules. It is not recommended to use this option anymore. The new Firewall Policy method should be used.

In Firewall Policy, firewall rules can consist of dnat rules, network rules, and application rules.

Application rules can be used to specify security policies at the application level (Layer 7). This includes policies such as FQDN filtering at the application level, web categorization filtering, threat intelligence filtering, TLS inspection, and IDPS.

Network rules can be used to allow or deny connections at the network level (Layer 3 and Layer 4). This includes basic network filtering and FQDN filtering at the network level (which relies on a DNS proxy being configured).

DNAT rules can be used to specify rules to translate inbound network requests for delivery to internal services.

Hands-on exercise 3 – deploying Azure Firewall into a VNet and a Virtual WAN Hub

Here are the tasks that we will complete in this exercise:

- **Task 1**: Deploy an Azure Firewall test environment template with the Azure CLI
- **Task 2**: Review the firewall service and the firewall policy
- **Task 3**: Test connectivity through the firewall

Task 1 – deploying an Azure Firewall test environment template with the Azure CLI

The first thing that we will do is deploy a test environment with Azure Firewall and test resources:

1. Open a web browser and go to the Azure Cloud Shell page – `https://shell.azure.com`. If you are prompted, log in with your Azure admin credentials. Check that the environment dropdown from the left-hand side of the Shell window says **Bash**.

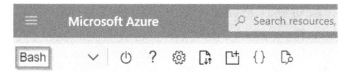

Figure 8.45 – Opening CloudShell (Bash)

2. Run the following command to deploy a template with an Azure Firewall test environment. Replace `<Complex_Password>` with a password, which you will need to access the test virtual machine post-deployment:

```
az deployment group create --name AzFW-Deployment-With-Policy
--resource-group "CharisTechRG-C8" --template-uri "https://
raw.githubusercontent.com/Azure/azure-quickstart-templates/
master/quickstarts/microsoft.network/azurefirewall-premium/
azuredeploy.json" --parameters remoteAccessUsername=azureuser
remoteAccessPassword=<Complex_Password>
```

3. The template will create the following resources:

   - A virtual network (`10.0.0.0/16`) with 3 subnets:

     - **WorkerSubnet** (`10.0.10.0/24`)

     - **AzureBastionSubnet** (`10.0.20.0/24`)

     - **AzureFirewallSubnet** (`10.0.100.0/24`)

   - A private Windows VM in **WorkerSubnet** named **WorkerVM**

   - A Bastion host in the virtual network

   - A route table attached to **WorkerSubnet** with a user-defined route pointing `0.0.0.0/0` to **AzureFirewall**

   - A Key Vault resource:

     - An access policy that grants the managed identity permissions to get and list secrets

- A self-signed root CA stored in Key Vault

- An intermediate CA deployed on **WorkerVM**

- An **AzureFirewall** policy with the following rules:

  - An application rule that allows HTTPS traffic from any source to `*azure.com` and `*microsoft.com`

  - An application rule that allows HTTPS traffic from any source to the **Business** and **Web-based email** web categories

  - An application rule that denies HTTPS traffic to `azure.microsoft.com/en-us/community/events` and `azure.microsoft.com/en-us/community/events/*`

  - TLS inspection enabled

  - IDPS enabled

Task 2 – reviewing the firewall service and the firewall policy

In this task, we will review the firewall service and the firewall policy that was created:

1. On the Azure portal home page, in the search box, type `Firewall` and select **Firewalls** when it appears.

Figure 8.46 – Selecting the Firewalls service

2. In the **Firewalls** window, select **DemoFirewall**.

3. In the **Overview** section, review the values of **Firewall SKU**, **Firewall subnet**, and **Firewall private IP**. Click on **DemoFirewallPolicy** to review the settings in the firewall policy that is deployed for this firewall.

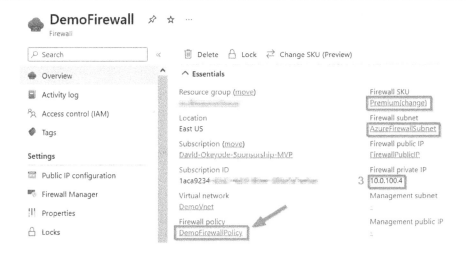

Figure 8.47 – Reviewing the firewall settings and clicking on the firewall policy

4. In the **DemoFirewallPolicy** window, click on **Application rules** to review the existing application rules. You will see five rules that belong to two rule collection groups here. Select **AllowAzure**, then click on **Edit**.

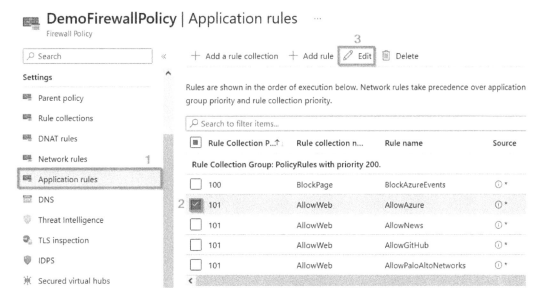

Figure 8.48 – Editing an existing application rule

5. In the **Edit application rules** window, notice that FQDN filtering and **TLS inspection** are configured. Click on **Cancel** without making any changes.

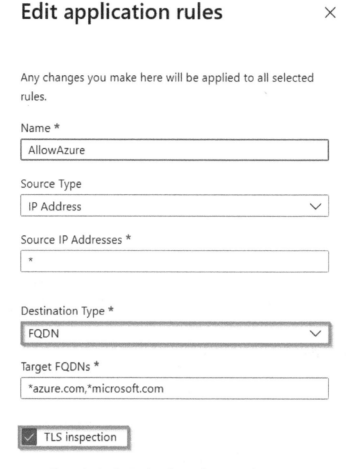

Figure 8.49 – Reviewing the application rule settings

6. Review other configurations such as **Threat Intelligence**, **TLS inspection**, **IDPS**, and **Private IP ranges (SNAT)** in the firewall policy without making any changes.

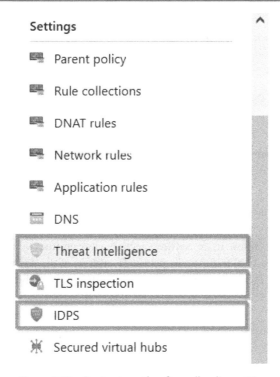

Figure 8.50 – Reviewing other firewall policy settings

7. On the Azure portal home page, in the search box, type `WorkerRoute` and select the **WorkerRoute** route table when it appears.

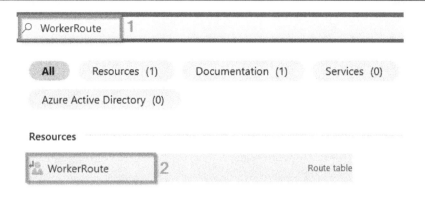

Figure 8.51 – Selecting the WorkerRoute route table

8. In the **WorkerRoute** window, in the **Settings** section, click on **Routes**. You should see a single route entry that forwards all traffic to the private IP address of the Azure Firewall service that you reviewed earlier. This route table is associated with **WorkerSubnet**, where **WorkerVM** is deployed.

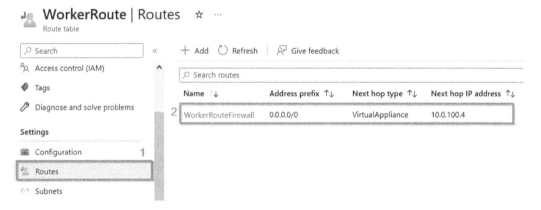

Figure 8.52 – Review the route table associated with the backend subnet

Task 3 – testing connectivity through the firewall

In the final task in this exercise, we will validate the firewall policy from **WorkerVM**:

1. On the Azure portal home page, in the search box, type WorkerVM and select the **WorkerVM** virtual machine when it appears.

Figure 8.53 – Selecting the WorkerVM virtual machine

2. In the **WorkerVM** window, click on **Connect**, then click on **Bastion**.

Figure 8.54 – Selecting the option to connect to the VM using Bastion

3. In the **WorkerVM | Bastion** window, configure the following and click on **Connect**:

    *   **Username**: azureuser
    *   **Authentication Type: Password**
    *   **Password**: Enter the password that you specified during the template deployment
    *   **Open in new browser tab**: Selected
    *   Click **Connect**

If prompted, enable the pop-up window for the connection to be successful.

Azure Bastion protects your virtual machines by providing lightweight, browser-based connectivity without the need to expose them through public IP addresses. Deploying will automatically create a Bastion host on a subnet in your virtual network. Learn more ☐

Using Bastion: **DemoBastion**, Provisioning State: **Succeeded**

Please enter username and password to your virtual machine to connect using Bastion.

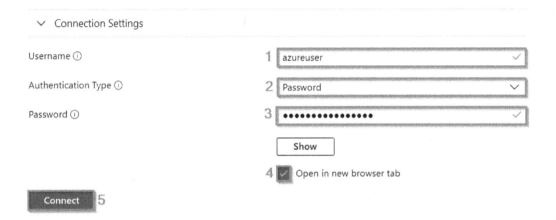

Figure 8.55 – Configure the VM credentials and initiate the connection to the VM

4. In **WorkerVM**, open a web browser and test the following URLs. You should receive the results specified here:

- `https://www.microsoft.com` – Allowed

- `https://www.azure.com` – Allowed

- `https://azure.microsoft.com/en-us/community/events` – Denied

Action: Deny. Reason: Policy: DemoFirewallPolicy. Rule Collection Group: PolicyRules. Rule Collection: BlockPage. Rule: BlockAzureEvents.

Figure 8.56 – Testing the firewall policies

Well done! You have successfully implemented and verified an Azure Firewall service in a virtual network. In the upcoming section, we will discuss another important network perimeter security feature in Azure – WAF.

Implementing a WAF in Azure

Web and API applications are popular workload types to host in Azure virtual networks. They are also frequently targeted by malicious attacks exploiting well-known vulnerabilities such as SQL injection, cross-site scripting, and code injection. To complement secure coding practices for web application development, a **WAF** can be deployed at the network perimeter as an additional layer of protection against these types of exploits and vulnerabilities. Azure WAF is not a standalone service in Azure. Instead, it is a capability that can be integrated into two Azure traffic management services – Azure Application Gateway and Azure Front Door.

Azure Application Gateway is a regional-level application delivery service that can be deployed with a WAF to protect public-facing or internal workloads in an Azure virtual network. It can be deployed into a designated subnet within our Azure virtual networks, and we can apply a WAF policy to it (see *Figure 8.57*). We will cover this service in greater detail in the next chapter of this book.

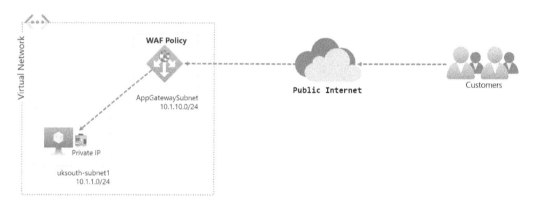

Figure 8.57 – Azure Application Gateway architecture

Azure Front Door is a global edge application delivery service that can integrate with WAF to protect public-facing web services at the edge. It uses the anycast protocol with split TCP and Microsoft's global network to improve global connectivity and performance for our web applications (see *Figure 8.58*). This service will be discussed further in the next chapter of this book.

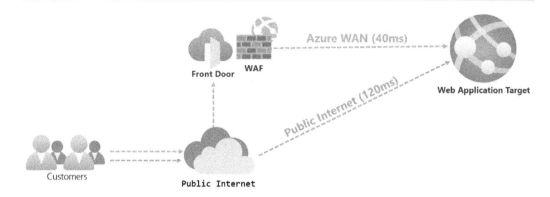

Figure 8.58 – Azure Front Door WAF

Figure 8.58 shows how Front Door receives client requests through a point of presence that is close to end users and uses the Microsoft high throughput backbone network to accelerate delivery to the backend application instead of the traffic being routed entirely over the public internet. Azure WAF, when integrated with Front Door, stops application DoS and targeted application attacks at the Azure network edge.

Understanding managed rule sets and WAF policies

To identify potential web application attacks, Azure WAF compares received requests to a set of rules (rule sets) designed to identify attack patterns. Rule sets can either be **managed rule sets** or **custom rule sets**. Managed rule sets are authored and maintained by Microsoft while custom rule sets are authored and maintained by the customer. When both are present, custom rule sets are always processed before managed rule sets.

Rule sets (both managed and custom) are configured within a WAF policy resource and applied to either a Front Door or an Application Gateway instance (see *Figure 8.59*). A WAF policy is a standalone resource type that is managed independently in Azure. We can create up to 100 WAF policies in an Azure subscription.

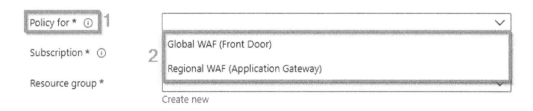

Figure 8.59 – Applying a WAF policy

Azure WAF supports the following managed rule sets (see *Figure 8.60*):

- The **Open Web Application Security Project (OWASP) Core Rule Set (CRS)**, which is based on the OWASP ModSecurity CRS. This managed rule set can only be applied to an Azure Application Gateway (regional WAF) instance. It is not supported for Azure Front Door.

  At present, there are three versions of this rule set available: 3.2, 3.1, and 3.0. Newer versions are typically released by OWASP to address new types of attacks or improve the accuracy of existing rules. Upgrading to the latest CRS version can help ensure that our web applications are protected against the latest threats.

  The latest version of this rule set, version 3.2, uses a newer WAF engine that has improved performance and scalability.

- The **Microsoft_DefaultRuleSet (DRS)**, which includes rules authored by the Microsoft Threat Intelligence team in addition to the rules based on the OWASP ModSecurity CRS. This managed rule set can only be applied to an Azure Front Door Premium instance and is not supported for the Front Door Standard tier or Application Gateway instances.

  There are currently three versions of this rule set available: 2.1, 2.0, and 1.1. The versions are updated as new updates are added to the OWASP core rule set. For instance, **Microsoft_DefaultRuleSet_2.1** is based on the OWASP CRS 3.3.2, while **Microsoft_DefaultRuleSet_2.0** is based on the OWASP CRS 3.2.

- The **Microsoft_BotManagerRuleSet (BRS)**, which includes rules authored by the Microsoft Threat Intelligence team to provide security against bots engaged in scraping, crawling, and vulnerability scanning. This managed rule set can be applied to an Azure Front Door Premium instance and an Application Gateway instance, but it is not supported for the Front Door Standard tier.

  There are two versions of the rule set currently available: version 0.1 and version 1.0. The previous version, 0.1, can only detect known bad bots based on IP reputation. In contrast, the current version, 1.0, can detect bad bots, good bots, and unknown bots based on IP reputation, user-agent headers, and other indicators that form signatures managed by Microsoft.

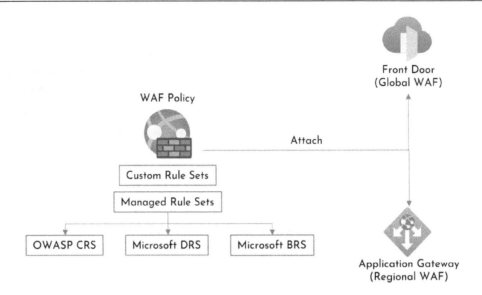

Figure 8.60 – Azure WAF policies and rule sets

> **Note**
>
> Bots can be classified as bad, good, or unknown. Bad bots are those that come from malicious IP addresses or have falsified identities. These malicious IP addresses are sourced from the Microsoft Threat Intelligence feed, which is updated hourly. On the other hand, good bots are validated search engines.
>
> Unknown bots comprise various bot groups that have identified themselves as bots, such as market analyzers, feed fetchers, and data collection agents. The classification of unknown bots is based on their published user agents without additional validation.

Understanding custom rule sets

Azure WAF provides the ability to create custom rules to address unique application requirements. These rules can be based on a variety of variables such as source IPs, geolocation, request URIs, request headers, request body, post arguments, and more (see *Figure 8.61*). We can configure up to 100 custom rules in a WAF policy.

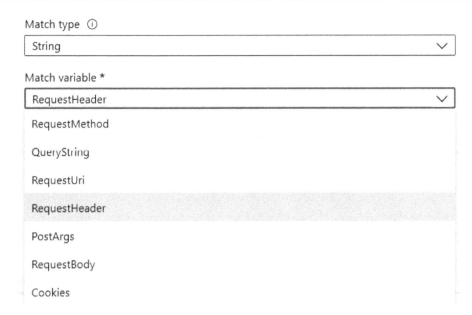

Figure 8.61 – Some custom rule match variables

A common use case for custom rule sets is to enable filtering or blocking of traffic from specific geographic locations, also known as geo-filtering (see *Figure 8.62*). This is useful for complying with regulations that mandate blocking requests from certain regions.

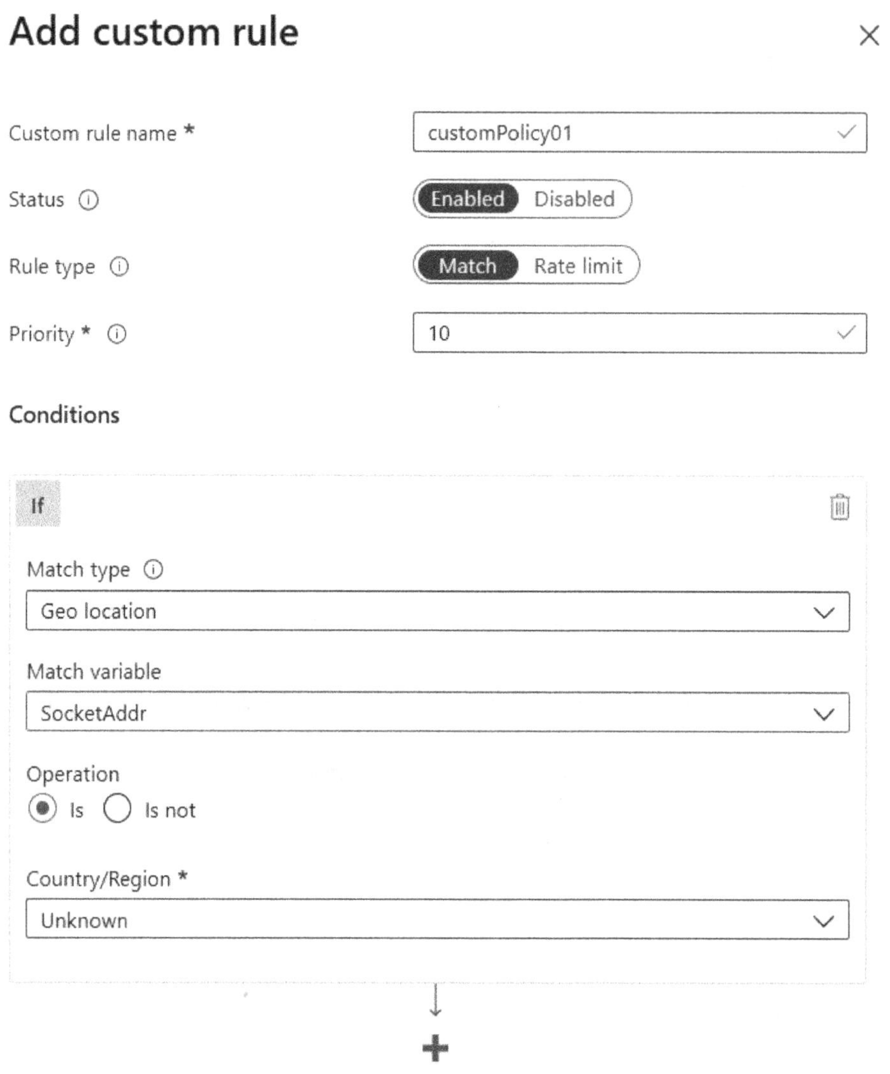

Add custom rule   ✕

Custom rule name *	customPolicy01	✓

Status ⓘ   (**Enabled** Disabled)

Rule type ⓘ   (**Match** Rate limit)

Priority * ⓘ   10   ✓

Conditions

If   🗑

Match type ⓘ

Geo location   ⌄

Match variable

SocketAddr   ⌄

Operation

◉ Is   ◯ Is not

Country/Region *

Unknown   ⌄

↓

╋

Figure 8.62 – Example custom rule

Another common use case for custom rules is to apply rate limiting to detect and block abnormally high levels of traffic from any IP address. This can be an effective way to mitigate certain types of DoS attacks or protect against clients that may have been mistakenly misconfigured to send large volumes of requests in a short time period.

If you'd like to see some WAF custom rule examples, check out these documents: `https://learn. microsoft.com/en-us/azure/web-application-firewall/ag/custom-waf-rules- overview` and `https://learn.microsoft.com/en-us/azure/web-application- firewall/afds/waf-front-door-custom-rules`.

Understanding WAF policy modes and rule actions

When an incoming request matches the defined rules in a rule set (managed and custom), the WAF engine takes an action based on two configurations – the **WAF policy mode** and **rule action**.

An Azure WAF policy supports two modes – **Detection** and **Prevention** (see *Figure 8.63*):

Instance details

Policy name * ⓘ	charistechWafPolicy ✓
Resource group region ⓘ	East US
Policy state ⓘ	☑
Policy mode ⓘ	⦿ Prevention ◯ Detection

Figure 8.63 – Azure WAF policy modes

In the **Detection** mode, the WAF engine logs incoming requests that match the defined rules instead of blocking them. The request details are logged to the diagnostic logs, which can be forwarded to a service such as the Azure Log Analytics workspace for further analysis. In this mode, individual rule actions are ignored. For example, if the WAF policy mode is set to **Detection** and an individual rule action is set to **Block**, that action will be ignored if that rule is triggered.

This mode is particularly useful for monitoring traffic and identifying potential attacks without disrupting legitimate traffic. It is recommended to initially set the WAF policy to **Detection** mode for a new application and fine-tune the policies based on feedback from the logs over several weeks to ensure that legitimate traffic is not blocked.

In the **Prevention** mode, the WAF engine applies the rule action configuration whenever a rule is triggered. The available actions are: **Allow**, **Block**, **Log**, and **Redirect**. This can be customized on a rule-by-rule basis.

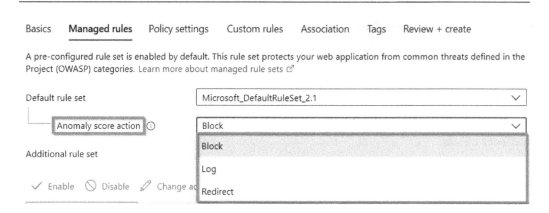

Figure 8.64 – WAF policy | Anomaly score action

The OWASP CRS versions 3.2 and above, as well as the Microsoft_DefaultRuleSet versions 2.0 and above, use an anomaly score to determine the appropriate action to take (as shown in *Figure 8.64*). When a request is received, the WAF engine analyzes the request and generates an anomaly score for each rule that has been matched, based on the scoring system shown in *Figure 8.65*.

Rule Severity	Anomaly Score
Critical	5
Error	4
Warning	3
Notice	2

Figure 8.65 – Azure WAF engine anomaly scoring

If the total anomaly score is below 5, the request is allowed to pass through to the web application. However, if the score is equal to or exceeds 5, the request is regarded as a possible attack, and the designated action (**Block**, **Log**, or **Redirect**) is applied, as demonstrated in *Figure 8.66*. For instance, a single critical rule match is adequate for the WAF engine to apply the configured action since the anomaly score is 5. A single warning rule match only raises the anomaly score by 3 and will not apply the configured action.

By default, a blocked request will return an HTTP 403 status code to the requesting client and write a **Blocked** action to the diagnostic logs. The response code and message can be customized as shown in *Figure 8.66* (marked as **1** and **2**). The following status codes are supported: HTTP 200 OK, HTTP 403 Forbidden, HTTP 405 Method not allowed, HTTP 406 Not acceptable, and HTTP 429 Too many requests.

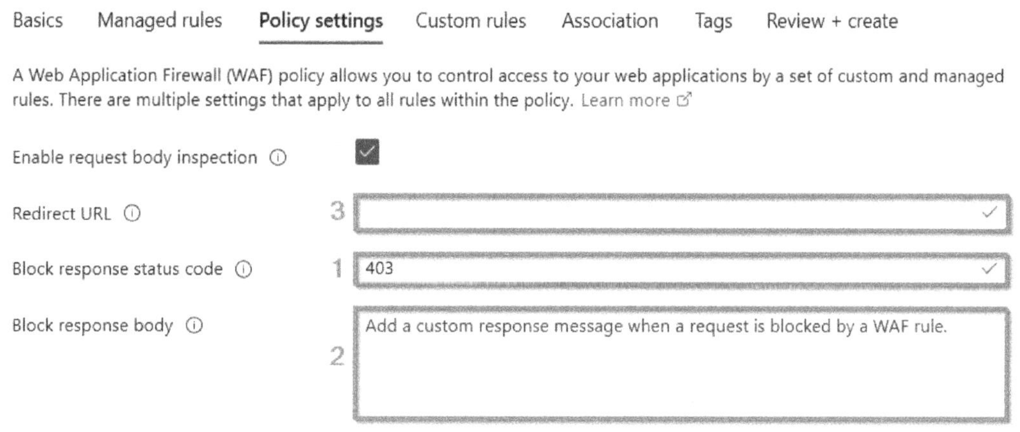

Basics   Managed rules   **Policy settings**   Custom rules   Association   Tags   Review + create

A Web Application Firewall (WAF) policy allows you to control access to your web applications by a set of custom and managed rules. There are multiple settings that apply to all rules within the policy. Learn more ⧉

Enable request body inspection ⓘ

Redirect URL ⓘ   3

Block response status code ⓘ   1   403

Block response body ⓘ   Add a custom response message when a request is blocked by a WAF rule.
2

Figure 8.66 – Azure WAF policy settings

For the redirect action, we can specify a **Redirect URL** option to send requests to when a matching rule is triggered (marked as **3** in *Figure 8.66*).

Understanding WAF policy associations

Once a WAF policy is set up with rule sets, it is important to associate it with one or more web applications for protection.

In the case of a WAF policy configured for Application Gateway (regional WAF), there are three levels at which it can be associated: the Application Gateway level, the individual listener level, or the route path level (see *Figure 8.67*). Here's a brief overview of each option:

- **The gateway** – This applies the WAF security policies to all web applications that are exposed on the Application Gateway resource. This is useful when we want to apply a default set of security policies to all web applications but may not be sufficient for applications with more complex security requirements.

- **An HTTP listener** – This applies the WAF security policies to a single web application on the gateway. This is useful when there are specific security requirements or compliance regulations that we want to apply to a particular application.

- **A route path** – This applies the WAF security policies to a single path of a web application! This is useful when we need to apply a set of custom security policies that are tailored to the specific requirements of a particular path of a web application. This is the most granular association that we can get.

Basics   Managed rules   Policy settings   Custom rules | Association | Tags   Review + create

Associated application gateways

Associate this WAF policy with a specific application gateway, listener, or route path. A WAF policy can be associate
policy associations with the selected application gateway. Learn more. ☐

➕ Add association   🗑 Remove association

Application Gateway	ociation type == **(blank)**	Application Gateway == **(blank)**	Resou
HTTP Listener	↑↓ **Application Gateway**	↑↓ Resou
Route Path		

Figure 8.67 – Associate an Application Gateway instance with a WAF policy

When configuring a WAF policy for Front Door (global WAF), the policy can only be associated at the **Domain** level (as shown in *Figure 8.68*). This is similar to applying the WAF security policies at the HTTP listener level for an Application Gateway instance. To meet specific security requirements, the policy can be associated with a single domain in a profile. Alternatively, to fulfill the baseline security requirements, the policy can be associated with multiple domains in a profile or all domains in a profile.

Associate a Front door profile   ✕

Front door profiles can be added and removed after a WAF policy is created.

Front door profile * ⓘ

contosoafd   ⌄

Domain

Multiple domains can be associated with a front door profile. Select those you want your WAF policy to apply to.

Domain *

contosoafd1   ⌄

Add   Cancel

Figure 8.68 – Associate a Front Door profile with a WAF policy

Understanding WAF policy limitations

Knowing the limits of any technology is important for proper planning, implementation, and usage. In this section, we will cover two critical limitations of the Azure WAF – the supported content types and the maximum HTTP body size that can be inspected.

The WAF engine can inspect the following content types:

- **Application Gateway Managed rules**: `application/json`; `application/xml`; `application/x-www-form-urlencoded`; and `multipart/form-data`

- **Application Gateway Custom rules**: `application/json`; `application/xml`; `text/xml`; `application/soap+xml`; `application/x-www-form-urlencoded`; and `multipart/form-data`

- **Front Door Managed rules (DRS 2.0 and above)**: `application/json`; `application/xml`; `application/x-www-form-urlencoded`; and `multipart/form-data`

- **Front Door Custom rules**: `application/x-www-form-urlencoded`

Although WebSockets are supported by Application Gateway, the WAF does not inspect traffic after the initial handshake between the client and server. Currently, WebSockets are not supported by Front Door.

By default, request body inspection is enabled and the latest version of the OWASP CRS (3.2) can inspect up to a 2-MB request body size (with a default of 128 KB). If the request includes a file upload, it can be inspected up to a maximum size of 4 GB (with a default of 100 MB). Only requests with **Content-Type** set to `multipart/form-data` are eligible for file uploads, and the content must be a part of a multipart form with a filename header to be considered a file upload. A Front Door WAF supports inspecting a maximum of 128 KB of the HTTP request body size.

If the WAF policy is in **Prevention** mode, it logs and blocks requests exceeding the size limit, while in **Detection** mode, it inspects the body up to the limit and ignores the rest. Request body inspection can be disabled, which allows messages larger than 128 KB to be sent to WAF but means that the contents of the HTTP message's body are not evaluated for vulnerabilities. In such cases, WAF continues to enforce its rules on headers, cookies, and the URI.

Implementing central management with Firewall Manager

In this chapter, we covered the application of network security configurations to safeguard the network perimeter. To protect virtual networks or public IP addresses from DDoS attacks, we can employ DDoS protection plans, deploy Azure Firewall in a virtual network or virtual WAN hub, and use Azure WAF policies on Application Gateway or Front Door instances. However, managing these security capabilities independently becomes ineffective when dealing with multiple Azure subscriptions and services spread across several regions.

This is where Azure Firewall Manager can help us. Firewall Manager provides centralized network security management across subscriptions and across regions. We can manage configuration and policies for Azure Firewall, Azure Application Gateway WAFs, Front Door WAFs, and DDoS protection plans from one place and deploy to networks and instances across subscriptions or regions. This significantly reduces the complexity of managing and deploying network perimeter security policies across multiple Azure subscriptions!

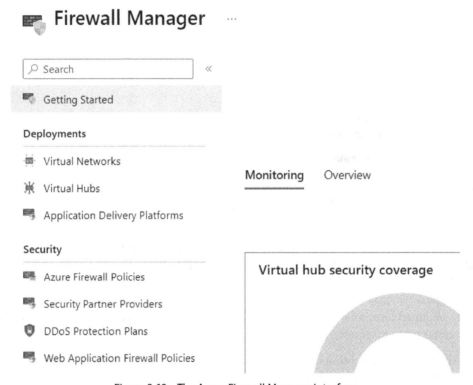

Figure 8.69 – The Azure Firewall Manager interface

Congratulations! You have made it to the end of this chapter.

Summary

In this chapter, we focused on securing the Azure virtual network perimeter using various methods. We covered the implementation of Azure DDoS Protection plans to prevent DDoS attacks, Azure Firewall to implement outbound traffic inspection, and a WAF to protect against common web application attacks. We also highlighted the importance of managing security capabilities across multiple Azure subscriptions and regions using Firewall Manager.

These insights align with important exam objectives and equip readers with the knowledge and skills needed to safeguard Azure virtual networks in the real world. In the next chapter, we will focus on network traffic management and load balancing in Azure. Looking forward to seeing you there!

Further reading

Refer to the following links to know more about the topics covered in this chapter:

- https://learn.microsoft.com/en-us/azure/ddos-protection/ddos-protection-overview
- https://learn.microsoft.com/en-us/azure/firewall/overview
- https://learn.microsoft.com/en-us/azure/web-application-firewall/afds/waf-front-door-drs
- https://learn.microsoft.com/en-us/azure/web-application-firewall/ag/waf-engine
- https://learn.microsoft.com/en-us/azure/firewall-manager/overview

Part 3: Design and Implement Traffic Management and Network Monitoring

This part comprises three pivotal chapters that focus on optimizing application delivery, enhancing platform service connectivity, and implementing robust network monitoring in the Azure environment. Throughout this part, we combine cutting-edge concepts with hands-on implementation, equipping you with the knowledge and practical skills needed to take your Azure networking expertise to the next level. Are you ready to fine-tune your application delivery, establish seamless platform service connectivity, and effectively monitor your Azure network? Let's embark on this enriching journey together! Let's get started!

This part comprises the following chapters:

- *Chapter 9, Design and Implement Application Delivery Services*
- *Chapter 10, Design and Implement Platform Service Connectivity*
- *Chapter 11, Monitoring Networks in Azure*

Designing and Implementing Application Delivery Services

In an increasingly connected world where applications and services are hosted on the cloud, load balancers are a critical component of any IT infrastructure. They ensure that traffic is distributed evenly among multiple service instances, thereby improving application performance, reliability, and scalability. Microsoft Azure provides a range of options to meet the diverse needs of its customers.

In this chapter, we will discuss the four main load-balancing services in Azure, look at things to consider when designing and implementing these services, and help you to understand how to select the best service for your application.

In this chapter, we will cover the following topics:

- Understanding Azure's load-balancing and application delivery services
- Designing and implementing an Azure Load Balancer service
- Designing and implementing an Azure Application Gateway service
- Designing and implementing an Azure Front Door service
- Designing and implementing an Azure Traffic Manager service
- Choosing an optimal load-balancing and application delivery solution

The topics are arranged to provide you with practical knowledge, hands-on implementation skills, and the required knowledge to succeed in the exam. Now, let's dive in and begin our journey!

Technical requirements

To follow along with the instructions in this chapter, you will need the following:

- A PC with an internet connection
- An Azure subscription

Understanding Azure's load-balancing and application delivery services

Application delivery and load balancing are two related but distinct concepts in the world of networking and web services. **Load balancing** refers to the distribution of incoming network traffic across multiple servers or resources in order to improve the overall performance, availability, and scalability of a service.

On the flip side, **application delivery** pertains to making software applications available to both internal users and external customers. It encompasses a wider range of functionalities beyond load balancing, including securing the application, optimizing application performance, and managing user authentication and access control.

Azure offers various services for load balancing and/or application delivery that we can leverage to distribute incoming network requests across application instances or handle application delivery functionalities. These services include Traffic Manager, Load Balancer, Front Door, and Application Gateway.

Understanding Azure load-balancing and application delivery services categories

Azure load-balancing services can be categorized based on their distribution approach (global or regional distribution) and traffic-handling capabilities (HTTP(S) or non-HTTP(S) traffic-handling capabilities).

When it comes to the global versus regional distribution categorization, global load-balancing/ application delivery services are designed to distribute traffic across resources in multiple Azure regions and even to resources in customer on-premises data centers (marked as *1* in *Figure 9.1*). On the other hand, regional load-balancing/application delivery services only distribute traffic to resources within a specific Azure region (marked as *2* in *Figure 9.1*):

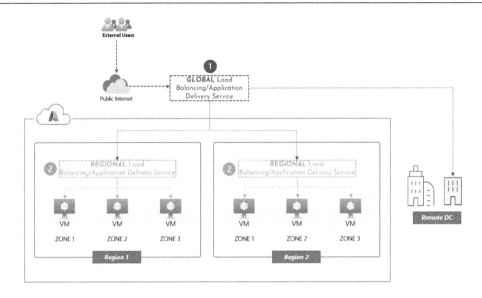

Figure 9.1 – Global and regional Azure load-balancing and app delivery services

In terms of traffic-handling capabilities, HTTP(S) load-balancing services operate as Layer 7 load balancers, accepting only HTTP(S) traffic. These services are optimized for web applications or other HTTP(S) endpoints and come with features such as **Secure Sockets Layer** (**SSL**) offload, **web application firewall** (**WAF**), path-based load balancing, and session affinity. On the other hand, non-HTTP/S load-balancing services can handle any protocol traffic, including non-HTTP(S) traffic, and are recommended for non-web workloads.

Figure 9.2 shows a list of Azure load-balancing/application delivery services in terms of these categories:

Azure Service	Supported Protocol	Global/Regional
Load Balancer	Any protocol including non-HTTP(S)	Regional or Global
Application Gateway	HTTP(S)	Regional
Front Door	HTTP(S)	Global
Traffic Manager	Any protocol including non-HTTP(S)	Global

Figure 9.2 – Azure load-balancing and app delivery services categorization

Let us dive deeper into these four services, beginning with Azure Load Balancer.

Designing and implementing an Azure Load Balancer service

Azure Load Balancer is a **pass-through network load balancer** that operates at Layer 4 of the **Open Systems Interconnection** (**OSI**) model. It can distribute network traffic for all **Transmission Control Protocol** (**TCP**) and **User Datagram Protocol** (**UDP**) protocols. Because it does not modify or analyze received traffic, it is the most performant load-balancing option in Azure.

> **What is a pass-through network load balancer?**
>
> A pass-through network load balancer is a type of load balancer that simply forwards traffic to backend services without modifying or analyzing the content. Unlike other types of load balancers, such as application load balancers, a pass-through network load balancer does not perform any application-level processing, such as SSL termination, header manipulation, or content inspection. Instead, it simply distributes incoming traffic across a pool of backend servers based on configured rules, such as round-robin, least connections, or IP hashing. Pass-through network load balancers are often used in scenarios where the backend servers handle the application-level processing, and the load balancer only needs to distribute traffic evenly across them. They are commonly used for non-HTTP(S) protocols such as UDP, **Structured Query Language** (**SQL**), MySQL, or **Simple Mail Transfer Protocol** (**SMTP**).

When planning an Azure Load Balancer implementation, the first decision to make is which **Stock-Keeping Unit** (**SKU**) to use. This can be done during deployment. Azure Load Balancer is available in three SKUs: **Basic**, **Standard**, and **Gateway** (see *Figure 9.3*). Each SKU is designed for specific use cases and offers different features and capabilities. Our choice of SKU should depend on our application's specific requirements and workload:

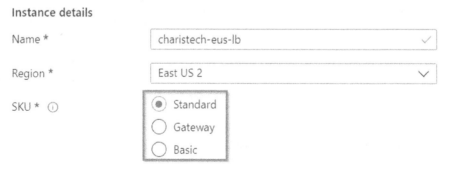

Figure 9.3 – Azure Load Balancer service tiers

Let's delve into each SKU, starting with the **Basic** SKU.

Understanding use cases for the Basic SKU

The **Basic** SKU is designed for simple load-balancing scenarios that do not require advanced features. Its functional, performance, security, and monitoring capabilities are limited in comparison to the **Standard** SKU (which we will cover in the next section of this chapter). For instance, it lacks valuable features such as outbound **Source Network Address Translation** (**SNAT**), availability zone support, metric collection for monitoring, and even a **service-level agreement** (**SLA**), meaning there is no guarantee of its availability!

It goes without saying that Microsoft does not advise using the **Basic** SKU for production workloads. Furthermore, it recently announced its retirement by September 2025. We're only mentioning this SKU for exam purposes, so please don't implement it.

> **Note**
> Microsoft has provided PowerShell scripts to upgrade existing **Basic** load balancers that customers may be using to the **Standard** SKU. The scripts can be accessed from this URL: `https://learn.microsoft.com/en-us/azure/load-balancer/load-balancer-basic-upgrade-guidance#upgrade-using-automated-scripts`.

Understanding use cases for the Standard SKU

The **Standard** SKU is a more advanced Layer 4 load-balancing option compared to the **Basic** SKU. As shown in *Figure 9.4*, the **Standard** SKU supports numerous features that are not available in the **Basic** SKU. It is ideal for workloads that require **high availability** (**HA**) across multiple availability zones, advanced security, and powerful monitoring and management capabilities:

Azure Service	Basic	Standard
Type	Public or Internal	Public or Internal
Tier	Regional only	Regional or Standard
Backend type	NIC based	IP based or NIC based
Backend pool endpoints	VMs in a single availability set	VMs and VMSS in a single network
Health probe types	TCP, HTTP	TCP, HTTP, HTTPS
Availability zone support	Not supported	Zone-redundant, Zonal or Non-Zonal
HA Ports	Not supported	Available for Internal Load Balancer
Diagnostics	Not supported	Azure Monitor multi-dimensional metrics
Secure by default	Open by default. NSG optional.	Closed to inbound flows. NSG required.
Outbound Rules	Not supported	Declarative outbound NAT configuration
TCP Reset on Idle	Inbound only	Available on any rule
Multiple front ends	Inbound only	Inbound and outbound
SLA	No SLA	99.99% SLA
Global VNet Peering Support	Not supported	Supported
NAT Gateway Support	Not supported	Supported
Private Link Support	Not supported	Supported
Global tier support (Preview)	Not supported	Supported

Figure 9.4 – Basic versus Standard load balancer

Choosing the type of load balancer to implement

The **Standard** load balancer can be implemented as a public or internal load balancer (*Figure 9.5*). We should choose the type of load balancer based on the requirements of our application:

Figure 9.5 – Selecting the load balancer type

A public load balancer is assigned a public IP address and used to distribute traffic from the internet to **virtual machines** (**VMs**) within a **virtual network** (**VNet**) (as indicated by *1* in *Figure 9.6*). In contrast, an internal load balancer is assigned a private IP address within a subnet and used to distribute traffic originating from internal clients (as indicated by *2* in *Figure 9.6*):

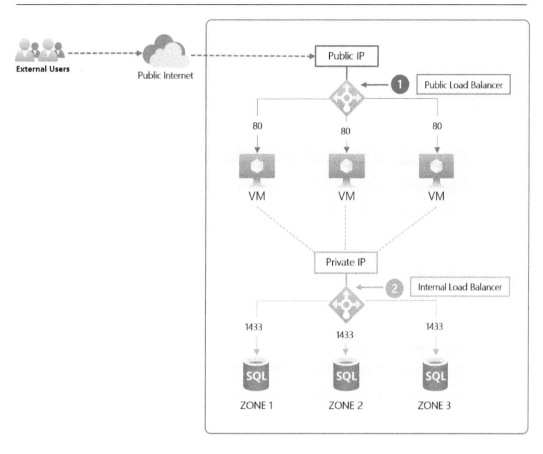

Figure 9.6 – Sample public and internal load balancer use case

Choosing the tier of the load balancer

If we are implementing a public **Standard** load balancer, we can opt for the **Global** (cross-region) tier, as shown in *Figure 9.7*. This option is only available for the public load balancer and not the internal one:

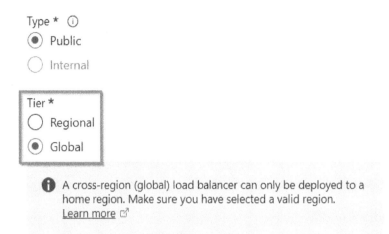

Figure 9.7 – Selecting the load balancer tier

The global (cross-region) load balancer can distribute traffic across multiple Azure regions. In this scenario, we deploy a global **Standard** load balancer in a "home region" with a backend pool of one or more regional load balancers (*Figure 9.8*):

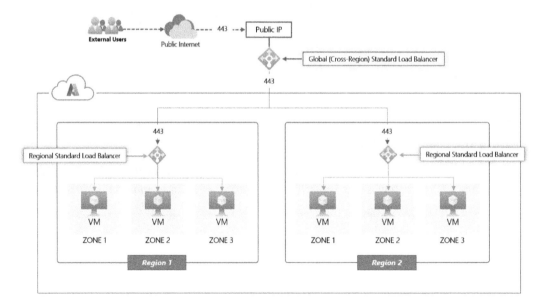

Figure 9.8 – Sample global load balancer implementation

When deploying a global (cross-region) load balancer, we need to specify a deployment region. This is referred to as the "home region" (*Figure 9.9*). At the time of writing, we can specify only nine regions as home regions. An updated list of possible home regions can be found here: `https://learn.microsoft.com/en-us/azure/load-balancer/cross-region-overview#home-regions`.

The region that we select does not influence how traffic is routed. For a global (cross-region) load balancer, the frontend IP configuration remains static and is advertised via Anycast to several other Azure regions, which are referred to as "participating regions" (*Figure 9.9*). At the time of writing, there are 22 participating regions. You can view an updated list of participating regions here: `https://learn.microsoft.com/en-us/azure/load-balancer/cross-region-overview#participating-regions`. Consequently, even if the home region experiences a disruption, traffic flow is not impacted as clients can still access the same IP address via the other regions:

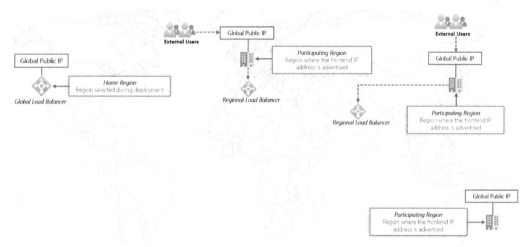

Figure 9.9 – Global load balancer home and participating regions

The global (cross-region) load balancer uses the **geo-proximity load-balancing algorithm** to determine the optimal routing path for network traffic. This algorithm directs requests to the nearest "participating region" based on the geographical location of the client initiating the request. The request is then transmitted via the Microsoft global network backbone to the closest regional load balancer (refer to *Figure 9.9*). By reducing the distance that network traffic has to travel, this approach helps minimize latency and improve overall performance.

Choosing the availability zone configuration option

One of the most significant benefits of the **Standard** SKU is that it supports traffic distribution to endpoints located in different availability zones for increased availability and redundancy, as depicted in *Figure 9.10*. To leverage this capability, it is necessary to deploy a load balancer in an Azure region that supports availability zones.

The **Standard** load balancer has three availability zone configuration options: **Zone-redundant**, **Zonal**, or **Non-zonal**.

A **zone-redundant** configuration allows the load balancer to distribute requests to resources in any zone while also providing protection against zone failure (*Figure 9.10*). In the event of a zone failure, requests are automatically redirected to resources in unaffected zones. This option provides the highest level of availability and redundancy. It is achieved by advertising the frontend IP address of the load balancer using Anycast across all zones in the region:

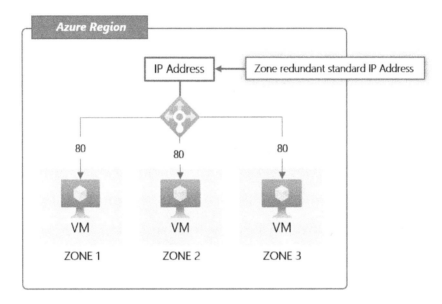

Figure 9.10 – Zone redundant Standard load balancer

A **zonal** configuration allows the load balancer to distribute requests to resources in a single zone (*Figure 9.11*). This configuration is optimal for scenarios where low latency is required within a zone. However, in the event of a zone failure, the load balancer will not remain functional. In scenarios such as this, it is typical to implement an additional load-balancing service, such as Azure Traffic Manager, to achieve some redundancy:

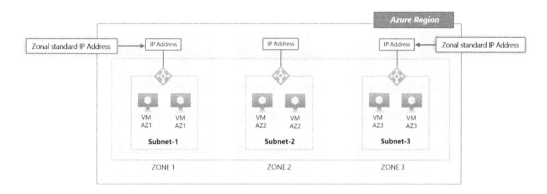

Figure 9.11 – Zonal Standard load balancer

A **non-zonal** configuration is relatively uncommon and is generally used to distribute requests to workloads that have not been pinned to a specific zone. This configuration is the only supported option if the resources are hosted in a region that does not yet support availability zones.

To configure zone-related properties, we specify the necessary setting in the frontend IP configuration of the load balancer, as illustrated in *Figure 9.12*. This setting must be specified at the time of deployment and cannot be modified or updated afterward:

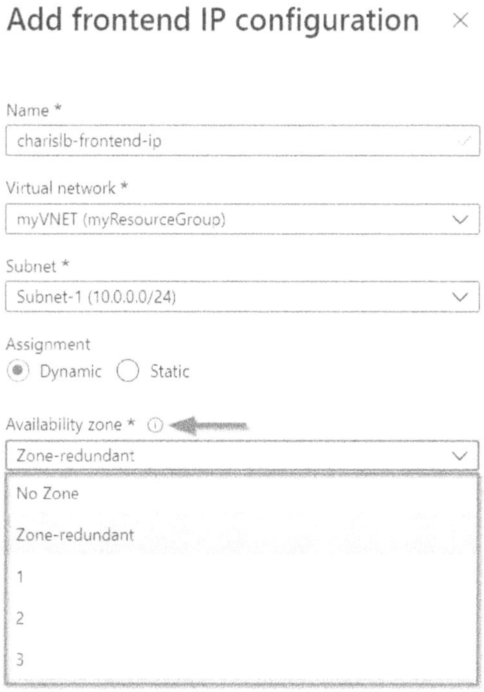

Add frontend IP configuration ×

Name *

charislb-frontend-ip

Virtual network *

myVNET (myResourceGroup)

Subnet *

Subnet-1 (10.0.0.0/24)

Assignment

◉ Dynamic   ○ Static

Availability zone * ⓘ ⟵

Zone-redundant

No Zone

Zone-redundant

1

2

3

Figure 9.12 – Configuring Standard load balancer zone properties

Selecting backend pools

The Azure **Standard** load balancer supports multiple types of backend pools, including VM scale sets, VMs, availability sets, and IP addresses. A backend pool is a set of VMs or other resources that receive network traffic from the load balancer.

In addition to the backend pool, the Azure **Standard** load balancer also uses a health probe to determine the availability of each resource in the pool. The health probe checks the status of each resource by sending a request to its IP address and checking for a response. The IP address used for the health probe is a well-known Azure address, which is 168.63.129.16. Traffic must be allowed from this IP address to backend instances so that they can successfully respond to health probes. There is an **AzureLoadBalancer** service tag that we can use for this purpose if we are defining this using a **network security group** (**NSG**).

Defining load balancer rules

Azure **Standard** load balancer rules are used to configure how traffic is distributed among backend resources. They allow you to specify which type of traffic to load balance and how to handle that traffic based on various conditions. There are three types of rules in an Azure **Standard** load balancer:

- **Load-balancing rules**: These rules are used to distribute traffic among backend resources based on factors such as session persistence, protocol, port, and health probes. For example, you can create a load-balancing rule to distribute HTTP traffic on port 80 among a set of backend VMs.

- **Inbound Network Address Translation (NAT) rules**: These rules are used to allow external clients to access internal resources behind the load balancer using NAT. Inbound NAT rules map an external port on the load balancer to an internal IP address and port on a backend resource. For example, you can create an inbound NAT rule to allow external clients to access a backend VM through a specific port.

- **Outbound rules**: These rules are used to control outbound traffic from backend resources. Outbound rules specify which backend resources can initiate outbound traffic, the protocol used for outbound traffic, and the destination IP address and port. For example, you can create an outbound rule to allow only certain VMs in a backend pool to initiate outbound traffic.

Let's head to the Azure environment and witness this in action!

Hands-on exercise 1 – Provisioning resources for this chapter's exercises

To follow along with the exercises in this chapter, we will provision some Azure resources to work with. We have prepared an **Azure Resource Manager** (**ARM**) template in the GitHub repository of this book for this purpose. The template will deploy load-balanced web servers across two Azure regions, as shown in *Figure 9.13*:

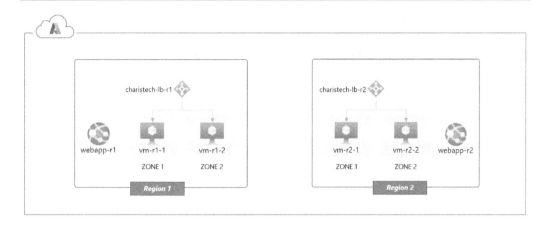

Figure 9.13 – Resources deployed via the provided ARM template

Here is the task that we will complete in this exercise:

- **Task 1**: Initialize the template deployment in GitHub, complete the parameters, and deploy the template to Azure

Let's get into this!

Task 1 – Initialize the template deployment in GitHub, complete parameters, and deploy the template to Azure

Follow these steps:

1. Open a web browser and browse to https://packt.link/C4sY0. This link will open the GitHub repository that has the ARM template to deploy the resources that we need.

2. In the GitHub repository that opens, click on **Deploy to Azure**:

Figure 9.14 – Starting the template deployment

3. If prompted to authenticate, sign in to the Azure portal with your administrative username and password.

4. In the **Custom Deployment** window, configure the following settings:

- **Subscription**: Select the subscription that you want to deploy the resources into.

- **Resource group**: **Create New** | **Name**: `CharisTechRG-C9` | **OK**

- **Region**: Select a region for the resource group. Ensure you match this to what you select for **First Region** (shown next).

- **First Region**: Select one of the available options—for example, **eastus2**.

- **Second Region**: Select one of the available options—for example, **eastus**.

- **Admin Username**: `azureuser`

- **Admin Password**: Enter a complex password. This will be the password for all deployed VM instances. Make a note of this as it will be needed for later exercises.

- **Vm Size**: Standard_D2s (or select the VM size that you verified in the first chapter of this book).

- Select **Review + create**.

- Select **Create**:

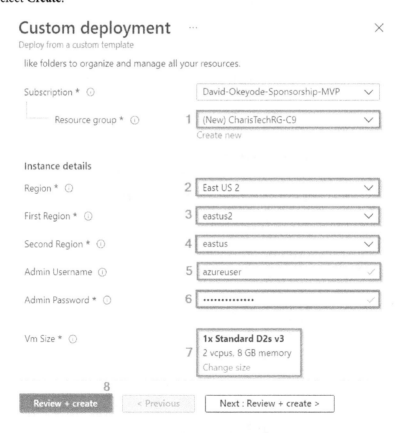

Figure 9.15 – Completing the template parameters

Hands-on exercise 2 – Creating and configuring a global (cross-region) load balancer

In this exercise, we will create a cross-region (global) load balancer and configure it to distribute incoming requests to workloads across two Azure regions, as shown in *Figure 9.16*:

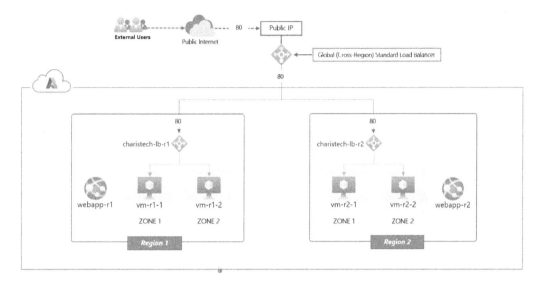

Figure 9.16 – Exercise 2 implementation

Here is the task that we will complete in this exercise:

- **Task 1**: Create and configure a global load balancer

Task 1 – Create and configure a global load balancer

Follow these steps:

1. In the search box at the top of the portal, enter Load balancer. Select **Load balancers** in the search results:

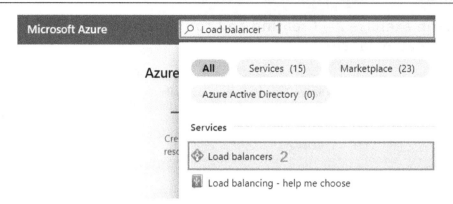

Figure 9.17 – Selecting Load balancers

2.   On the **Load balancer** page, select **+ Create**.

3.   In the **Basics** tab of the **Create load balancer** page, press *Enter*, or select the following information:

- **Subscription**: Select the subscription that you want to deploy the resources into

- **Resource group**: `CharisTechRG-C9`

- **Name**: **CharisTech-CrossRegion-LB**

- **Region**: Select the region that you used as your first region in the previous deployment

- **SKU: Standard**

- **Type: Public**

- **Tier: Global**

- Select **Next: Frontend IP configuration >**:

Project details

Subscription *   David-Okeyode

└── Resource group *   **1** CharisTechRG-C9
                                            Create new

Instance details

Name *   **2** CharisTech-CrossRegion-LB

Region *   **3** East US 2

SKU * ⓘ   **4** ⦿ Standard
                                            ○ Gateway
                                            ○ Basic

                                            ⓘ Microsoft recommends Standard SKU load balancer for production workloads.
                                            Learn more about pricing differences between Standard and Basic SKU ↗

Type * ⓘ   **5** ⦿ Public
                                            ○ Internal

Tier *   ○ Regional
                                      6 ⦿ Global

[Review + create] [< Previous] [**Next : Frontend IP configuration >**] **7** Download a template for automation

⏷Give feedback

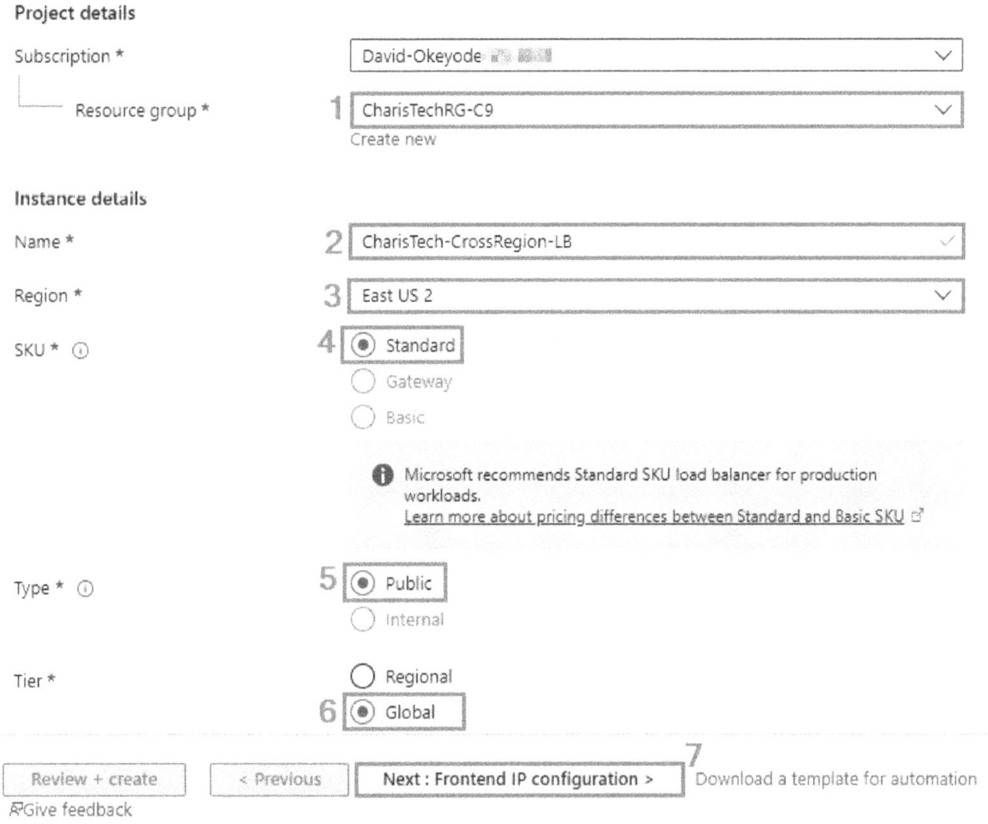

Figure 9.18 – Completing the load balancer basic parameters

4. In the **Frontend IP configuration** tab, select + **Add a frontend IP configuration**.

5. In the **Add frontend IP configuration** blade, configure the following settings:

    - **Name**: CharisTech-CrossRegion-LB-PIP

    - **IP version**: IPv4

    - **Public IP address**: charistech-lbPublicIP-cr

- Select **Add**:

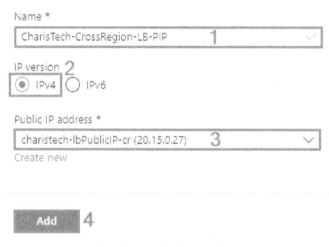

Add frontend IP configuration ×

Name *

| CharisTech-CrossRegion-LB-PIP   1 | ✓ |

IP version 2

(●) IPv4 (○) IPv6

Public IP address *

| charistech-lbPublicIP-cr (20.15.0.27)   3 | ✓ |

Create new

Add   4

Figure 9.19 – Configuring the frontend IP configuration

6. Select **Next: Backend pools** > at the bottom of the page.

7. In **Backend pools**, select + **Add a backend pool**.

8. In the **Add backend pool** window, configure the following settings:

- **Name**: charistech-vm-app-pool

- In the **Load balancers** section, select **charistech-lb-r1** in the **Load balancer** drop-down box and select **LoadBalancerFrontEnd-r1** in the **Frontend IP configuration** pull-down box

- On the second line, select **charistech-lb-r2** in the **Load balancer** pull-down box and select **LoadBalancerFrontEnd-r2** in the **Frontend IP configuration** pull-down box

- Verify that the configuration corresponds with the following screenshot and click **Save**:

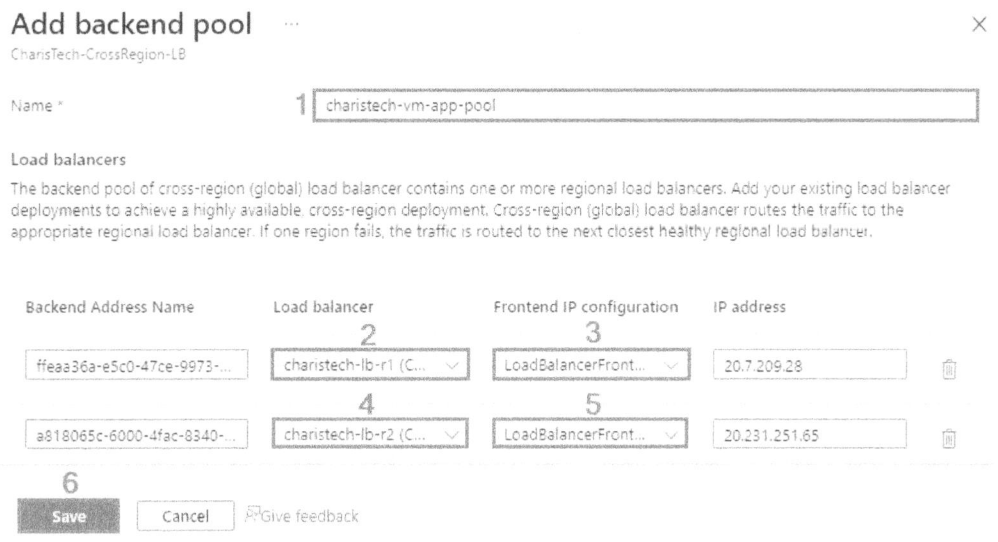

Add backend pool ...

CharisTech-CrossRegion-LB

Name *   1 | charistech-vm-app-pool

Load balancers

The backend pool of cross-region (global) load balancer contains one or more regional load balancers. Add your existing load balancer deployments to achieve a highly available, cross-region deployment. Cross-region (global) load balancer routes the traffic to the appropriate regional load balancer. If one region fails, the traffic is routed to the next closest healthy regional load balancer.

Backend Address Name	Load balancer	Frontend IP configuration	IP address
ffeaa36a-e5c0-47ce-9973-...	2 charistech-lb-r1 (C... ⌄	3 LoadBalancerFront... ⌄	20.7.209.28
a818065c-6000-4fac-8340-...	4 charistech-lb-r2 (C... ⌄	5 LoadBalancerFront... ⌄	20.231.251.65

6
Save   Cancel   Give feedback

Figure 9.20 – Adding regional load balancers as backend pools

9. Select **Next: Inbound rules** > at the bottom of the page.

10. In **Inbound rules**, select + **Add a load balancing rule**.

11. In the **Add load balancing rule** blade, configure the following settings:

- **Name**: HTTP-LB-Rule

- **IP Version**: IPv4

- **Frontend IP address**: **Ch
arisTech-CrossRegion-LB-PIP**

- **Backend pool**: **charistech-vm-app-pool**

- **Protocol**: TCP

- **Port**: 80

- **Session persistence: None**

- **Idle timeout (minutes): 4**

- **TCP reset: Enabled**

- **Floating IP: Disabled**

- Select **Add**:

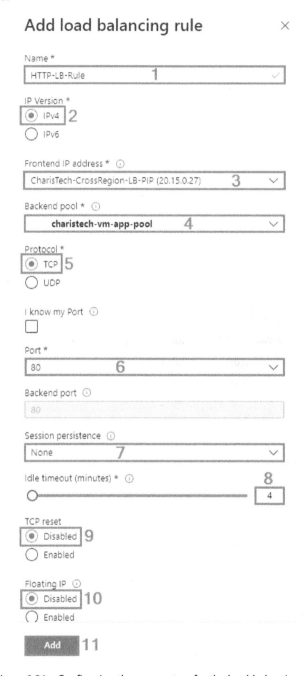

Figure 9.21 – Configuring the parameters for the load-balancing rule

12. Select **Review + create** at the bottom of the page.

13. Select **Create** in the **Review + create** tab.

14. Wait for a few minutes for the cross-region load balancer resource to be created. Click on **Go to resource**:

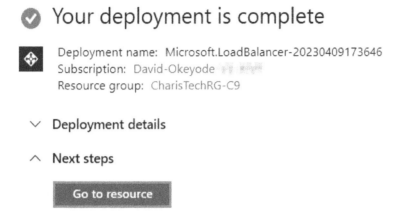

Figure 9.22 – Selecting Go to resource

15. On the **CharisTech-CrossRegion-LB** load balancer page, make a note of the public IP address of the resource:

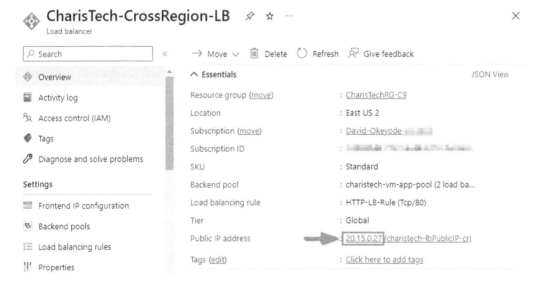

Figure 9.23 – Making a note of the load balancer's public IP

16. Open a new web browser and browse to `http://PUBLIC_IP_ADDRESS`. Replace `PUBLIC_IP_ADDRESS` with the public IP address that you made a note of in the previous step. You should see a web page with the name of the VM that served the request (*Figure 9.24*). If you have other browsers on your PC, browse to the same URL to test out the load balancing:

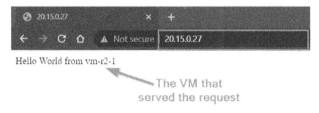

Figure 9.24 – The test web page

Well done! You have successfully deployed and validated a global (cross-region) load balancer on Azure. Now, let us delve into another Azure application delivery service—Azure Application Gateway.

Designing and implementing an Azure Application Gateway service

Azure Application Gateway is a regional service that provides Layer 7 load balancing, SSL/**Transport Layer Security** (**TLS**) termination, and WAF capabilities. It is optimized for web traffic and enables you to manage traffic to your web applications.

Understanding Azure Application Gateway tiers

When implementing Azure Application Gateway, one of the first decisions that we need to make is the service tier to implement. Azure Application Gateway offers four service-tier options: **Standard** (V1), **Standard V2**, **WAF** (V1), and **WAF V2** (*Figure 9.25*):

Figure 9.25 – Azure Application Gateway service tiers

The **Standard** tier is suitable for small-to-medium-scale applications that require basic load-balancing and SSL termination capabilities. It supports features such as SSL offload, session affinity, and URL-based routing. It does not, however, support autoscaling or WAF capabilities. This tier is ideal for non-critical workloads that do not require autoscaling, zonal availability, or advanced security features via WAF integration.

The **Standard V2** tier is designed for larger-scale applications that require advanced load-balancing, SSL termination, and traffic management capabilities. The **Standard V2** tier includes all the features of the **Standard** tier, plus support for autoscaling, and zonal availability.

The **WAF** tier is designed for small-to-medium-scale web applications that require advanced security features, such as protection against common web vulnerabilities such as SQL injection and **cross-site scripting** (**XSS**). The WAF tier includes all the features of the **Standard** tier, plus support for the WAF. The **WAF** tier allows us to create custom WAF policies to protect your web applications against known vulnerabilities and exploits.

The **WAF V2** tier is the most advanced tier of Azure Application Gateway, designed for large-scale web applications that require enterprise-grade security features. The **WAF V2** tier includes all the features of the **WAF** tier, plus support for the **Open Worldwide Application Security Protocol** (**OWASP**) Top 10 and Azure managed rules. The **WAF V2** tier also includes advanced analytics and reporting capabilities, which allows us to monitor and manage web traffic and security policies in real time.

Going forward in this chapter, we will be referring to the gateway tiers in groups, as follows:

- **V1 tiers**: Includes **Standard V1** and **WAF V1**

- **V2 tiers**: Includes **Standard V2** and **WAF V2**

- **Standard tiers**: Includes **Standard V1** and **Standard V2**

- **WAF tiers**: Includes **WAF V1** and **WAF V2**

> **Note**
>
> Microsoft provides a PowerShell script that can be used to migrate from V1 service tiers to V2 service tiers. The script will create a new resource and copy over the configuration. You can find out more here: `https://learn.microsoft.com/en-us/azure/application-gateway/migrate-v1-v2`.

Understanding the scalability and performance of the tiers

Azure Application Gateway uses compute instances in its backend to handle incoming traffic. For the **Standard** or **WAF** tiers, we need to specify both the number and size of the instances desired (*Figure 9.26*). This puts the burden of capacity planning on us:

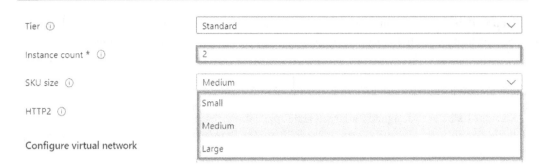

Figure 9.26 – Application Gateway V1 tier sizes

The **Standard** tier offers three size options: **Small**, **Medium**, and **Large**, while the **WAF** tier provides two size options: **Medium** and **Large**. Both options support a maximum of 32 instances for any of the sizes.

For the **Standard V2** and **WAF V2** tiers, we can implement autoscaling to automatically add or remove backend compute instances based on changing traffic-load patterns. This removes the requirement to choose a deployment size or instance count during provisioning. When we implement autoscaling, we need to specify a minimum instance count that will always be active and a maximum instance count that the resource can scale to (*Figure 9.27*). As of the time of writing, a maximum of 125 instances is supported:

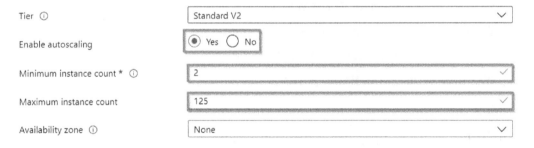

Figure 9.27 – Application Gateway V2 tiers' autoscaling settings

Considerations for the Application Gateway subnet

When deploying an application gateway in a VNet, a dedicated subnet must be used exclusively for this purpose, with no other resources sharing the same subnet. While multiple application gateway resources can be deployed within the same subnet, v1 and v2 tiers cannot be mixed. Microsoft recommends using a /24 size subnet, as each backend gateway instance will be assigned an IP address from the subnet range. A /24 size subnet is typically sufficient, as v1 Application Gateway tiers support up to 32 instances and v2 tiers can have up to 125 instances. However, if multiple gateway resources are deployed in the same subnet, a larger subnet size may be necessary. If needed, subnet sizes can be expanded using Azure PowerShell or the Azure CLI, provided there is unused address space in the VNet to expand to.

What about NSGs? Can we use NSGs to restrict network access to the application gateway subnet? The answer is *YES*! However, it is important to ensure that the necessary rules are in place for functionalities to work properly. This includes allowing additional ports required for Azure infrastructure communication, in addition to the ports used by the application.

For **Standard** and **WAF** tiers, inbound TCP ports 65503-65534 must be allowed from the **GatewayManager** service tag. For **Standard V2** and **WAF V2** tiers, inbound TCP ports 65200-65535 must be allowed from the **GatewayManager** service tag. Also, if the backend targets are hosted in a subnet, traffic must be allowed inbound from the **AzureLoadBalancer** tag as well.

What about **User-Defined Routes (UDRs)**? Can we use them in an application gateway subnet? The answer is *yes*, it is possible to use them, but it is *not* recommended due to potential issues with health status checks and logging consistency. If UDRs are used, it is important to ensure that all management/control-plane traffic is routed directly to the internet and not through a virtual appliance. However, it is best to avoid using UDRs altogether to avoid possible issues.

Understanding Azure Application Gateway components

An application gateway accepts, processes, and distributes incoming application traffic across multiple backend targets. To perform these functions, it relies on three key components (*Figure 9.28*): **frontend IP addresses**, which receive incoming traffic; **backend targets**, to which the requests are distributed; and **routing rules**, which dictate how the gateway processes and distributes the requests from the frontend to the backend targets:

Figure 9.28 – Application Gateway core components

Let us look at these three components in more detail, starting with the frontend IP address.

Configuring frontend IP addresses

Traffic enters the application gateway through its frontend IP address(es), which can be a public IP address, a private IP address, or a combination of both, as shown in *Figure 9.29*. A public IP address can serve as the point of entry for external clients, while a private IP address can serve as the point of entry for internal clients. The application gateway is limited to one (1) public IP and one (1) private IP at most:

Figure 9.29 – Frontend IP address options

For the **Standard V1** and **WAF V1** tiers, either a public IP address, a private IP address, or a combination of both can be used (*Figure 9.29*). On the other hand, for the **Standard V2** and **WAF V2** tiers, only a public IP address or both public and private IP addresses are supported. It was previously not possible to use only a private IP address as the frontend in V2 tiers, but Microsoft recently announced this capability in preview here: `https://azure.microsoft.com/en-us/updates/public-preview-private-application-gateway-v2/`.

Configuring backend targets

The term *"backend targets"* refers to a group of endpoints that an application gateway can send traffic to. Two types of targets can be configured: **backend pools** and **redirections** (as illustrated in *Figure 9.30*):

Figure 9.30 – Backend target types

A backend pool can be a collection of IP addresses and/or **fully qualified domain names** (**FQDNs**), a group of VM instances, or VM scale sets (*Figure 9.31*). In other words, backend pools represent the actual backend infrastructure that the application gateway is load-balancing traffic to. We can configure up to a maximum of 100 backend address pools and 1,200 backend targets per pool:

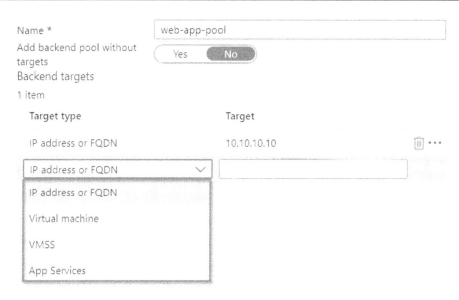

Figure 9.31 – Backend pool types

Redirections, on the other hand, are used to redirect incoming traffic from the application gateway to an **external site** or a **listener** (*Figure 9.32*).

A **listener** refers to an endpoint (different HTTP/HTTPS listener) within the same application gateway. This can be useful when we want to redirect insecure (HTTP) requests to a secure (HTTPS) listener within the same gateway:

Figure 9.32 – Selecting a redirection target

An **external site** refers to an endpoint outside of the application gateway, such as a different web server or a cloud service. This can be useful in scenarios where, for example, a web application is moved to a new URL, and we want to redirect all incoming traffic to the new URL.

When implementing a redirection backend target (external or listener), we can specify one of four redirection types—**Permanent**, **Temporary**, **Found**, and **See other** (*Figure 9.33*). The redirection type that we specify determines the HTTP response code that will be returned to the requesting client:

Figure 9.33 – Selecting a redirection type

For **Permanent** redirection, the application gateway sends an HTTP 301 response code to the client, indicating that the requested resource has been permanently moved to a new location. This type of redirection causes clients, including search engines, to automatically update their index to reflect the change.

On the other hand, **Temporary** redirection sends an HTTP 302 response code to the client, indicating that the redirection is temporary and the client should continue to use the original URL for future requests. Search engines will not update their index for this type of redirection.

Found redirection is similar to **Temporary** redirection in that it also sends an HTTP 302 response code to the client, but it is used specifically when the requested resource is found at a different URL.

Finally, **See other** redirection sends an HTTP 303 response code to the client, indicating that the request can be fulfilled by accessing a different resource or URL. This type of redirection is similar to **Temporary** redirection but is intended to be used for non-GET requests.

Configuring routing rules

Routing rules in an application gateway are used to determine how traffic should be directed and processed by the gateway. It consists of two main components—the **HTTP/HTTPS listener** and the **backend setting** (*Figure 9.34*).

The HTTP/HTTPS listener specifies the communication settings between the clients and the application gateway, while the backend setting defines the communication settings between the application gateway and the backend pool endpoints. Let us look at these components and their configuration options in detail:

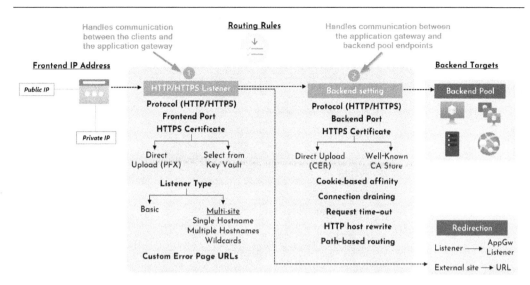

Figure 9.34 – Routing rules components

Understanding the HTTP/HTTPS listener

The HTTP listener in an application gateway routing rule plays a critical role in managing traffic to backend services and ensuring that requests are properly routed and load-balanced. It is responsible for receiving incoming web requests to a frontend IP address on a specified port, inspecting the request headers, such as the host header, to determine whether it matches configured options, and performing SSL/TLS termination to decrypt incoming HTTPS traffic.

Up to 200 listeners can be configured for **Standard** tiers, but only 100 of them can be active. An active listener is one that is linked to a rule and directs traffic to a backend pool. Any listener that only redirects traffic is not counted as active. This listener limit also applies to the **WAF V2** tier when using **Core Rule Set** (**CRS**) 3.2 or higher. However, for **WAF** and **WAF V2** tiers that are using the CRS 3.1 or lower, only a maximum of 40 listeners are supported.

In *Figure 9.35*, you can find six key configuration options that can be defined for an HTTP listener:

Figure 9.35 – Listener configuration options

These options are detailed here with their corresponding numbers:

- **Frontend IP** (*1*): This setting specifies the frontend IP address that will be associated with the listener. It is where incoming requests will be received.

- **Listener type** (*2*): There are two types of listeners available: **Basic** and **Multi site**. A **Basic** listener is used when there is only one website or application to be served, while a **Multi site** listener can be used to receive traffic for different websites based on the host header of incoming requests.

- **Error page url** (*3*): This setting allows us to define custom error pages at the listener level for HTTP 502 (Bad gateway) or HTTP 403 (Unauthorized access) error messages.

- **Protocol** (HTTP/HTTPS) (*4*): This setting determines whether traffic between the client and the listener will be encrypted. HTTP traffic is unencrypted, while HTTPS traffic is encrypted using SSL/TLS.

- **Port** (*5*): This setting specifies the frontend port for the listener. We can use well-known ports such as 80 and 443, or any port between 1 and 65502 (v1 tiers) or 1 to 65199 (v2 tiers).

- **HTTPS certificate** (6): This setting is used to define the certificate that will be used to establish a secure connection with the client using SSL/TLS if HTTPS is configured as the protocol. We can either upload a **Personal Information Exchange (PFX)** certificate file directly or select a certificate stored in Azure Key Vault, which requires a managed identity for access.

Understanding the backend setting

When routing requests to a backend pool, it is necessary to create a backend setting for the routing rule. This setting determines how traffic from the HTTP listeners will be handled when being sent to the endpoints in the backend pool.

Figure 9.36 highlights nine configuration options that can be defined for a backend setting:

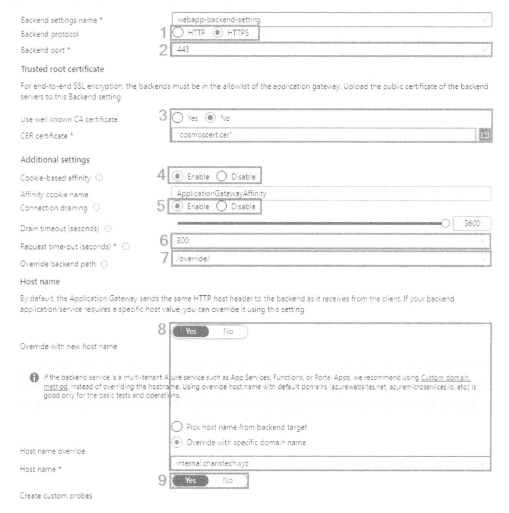

Figure 9.36 – Backend setting configuration options

These options are detailed here with their corresponding numbers:

- **Backend protocol** (*1*): This setting determines whether traffic between the gateway and the backend targets will be encrypted. When configuring this setting, you must ensure that the backend servers also support the same protocol. If HTTPS is configured for the listener and you have a requirement to enforce end-to-end TLS, you should configure HTTPS here.

- **Backend port** (*2*): This setting refers to the port number that the backend pool endpoints are listening on to receive incoming traffic from the application gateway. By default, the application gateway uses port 80 for HTTP and port 443 for HTTPS, but you can configure it to use any valid port number.

- **HTTPS certificate** (*3*): This setting is used to define the trusted root certificate that will be used to validate the SSL/TLS certificate presented by backend servers if HTTPS is configured as the protocol. If we are using a self-signed certificate or a certificate signed by an internal **Certificate Authority** (**CA**), we must upload the matching public certificate in the .CER format. Alternatively, if the certificate on the backend pool is signed by a trusted public CA, we can set the **Use well known CA certificate** option to **Yes** and skip uploading a public certificate.

- **Cookie-based affinity** (*4*): This setting is used to enable session affinity or sticky sessions. When enabled, Application Gateway sets an affinity cookie in the response sent back to the client. This cookie contains a hash value that includes the session details, including the identity of the backend server that served the client's initial request. Subsequent requests from a client with the cookie will be routed to the same backend server. This feature is useful when we want to keep a user session pinned to the same backend server where the session state might have been saved locally. The default name for the affinity cookie is **ApplicationGatewayAffinity**, but it can be customized.

- **Connection draining** (*5*): This setting is useful in smoothly removing backend pool members during planned service updates. When enabled, Application Gateway will stop sending new connections to backend pool members that are being deregistered. Application Gateway will also wait for existing connections to complete within a configurable time range of 1 to 3,600 seconds (drain timeout).

- **Request time-out** (*6*): This setting specifies the maximum amount of time, in seconds, that the application gateway will wait for a response from a backend pool endpoint before timing out the request and returning a "connection timed out" error message. It can be configured to any value within the range of 1 to 86,400 seconds (24 hours).

- **Override backend path** (*7*): This setting can be used to modify the path of incoming requests before they are forwarded to the backend servers. By default, when requests are received by the HTTP/HTTPS listener, the path in the incoming request is forwarded as-is to the backend servers. However, in some cases, we may want to modify the path to match the path expected by the backend server. For example, if the backend server expects requests to be sent to a specific path such as /api/v1, but the requests received by the application gateway have a different path, such as /myapp/v1, we can use the **Override backend path** setting to modify the path before it is forwarded to the backend server.

- **Override with new host name** (*8*): This setting can be used to modify the hostname in the incoming HTTP request with a new hostname before they are forwarded to the backend servers. This can be useful in scenarios where the original hostname in the incoming HTTP request does not match the backend server's hostname or IP address. For example, if we have a backend server that is accessible internally as internal.app, but the hostname in the incoming HTTP request points to external.app, we can use this setting to replace the incoming hostname by specifying the hostname expected by the backend server in this setting.

- **Create custom probes** (*9*): This allows us to define and configure custom health checks for the backend servers. We can configure custom probes to use HTTP or HTTPS and specify the URL path to send requests to and a response code that the backend server should return for the probe to be considered successful. If the response code does not match or if the request times out, the backend server is considered unhealthy, and the application gateway will stop sending traffic to it.

Let's shift our focus to another Layer 7 load-balancing service available in Azure—Front Door.

Designing and implementing an Azure Front Door load balancer service

Azure Front Door is a service that delivers applications and caches content using a network of globally distributed edge nodes. It offers capabilities such as global load balancing, dynamic and static content acceleration, and web application protection at the global edge for web applications and APIs. Unlike the regional Application Gateway, Front Door is a global service that can serve requests and content for endpoints distributed across multiple Azure regions or even those outside of Azure.

In *Figure 9.37*, the Front Door service receives client requests from end users through a nearby point of presence (or edge location) using an anycast public IP address. It then leverages Microsoft's high-throughput backbone network to accelerate delivery to the backend application instead of routing traffic entirely over the public internet. Azure Front Door has over 150 **points of presence** (**PoP**) distributed globally:

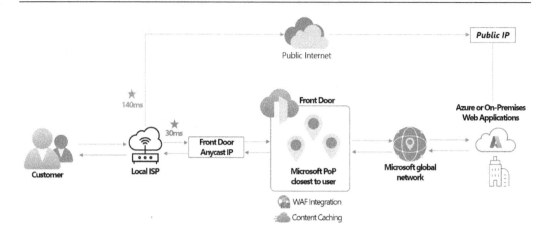

Figure 9.37 – Front Door content acceleration

Front Door also offers content caching and security for web applications at the global edge via its integration with Microsoft Azure **Content Delivery Network** (**CDN**) and Azure WAF.

Understanding Azure Front Door tiers

When setting up the Azure Front Door service, one of the primary decisions we must make is which service tier to implement. Front Door offers three options: **Standard**, **Premium**, and **Classic**. The **Classic** tier has been available for a long time and uses the `Microsoft.Network` resource provider, while the **Standard/Premium** tiers are newer and use the `Microsoft.Cdn` resource provider namespace.

The **Standard** and **Premium** tiers combine the capabilities of the **Classic** tier and the capabilities of another Azure service—Azure CDN from Microsoft. Microsoft no longer recommends the **Classic** tier due to its limitations, such as the absence of content caching, no support for non-internet facing backends via private link delivery, and no support for the newer enhanced rules engine and advanced diagnostics. Therefore, our focus in this chapter will primarily be on the **Standard/Premium** tiers (*Figure 9.38*), with only brief references made to the **Classic** tier when relevant to the discussion:

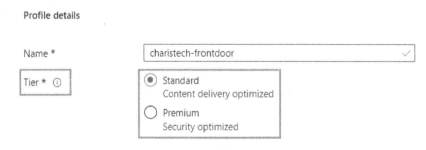

Figure 9.38 – Azure Firewall service tiers

If you currently use the **Classic** tier, Microsoft provides a zero-downtime migration option to transfer to the newer **Standard** and **Premium** tiers. However, this offering is presently in public preview. It is strongly recommended that you follow this process if you intend to migrate because there may be some "breaking changes," such as the resource provider changes that we discussed earlier.

To understand the differences between the tiers, please refer to *Figure 9.39*, which shows a feature comparison between the three service-tier options:

Features and optimization	Standard	Premium	Classic
Static file delivery	Yes	Yes	Yes
Dynamic site delivery	Yes	Yes	Yes
Custom domains	Yes	Yes	Yes
Cache manage (purge, rules, and compression)	Yes	Yes	Yes
Regular expression in rules engine	Yes	Yes	No
Advanced analytics/built-in reports	Yes	Yes	No
Health probe log	Yes	Yes	No
Custom Web Application Firewall (WAF) rules	Yes	Yes	Yes
Microsoft managed rule set	No	Yes	Yes - DRS 1.1 or below
Bot protection	No	Yes	Yes - BRS 1.0
Private link connection to origin	No	Yes	No

Figure 9.39 – Feature comparison table between the Standard, Premium, and Classic tier options

Understanding Front Door components

An instance of the Azure Front Door service is referred to as a **Front Door profile**. We can create up to 500 **Standard** or **Premium** tier profiles in an Azure subscription. To perform its functions, Front Door relies on three key components (*Figure 9.40*)—an **endpoint**, which receives incoming traffic; **origin groups**, to which requests are distributed or that host the original content; and **routes**, which map frontend endpoint domains to backend origin groups:

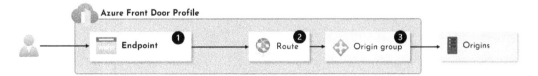

Figure 9.40 – The three core Front Door components

Let's examine these components more closely, beginning with the endpoint.

Configuring a Front Door endpoint

A Front Door endpoint is an entry point that receives incoming requests for our application. The number of endpoints that can be created for a **Standard** tier resource is limited to 10, while for a **Premium** tier resource, it can be extended up to 25 endpoints.

When an endpoint is created, a default domain name will be automatically generated for it. The default domain name combines the endpoint's designated name, a random hash value, and Front Door's base domain name, which is .z01.azurefd.net (*Figure 9.41*).

The random hash value (*Figure 9.41*) is added as a protective measure against subdomain takeover attacks, in which an attacker creates a Front Door resource using a previously used endpoint name to intercept incoming requests:

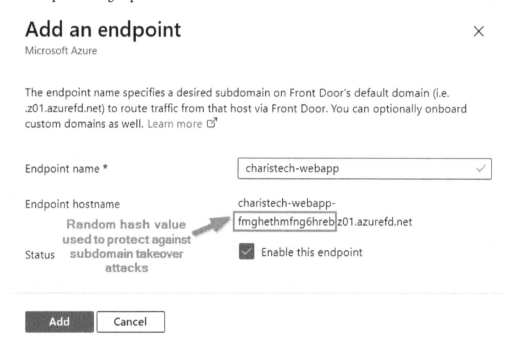

Figure 9.41 – Random hash value added to endpoint hostname

Adding custom domains to a Front Door endpoint

We can optionally onboard custom domains to a Front Door endpoint (*Figure 9.42*). We can add up to 100 custom domains per Front Door profile for a **Standard** tier resource, and up to 500 custom domains for a **Premium** tier resource:

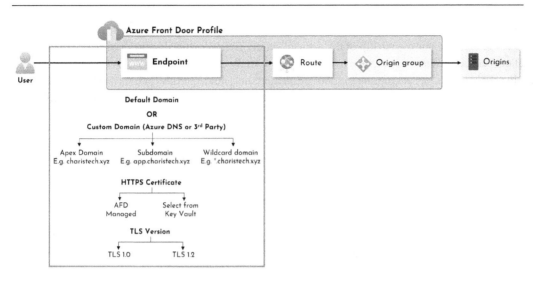

Figure 9.42 – Front Door endpoint configuration options

The DNS zone hosting the custom domain can be managed by either the Azure DNS service or a third-party service, as shown in *Figure 9.43*. We can specify this option when we add the domain:

Figure 9.43 – DNS management options

Azure Front Door supports adding three types of custom domain names—apex domains, subdomains, and wildcard domains (*Figure 9.42*). Let's look at these in more detail:

- An **apex domain**, also known as the root domain, is the highest level of a domain name and does not include any subdomains. For instance, `charistech.xyz` is an example of an apex domain.

- A **subdomain** is part of a larger domain name that is created by adding a prefix to the apex domain. For example, `webapp.charistech.xyz` is a subdomain. The most frequently added type of custom domain name to Front Door is a subdomain.

- A **wildcard domain** is a domain name that matches multiple subdomains with a single domain name, and it is denoted by an asterisk (`*`) as the leftmost part of the domain name. For example, `*.charistech.xyz` can match `app.charistech.xyz` and `webapp.charistech.xyz`, among others.

After adding a custom domain to our Azure Front Door resource, we must complete a validation process to confirm our ownership of the domain name. This is a crucial security measure to ensure that only authorized users can use a custom domain with the Azure Front Door service and to protect against malicious actors attempting to spoof a domain that is not rightfully theirs. Without completing this, the domain status will remain in a **Pending** state (*Figure 9.44*), and Azure Front Door will not accept traffic for that custom domain name:

Figure 9.44 – Pending domain validation state

The validation process involves adding a **TXT record** provided by Azure Front Door to our DNS zone (*Figure 9.45*). Once the TXT record is created, Azure Front Door will verify its existence, and the status of the domain will be changed to **Approved**. If the validation process is not completed within 7 days, the attempt will time out, and the domain status will be changed to **Timeout**. In this case, we will need to regenerate the DNS record value and add it:

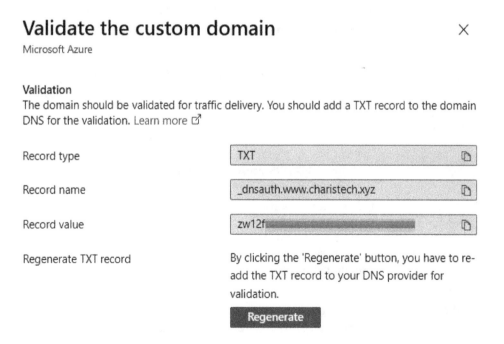

Figure 9.45 – Sample TXT record for domain validation

The validation process varies based on the DNS zone hosting the custom domain. If the DNS zone is managed by the Azure DNS service, Azure Front Door can automatically create a TXT record in the DNS zone and complete the validation without any additional action required from the user. If the DNS zone is not managed by Azure DNS, we need to manually create a TXT record in the DNS zone with the provided name and value.

It is crucial to note that the domain validation process needs to be repeated whenever the domain configuration is changed to ensure the ongoing security of the Azure Front Door service.

> **Note**
>
> Once the custom domain has been successfully validated, we can remove the TXT record from the DNS zone without any concerns.

Certificate support for custom domains

When we add a custom domain to a Front Door endpoint, HTTPS is enforced and we need to specify the SSL/TLS certificate to use to establish a secure connection with clients. Two options are available, as shown in *Figure 9.46*—using a Front Door managed certificate or using our own certificate that is kept in Azure Key Vault (this is referred to as **Bring Your Own Certificate (BYOC)**):

HTTPS
Enable HTTPS protocol for a custom domain that's associated with Front Door to ensure that sensitive data is delivered securely via SSL/TLS encryption when sent across the Internet.
Learn more

HTTPS   ◉ AFD managed (Recommended)
                    ○ Bring Your Own Certificate (BYOC)

Minimum TLS version ○ TLS 1.0 ◉ TLS 1.2

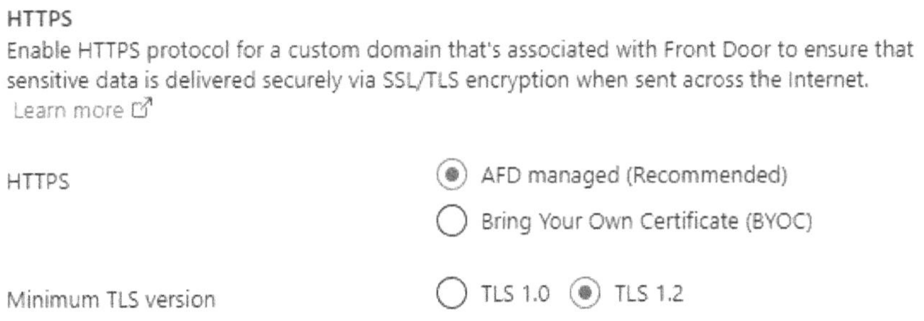

Figure 9.46 – Custom domain certificate options

It is recommended to use the Front Door managed certificate option as it minimizes the operational costs of having to manage certificate rotation, since the Front Door service will automatically issue and rotate the certificate for us. However, it is not always available for every scenario. Front Door managed certificates are available for apex domains and subdomains but *NOT* for wildcard domains! Also, renewal for apex domain certificates requires domain revalidation.

Adding origin groups and origins

In Azure Front Door, origin groups define a collection of backend targets (referred to as "origins") that host applications or content that will be served to requesting clients. Front Door supports both Azure and non-Azure origins to an origin group. Azure origins that are supported include Blob Storage, App Service, Static Web Apps, API Management, Application Gateway, public IP addresses, Traffic Manager, and Container Instances. In addition to these Azure origins, Front Door also supports any HTTP/HTTPS endpoint through its **Custom** origin type, allowing for greater flexibility in serving content to clients.

The recommended approach is to add backend endpoints (origins) that are responsible for serving the same application, content, or API to an origin group in Front Door. This enables Front Door to manage traffic distribution across origins and enables failover in case of an origin failure.

Figure 9.47 shows the various configuration setting options that we can implement for origin groups and origins in Front Door:

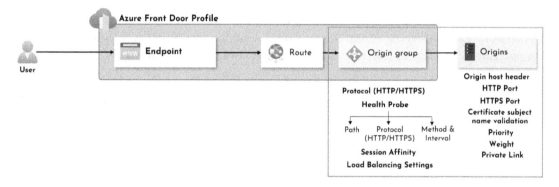

Figure 9.47 – Front Door origin and origin group configuration options

Let us review some of these key configuration settings, starting with origins. When we add an origin to an origin group, we can define the following configuration settings (*Figure 9.48*):

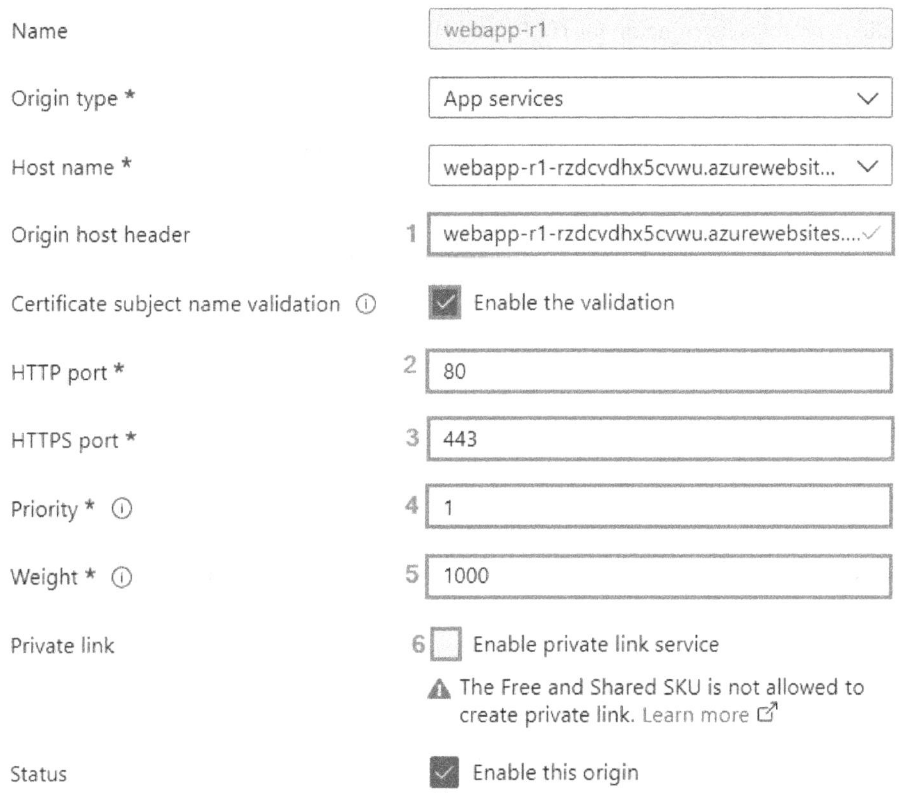

Name	webapp-r1	
Origin type *	App services	∨
Host name *	webapp-r1-rzdcvdhx5cvwu.azurewebsit...	∨
Origin host header	1 webapp-r1-rzdcvdhx5cvwu.azurewebsites....✓	
Certificate subject name validation ⓘ	✓ Enable the validation	
HTTP port *	2 80	
HTTPS port *	3 443	
Priority * ⓘ	4 1	
Weight * ⓘ	5 1000	
Private link	6 ☐ Enable private link service	
	⚠ The Free and Shared SKU is not allowed to create private link. Learn more ⌕	
Status	✓ Enable this origin	

Figure 9.48 – Origin configuration settings

- **Origin host header**: This setting specifies the host-header value sent to the backend for each request. This should match the domain name that the backend is expecting. This setting can be used to modify the hostname in the incoming HTTP request with a new hostname before they are forwarded to the backend servers. For example, if we have a backend server that is accessible internally as `internal.app` but the hostname in the incoming HTTP request points to `external.app`, we can use this setting to replace the incoming hostname by specifying the hostname expected by the backend server in this setting.

- **Certificate subject name validation**: If this setting is enabled, Azure Front Door will validate whether the request hostname matches the hostname in the certificate provided by the origin, whenever it establishes a TLS connection to a backend origin target. From a security standpoint, it is not recommended to enable this setting.

- **HTTP port** and **HTTPS port**: These settings can be used to specify the port numbers that the backend origin is listening on for HTTP and HTTPS connections.

- **Priority**: We can use this setting to assign the priority order in which requests are sent to different origins. The lower the priority number, the higher the priority of the origin. For example, we have three origins configured in Azure Front Door: origin A, origin B, and origin C. If the goal is to send requests to origin A as the primary origin, but it's unavailable, we want to send requests to origin B as the secondary origin, and if both origin A and origin B are unavailable, we want to send requests to origin C as the last resort. To achieve this, we can assign origin A a priority number of 1, origin B a priority number of 2, and origin C a priority number of 3. In this way, when requests come to Azure Front Door, it will send them to origin A first, and if it's not available, it will send them to origin B. If neither origin A nor origin B is available, Azure Front Door will send requests to origin C. The value that we specify must be between 1 and 5.

- **Weight**: When multiple origins have the same priority number in Azure Front Door, the weight configuration comes into play to determine how incoming requests are distributed across them. The weight configuration allows us to allocate a percentage of traffic to each origin, based on the weight we assign to it. This means that we can distribute traffic evenly across origins with the same priority or allocate more traffic to certain origins, depending on their weight. The value that we specify must be between 1 and 1,000.

- **Private link**: At the time of writing, only three origin types support private link connectivity from Front Door—Blob Storage, App Service, and internal load balancers.

When origin groups are added to Front Door, we can define the following configuration settings (*Figure 9.49*):

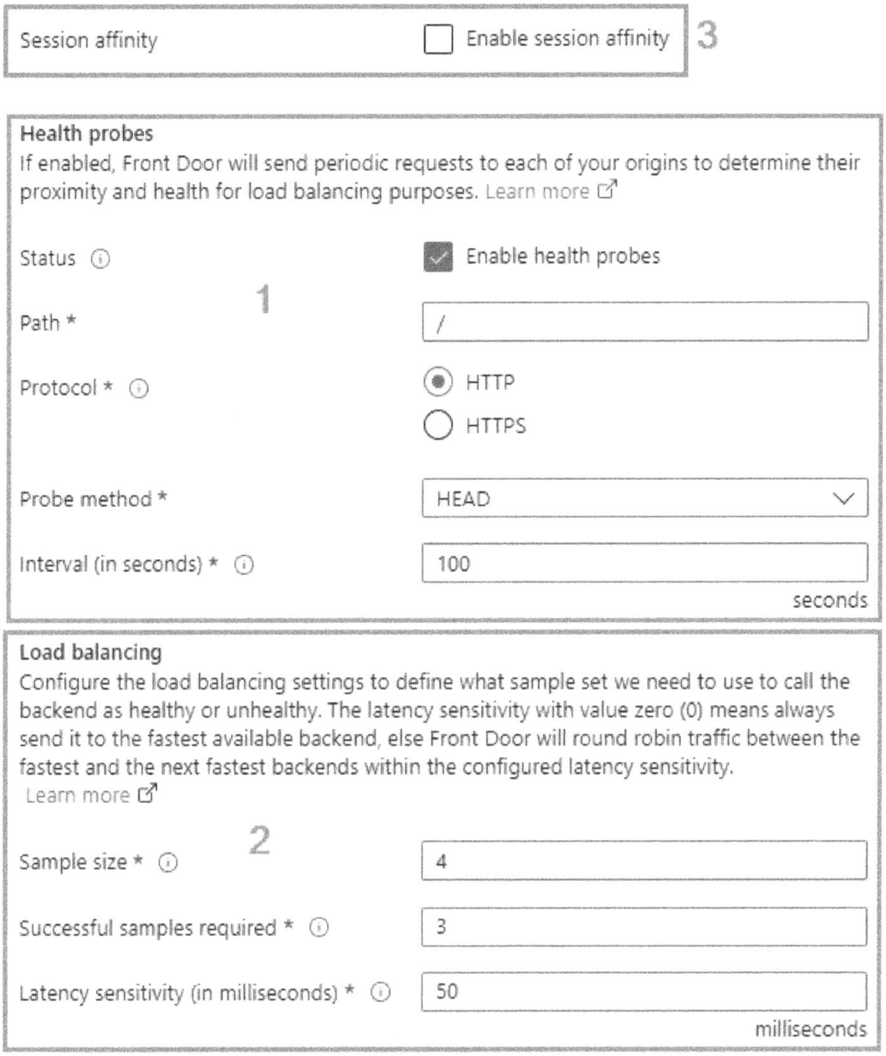

| Session affinity | ☐ Enable session affinity | 3 |

Health probes

If enabled, Front Door will send periodic requests to each of your origins to determine their proximity and health for load balancing purposes. Learn more ☐

Status ⓘ   ☑ Enable health probes

                        1

Path *   /

Protocol * ⓘ   ⦿ HTTP
                  ◯ HTTPS

Probe method *   HEAD   ⌄

Interval (in seconds) * ⓘ   100

                                            seconds

Load balancing

Configure the load balancing settings to define what sample set we need to use to call the backend as healthy or unhealthy. The latency sensitivity with value zero (0) means always send it to the fastest available backend, else Front Door will round robin traffic between the fastest and the next fastest backends within the configured latency sensitivity.
Learn more ☐

                        2

Sample size * ⓘ   4

Successful samples required * ⓘ   3

Latency sensitivity (in milliseconds) * ⓘ   50

                                            milliseconds

Figure 9.49 – Origin group configuration settings

- **Health-probe settings** (*1*): Azure Front Door conducts periodic HTTP/HTTPS probe requests to each of the configured origins to determine their proximity and health status for load-balancing end-user requests. The health-probe settings for an origin group define how Front Door polls the health status of application backends. This includes the URL path to send the probes to, the protocol to use for the probe (HTTP or HTTPS), the HTTP method to use for sending health probes (GET or HEAD), and the frequency of health probes to the origins. Note that to reduce the load and cost on the backend origins, using HEAD requests for health probes is recommended.

- **Load-balancing settings** (*2*): Load-balancing configuration settings for an origin group determine how Azure Front Door evaluates health probes to conclude whether an origin is healthy or unhealthy. These settings also determine how to balance traffic among different origins in the origin group. The following load-balancing settings are available:

  - **Sample size** defines the number of health-probe samples to consider when evaluating origin health.

  - **Successful samples required** defines the minimum number of successful health-probe samples required to declare an origin as healthy. For example, if the Front Door health-probe interval is 100 seconds, the sample size is 4, and the successful sample size is 3, Azure Front Door evaluates the last 4 health-probe samples over a 400-second period (4 x 100). The origin is considered healthy if at least 3 of the samples are successful.

  - **Latency sensitivity (in milliseconds)**: This setting is useful for implementing latency-based traffic routing. Suppose the latency sensitivity is configured to 30 milliseconds, and Front Door has three origins with the following edge-to-origin latencies: origin A—15 milliseconds, origin B—30 milliseconds, and origin C—60 milliseconds. In this scenario, only origin A and origin B will be considered eligible since the latency of origin C exceeds the configured latency sensitivity. When the setting is configured to 0 milliseconds, the request is directed to the origin with the lowest latency, and the weightings assigned to origins are not considered unless multiple origins have exactly the same network latency.

- **Session affinity** (*3*): Azure Front Door forwards requests to different origins by default, without session affinity. However, some stateful applications or certain scenarios may require that subsequent requests from the same user are processed by the same origin as the initial request. In this case, enabling the **Session affinity** feature allows Front Door to add a session affinity cookie to the response sent back to the client. It's worth noting that if the response from the origin to Front Door is cacheable, a session affinity cookie will not be added, to avoid disrupting the cookies of other clients requesting the same resource.

Configuring routes and rule sets

A Front Door route defines the association between the frontend of Front Door (endpoint domains) and the backend of Front Door (origin groups). We can add up to 100 routes to a **Standard** tier resource and up to 200 routes to a **Premium** tier resource. Route settings consist of two primary components: the "frontend side" and the "backend side," as illustrated in *Figure 9.50*:

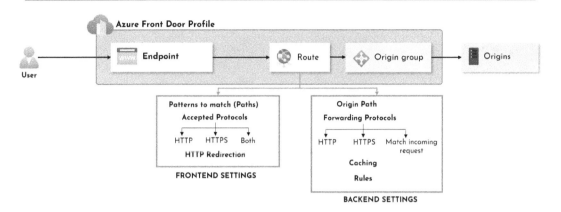

Figure 9.50 – Front Door route configuration settings

The "frontend side" defines the traffic that will be handled by the route and how incoming insecure requests (HTTP traffic) will be handled (note that HTTPS is mandatory for custom domains). We can configure the following settings for this side:

- **Patterns to match**: This setting defines the URL path patterns that the route will accept. For example, if we set this to /users/* for the www.charistech.xyz endpoint domain, requests with the URL path of www.charistech.xyz/users/* will be handled by this route.

- **Accepted protocols** and **HTTP redirection**: For custom domains, only HTTPS requests will be accepted. For the default domain (.z01.azurefd.net), both HTTP and HTTPS requests can be configured. We can also use the HTTPS redirection setting to redirect incoming HTTP requests from the clients to use the HTTPS protocol.

The "backend side" determines how the specified request will be fulfilled and how Front Door will connect with the target destinations (origins). We can configure the following settings for this side:

- **Origin path**: This setting allows us to specify a particular path or endpoint on the target destination (origin) where the requested content should be fetched from.

- **Caching**: Enabling this setting allows Front Door to cache static content for optimized content delivery to clients. We can customize how Front Door caches content from backend services when query strings are used, as shown in *Figure 9.51*:

Figure 9.51 – Caching behavior options

- **Query string caching behavior**: The various options are set out here:

  - **Ignore Query String**: This option tells Front Door to ignore query string parameters when caching content. If two requests have the same URL but different query strings, they will be treated as identical and the cached content for one request will be used for the other.

  - **Use Query String**: This option tells Front Door to use the entire query string when caching content. If two requests have the same URL but different query strings, they will be treated as different and the content for each request will be cached separately.

  - **Ignore Specified Query Strings**: This option allows us to specify which query string parameters to ignore when caching content. We can enter a comma-separated list of parameter names that Front Door should ignore when caching content. If two requests have the same URL but different values for the specified query string parameters, they will be treated as identical and the cached content for one request will be used for the other.

  - **Include Specified Query Strings**: This option allows us to specify which query string parameters to include when caching content. We can enter a comma-separated list of parameter names that Front Door should use when caching content. If two requests have the same URL but different values for the specified query string parameters, they will be treated as different and the content for each request will be cached separately.

- **Compression**: We can also enable compression to improve the response time and reduce the amount of data transmitted over the network. This feature is particularly useful when serving content to clients with limited bandwidth or high-latency connections.

Overriding rules with a rule set

To perform more granular processing or customizations beyond the capabilities of routes in Front Door, we can use **rule sets**. Rule sets are a set of rules that can be applied to incoming traffic to Front Door. They allow for granular customization of how requests are handled at the Front Door edge and can even override the origin group for a given request. In a **Standard** tier resource, we can have a maximum of 100 rule sets, while in a **Premium** tier resource, we can have up to 200 rule sets.

At an implementation level, a rule set consists of a set of **if-then** definitions known as rules. Each rule outlines the criteria that need to be assessed for incoming requests and the corresponding action to take if the criteria are met (as shown in *Figure 9.52*). Each rule can perform a specific action, such as routing traffic to a specific backend, redirecting traffic to a different URL, or modifying the URL path before forwarding the request to an origin:

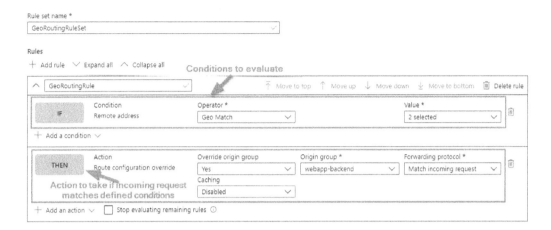

Figure 9.52 – Rule set configuration

Here's an example of how Front Door rule sets can be used in a real-world scenario. Suppose we have a web application that is deployed across multiple regions, and we want to ensure that incoming traffic is always directed to the region that is closest to the user. To achieve this, we could create a rule set that includes a rule for each region, with each rule defining the backend that should be used for traffic originating from that region. Here's an example:

- **Rule 1**: If traffic originates from North America, direct it to the North America backend

- **Rule 2**: If traffic originates from Europe, direct it to the Europe backend

- **Rule 3**: If traffic originates from Asia, direct it to the Asia backend

With this rule set in place, incoming traffic to our application will be automatically routed to the backend that is closest to the user, based on their geographic location.

Other use cases include the following:

- Directing requests to the mobile or desktop version of our application based on the type of client device

- Adding, modifying, or removing request/response headers to obscure sensitive information or capture crucial details through headers

- Rewriting the request URL path and forwarding the request to the appropriate origin in an origin group

- Modifying the caching configuration of a route dynamically based on incoming requests

Enough discussion for now—let's return to our Azure environment and implement the Azure Front Door service!

Hands-on exercise 1 – Creating and configuring an Azure Front Door service

In this exercise, we will set up an Azure Front Door configuration that pools two instances of a web application that runs in different Azure regions. This configuration directs traffic to the nearest site that runs the application. Azure Front Door continuously monitors the web application. It will demonstrate automatic failover to the next available site when the nearest site is unavailable.

Here are the tasks that we will complete in this exercise:

- **Task 1**: Create and configure an Azure Front Door service
- **Task 2**: Verify application access through Front Door

Task 1 – Create and configure an Azure Front Door service

Follow these steps:

1. Sign in to the Azure portal.

2. From the home page or the Azure menu, select + **Create a resource**. Search for **Front Door and CDN profiles**. Then, select **Create | Front Door and CDN profiles**.

3. On the **Compare offerings** page, select **Custom create**. Then, select **Continue to create a Front Door**.

4. On the **Basics** tab, configure the following settings, and then select **Next: Secrets >**:

    - **Subscription**: Select the subscription that you want to deploy the resources into

    - **Resource group**: CharisTechRG-C9

    - **Name: CharisTech-FrontDoor-Profile** (replace XXXXX with a random number as a unique name is required)

    - Select **Next: Secrets >**

The network configuration is shown in *Figure 9.53*:

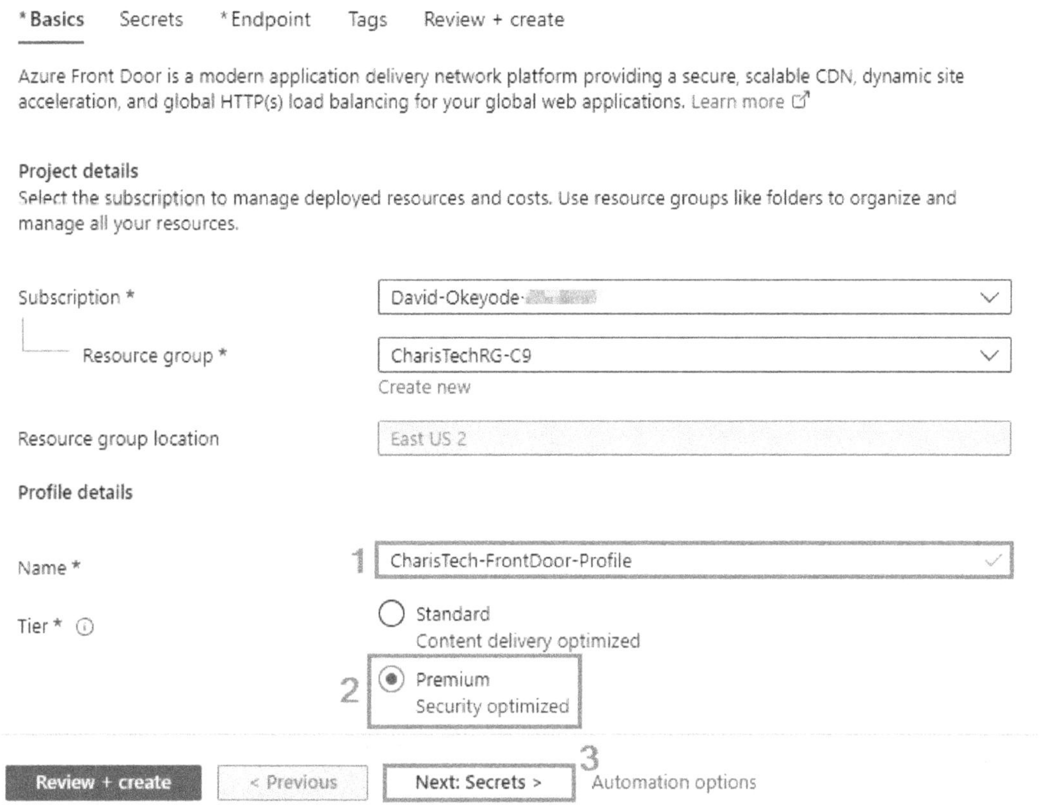

*Basics   Secrets   *Endpoint   Tags   Review + create

Azure Front Door is a modern application delivery network platform providing a secure, scalable CDN, dynamic site acceleration, and global HTTP(s) load balancing for your global web applications. Learn more ☐

Project details
Select the subscription to manage deployed resources and costs. Use resource groups like folders to organize and manage all your resources.

Subscription *	David-Okeyode⸳⸻⸻⸻ ⌄
Resource group *	CharisTechRG-C9 ⌄
	Create new
Resource group location	East US 2

Profile details

Name *	1 CharisTech-FrontDoor-Profile ✓
Tier * ⓘ	◯ Standard Content delivery optimized
	2 ◉ Premium Security optimized

3

Review + create	< Previous	Next: Secrets >	Automation options

Figure 9.53 – Basic Front Door configuration

5. On the **Secrets** tab, click **Next: Endpoint >**.

6. On the **Endpoint** tab, click **Add an endpoint** and configure the following settings:

    - **Endpoint name**: `charistech-webapp`

    - **Status: Enable this endpoint** selected

    - Click **Add**

The process is shown in *Figure 9.54*:

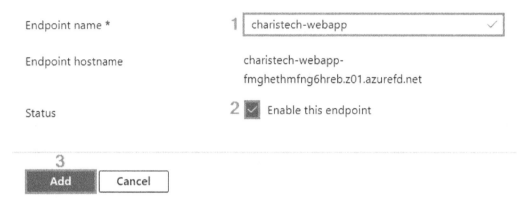

Figure 9.54 – Adding a Front Door endpoint

7. Still on the **Endpoint** tab, click + **Add a route** to configure routing to the web app origin:

Figure 9.55 – Adding a route from the endpoint page

8. On the **Add a route** page, configure the following settings:

    *   **Name**: `charistech-webapp-endpoint-to-backend-route`

    *   **Domains**: `charistech-webapp-xxxxxxxxx.z01.azurefd.net`

    *   **Patterns to match**: `/*` (This sets all the URLs this route will accept. This setting will accept all URL paths.)

    *   **Accepted protocols**: **HTTP** and **HTTPS** (This sets the protocols that this route will accept. This setting will accept both HTTP and HTTPS requests.)

    *   **Redirect**: **Redirect all traffic to use HTTPS** selected (This setting will redirect all HTTP traffic to the HTTPS endpoint.)

    *   **Origin group**: Add a new origin group

9. In the **Add an origin group** blade, configure the following settings:

    *   **Name**: `webapp-backend`

    *   Select + **Add an origin**

10. In the **Add an origin** blade, configure the following settings:

    *   **Name**: `webapp-r1`

    *   **Origin type**: **App services**

    *   **Host name**: `webapp-r1-<random_characters>.azurewebsites.net`

- Select **Add** to add the origin to the origin group:

Add an origin

Microsoft Azure

← Go back to origin group

Name *	**1**	webapp-r1 ✓
Origin type *	**2**	App services ∨
Host name *	**3**	webapp-r1-rzdcvdhx5cvwu.azurewebsit... ∨
Origin host header		webapp-r1-rzdcvdhx5cvwu.azurewebsites...✓
Certificate subject name validation ⓘ		✓ Enable the validation
HTTP port *		80
HTTPS port *		443
Priority * ⓘ		1
Weight * ⓘ		1000

4

Add · Cancel

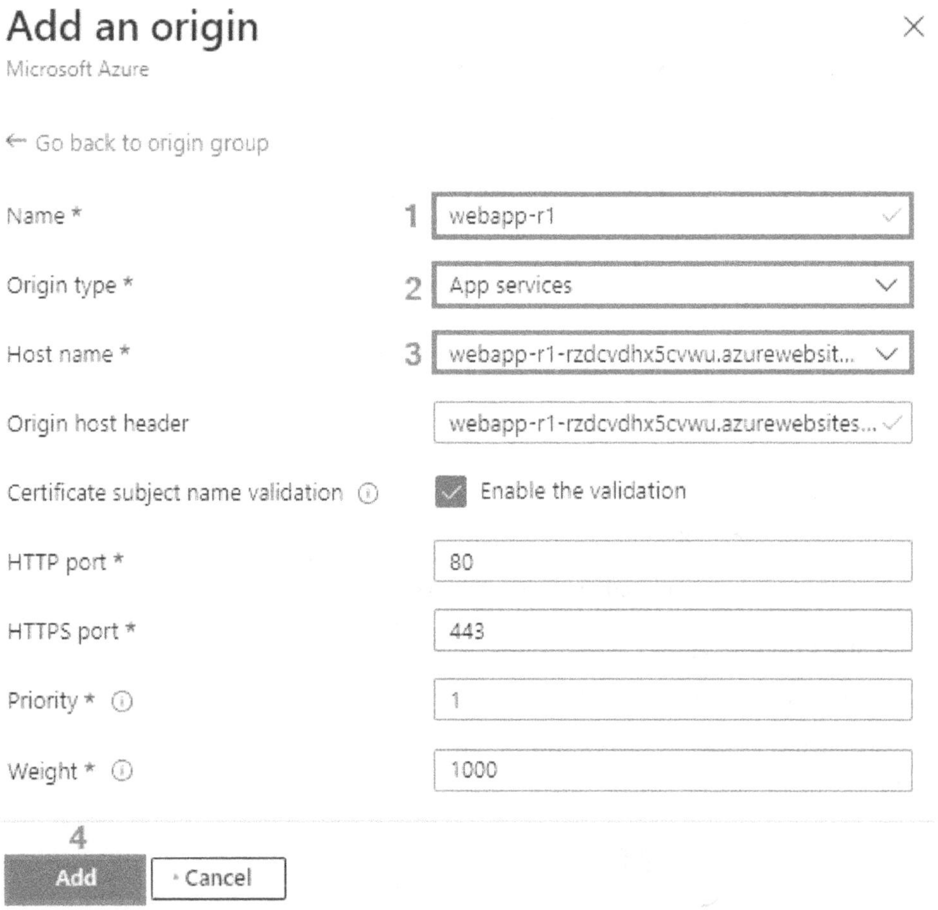

Figure 9.56 – Adding an origin to Front Door

11. Repeat *steps 9-10* to add the second web app as an origin and configure it as follows:

- **Name**: webapp-r2
- **Origin type**: **App services**
- **Host name**: **webapp-r2-<random_characters>.azurewebsites.net**
- Select **Add** to add the origin to the origin group

12. Back in the **Add an origin group blade**, leave the other settings at their defaults, and click **Add** to add the origin group:

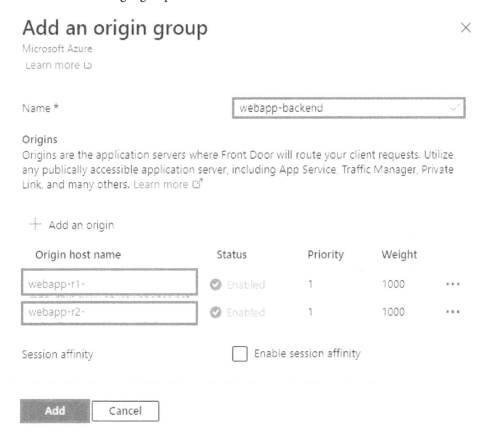

Figure 9.57 – Adding an origin group to Front Door

13. Back in the **Add a route** window, configure the following settings:

- **Origin path**: Leave blank
- **Forwarding protocol**: Match incoming request
- **Caching**: Not selected
- Click **Add** to add the route to the Front Door profile

14. Back in the **Endpoint** tab of the page to create a Front Door profile, in the **Security policy** section, select + **Add a policy** to apply a WAF policy to the Front Door profile:

Figure 9.58 – Adding a security policy from the endpoint page

15. On the **Add security policy** page, configure the following settings:

    • **Name**: `charistech-webapp-waf-policy`

    • **Domains: charistech-webapp-<random_characters>.z01.azurefd.net**

    • **WAF Policy**: Click on **Create New** to create a new security policy:

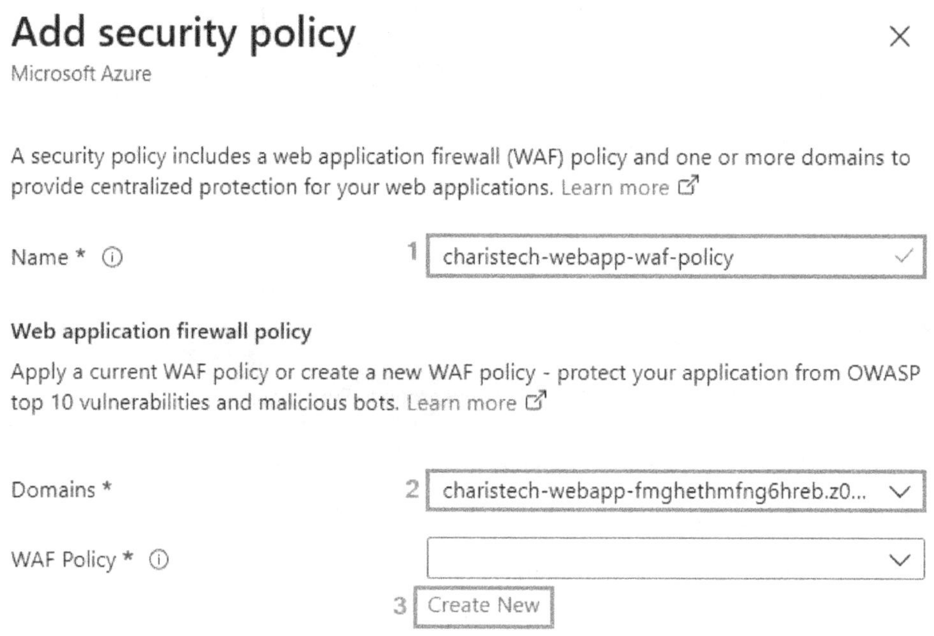

Add security policy   ✕

Microsoft Azure

A security policy includes a web application firewall (WAF) policy and one or more domains to provide centralized protection for your web applications. Learn more ☐↗

Name * ⓘ   1 | charistech-webapp-waf-policy   ✓ |

Web application firewall policy

Apply a current WAF policy or create a new WAF policy - protect your application from OWASP top 10 vulnerabilities and malicious bots. Learn more ☐↗

Domains *   2 | charistech-webapp-fmghethmfng6hreb.z0...   ∨ |

WAF Policy * ⓘ | ∨ |

                                   3 | Create New |

Figure 9.59 – Adding a security policy

16. On the **Create a new WAF policy** blade, configure the following settings:

   - **Name**: `charistechWebappWafPolicy`

   - **Add bot protection**: Not selected

   - Click **Create**

17. Back on the **Add security policy** blade, click on **Save** to add the policy:

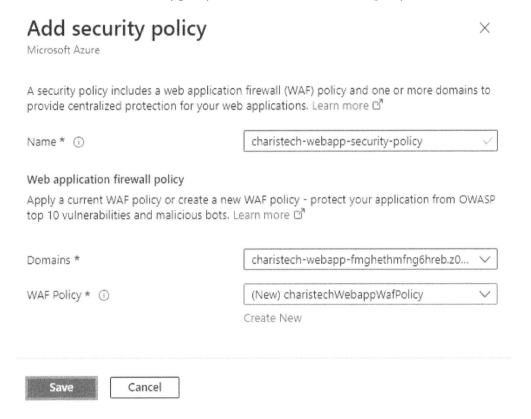

Add security policy

Microsoft Azure

X

A security policy includes a web application firewall (WAF) policy and one or more domains to provide centralized protection for your web applications. Learn more ⬀

Name * ⓘ   charistech-webapp-security-policy   ✓

Web application firewall policy

Apply a current WAF policy or create a new WAF policy - protect your application from OWASP top 10 vulnerabilities and malicious bots. Learn more ⬀

Domains *   charistech-webapp-fmghethmfng6hreb.z0... ∨

WAF Policy * ⓘ   (New) charistechWebappWafPolicy   ∨
                             Create New

Save   Cancel

Figure 9.60 – Saving the configuration

18. Select **Review + create**, and then **Create** to deploy the Azure Front Door profile. It will take a few minutes for configurations to be propagated to all edge locations.

Task 2 – Verify application access through Front Door

Follow these steps:

1. After the deployment completes, click on **Go to resource**:

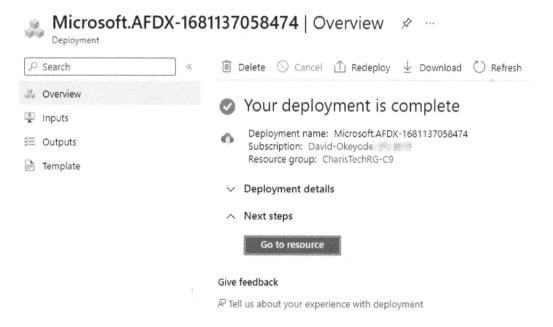

Figure 9.61 – Clicking to go to the resource

2.   In the **Overview** section, in the **Properties** tab, make a note of the **Endpoint hostname** value:

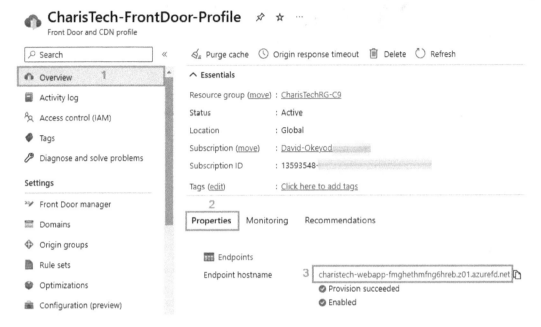

Figure 9.62 – Making a note of the Front Door endpoint hostname

3.   Open a new browser tab and browse to the following, replacing FRONT_DOOR_HOST_NAME with the name that you made a note of in the previous step:

- http://FRONT_DOOR_ENDPOINT_HOSTNAME (this should be redirected to HTTPS)

- https:// FRONT_DOOR_ENDPOINT_HOSTNAME

You should see the region that served the application request. You can try other browsers or devices to see the region that you are directed to:

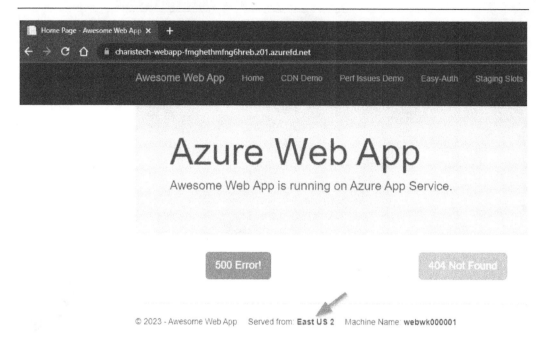

Figure 9.63 – Validating application access through Front Door

Designing and implementing an Azure Traffic Manager service

Azure Traffic Manager is a DNS-based traffic load balancer that routes incoming client requests to the most suitable endpoint based on routing rules configured by the user. It is important to note that Traffic Manager is not an inline load-balancing service like the three other services that we have discussed so far. Instead, it uses DNS to redirect a client to an available backend target.

Figure 9.64 provides an overview of the Traffic Manager request routing process:

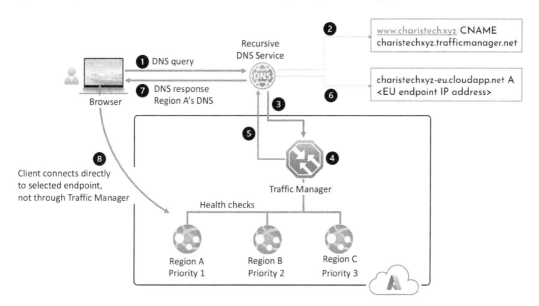

Figure 9.64 – Traffic Manager request routing process

The request routing process in Azure Traffic Manager involves several steps, as explained next using an example:

1. When the client needs to resolve the name `partners.contoso.com`, it sends a DNS query to its configured recursive DNS service. This service contacts the various authoritative DNS services across the internet to resolve the DNS name. For example, let's suppose the user wants to access the website `www.charistech.xyz`.

2. The recursive DNS service first finds the name servers for the `charistech.xyz` domain and requests the `www.charistech.xyz` DNS record. The `charistech.xyz` DNS servers respond with a CNAME record that points to `charistechxyz.trafficmanager.net`.

3. The recursive DNS service then finds the name servers for the `trafficmanager.net` domain, which are provided by the Azure Traffic Manager service. It sends a request for the `charistechxyz.trafficmanager.net` DNS record to those DNS servers.

4. The Traffic Manager name servers receive the request and select an endpoint based on the configured state and health of each endpoint, as determined by the Traffic Manager health checks, and the chosen traffic-routing method (we will discuss traffic-routing methods in the next section).

5. The selected endpoint is returned as another DNS CNAME record—for example, `charistechxyz-eu.cloudapp.net`.

6. The recursive DNS service finds the name servers for the `cloudapp.net` domain and requests the `charistechxyz-eu.cloudapp.net` DNS record. A DNS A record containing the IP address of the EU-based service endpoint is returned.

7. The recursive DNS service consolidates the results and returns a single DNS response to the client.

8. The client then connects directly to the application service endpoint, not through Traffic Manager, but by using the given IP address. As it is an HTTPS endpoint, the client performs the necessary SSL/TLS handshake and makes the necessary web requests.

Azure Traffic Manager continuously monitors the health of each endpoint and updates its routing policy accordingly. If an endpoint becomes unavailable, Azure Traffic Manager will automatically route traffic to the next available endpoint.

Configuring a traffic routing method

Several routing methods can be used in Azure Traffic Manager (*Figure 9.65*):

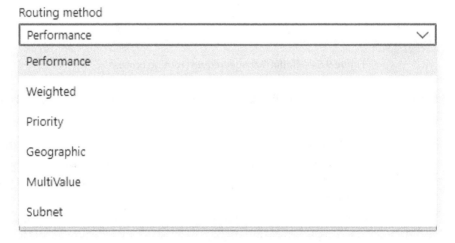

Figure 9.65 – Traffic Manager routing options

The various routing methods are described in more detail here:

- **Priority**: This method sends traffic to a specific endpoint based on the configured priority value. The endpoint with the highest priority is chosen first. For example, we can configure a primary endpoint in one region and a secondary endpoint in another region. If the primary endpoint is unavailable, traffic will be sent to the secondary endpoint.

- **Weighted**: This method distributes traffic across endpoints based on user-defined weights. For example, we can allocate 50% of the traffic to one endpoint and 50% to another.

- **Performance**: This method routes traffic to the endpoint with the lowest latency. For example, if we have endpoints in multiple regions, Traffic Manager can route traffic to the endpoint that provides the best performance for a specific user.

- **Geographic**: This method routes traffic based on the user's geographic location. Traffic is sent to the endpoint that is closest to the user. For example, if we have endpoints in Europe and the US, Traffic Manager can send traffic to the endpoint that is closest to the user's location.

- **MultiValue**: This method sends traffic to multiple endpoints that are healthy and meet the criteria defined in the routing rule. For example, if we have endpoints in multiple regions and want to send traffic to all available endpoints, we can use this method.

Overall, Azure Traffic Manager provides flexible and powerful routing options to distribute traffic across multiple endpoints in a way that is optimized for your application's needs.

Configuring Traffic Manager endpoints

Azure Traffic Manager supports the following types of endpoints:

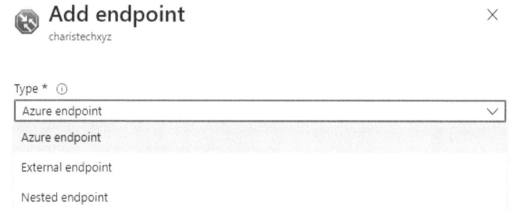

Figure 9.66 – Traffic Manager endpoint options

- **Azure endpoints**: These are used to route traffic to Azure resources such as Azure web apps, Azure VMs, a public IP address, or Azure Cloud Services.

- **External endpoints**: These are used to route traffic to external resources such as websites hosted outside of Azure or other non-Azure resources that have a publicly accessible IP address.

- **Nested endpoints**: These are used when an endpoint is another Traffic Manager profile. This allows for the creation of hierarchical or nested Traffic Manager profiles, where one profile can route traffic to another Traffic Manager profile.

Choosing an optimal load-balancing and application delivery solution

The Azure load-balancing decision tree takes into account various factors when selecting the appropriate load-balancing options. The **Help me choose default** tab in Azure load balancing considers the following factors:

- **Traffic type**: Is the application web-based (HTTP/HTTPS)? Is it a public or private application?

- **Global versus regional**: Do you need to load balance VMs or containers within a VNet? Or do you need to load balance scale units/deployments across different regions, or both?

- **Availability**: What is the required SLA for the application?

- **Cost**: In addition to the cost of the load-balancing service itself, consider the cost of managing a solution built on that service.

- **Features and limitations**: What are the overall limitations of each load-balancing service? Refer to the service limits to identify the constraints.

The flowchart shown in *Figure 9.67* provides guidance on selecting the appropriate load-balancing solution for your application. However, it should be treated as a starting point because every application has unique requirements. Therefore, it is recommended to perform a more detailed evaluation after using the flowchart's recommendations:

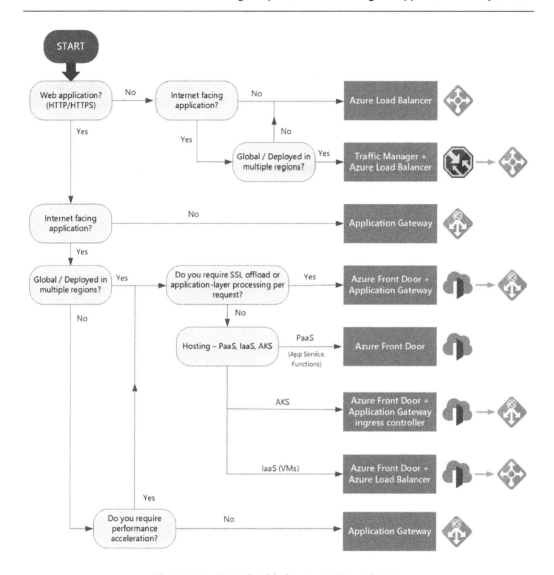

Figure 9.67 – Azure load-balancing option selection

If your application consists of multiple workloads, evaluate each workload separately. A complete solution may require incorporating two or more load-balancing solutions.

Summary

In this chapter, we delved into the topic of load-balancing and application delivery services in Azure. We discussed the importance of load balancing for ensuring the HA and scalability of applications and covered the design and implementation of several Azure load-balancing solutions, including Azure Load Balancer, Azure Application Gateway, Azure Front Door, and Azure Traffic Manager.

We explored the differences between these solutions and their various use cases and provided guidance on how to choose the optimal solution based on specific requirements. This chapter equipped you with a solid understanding of Azure's load-balancing and application delivery services and the skills needed to design and implement these solutions.

In the next chapter, we will expand on our understanding of Azure networking by concentrating on establishing private connectivity to Azure platform services. See you there!

10

Designing and Implementing Platform Service Connectivity

Azure offers various platform services, such as Azure SQL Database, Azure Storage, Azure Key Vault, and Azure App Service, that are widely used by organizations. These services come with several advantages, such as easy deployment, automatic scaling, built-in backups, and high availability. While it is advisable to deploy platform services in a customer-managed virtual network for better control over network traffic, this may not always be possible, mainly due to technical limitations. When deploying platform services outside of customer-managed virtual networks, there are three main options available for controlling network connections to the services in Azure. This chapter will provide you with a clear understanding of these three options. It will also guide you in determining the appropriate option to use based on your specific use case. By the end of this chapter, you will have a good understanding of the following:

- The platform service firewall and its exceptions
- Implementing service endpoints
- Implementing private endpoints

We have arranged these topics so that they match the exam objectives. Let's get started!

Technical requirements

To follow along with the instructions in this chapter, you will need the following:

- A PC with an internet connection
- An Azure subscription

Implementing platform service network security

Services such as Azure Storage and Azure Key Vault cannot be deployed into a customer-managed Azure virtual network. At the time of writing, only 29 platform services can be deployed to a customer-managed virtual network. Additionally, deploying supported services in a private network can be expensive. For example, deploying an Azure App Service into a private network with App Service Environment costs more than deploying a normal App Service.

When deploying platform services outside of customer-managed virtual networks, there are options available for controlling network connections to the services in Azure. These options include the *platform service firewall*, *private endpoints*, and *service endpoints* (see *Figure 10.1*):

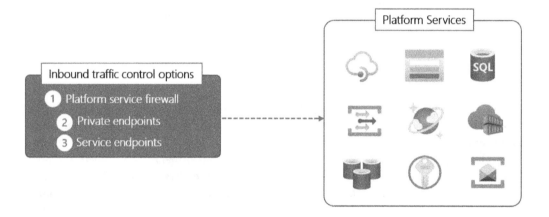

Figure 10.1 – Options for controlling inbound network connections to platform services in Azure

Let's get started with the platform service firewall option!

> **Note**
>
> For an updated list of platform services that can be deployed into a customer-managed virtual network, please refer to this URL: `https://learn.microsoft.com/en-us/azure/virtual-network/virtual-network-for-azure-services#services-that-can-be-deployed-into-a-virtual-network`.

Understanding the platform service firewall and its exceptions

In their default configuration, most platform services in Azure have public endpoints that allow network connections from any network, including the internet (see *Figure 10.2*). However, this may not be suitable for organizations that require more restricted incoming requests due to security or compliance concerns:

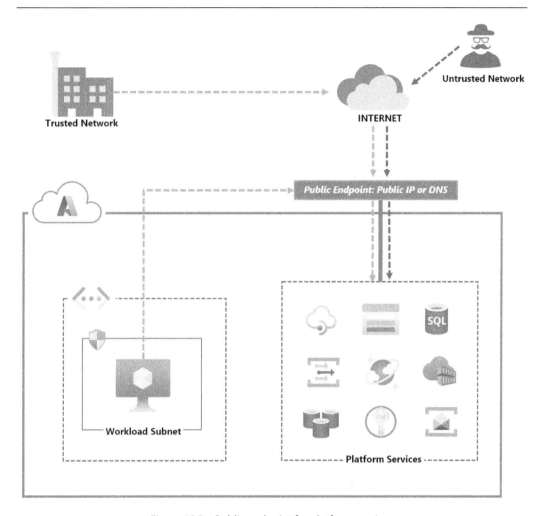

Figure 10.2 – Public endpoint for platform services

The Azure platform service firewall is a network security feature that enables you to restrict network access to platform services from specific IP addresses or IP ranges. It works by allowing or blocking traffic based on the source IP address. It is designed to act as an additional layer of defense against unauthorized network access from the internet or other untrusted networks (see *Figure 10.3*).

This option works well for clients that use a static IP address or a known IP range, and if communication over the internet is not disallowed by policy. To allow access to Azure services, such as Web App or Logic App, we can refer to the list of publicly documented data center IP addresses for Azure services, which can be found at `https://www.microsoft.com/download/details.aspx?id=56519`:

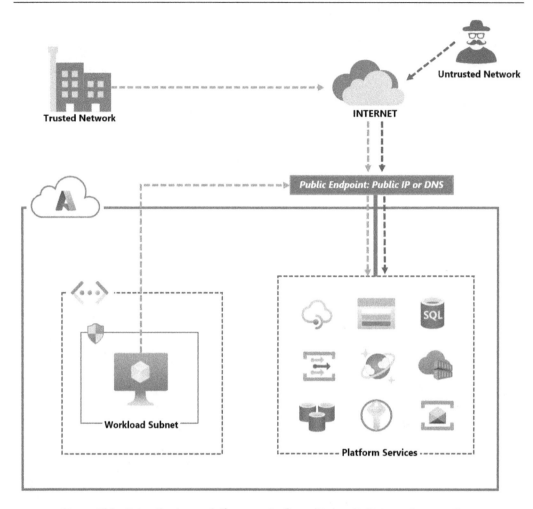

Figure 10.3 – Using the Azure platform service firewall to control inbound connections

Figure 10.4 shows a platform service firewall configuration for an Azure Key Vault resource that allows network access only when the request originates from two trusted IP addresses (`1.1.1.1` and `2.2.2.2`). Any network connection originating from an IP address that is not listed will be blocked! This also applies to performing data plane operations from the Azure portal:

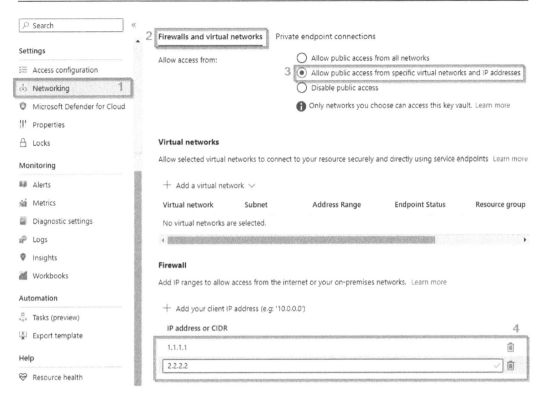

Figure 10.4 – Sample firewall rule for an Azure PaaS service

That being said, we need to be a bit careful when implementing this option! The reason is that when we configure a firewall for supported PaaS services, all requests that are not explicitly allowed are blocked. While this may not sound like a bad thing, it can impact the functionality of certain features that rely on interactions with other Azure services. For example, if we want to use the Azure Backup service to protect VM disks stored in a storage account, we need to allow the IP addresses of the Azure Backup service explicitly; otherwise, the backup process will fail. However, keeping track of IP addresses used by Microsoft services can be challenging since they are dynamic and can change. To handle this, we can configure an exception by allowing trusted Microsoft services, as shown in *Figure 10.5*:

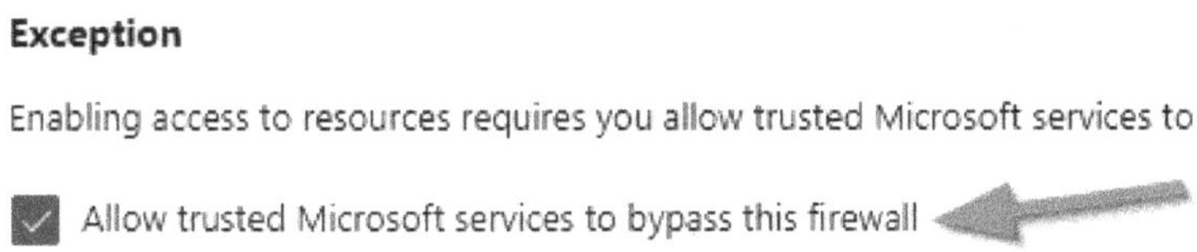

Exception

Enabling access to resources requires you allow trusted Microsoft services to bypass firewall.

✓ Allow trusted Microsoft services to bypass this firewall

Figure 10.5 – Adding a platform service firewall exception

What are trusted Microsoft services?

Trusted services include services where Microsoft controls all the code that runs on the service. For example, Azure DevOps is not on the list since users can write custom code to run on it. There are currently 30 services on the list here: `https://learn.microsoft.com/en-us/azure/key-vault/general/overview-vnet-service-endpoints#trusted-services`.

Understanding service endpoints

In addition to the public endpoints that we discussed earlier, many services also offer a service endpoint. A service endpoint exposes the service to resources in an Azure subnet via an optimized route using the Azure backbone network (indicated as *2* in *Figure 10.6*), rather than through an internet-reachable public endpoint. This is useful when we want to limit network access to services hosted in particular Azure subnets. For example, if a virtual machine in an Azure subnet needs to store data in Azure Blob storage, we can create a service endpoint for **Microsoft.Storage** for the subnet where the virtual machine is located. At the time of writing, 15 services support service endpoints. The list can be found at `https://learn.microsoft.com/en-us/azure/virtual-network/virtual-network-service-endpoints-overview`:

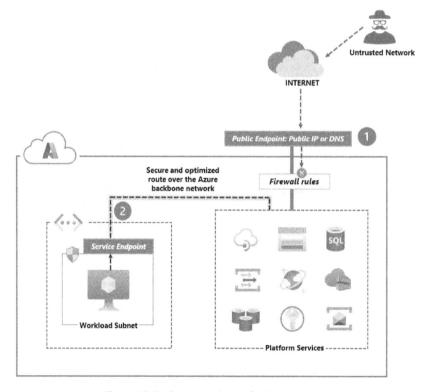

Figure 10.6 – Azure service endpoint scenario

To implement service endpoints, there are two main steps that we need to take. The first step is to enable the service endpoint on the subnet that needs access to the Azure service (shown in *Figure 10.7*). This is a network-side operation:

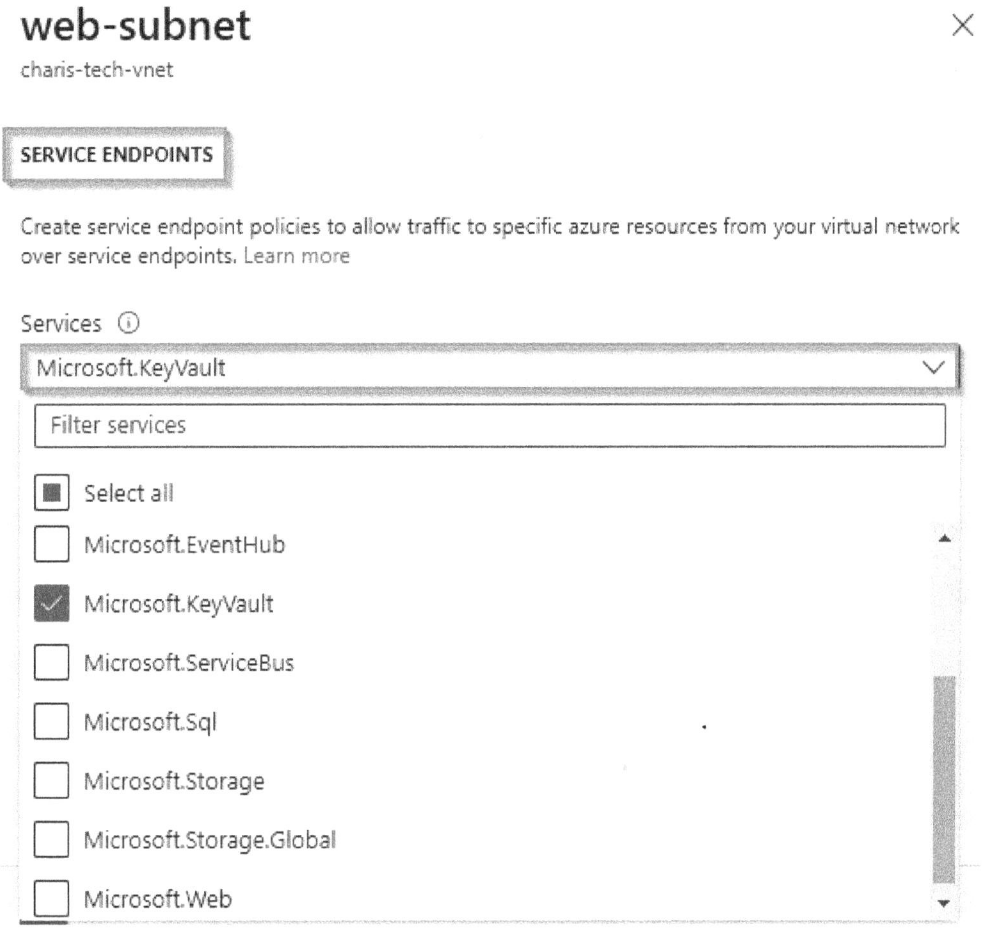

web-subnet   ×

charis-tech-vnet

SERVICE ENDPOINTS

Create service endpoint policies to allow traffic to specific azure resources from your virtual network over service endpoints. Learn more

Services ⓘ

Microsoft.KeyVault   ∨

Filter services

■ Select all

☐ Microsoft.EventHub

☑ Microsoft.KeyVault

☐ Microsoft.ServiceBus

☐ Microsoft.Sql

☐ Microsoft.Storage

☐ Microsoft.Storage.Global

☐ Microsoft.Web

Figure 10.7 – Enabling the service endpoint for a subnet

The second step is to grant access to our subnet at the destination service level (as shown in *Figure 10.8*). This is a resource-side operation:

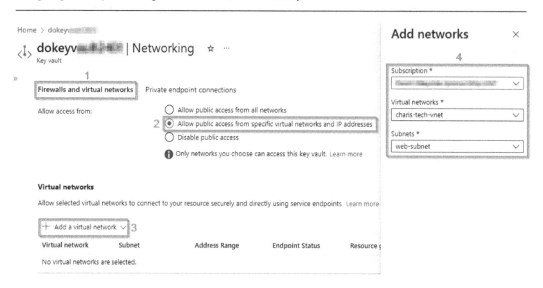

Figure 10.8 – Firewall access for a service endpoint

There are a few points to keep in mind when using the service endpoint option. First, the service endpoint is not supported across AD tenants for most services, except for Azure Storage and Azure Key Vault. For example, if we have a virtual network in one AD tenant, we can use a service endpoint to access an Azure Storage Account or Key Vault resource in another Azure AD tenant, but not for other services as they belong to different AD tenants.

Also, virtual networks created in different regions can access most Azure services in another region through service endpoints, except for Azure Storage and Azure SQL Database, which are regional and require both the virtual network and Azure service to be in the same region. For example, a virtual network in one region can use a service endpoint to access an Azure Cosmos DB account in another region but cannot do the same for an Azure Storage account.

Understanding service endpoint policies

Service endpoint policies allow us to control the Azure service that will be reachable via a service endpoint configuration. They provide an additional layer of security to ensure that a service endpoint configuration cannot be used to access all instances of a resource. For example, if we have multiple storage accounts in our Azure subscription, we can use a service endpoint policy to limit access to a specific storage account. Service endpoint policies are created and managed at the Azure subscription level and can be applied to multiple subnets in our environment.

At the time of writing this book, only **Microsoft.Storage** is available with service endpoint policies. We can scope access to one of three options: **All accounts in subscription**, **All accounts in resource group**, or **Single account** (see *Figure 10.9*):

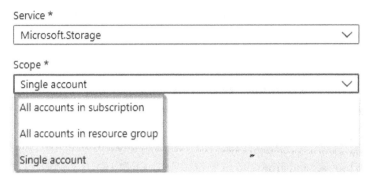

Figure 10.9 – The scope options of a service endpoint policy

Having understood platform services, we will now move on to hands-on exercises to get a better grip on the lessons we learned.

Hands-on exercise 1 – provisioning the resources for this chapter's exercises

To follow along with the exercises in this chapter, we will provision some Azure resources to work with. We have prepared an Azure ARM template in the GitHub repository of this book for this purpose. The template will deploy a virtual machine, a storage account (with a file share), and an app service web app in the specified Azure region, as shown in *Figure 10.10*:

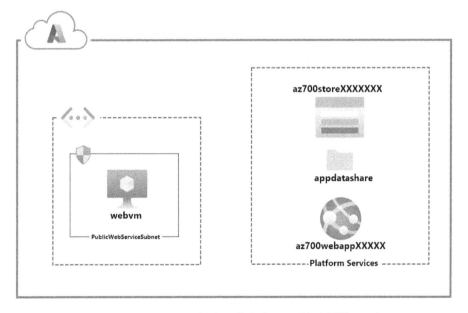

Figure 10.10 – Resources deployed via the provided ARM template

In this exercise, we will initialize the template deployment in GitHub, complete the necessary parameters, and deploy the template to Azure.

Let's get into this!

Task 1 – initializing the template deployment in GitHub, completing the parameters, and deploying the template to Azure

The steps are as follows:

1. Open a web browser and browse to `https://packt.link/yfcGl`.

    This link will open the GitHub repository that contains the ARM template for deploying the resources that we need.

2. In the GitHub repository that opens, click **Deploy to Azure**:

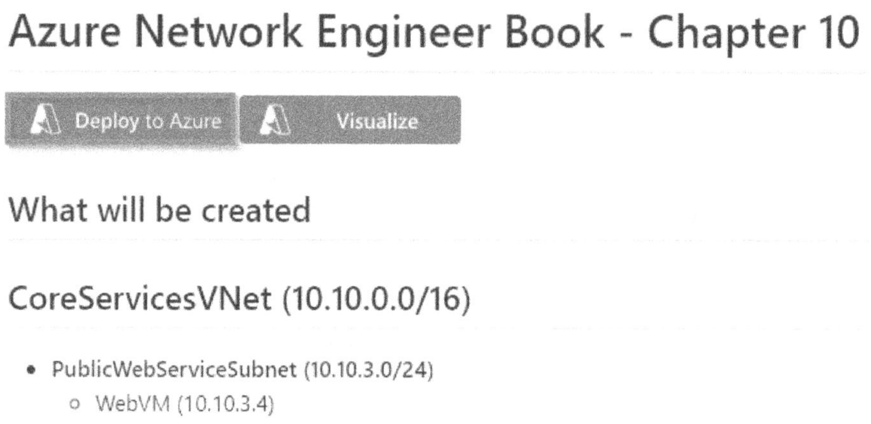

Azure Network Engineer Book - Chapter 10

What will be created

CoreServicesVNet (10.10.0.0/16)

- PublicWebServiceSubnet (10.10.3.0/24)
  - WebVM (10.10.3.4)

Figure 10.11 – Starting the template deployment

3. If you're prompted to authenticate, sign in to the Azure portal with your administrative username and password.

4. In the **Custom Deployment** window, configure the following:

    - **Subscription**: Select the subscription that you want to deploy the resources into.

    - **Resource Group**: **Create New** | **Name**: `CharisTechRG-C10` | **OK**.

    - **Region**: Select a region for the resource group and all the resources that will be created.

    - **VM Size**: **Standard_B2s** (or select the VM size that you verified in *Chapter 1*).

    - **Admin Username**: `azureuser`.

    - **Admin Password**: Enter a complex password. This will be the password for all deployed VM instances. Make a note of this as it will be needed for later exercises.

- Select **Review + create**:

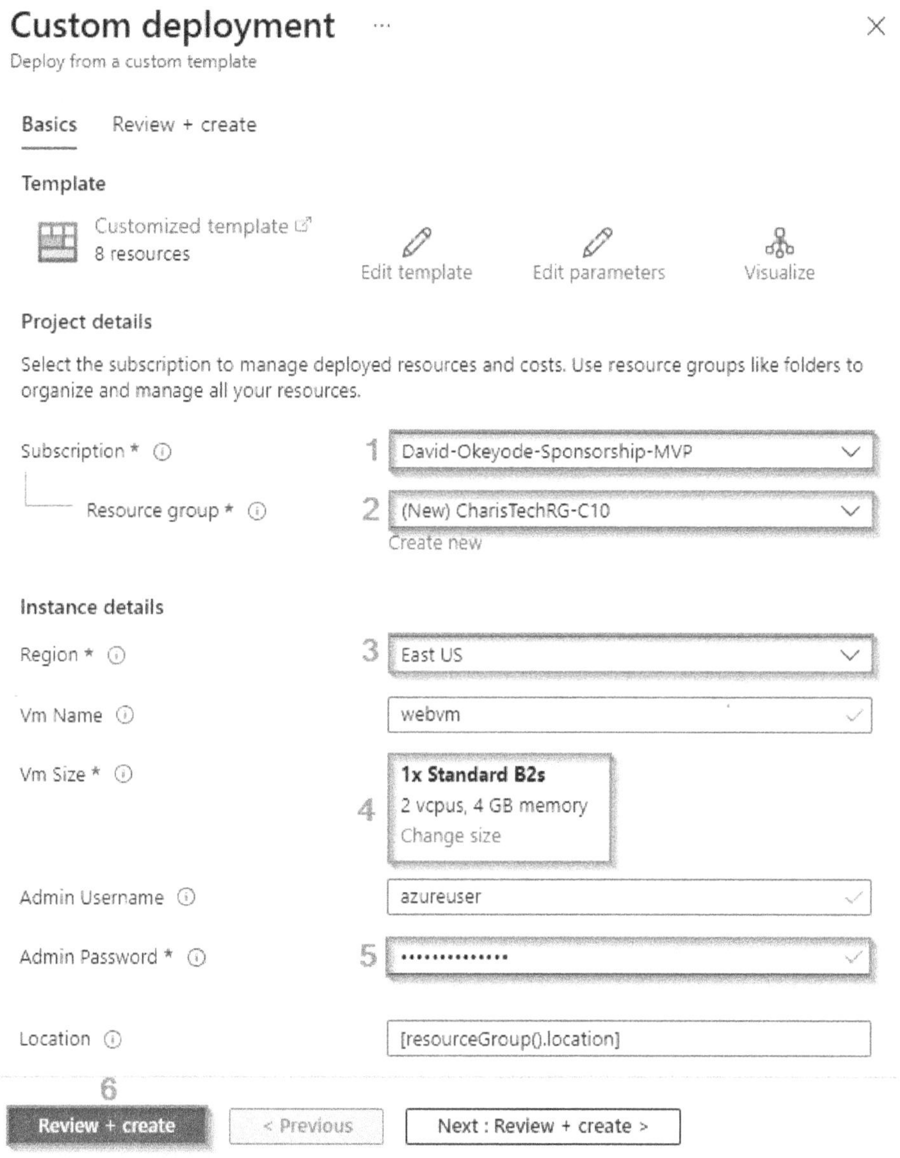

Custom deployment · · ·   ✕
Deploy from a custom template

Basics   Review + create

Template

⊞   Customized template ↗
      8 resources
                              ✎   ✎   ⊹
                          Edit template   Edit parameters   Visualize

Project details

Select the subscription to manage deployed resources and costs. Use resource groups like folders to organize and manage all your resources.

Subscription * ⓘ	1	David-Okeyode-Sponsorship-MVP	⌄

Resource group * ⓘ   2 (New) CharisTechRG-C10   ⌄
                          Create new

Instance details

Region * ⓘ	3	East US	⌄

Vm Name ⓘ   webvm   ✓

Vm Size * ⓘ   **1x Standard B2s**
                  4 2 vcpus, 4 GB memory
                     Change size

Admin Username ⓘ   azureuser   ✓

Admin Password * ⓘ 5 ············   ✓

Location ⓘ   [resourceGroup().location]

6

Review + create	< Previous	Next : Review + create >

Figure 10.12 – Completing the template parameters

5. After the validation has passed, click **Create**.

6. Wait for the deployment to complete before moving on to the next exercise.

Hands-on exercise 2 – configuring service endpoints for a storage account

Here are the exercises that we will complete in this exercise:

- Task 1 – Obtaining file share mounting information
- Task 2 – Configuring service endpoint access to the storage account
- Task 3 – Testing service endpoint connectivity to the storage account from the private subnet
- Task 4 – Testing the storage account's connection from an external network to confirm that access is denied
- Task 5 – Configuring a service endpoint policy

Let's go through the steps to accomplish these tasks.

Task 1 – obtaining file share mounting information

The steps are as follows:

1. In the Azure portal, in the **Search resources, services, and docs** textbox at the top of the Azure portal page, type `az700store` and select the displayed storage account:

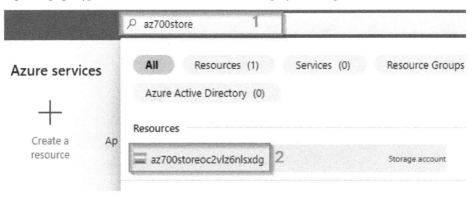

Figure 10.13 – Searching for the storage account

2. In the **Data storage** section, click **File shares** and select the **appdatashare** share:

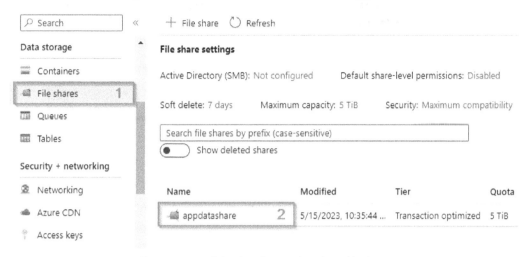

Figure 10.14 – Selecting the appdatashare file share

3. In the **appdatashare** window, click **Connect**, select the **Windows** tab, and fill in the following:

-   **Drive letter**: Leave the default setting
-   **Authentication method: Storage account key**
-   Click **Show Script**:

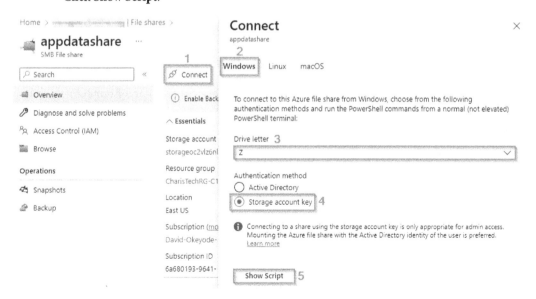

Figure 10.15 – Copying the connection information for the file share

4.   Make a note of the mount command. You can copy the information into a Notepad document. This information will be required in the later steps of this exercise. Close the **Connect** blade, then close the **appdatashare** blade:

```
Hide Script
```

```
$connectTestResult = Test-NetConnection -ComputerName
                              .file.core.windows.net -Port 445
if ($connectTestResult.TcpTestSucceeded) {
    # Save the password so the drive will persist on reboot
    cmd.exe /C "cmdkey /add:"storageoc2vlz6nlsxdg.file.core.windows.net"
/user:"localhost\                      "
/pass:"j                            7BEjsX1ycNfa7ymorAVKmTMhSqOcxdakCoGf
QPVvwnB+vbp1ah+ASt8IkU8Q=="""
    # Mount the drive
    New-PSDrive -Name Z -PSProvider FileSystem -Root
"\\                      .file.core.windows.net\appdatashare" -Persist
} else {
    Write-Error -Message "Unable to reach the Azure storage account via port 445.
Check to make sure your organization or ISP is not blocking port 445, or use Azure
P2S VPN, Azure S2S VPN, or Express Route to tunnel SMB traffic over a different
port."
}
                              Click to copy the script ━━━━▶ 🗅
```

Figure 10.16 – Copying the PowerShell script to mount the file share

Task 2 – configuring service endpoint access to the storage account

In this task, we will streamline the process by enabling the service endpoint for our subnet while simultaneously granting access at the service level, rather than carrying out these actions separately in two steps:

1.   Still on the **Storage account** blade, in the **Security + networking** section, click **Networking**, then **Firewalls and virtual networks**:

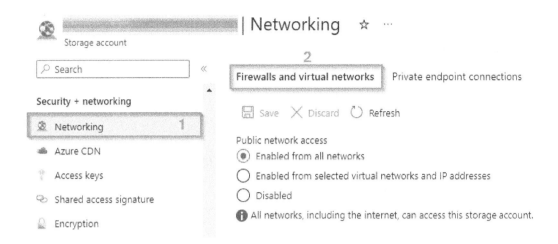

Figure 10.17 – Adding a service endpoint connection

2. In the **Public network access** section, select **Enabled from selected virtual networks and IP addresses**, then click + **Add existing virtual network**:

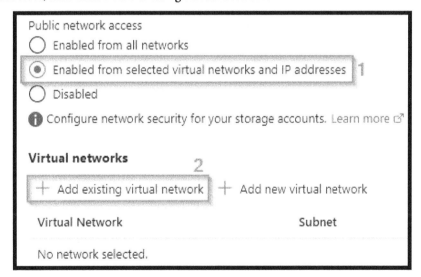

Figure 10.18 – Adding a virtual network configuration

3. In the **Add networks** blade, configure the following:

    • **Subscription**: Select your subscription

    • **Virtual networks: CoreServicesVnet**

- **Subnets: PublicWebServiceSubnet**

- Click **Enable**:

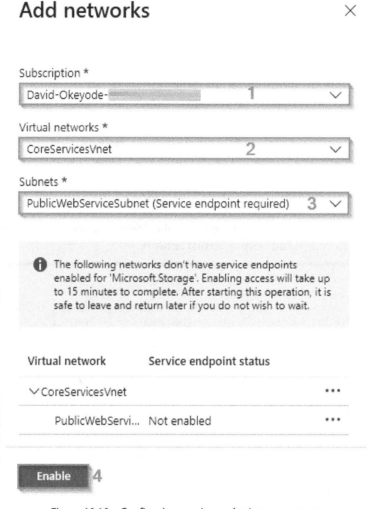

Figure 10.19 – Configuring service endpoint parameters

4. This will enable the service endpoint for **PublicWebServiceSubnet**. You will get a confirmation when this is completed, as shown here. Click **Add** to proceed with this process:

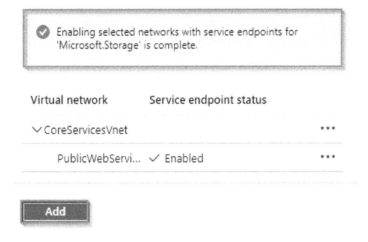

Figure 10.20 – Adding the new service connection

5.   Click **Save** to complete this process:

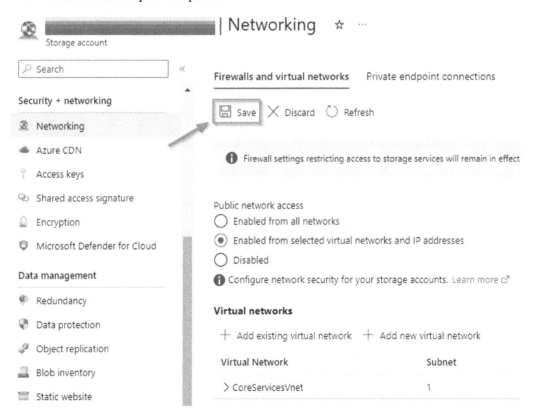

Figure 10.21 – Saving the configuration

Now that we have configured the service endpoint, we will test access to the storage account by mounting the **appdatashare** file share on the Windows VM. Since it is connected to the **PublicWebServiceSubnet** subnet, if the mounting process is successful, this means that the subnet has access to the storage account.

Task 3 – testing service endpoint connectivity to the storage account from the private subnet

This task aims to use the Bastion service to establish a connection with the virtual machine and confirm connectivity to the storage account via the service endpoint. We will accomplish this by mounting the file share:

1. On the Azure portal home page, in the search box, type WebVM and select the **WebVM** virtual machine when it appears:

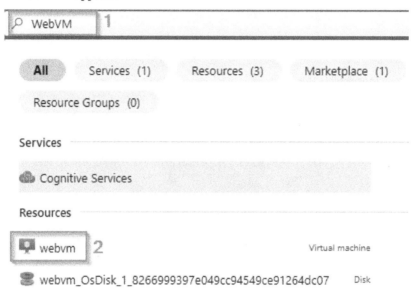

Figure 10.22 – Selecting the WebVM virtual machine

2.   In the **WebVM** window, in the **Settings** section, click **Connect**, then **Bastion**. Click **Use Bastion**:

Figure 10.23 – Selecting the option to connect to the VM using Bastion

3.   In the **WebVM | Bastion** window, configure the following and click **Connect**:

- **Username**: `azureuser`
- **Authentication Type**: **Password**
- **Password**: Enter the password that you specified during the template deployment
- **Open in new browser tab**: Selected

If prompted, enable a pop-up window for the connection to be successful. Also, allow clipboard access if prompted:

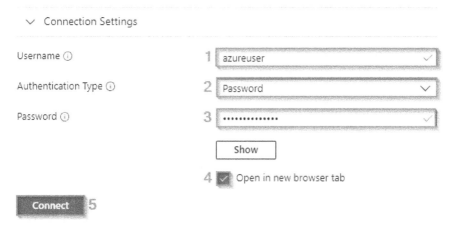

Figure 10.24 – Configuring the VM credentials and initiating a connection to the VM

4. In WebVM, open Windows PowerShell and run the commands you copied in *Task 1* of this exercise to mount the **appdatashare** file share on the Windows VM. It is recommended to paste the script into Notepad on the VM first and then copy it from there. Sometimes, pasting the script directly via Bastion messes it up:

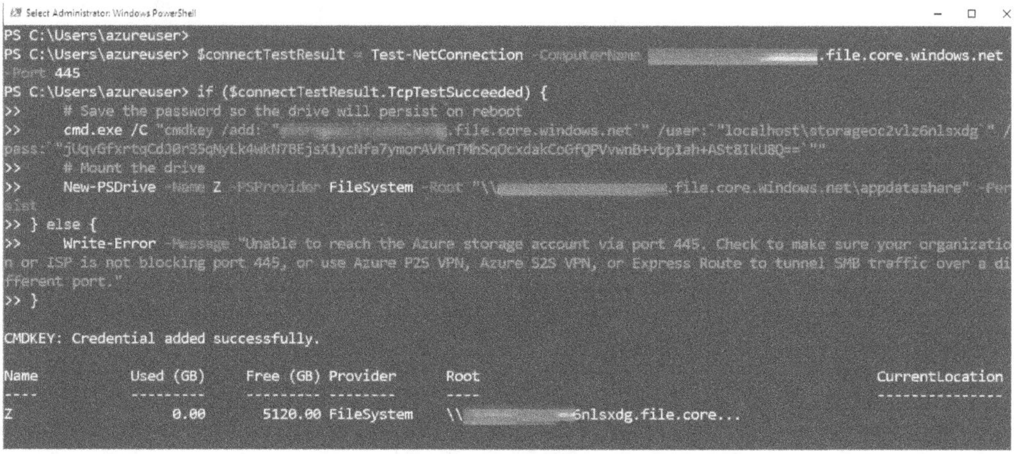

Figure 10.25 – Running the script to mount the file share

Keep the Bastion session open as it will be required in the third hands-on exercise of this chapter.

Task 4 – testing the storage account's connection from an external network to confirm that access is denied

The steps are as follows:

1. Back in the Azure portal, open the **Storage account** blade. Then, in the **Data storage** section, select **File shares**. Click **appdatashare**:

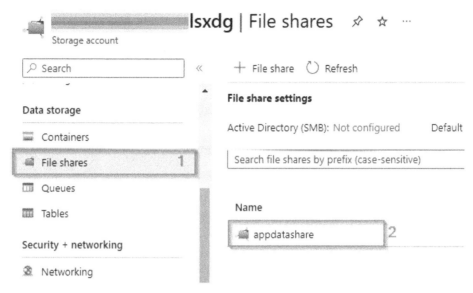

Figure 10.26 – Attempting to access the file share from the portal over the internet

2. In the **appdatashare** window, click **Browse** to attempt to access the file share. You will get an error informing you that you do not have access to the file share, as shown in the following screenshot. This confirms that access to the public internet and any other network is now restricted:

Figure 10.27 – Reviewing the access denied message

Task 5 – configuring a service endpoint policy

The objective of this task is to create a service endpoint policy that limits access to a specific storage account rather than allowing access to all storage accounts. Additionally, we will associate this policy with the **PublicWebServiceSubnet** subnet:

1. In the Azure portal, click on the **Microsoft Azure** icon in the top-left section to go to the home page, then click + **Create a resource**:

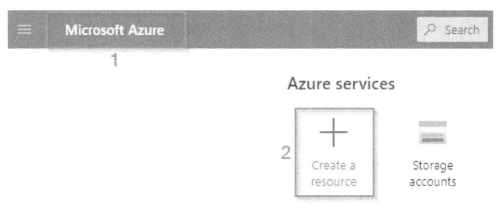

Figure 10.28 – Adding a resource in Azure

2. In the search pane, type `service endpoint policy` and press *Enter*. From the search results, select the **Service endpoint policy** option and click on the **Create** button:

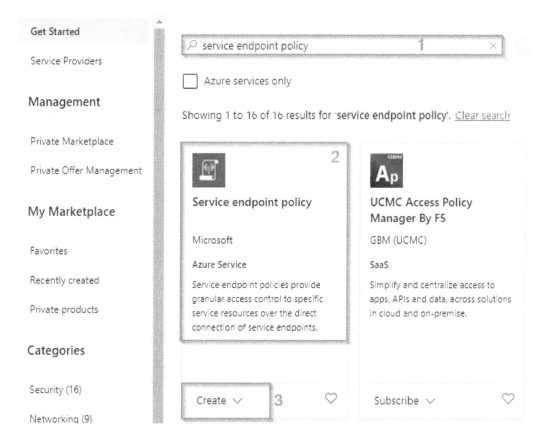

Figure 10.29 – Searching for service endpoint policy

3. In the **Create service endpoint policy** window, configure the following:

    •   **Subscription**: Select your Azure subscription

    •   **Resource group: CharisTechRG-C10**

    •   **Name: PublicWebSubnet-SE-Policy**

    •   **Location**: Select the same location as the other resources

- Click **Next : Policy definitions >**:

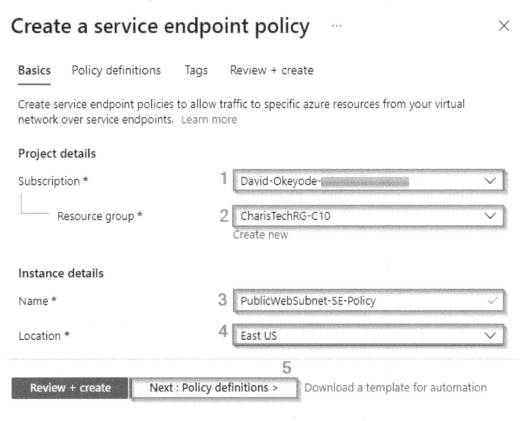

Figure 10.30 – Configuring the parameters for a service endpoint policy

4. In the **Policy definitions** tab, select **+ Add a resource** and configure the following:

- **Service: Microsoft.Storage** (only **Microsoft.Storage** is available with service endpoint policies)

- **Scope: Single Account**

- **Subscription**: Select your Azure subscription

- **Resource group: CharisTechRG-C10**

- **Resource**: Select the storage resource that starts with az700

- Click **Add** to finish adding the resource:

Home > Create a resource > Market

Add a resource   ✕

Create a service endp

```
            1
Basics  | Policy definitions |  Tags
```

This policy will allow access only to the
denied.

Resources
+ Add a resource 2

Service   Allowed R

Add a resource to get started

Aliases
+ Add an alias

Service Alias

Add an alias to get started

Service *

Microsoft.Storage   3 ∨

Scope *

Single account   4 ∨

Subscription *

David-Okeyode-   5 ∨

Resource group *

CharisTechRG-C10   6 ∨

Resource *

sxdg   7 ∨

Add 8

Figure 10.31 – Adding a policy definition resource

5. Select **Review + create**. After the validation has passed, click **Create**. This creates the service endpoint policy. After completion, click **Go to resource**.

6. In the **PublicWebSubnet-SE-Policy** window, in the **Settings** section, click **Associated subnets**, then + **Edit subnet association**:

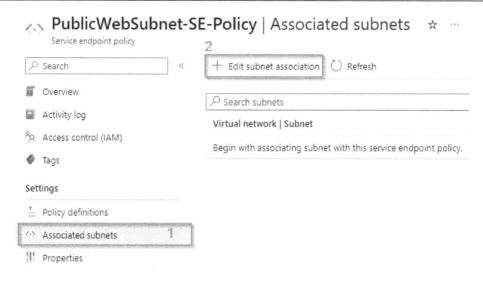

Figure 10.32 – Modifying the subnet association for the service endpoint policy

7. In the **Edit subnet association** blade, configure the following:

- **Virtual network: CoreServicesVnet**

- **PublicWebServiceSubnet**: Selected

- Click **Apply** to complete the process of associating the service endpoint policy with the subnet:

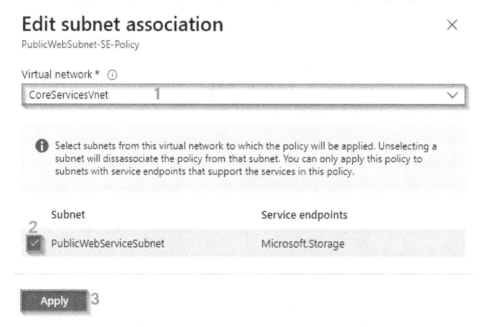

Figure 10.33 – Adding a virtual network and subnet

Well done! You have successfully implemented the service endpoint option, together with a service endpoint policy. In the next section, we will discuss the third option for controlling network traffic to platform services in Azure – the private endpoint.

Designing and implementing Azure Private Link and Azure private endpoints

Azure Private Link (marked as *1* in *Figure 10.34*) is a feature that allows us to establish private and secure connections to supported Azure platform services and customer-owned/partner services hosted in Azure. These connections are made through a virtual network interface located within our virtual network, which is known as a private endpoint (marked as *2* in *Figure 10.34*).

Network communication between our virtual network and the service uses Microsoft's backbone network and is encrypted. This provides a fully private experience for platform service access as there is no need to use the public endpoint or the service endpoint for access. At the time of writing, 46 platform services support private link/private endpoint access. For an up-to-date list of the supported services, please visit the following URL: `https://learn.microsoft.com/en-us/azure/private-link/availability`.

Private Link/private endpoints offer an advantage over the service endpoint option discussed previously. They allow on-premises networks to access platform services privately, over an ExpressRoute or VPN connection through the private endpoint (see *Figure 10.34*). The service endpoint option does not support this scenario at the time of writing:

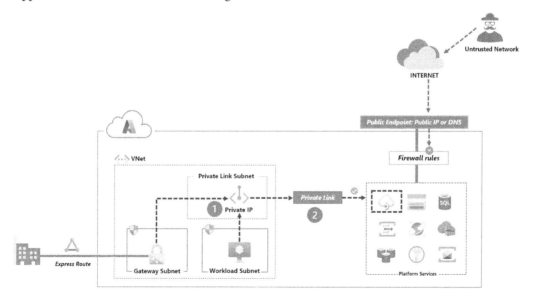

Figure 10.34 – Sample private endpoint implementation

Azure Private Link service considerations

Before creating an Azure Private Link service, it's important to consider the different components involved and how they relate to our Azure architecture.

If we have implemented a virtual WAN architecture, private endpoints can only be deployed on spoke virtual networks connected to the virtual hub. Implementing private endpoints directly in the virtual hub is not supported.

If we have a requirement to log or filter traffic to private endpoints, we can implement a network virtual appliance in the hub VNet for traffic analysis between spokes, between hub and spokes, and between on-premises components and Azure networks.

We can also use a **network security group** (**NSG**) to restrict access from the hub or on-premises systems to private endpoints by associating an NSG with the endpoint subnet and configuring appropriate inbound rules.

When planning our private endpoint implementation, it is recommended to implement the principle of least privilege. This should guide our decision to either place each private endpoint in a separate subnet or aggregate multiple private endpoints into a dedicated spoke subnet.

Integrating a Private Link service with DNS

Supported Azure services can be accessed over private endpoints, but you need to register those private endpoint records in a corresponding private DNS zone. The required DNS records can be automatically generated if we implement DNS using the Azure Private DNS zone service with the recommended naming scheme for the zone. For Azure services, use the recommended zone names, as described at `https://learn.microsoft.com/en-us/azure/private-link/private-endpoint-dns#azure-services-dns-zone-configuration`.

That's enough discussion for now – let's proceed to implement this in practice.

Hands-on exercise 3 – configuring an Azure private endpoint for an Azure WebApp

Here are the exercises that we will complete in this exercise:

- **Task 1**: Creating a private endpoint for the web app
- **Task 2**: Testing connectivity to the web app via the private endpoint
- **Task 3**: Testing connectivity to the web app from an external network
- **Task 4**: Cleaning up resources

Let's go through the steps to accomplish these tasks.

Task 1 – creating a private endpoint for the web app

The steps are as follows:

1. In the Azure portal, in the **Search resources, services, and docs** text box at the top of the Azure portal page, type `az700webapp` and select the displayed web app:

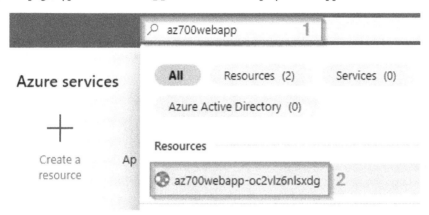

Figure 10.35 – Searching for the storage account

2. In the **Web App** window, make a note of the web app's name; you will need it for testing later in this exercise:

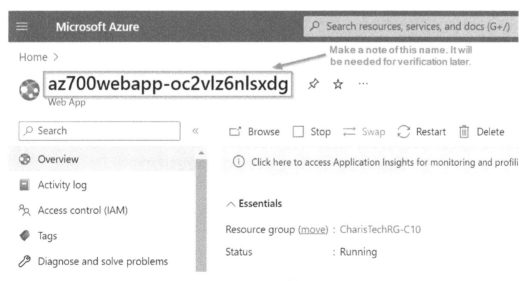

Figure 10.36 – Making a note of the web app's name

3. In the left-hand menu, in the **Settings** section, select **Networking**, then select the **Private endpoints** link:

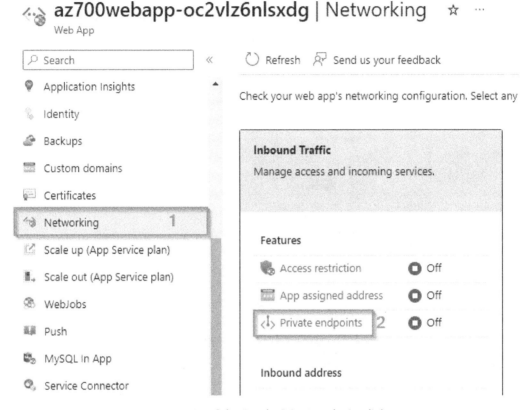

Figure 10.37 – Selecting the Private endpoints link

4. In the **Private Endpoint connections** window, click **+ Add**, then **Advanced**:

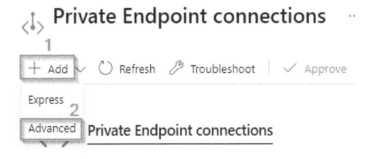

Figure 10.38 – Selecting the Advanced option

5. In the **Create a private endpoint** window, in the **Basics** tab, configure the following:

- **Name**: **az700webapp-endpoint**
- **Network Interface Name**: Leave the default value as is
- **Region**: Select the same region that previous resources were deployed into
- Click **Next : Resource >**:

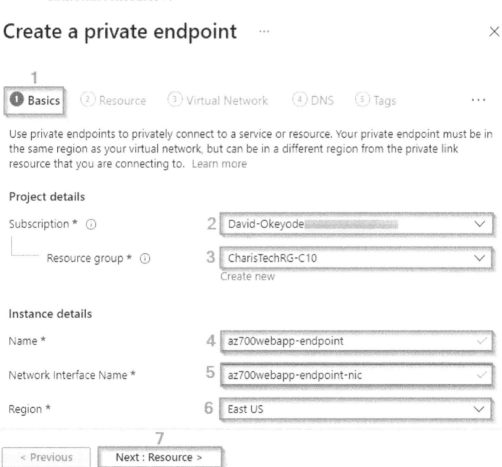

Figure 10.39 – Configuring the parameters

6. On the **Resource** tab, leave the default settings as they are and click **Next : Virtual Network >**.

7.   On the **Virtual Network** tab, configure the following:

  - **Virtual network: CoreServicesVnet (CharisTechRG-C10)**
  - **Subnet**: **PublicWebServiceSubnet**
  - **Private IP configuration: Dynamically allocate IP address**
  - Click **Next : DNS >**:

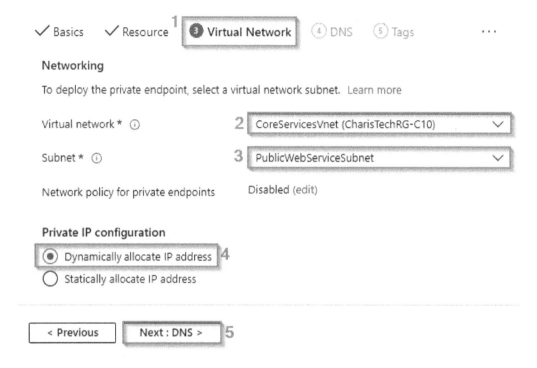

Figure 10.40 – Configuring the virtual network parameters

8.   On the **DNS** tab, configure the following:

  - **Integrate with private DNS zone: Yes**
  - **Subscription**: Select your Azure subscription
  - **Resource group: CharisTechRG-C10**
  - Leave the other settings with their default values

- Click **Next : Tags >**:

Figure 10.41 – Configuring the DNS parameters

9. On the **Tags** tab, click **Next : Review + create >**.

10. On the **Review + create** tab, click **Create**:

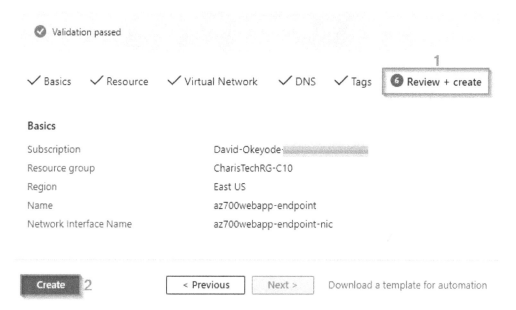

Figure 10.42 – Creating the private endpoint

Task 2 – testing connectivity to the web app via the private endpoint

The steps are as follows:

1. In the Windows PowerShell session of the Bastion connection to WebVM, type the following command to verify the DNS resolution for the web app. Replace <webapp-name> with the name of the web app that you made a note of earlier:

    ```
    nslookup <webapp-name>.azurewebsites.net
    ```

> **Note**
>
> If the session is closed, follow *Hands-on exercise 2*, *Task 3*, *steps 1* to *6* of this chapter.

2. You'll receive an output similar to what is displayed here. Notice that the DNS name now resolves to a private IP address. This address is in the same subnet as the VM (**PublicWebServiceVnet**):

Figure 10.43 – Performing a name resolution lookup

3. Open Internet Explorer and enter the URL of the web app, https://<webapp-name>. azurewebsites.net. Replace <webapp-name> with the name of the web app that you made a note of earlier. Verify that you can see a web page, similar to what's shown in *Figure 10.44*. Close the connection to the virtual machine:

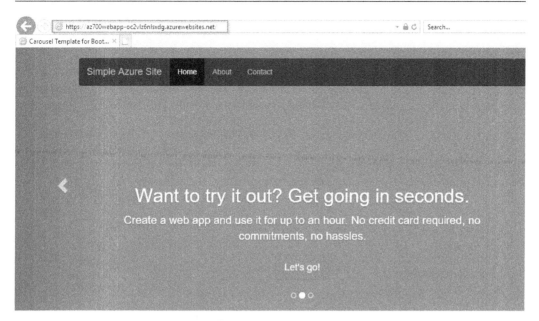

Figure 10.44 – Verifying the web app's private connectivity

Task 3 – testing connectivity to the web app from an external network

On your PC, browse to the URL of the web app, `https://<webapp-name>.azurewebsites.net`. Replace `<webapp-name>` with the name of the web app that you made a note of earlier. Verify that you got an error message similar to what's shown in *Figure 10.45*. Close the browser:

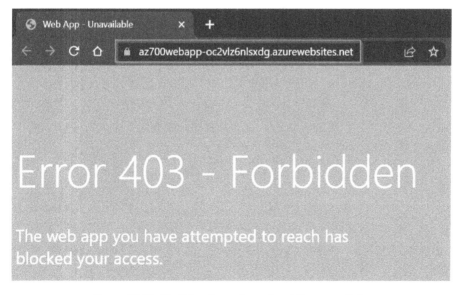

Figure 10.45 – Verifying the web app's public connectivity

Task 4 – cleaning up resources

The steps are as follows:

1. In the Azure portal, in the **Search resources, services, and docs** textbox at the top of the Azure portal page, type CharisTechRG-C10 and select the displayed resource group:

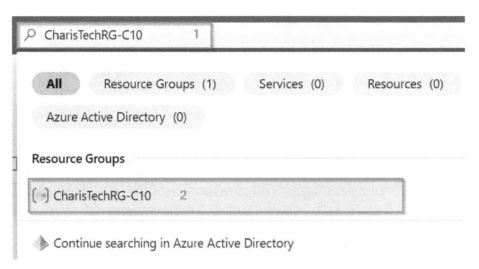

Figure 10.46 – Searching for the resource group

2. In the **Resource group** window, click **Delete resource group**:

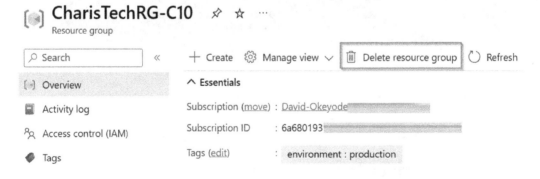

Figure 10.47 – Deleting the resource group

3. In the **Delete a resource group** window, do the following:

- **Apply force delete for selected Virtual machines and Virtual machine scale sets**: Selected
- **Enter resource group name to confirm deletion**: `CharisTechRG-C10`
- Click **Delete** to start the resource group deletion process
- Again, click **Delete**, when prompted, to confirm the deletion:

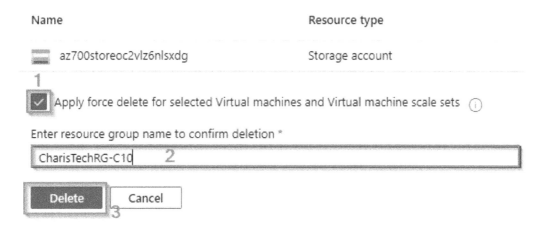

Delete a resource group   ✕

The following resource group and all its dependent resources will be permanently deleted.

Resource group to be deleted

[◀] CharisTechRG-C10 ⎘

Dependent resources to be deleted (20)

All dependent resources, including hidden types, are shown

Name	Resource type
az700storeoc2vlz6nlsxdg	Storage account

1

☑ Apply force delete for selected Virtual machines and Virtual machine scale sets ⓘ

Enter resource group name to confirm deletion *

| CharisTechRG-C10   2 |

[Delete] [Cancel]
3

Figure 10.48 – Confirming resource group deletion

Congratulations! You have completed this exercise.

Summary

In this chapter, we provided insights into the options available for managing network connections to Azure platform services. We discussed and implemented a platform service firewall and exceptions, a service endpoint, and a private endpoint. This chapter has provided you with the knowledge and skills necessary to control network connections to Azure platform services effectively. This information is also crucial for the AZ-700 – Azure Network Engineer certification exam.

In the final chapter of this book, we will focus on network monitoring in Azure. Thank you, and we look forward to seeing you there!

Further reading

Refer to the following links for more information about the topics covered in this chapter:

- *Virtual Network service endpoints*: https://learn.microsoft.com/en-us/azure/virtual-network/virtual-network-service-endpoints-overview

- *Private Link documentation*: https://learn.microsoft.com/en-us/azure/private-link/

11

Monitoring Networks in Azure

Network monitoring and diagnostics are essential components for maintaining the smooth functioning and optimal performance of a network infrastructure. This includes real-time monitoring of network services, systems, and traffic to detect problems early before they escalate into major disruptions. By identifying issues promptly, network engineers can take proactive measures to address them, minimizing network downtime and service interruptions. In this chapter, we will cover Azure services and tools that we can use to monitor and diagnose network services.

By the end of this chapter, you will have a good understanding of the following:

- Understanding the network monitoring tools of Network Watcher
- Understanding the network diagnostic tools of Network Watcher
- Understanding NSG flow logs

We have arranged the topics to match the exam objectives. Let's get started!

Technical requirements

To follow along with the instructions in this chapter, you will need the following:

- A PC with an internet connection
- An Azure subscription

Introducing Azure Network Watcher for monitoring, network diagnostics, and logs

Azure Network Watcher is a collection of tools used to monitor and diagnose network connectivity in Azure. It focuses on monitoring and maintaining the network health of **Infrastructure-as-a-Service** (**IaaS**) products such as VM, VNets, load balancers, and application gateways. It is important to note that Network Watcher is not suitable for monitoring **Platform-as-a-Service** (**PaaS**) resources or conduct ing web analytics. The tools in Network Watcher fall into two main categories – network monitoring and network diagnostics (see *Figure 11.1*).

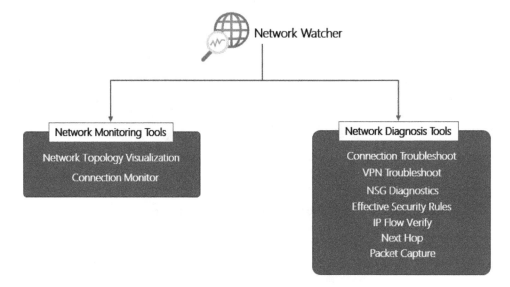

Figure 11.1 – Azure Network Watcher tool categories

The network monitoring tools are useful for gaining visibility of the existing state of our networks in Azure, while the network diagnostics tools are useful for troubleshooting and identifying the root cause of network-related problems.

From a design perspective, Network Watcher is a regional service and can only interact with resources located in the same region. This means that we will need to create an instance of Network Watcher in all regions where we plan to use its tools.

Understanding the network monitoring tools of Network Watcher

Network Watcher's *monitoring tools* are useful for gaining valuable insight into the current status of our Azure networks. There are two main tools that fall into this category – topology visualization and Connection Monitor. Let us review their functionalities.

Topology visualization

As VNets grow in size and complexity, it becomes challenging to understand the resources that they contain and the relationships between them. The topology visualization tool in Network Watcher addresses this challenge by providing network administrators and engineers with the ability to visualize the network topology.

By using this tool, administrators can create a visual representation of the resources within a VNet and their relationships. An editable version of the picture can also be downloaded in the SVG format. This helps to easily determine the subnets within a VNet, the network interfaces connected to each subnet, and the association of network interfaces with **virtual machines** (**VMs**). They can also identify the public IP addresses associated with network interfaces. An example of this can be seen in *Figure 11.2*.

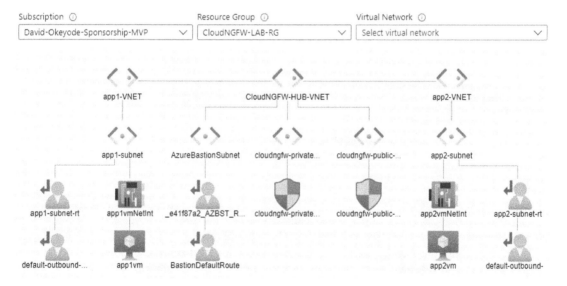

Figure 11.2 – Network topology visualization in Network Watcher

To use this feature, the only requirement is to have a network watcher resource enabled in the same region as the VNet for which we want to generate the topology. Also, there is no additional cost to using this feature.

It is important to note that the visualization options for this feature are limited in several ways. For example, it only supports visualization of the following resource types: virtual network, subnet, network interface, network security group, load balancer, load balancer health probe, public IP, VNet peering, VNet gateway, VPN gateway connection, VM, and VM scale set.

It also lacks the capability to visualize network resource relationships across multiple subscriptions, resource groups, and locations. For example, it cannot be used to visualize peering between two VNets located in different subscriptions.

There is a newer topology visualization tool in Azure Monitor Networks Insights that offers topology visualization with support for additional resources, including application gateways, ExpressRoute circuits, PrivateLink endpoints, and PrivateLink services. It can also be used to visualize network resource relationships across multiple subscriptions, resource groups, and locations. It is currently in preview at the time of writing. Please refer to *Figure 11.3* for a comparison of these two options.

Capabilities	Topology Visualization (Network Watcher)	Network Insights Topology (Azure Monitor)
Supported Resources: Virtual Network, Subnet, Network Interface, Network Security Group, Load Balancer, Load Balancer Health probe, Public IP, Virtual Network Peering, Virtual network gateway, VPN Gateway Connection, Virtual Machine, and Virtual Machine Scale Set	✓	✓
Supported Resources: Application gateways, ExpressRoute Circuits, PrivateLink Endpoints, and PrivateLink Services	✗	✓
Cross-subscription, cross resource groups and cross location network resource visualization	✗	✓

Figure 11.3 – Comparing the topology visualization options

> **Note**
> While the newer topology visualization tool in Azure Monitor offers a more comprehensive experience, it does have a limitation when it comes to viewing all resources within a VNet from a single pane, as we could in Network Watcher. I have found this capability to be occasionally useful. Hopefully, the team at Microsoft will work toward consolidating these tools to reduce confusion and provide a unified experience for network topology visualization in Azure.

Connection monitor

The connection monitor feature of Network Watcher enables us to monitor network connectivity and metrics for Azure and hybrid networks. We can define continuous network connectivity tests that will be performed between source endpoints and specified destination endpoints (see *Figure 11.4*).

The source endpoint can be an individual Azure VM, an instance within an Azure VM scale set, or a VM located on-premises. The destination endpoint can be other reachable Azure VMs, non-Azure VMs, or any external IPv4 address/URL.

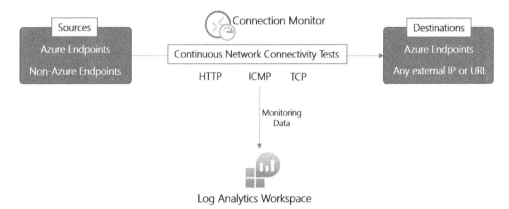

Figure 11.4 – Connection Monitor components

With connection monitor, we can configure connectivity checks using HTTP, TCP, or ICMP protocols to verify the reachability. We can also define the probing frequency (how frequently connection tests are performed) and the success criteria (see *Figure 11.5*).

New configuration   Choose existing

Test configuration name *

| ssh-test-configuration | ✓ |

Protocol ⓘ

| TCP | ⌄ |

HTTP

TCP

ICMP

☐ Listen on port ⓘ

Test Frequency ⓘ

| Every 30 seconds | ⌄ |

Success Threshold ⓘ

Checks failed (%)   Round trip time (ms)

Figure 11.5 – Configuring Connection Monitor

Connection Monitor relies on agents that are installed on source endpoints to perform connectivity tests and collect data related to connection health. The agent simulates network traffic between source and destination endpoints to measure key parameters such as latency, packet loss, and connectivity status. The monitoring data is collected and stored in a Log Analytics workspace.

The agent to install on the source endpoint depends on whether the source VM is hosted on Azure or on-premises. For Azure sources (Azure VMs and VM scale set instances), we can install the Network Watcher VM extension. For non-Azure sources (on-premises VMs), we can install **Azure Monitor Agent (AMA)** or the legacy Log Analytics agent.

> **Note**
>
> It is worth mentioning that Network Watcher includes two legacy tools that are no longer available for new deployments – the legacy Connection Monitor (classic) tool and the Network Performance Monitor tool. However, the functionality of these legacy tools has been integrated into the new Connection Monitor tool.
>
> For users who previously implemented the legacy Connection Monitor or Network Performance Monitor tool, Microsoft has provided comprehensive documentation on how to transition to the new Connection Monitor tool. You can access the documentation here: `https://learn.microsoft.com/en-us/azure/network-watcher/migrate-to-connection-monitor-from-network-performance-monitor` and `https://learn.microsoft.com/en-us/azure/network-watcher/migrate-to-connection-monitor-from-connection-monitor-classic`.

There are several use cases for Connection Monitor. Here are some key ones:

- Timely detection of network issues between a source and a destination, such as traffic blackholing or routing errors. For example, the feature can be used in a scenario where we have a web server VM that communicates with a database server VM. If someone in our organization applies a custom route or network security rule that accidentally makes the database server VM or its associated subnet unreachable from the web server, Connection Monitor will swiftly identify the connectivity problem and provide notifications, detailing the root cause of the issue.

- It can also be used to monitor and compare network latencies, such as those between VMs located in different Azure regions or between on-premises VMs and several cloud targets. For example, if an organization has VMs or scale sets in the east US region and wants to connect with VMs or scale sets in the central US region, Connection Monitor can be used to monitor the network latency between these regions.

We will implement Connection Monitor when we get to the hands-on exercises in this chapter, so stay tuned for that!

Understanding the Network diagnostic tools of Network Watcher

Network Watcher's *diagnostic tools* are useful for troubleshooting and identifying the root cause of network-related problems. There are seven main tools that fall into this category – connection troubleshoot, IP flow verify, NSG diagnostics, next hop, VPN troubleshoot, packet capture, and effective security rules. In this section, we will explore six of these tools, starting with connection troubleshoot.

Connection troubleshoot

The connection troubleshoot tool in Network Watcher is similar to the Connection Monitor tool discussed earlier, in that it allows users to validate network communication between a source and a destination endpoint. However, there are key differences between the two. While Connection Monitor provides continuous monitoring of network connectivity, connection troubleshoot allows us to perform tests on demand, which is useful for troubleshooting scenarios.

Connection troubleshoot also supports a wider range of source types beyond Azure and non-Azure VMs. It supports Azure Bastion instances, and Application Gateway v2 as source endpoints (see *Figure 11.6*).

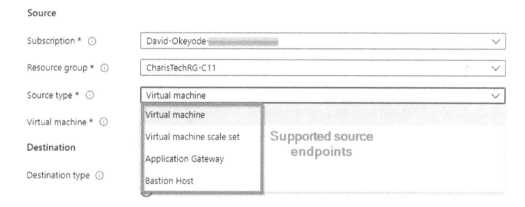

Figure 11.6 – Connection troubleshoot-supported source endpoints

The destination endpoint for connection troubleshoot can be Azure VMs, non-Azure VMs, **fully qualified domain names (FQDNs)**, **uniform resource identifiers (URIs)**, or specific IPv4 and IPv6 addresses. Connection troubleshoot only supports TCP and ICMP checks and does not provide HTTP support to test connections.

To use this feature, we need to have a network watcher resource enabled in the same region as the target resource. Also, if the source endpoint is an Azure VM or a VM scale set instance, it needs to have the Azure Network Watcher extension installed.

There are several use cases for this feature. Here are some key ones:

- Troubleshooting connection latency issues between a source and a destination endpoint

- Troubleshooting connectivity issues between a source and a destination endpoint, including DNS resolution failures, misconfigured or missing routes, **Network Security Group** (**NSG**) rules that block traffic, missing address resolution protocol entries for Azure ExpressRoute circuits, and servers not listening on designated destination ports

IP flow verify

Network Watcher IP flow verify checks whether a packet is allowed or denied from a VM based on five-tuple information. This is useful if we need to quickly diagnose connectivity between an Azure VM and an internet endpoint or an on-premises endpoint. It is also useful to check whether a rule in an NSG blocks inbound or outbound traffic to or from a VM.

Figure 11.7 shows an example IP flow verify check. This check is used to verify whether a remote host, with an IP address of 10.10.3.4 and a source port of 10000, is allowed to communicate with the **dataVM** VM on TCP port 22.

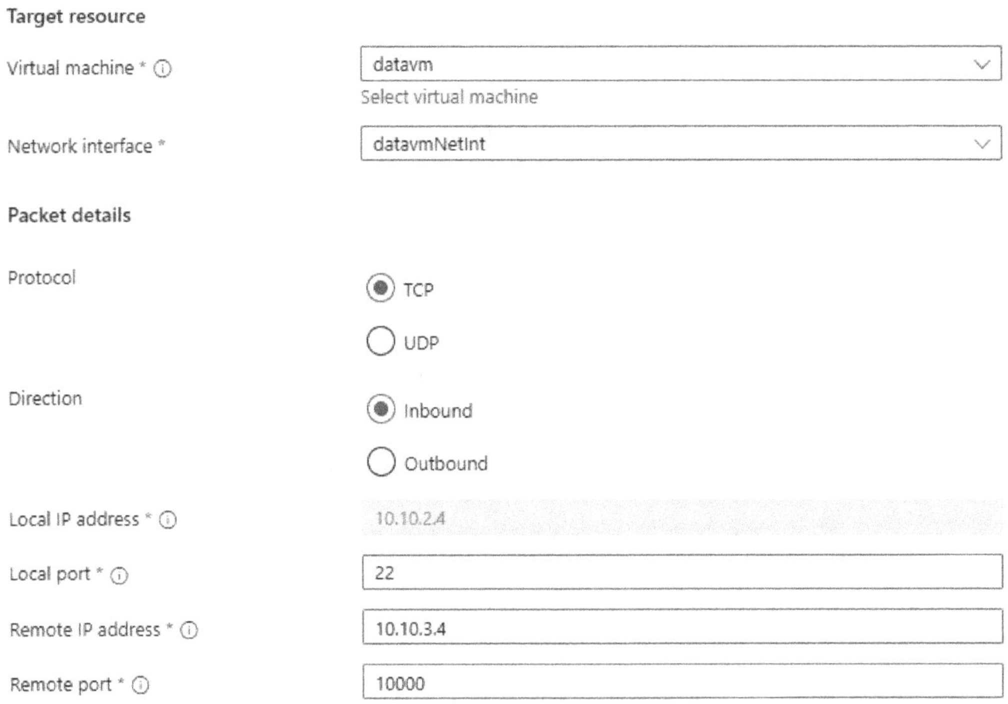

Target resource

Virtual machine * ⓘ

> datavm ⌄
> Select virtual machine

Network interface *

> datavmNetInt ⌄

Packet details

Protocol

> ◉ TCP
> ○ UDP

Direction

> ◉ Inbound
> ○ Outbound

Local IP address * ⓘ   10.10.2.4

Local port * ⓘ

> 22

Remote IP address * ⓘ

> 10.10.3.4

Remote port * ⓘ

> 10000

Figure 11.7 – An example of an IP flow verify check

IP flow verify will look at the rules for all NSGs applied to the network interface of the VM and returns a result on whether the traffic is allowed or denied, as well as the responsible NSG rule (see *Figure 11.8*).

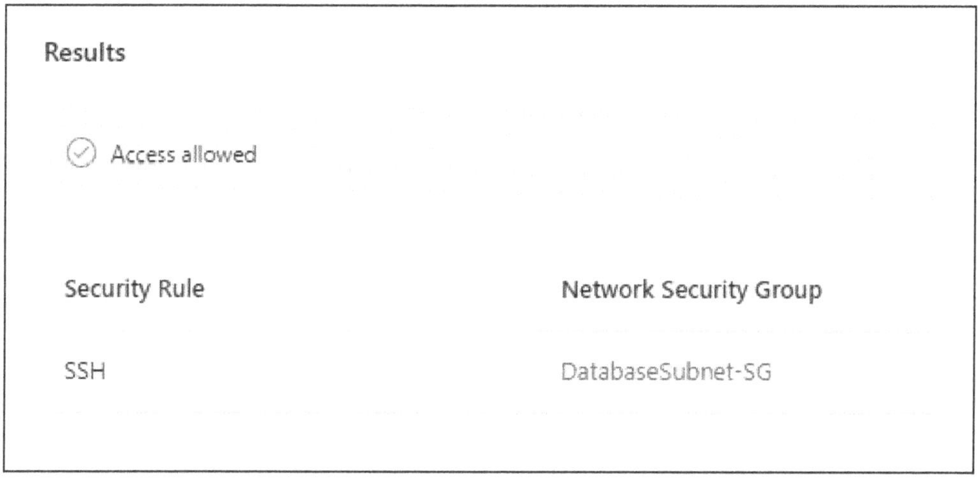

Results

⊘ Access allowed

Security Rule   Network Security Group

SSH   DatabaseSubnet-SG

Figure 11.8 – An example of an IP Flow Verify result

The only prerequisite to using IP flow verify is having a Network Watcher resource enabled in the same region as the target resource. It can be used alongside other similar features such as effective security rules. Also, there's no extra cost associated with this feature.

NSG diagnostics

NSG diagnostics is an Azure Network Watcher tool that can be used to verify whether our NSG rules are configured correctly. It examines all applicable NSG rules between the specified source endpoint and the target resource to determine whether traffic is allowed or denied. *Figure 11.9* shows an example of an NSG diagnostics check. This check is used to verify whether applicable NSG rules allow communication from a remote host with an IP address of 10.10.3.4 to a target host of 10.10.2.4 on TCP port 22.

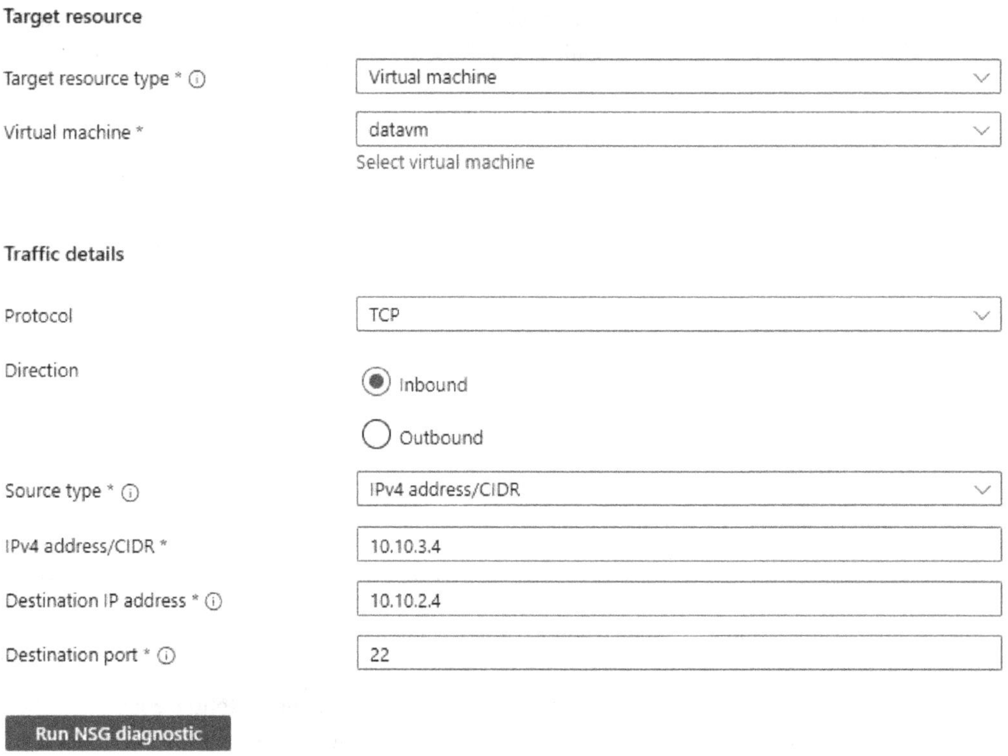

Target resource
Target resource type *
Virtual machine
Virtual machine *
datavm
Select virtual machine
Traffic details
Protocol
TCP
Direction
Inbound
Outbound
Source type *
IPv4 address/CIDR
IPv4 address/CIDR *
10.10.3.4
Destination IP address *
10.10.2.4
Destination port *
22
Run NSG diagnostic

Figure 11.9 – An example of an NSG diagnostics check

Figure 11.10 shows the result of this check:

Results
Traffic will be allowed if all NSGs allow it.
Traffic status: Allowed
NSG name
Applied to
Applied action
Additional info
DatabaseSubnet-SG
datavmNetInt
Allow
View details

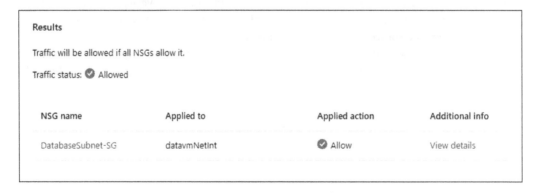

Figure 11.10 – An example of an NSG Diagnostics result

Because this tool only simulates the specified flow, it does not require an agent or extension installation.

Next hop

The next hop tool in Network Watcher can be used to determine the next hop for outbound traffic from a specified Azure VM to a specified destination IP address (see *Figure 11.11*). The main use case for this tool is troubleshooting routing issues.

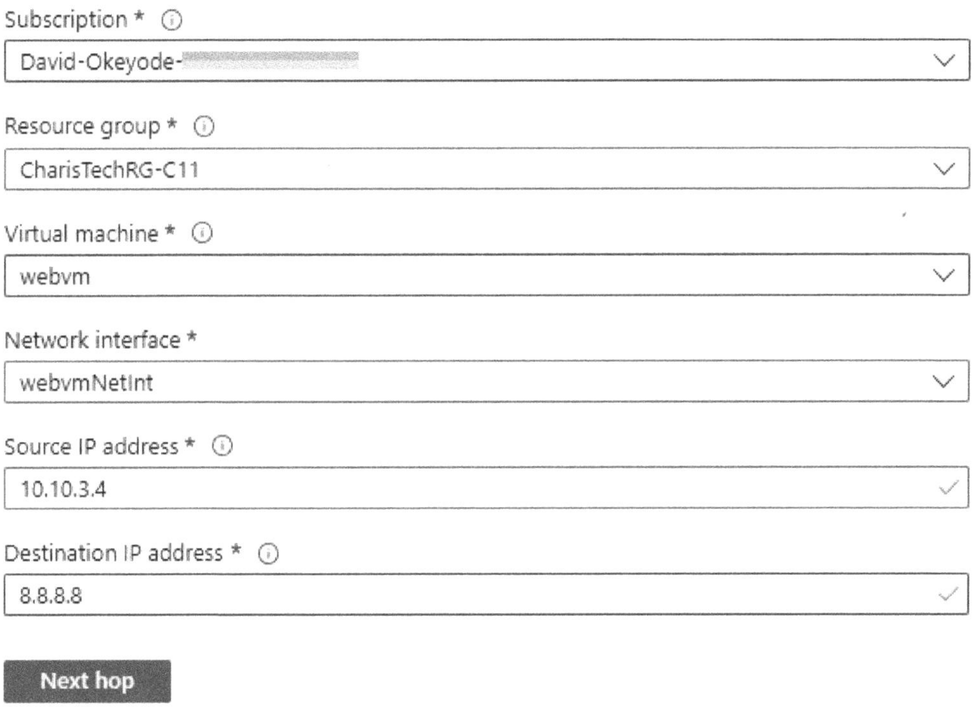

Subscription * ⓘ

David-Okeyode-

Resource group * ⓘ

CharisTechRG-C11

Virtual machine * ⓘ

webvm

Network interface *

webvmNetInt

Source IP address * ⓘ

10.10.3.4

Destination IP address * ⓘ

8.8.8.8

Next hop

Figure 11.11 – An example of a next hop check

The result of the check shows the applicable route table and the next hop (see *Figure 11.12*).

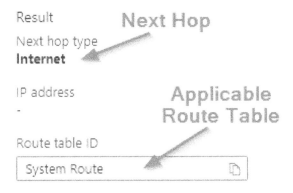

Figure 11.12 – An example of a next hop check result

VPN troubleshoot

The VPN troubleshoot tool in Network Watcher can be used to troubleshoot VPN connectivity issues between an on-premises (or remote) gateway device and Azure VPN Gateway. The following gateway types are supported:

- **Supported gateway types**: VPN gateway (route-based)
- **Unsupported gateway types**: ExpressRoute gateway and VPN gateway (policy-based)

Initiating the VPN troubleshoot operation can take some minutes to complete, and there is a limitation of only one VPN troubleshoot operation per subscription at a time.

Packet capture

Azure Network Watcher's packet capture feature can be used to capture raw data packets going in and out of a VM or a scale set instance. This is useful for scenarios where we need to perform more detailed troubleshooting that requires us to analyze raw packets. The captured data can be analyzed to identify network issues, compile network statistics, detect network breaches, or debug interactions between clients and servers.

With this feature, packet captures can be started remotely without needing to directly connect to the VM. The captured data can be stored either on our local system or in an Azure storage account (see *Figure 11.13*). We can also apply filters to selectively capture the network traffic that we are interested in. This feature requires the Azure Network Watcher extension to be installed on the specified VM.

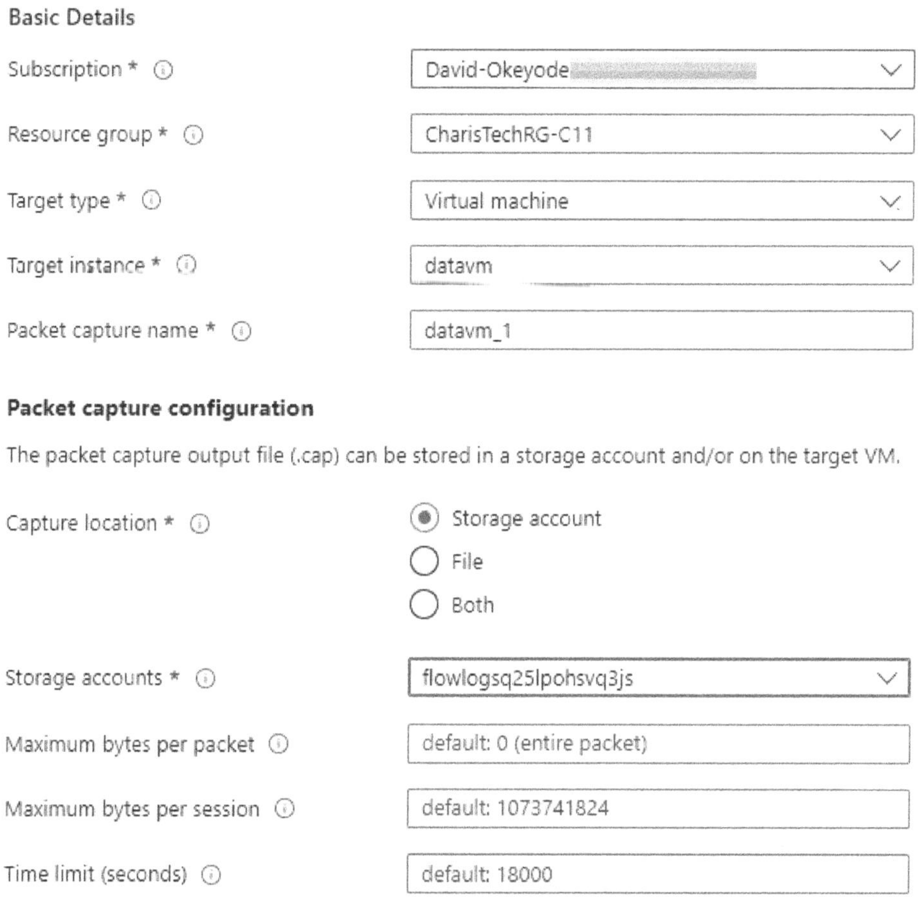

Basic Details

Subscription * ⓘ

David-Okeyode   ∨

Resource group * ⓘ

CharisTechRG-C11   ∨

Target type * ⓘ

Virtual machine   ∨

Target instance * ⓘ

datavm   ∨

Packet capture name * ⓘ

datavm_1

Packet capture configuration

The packet capture output file (.cap) can be stored in a storage account and/or on the target VM.

Capture location * ⓘ

◉ Storage account

◯ File

◯ Both

Storage accounts * ⓘ

flowlogsq25lpohsvq3js   ∨

Maximum bytes per packet ⓘ

default: 0 (entire packet)

Maximum bytes per session ⓘ

default: 1073741824

Time limit (seconds) ⓘ

default: 18000

Figure 11.13 – Configuring packet capture in Network Watcher

Now that we have learned about the monitoring and diagnostic tools in Network Watcher, it is time to gain hands-on experience with some of the capabilities that we have discussed.

Hands-on exercise 1 – provisioning the resources for the chapter's exercises

To follow along with the exercises in this chapter, we will provision some Azure resources to work with. We have prepared an Azure ARM template in the GitHub repository of this book for this purpose. The template will deploy a VM, a storage account (with a file share), and an App Service web app in the specified Azure region, as shown in *Figure 11.14*.

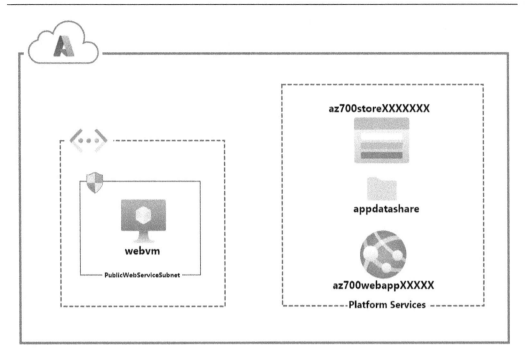

Figure 11.14 – Resources deployed via the provided ARM template

Here are the tasks that we will complete in this exercise:

- **Task 1**: Initialize template deployment in GitHub, complete the parameters, and deploy a template to Azure

Let's get into this!

Task 1 – initialize template deployment in GitHub, complete the parameters, and deploy a template to Azure

The steps are:

1. Open a web browser and navigate to `https://packt.link/AdmXo`.
2. This link will open the GitHub repository that has the ARM template to deploy the resources that we need.

3. In the GitHub repository that opens, click on **Deploy to Azure**.

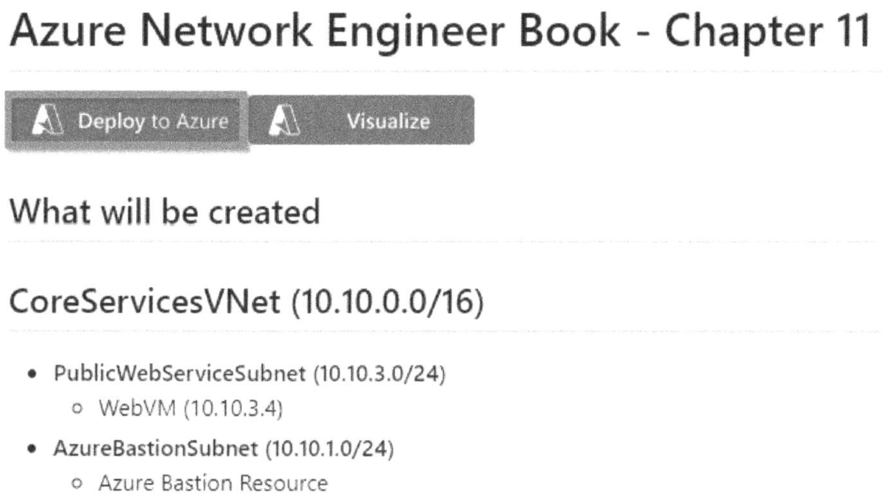
Azure Network Engineer Book - Chapter 11
Deploy to Azure
Visualize
What will be created
CoreServicesVNet (10.10.0.0/16)
PublicWebServiceSubnet (10.10.3.0/24)
WebVM (10.10.3.4)
AzureBastionSubnet (10.10.1.0/24)
Azure Bastion Resource

Figure 11.15 – Starting the template deployment

4. If prompted to authenticate, sign in to the Azure portal with your administrative username and password.
5. In the **Custom Deployment** window, configure the following:
   - **Subscription**: Select the subscription that you want to deploy the resources into.
   - **Resource group**: **Create New** | **Name** – `CharisTechRG-C11` | **OK**.
   - **Region**: Select a region for the resource group and all the resources that will be created.
   - **Vm Size**: **Standard_B2s** (or select the VM size that you verified in the first chapter of this book).
   - **Admin Username**: `azureuser`.
   - **Admin Password**: Enter a complex password. This will be the password for all deployed VM instances. Make a note of this, as it will be needed for later exercises.

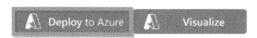

- Select **Review + Create**.

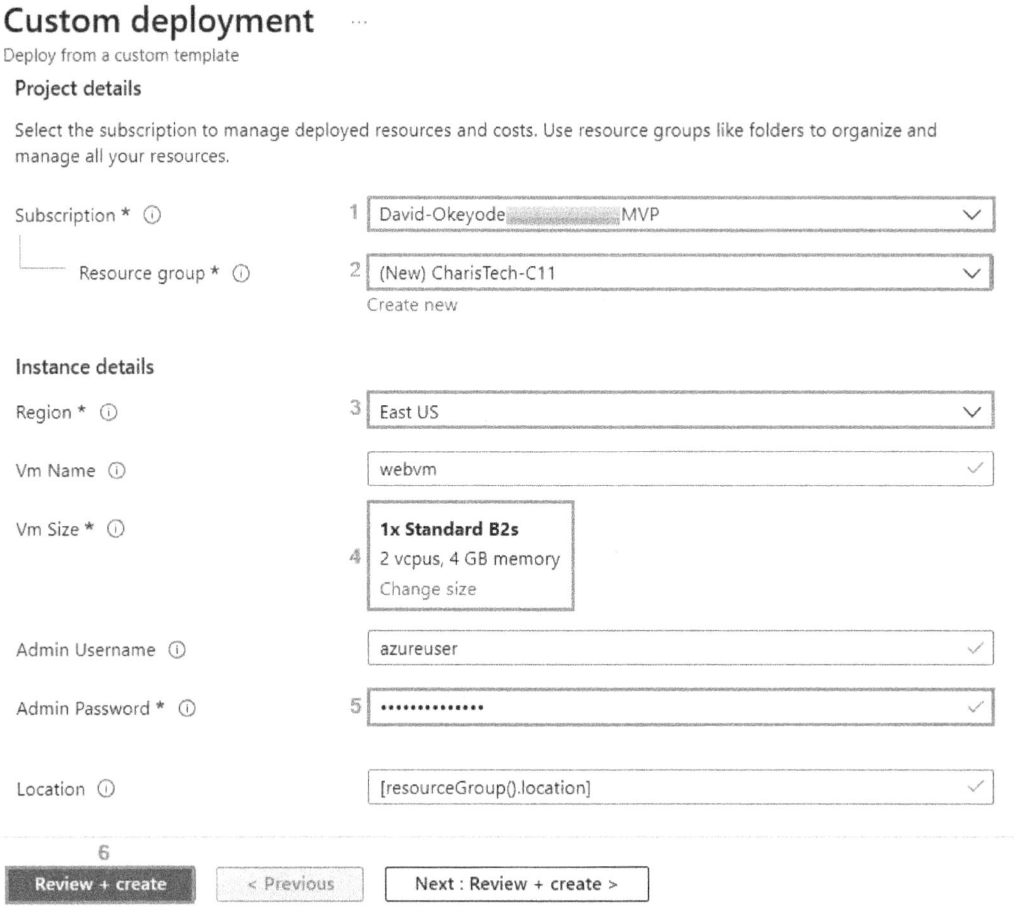

Custom deployment   ...

Deploy from a custom template

Project details

Select the subscription to manage deployed resources and costs. Use resource groups like folders to organize and manage all your resources.

Subscription * ⓘ   1 | David-Okeyode_____MVP   ⌄ |

       Resource group * ⓘ   2 | (New) CharisTech-C11   ⌄ |
                         Create new

Instance details

Region * ⓘ   3 | East US   ⌄ |

Vm Name ⓘ | webvm   ✓ |

Vm Size * ⓘ   4 | **1x Standard B2s**
2 vcpus, 4 GB memory
Change size |

Admin Username ⓘ | azureuser   ✓ |

Admin Password * ⓘ   5 | ••••••••••••••   ✓ |

Location ⓘ | [resourceGroup().location]   ✓ |

6

[Review + create]   [< Previous]   [Next : Review + create >]

Figure 11.16 – Complete the template parameters

6. After the validation has passed, select **Create**.

7. Wait for the deployment to complete before moving to the next exercise.

Hands-on exercise 2 – implementing the network monitoring tools of Network Watcher

Here are the exercises that we will complete in this exercise:

- **Task 1**: Visualize the topology of an Azure VNet
- **Task 2**: Create an Azure Network Watcher connection monitor
- **Task 3**: Trigger a network issue and review Connection Monitor

Let us go through the steps to accomplish these tasks:

Task 1 – visualize the topology of an Azure VNet

The steps are:

1. In the Azure portal, in the **Search resources, services, and docs** textbox at the top of the Azure portal page, type `network watcher`. Select **Network Watcher** from the search results.

2. In the **Network Watcher** window, in the **Monitoring** section, select **Topology** and specify the following:

    - **Subscription**: Select the Azure subscription that you deployed the resources into
    - **Resource Group**: **CharisTechRG-C11**
    - **Virtual Network**: **CoreServicesVnet**

Figure 11.17 – Specify the network to visualize

3. Review the topology. You can see the subnets in the VNet, the network interfaces, and the route tables that are associated with each subnet.

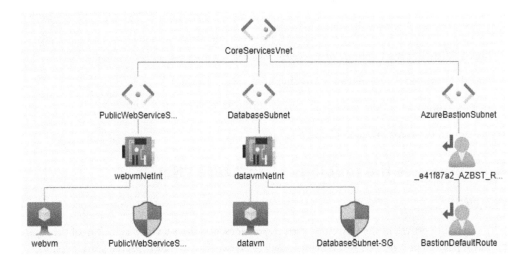

Figure 11.18 – Review the network topology

Task 2 – create an Azure Network Watcher connection monitor

The steps are:

1. In the **Network Watcher** window, in the **Monitoring** section (left pane), select **Connection monitor** and then **+ Create**.

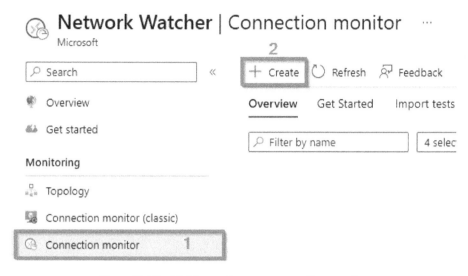

Figure 11.19 – Click to create a new connection monitor

2. On the **Basics** pane, specify the following details:

    • **Connection Monitor Name**: `webvm-to-dbvm-monitor`

    • **Subscription**: Select the subscription where the resources are deployed

    • **Region**: **East US**

    • **Workspace configuration**: Select **Use workspace created by connection monitor (default)**

- Click **Next : Test groups >>**

Create Connection Monitor ···
Microsoft

| **Basics** | Test groups | Create alert | Review + create |

Connection Monitor enables you to monitor connectivity in your Azure and hybrid network. Select your preferred subscription and region from which monitoring will be performed. Use workspace configuration to store monitoring data generated by Connection Monitor tests in Log Analytics workspace. Complete the Basics tab then proceed to Test Groups tab. Learn more ↗

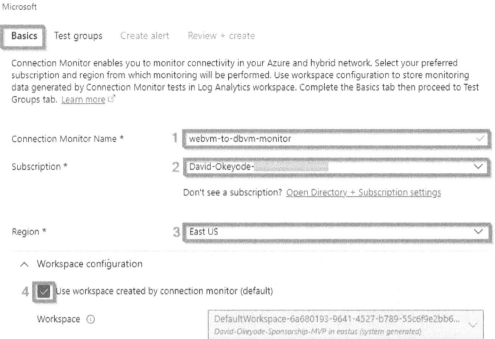

Connection Monitor Name *   1 webvm-to-dbvm-monitor

Subscription *   2 David-Okeyode-

Don't see a subscription? Open Directory + Subscription settings

Region *   3 East US

∧ Workspace configuration

4 ☑ Use workspace created by connection monitor (default)

Workspace ⓘ   DefaultWorkspace-6a680193-9641-4527-b789-55c6f9e2bb6...
                    David-Okeyode-Sponsorship-MVP in eastus (system generated)

Figure 11.20 – Specify Connection Monitor parameters

3. In the **Add test group details** window, specify the following:

    - **Test group name: web-app-test-group**

    - Click on **Add sources**

4. In the **Add Sources** window, specify the following under the **Azure endpoints** tab:

    - **Type**: **Virtual Machines**

    - Select **Subnet**

    - **Subscription**: Select the subscription where the resources are deployed

    - Select **PublicWebServiceSubnet**

- Click on **Add endpoints**

Figure 11.21 – Specify the test sources

5. Back in the **Add test group details** window, select **Add destinations**.

6. In the **Add Destinations** window, specify the following under the **Azure endpoints** tab:

- **Type: Virtual Machines**

- Select **Subnet**

- **Subscription**: Select the subscription where the resources are deployed

- Select **DatabaseSubnet**

- Click on **Add endpoints**

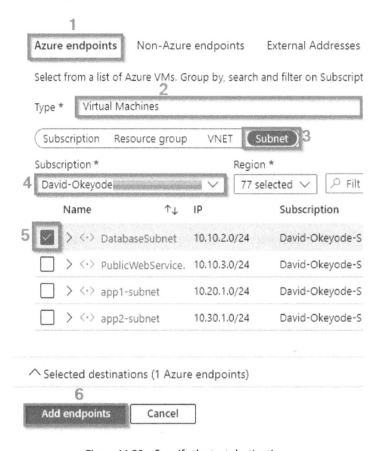

Figure 11.22 – Specify the test destinations

7. Back in the **Add test group details** window, select **Add Test configuration**.

8. In the **Add Test configuration** window, specify the following under the **New configuration** tab:

    - **Test configuration name**: `ssh-test-configuration`

    - **Protocol**: TCP

    - **Destination port**: `22`

    - **Test Frequency**: **Every 30 seconds**

    - **Checks failed (%)**: **5** (this specifies the percentage of checks that can fail when the connectivity is tested)

- **Round trip time (ms)**: **10** (the specifies the maximum allowed round trip latency between the source and the destination)

- Click on **Add Test configuration**

Figure 11.23 – Specify the test configuration parameters

9.   Back in the **Add test group details** window, select **Add Test Group**.

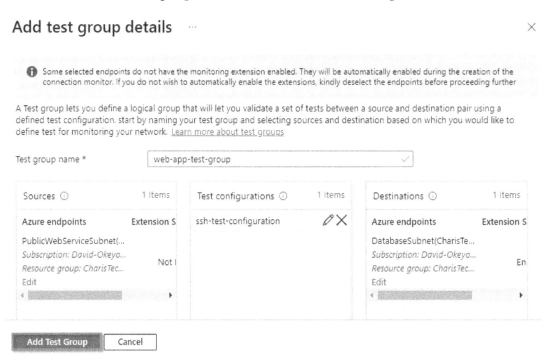

Figure 11.24 – Click to add a test group

10. Click on **Next: Create Alert >>**. Learn more about creating alerts.

11. In the **Create alert** tab, enable the **Create alert** option, and then click on **Select action group**.

Figure 11.25 – Select the option to create an alert

12. In the **Select action group** window, specify the following:

- **Subscription**: Select the subscription where the resources are deployed
- Click on **Select action group**
- Select **network-ops-action-group**

- Click on **Done**

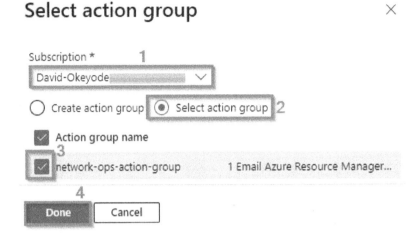

Figure 11.26 – Select an action group

13. At the bottom of the pane, select **Next: Review + create**.

14. Then, select **Create**. This will begin the process of installing the Azure Network Watcher extension on the VMs and setting up connection monitor.

Task 3 – Trigger a network issue and review Connection Monitor

The steps are:

1. Open Cloud Shell and run the following command to trigger a network issue. The command will block inbound SSH connectivity to the DataVM:

```
az network nsg rule update -g "CharisTechRG-C11" --nsg-name
"DatabaseSubnet-SG" -n "SSH" --access Deny
```

2. Back in the **Network Watcher | Connection monitor** window, click on **Refresh** until a **Fail** notification is displayed, as shown here.

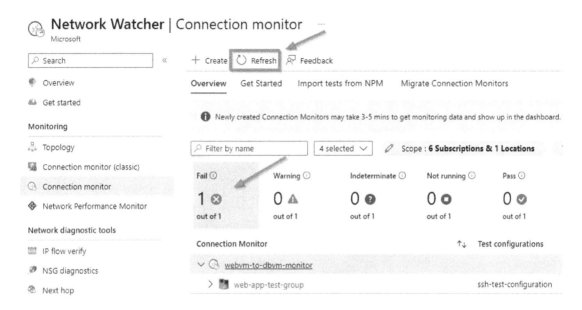

Figure 11.27 – Refresh until the failed notification is displayed

3.   Click on the connection monitor configuration to review the metrics.

Understanding NSG flow logs

Flow logs are a feature of Azure Network Watcher that records all IP flows moving in and out of an NSG. To filter network traffic to and from Azure resources within a VNet subnet, we can implement NSGs (see *Figure 11.28*). Rules can then be configured in an NSG to allow or deny traffic by source/destination IP address, source/destination port, and protocol (known as the five-tuple). We can associate an NSG at the subnet level or the VM NIC level (see *Figure 11.28*).

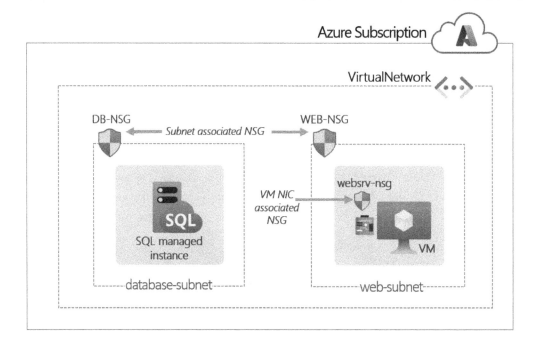

Figure 11.28 – The NSG at the subnet and VM NIC levels

When enabled, NSG flow logs will record IP flows through the NSG, outside the path of the network traffic, so there is no latency impact. The logs are written in JSON format and can be stored in an Azure Blob Storage container. We can specify the retention period at configuration time, as shown in the following screenshot (see *Figure 11.29*). We can also collect the logs in a Log Analytics workspace (if **Traffic Analytics** is enabled), where the retention period of the workspace applies.

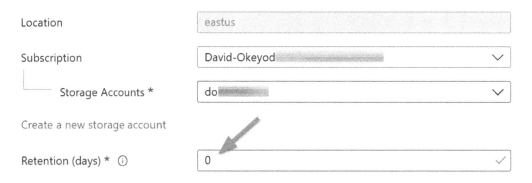

Figure 11.29 – Configuring the flow log retention period

> **Note**
>
> For information on the NSG flow log format, please refer to this document: `https://learn.microsoft.com/en-us/azure/network-watcher/network-watcher-nsg-flow-logging-overview#log-format`.

NSG flow logs limitations and use cases

That being said, please be aware that NSG flow logs do not log every network flow for a subnet or VM NIC! There are certain considerations and limitations that you should be aware of, as highlighted here:

- **NSG flow logs are associated with an NSG resource**: Network flows will only be logged where there is an associated NSG resource that has flow logs enabled.

- **NSG flow logging is not supported for certain scenarios**: Some of these "blind spots" are partly due to platform limitations and partly because some network flow implementation bypasses the NSGs applied at the subnet level! Those cases are highlighted here:

  - **Application Gateway v2 SKU**: NSG flow logging does not work properly (and is not currently supported) for NSGs that are associated with an Application Gateway v2 subnet. This limitation does not affect Application Gateway v1 SKUs: `https://docs.microsoft.com/en-us/azure/application-gateway/application-gateway-faq#are-nsg-flow-logs-supported-on-nsgs-associated-to-application-gateway-v2-subnet`.

  - **Azure Container Instances (ACIs)**: NSGs can also be applied to the subnet of container groups that are deployed into a private VNet subnet, but NSG flow logs are not supported: `https://docs.microsoft.com/en-us/azure/network-watcher/network-watcher-nsg-flow-logging-overview#nsg-flow-logging-considerations`.

  - **Logic apps**: Logic app workflows that need access to private network resources can be configured to run in an **Integrated Service Environment** (ISE), deployed into a VNet subnet. Even though NSGs are allowed for the subnet, NSG flow logs are not currently supported: `https://docs.microsoft.com/en-us/azure/network-watcher/network-watcher-nsg-flow-logging-overview#nsg-flow-logging-considerations`.

  - **Azure Firewall, VPN gateway, and ExpressRoute gateway**: Associating an NSG with Azure Firewall, VPN gateway, or ExpressRoute gateway subnets is disabled to prevent service interruption, so NSG flow logs cannot be used to collect network flow logs: `https://docs.microsoft.com/en-us/azure/firewall/firewall-faq#are-network-security-groups--nsgs--supported-on-the-azurefirewallsubnet`.

There are several use cases for the NSG flow logs feature. Here are some key ones:

- Detecting unknown or unwanted traffic

- Monitoring traffic volumes and bandwidth usage for anomalies

- Exporting flow logs to our preferred analytics and visualization tools to establish monitoring dashboards

- Identifying the main data users in your network

- Use flow data to confirm network isolation and compliance with company access rules

Now that you have some understanding of the NSG flow log capability of Network Watcher, it's time to put this knowledge into practice and proceed with the implementation.

Hands-on exercise 3 – enabling NSG flow logs

Here are the exercises that we will complete in this exercise:

- **Task 1**: Enable an NSG flow log

- **Task 2**: Download and review the flow log

Let us go through the steps to accomplish these tasks.

Task 1 – enable an NSG flow log

The steps are:

1. In the Azure portal, in the **Search resources, services, and docs** textbox at the top of the Azure portal page, type `network watcher`. Select **Network Watcher** from the search results.

2. On the left page, in the **Logs** section, select **Flow logs**.

3. In **Network Watcher | Flow logs**, select **+ Create**.

4. In the **Create a flow log** window, in the **Basics** tab, configure the following:

    - **Subscription**: Select your Azure subscription, the subscription of your VM, and its NSG

- Click on + **Select resource**

Figure 11.30 – Click to select the NSG resources to monitor

5.   In the **Select network security group** window, select the following NSGs – **PublicWeb ServiceSubnet-SG** and **DatabaseSubnet-SG**. Click on **Confirm selection**.

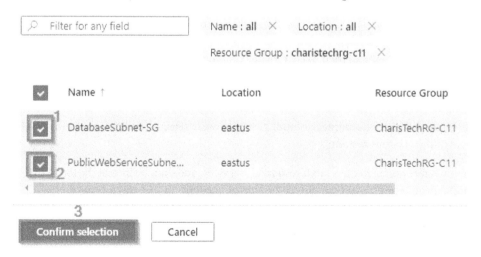

Figure 11.31 – Select an NSG

6. Back in the **Create a flow log** window, configure the following:

    *   **Subscription**: Select your Azure subscription and the subscription of the storage account

    *   **Storage Accounts**: Select the storage account that has `flowlogs` in the name

    *   **Retention (days)**: 5

    *   Select **Review + create**

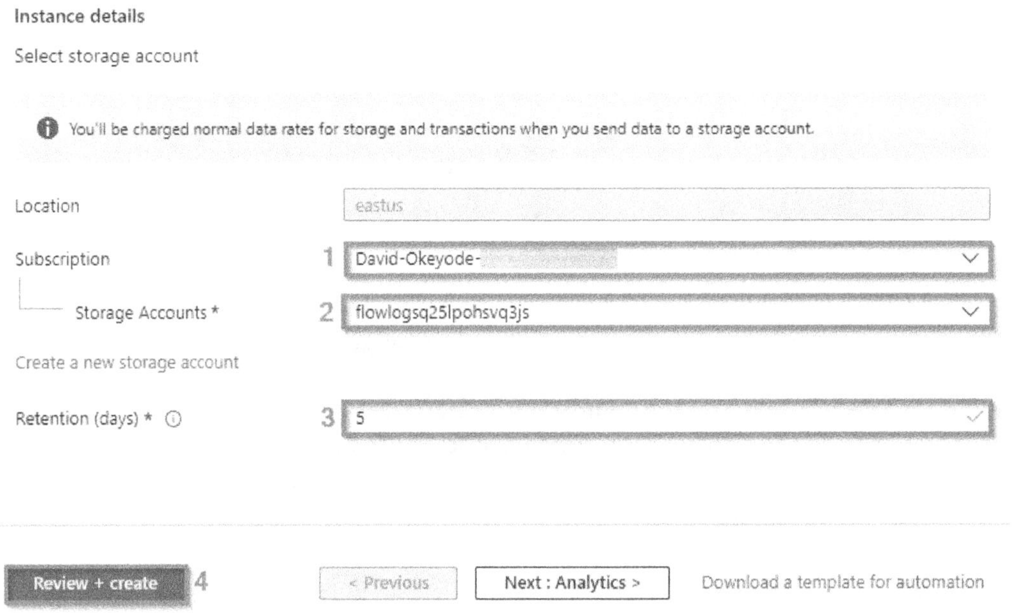

Instance details

Select storage account

> ℹ You'll be charged normal data rates for storage and transactions when you send data to a storage account.

Location	eastus
Subscription	1 David-Okeyode- ⌄
Storage Accounts *	2 flowlogsq25lpohsvq3js ⌄
Create a new storage account	
Retention (days) * ⓘ	3 5 ✓

Review + create 4   < Previous   Next : Analytics >   Download a template for automation

Figure 11.32 – Configure the storage account to store the logs

7. Review the settings, and then select **Create**. Wait for the deployment to complete.

Task 2 – download and review the flow log

In this task, we will go to the storage account you previously selected and download the NSG flow log created in the previous section:

1. In the Azure portal, in the **Search resources, services, and docs** textbox at the top of the Azure portal page, type `flowlogs`. Select the storage accounts in the search results.

2. On the left pane, in the **Data storage** section, select **Containers**.

3. Select the **insights-logs-networksecuritygroupflowevent** container.

4. In the container, navigate the folder hierarchy until you get to the `PT1H.json` file. NSG log files are written to a folder hierarchy that follows the following naming convention: `https://{storageAccountName}.blob.core.windows.net/insights-logs-networksecuritygroupflowevent/resourceId=/SUBSCRIPTIONS/{subscriptionID}/RESOURCEGROUPS/{resourceGroupName}/PROVIDERS/MICROSOFT.NETWORK/NETWORKSECURITYGROUPS/{networSecurityGroupName}/y={year}/m={month}/d={day}/h={hour}/m=00/macAddress={macAddress}/PT1H.json`.

5. Select the ellipsis **...** to the right of the `PT1H.json` file, and then select **Download**.

6. Open the downloaded `PT1H.json` file using a text editor of your choice. The following example is a section taken from the downloaded `PT1H.json` file, which shows a flow processed by the **DefaultRule_AllowInternetOutBound** rule.

Congratulations! You have successfully completed the final hands-on lab in this book!

Summary

Congratulations! You have come to the end of this not just this chapter but also this book! In this final chapter, we explored and implemented key functionalities of the Azure Network Watcher service. We covered its network monitoring and diagnostic tools and also discussed NSG flow logs and their implementation. The information covered in this chapter has provided you with the skills needed to effectively monitor and diagnose network connectivity issues in Azure. This knowledge forms a critical part of the "Monitor Networks" objective for the *AZ-700 – Azure Network Engineer Associate* certification exam.

Further reading

Azure Network Watcher documentation: `https://learn.microsoft.com/en-us/azure/network-watcher/`

Index

A

active-active mode 159-162
active-passive mode 159-160
any-to-any IPVPN connection 204
apex domain 383
application DDoS attacks 287
application delivery 348
Application Gateway subnet
  considerations 370
authentication type 180
Autonomous System Numbers
    (ASNs) 111, 115
Availability Zones (AZs) 8, 215, 315
Azure
  BGP-enabled VPN connection,
    implementing 168
  dual-stack VNet, creating 26
  scalable network topology, designing 236
  single-stack VNet, creating 17
  Web Application Firewall (WAF),
    implementing 331, 332
Azure Active Directory (Azure AD) 184

Azure application delivery services
  categories 348, 349
  selecting 408, 409
Azure Application Gateway components 371
  backend targets, configuring 372-374
  frontend IP addresses, configuring 371, 372
  routing rules, configuring 374
Azure Application Gateway service
  designing 368
  implementing 368
Azure Application Gateway tiers 368, 369
  performance 369
  scalability 369
  Standard tier 369
  Standard V2 tier 369
  WAF tier 369
  WAF V2 tier 369
AzureBastionSubnet 16
Azure certificate 183
Azure certificate authentication
  used, for implementing P2S
      VPN connection 184
Azure Container Instances (ACIs) 477
Azure DDoS Protection pricing
  reference link 289
Azure DDoS Protection service
    tiers 287-289

Azure DNS name server information
reviewing 76
Azure Firewall
deploying, in virtual hub 280-282
implementing 310
Azure Firewall deployment
considerations 320-322
Azure Firewall, features 310
advanced threat protection
capabilities 317, 318
enterprise integration capabilities 318, 319
network filtering 311-315
reliability and performance
capabilities 315, 316
Azure Firewall service tiers 310
AzureFirewallSubnet 16
Azure Firewall test environment template
deploying, with Azure CLI 323, 324
Azure Front Door service
application access, verifying
through 402, 403
components 381
configuring 394-401
creating 394-401
designing 379, 380
implementing 379, 380
tiers 380, 381
Azure Front Door service, components
Front Door endpoint, configuring 382
origin groups, adding 386-390
origins, adding 386-390
routes, configuring 390-392
rule set, overriding 392, 393
rule sets, configuring 390-392
rules, overriding 392, 393
Azure Front Door service, tiers
Classic tier 381
Premium tier 380

Standard tier 380
**Azure hybrid network connection
options 152**
Azure Load Balancer service
Basic SKU, use cases 351
designing 350
global load balancer, configuring 361
global load balancer, creating 361
implementing 350
parameters, completing 359, 360
resources, provisioning 358, 359
Standard SKU, use cases 351
template, deploying to Azure 359, 360
template deployment, initializing
in GitHub 359, 360
Azure load-balancing services
categories 348, 349
selecting 408, 409
Azure Monitor Agent (AMA) 454
Azure Network Watcher 450
diagnostic tools 455
network monitoring tools 451
network monitoring tools,
implementing 465
used, for monitoring network
diagnostics and logs 450
Azure Private DNS 61, 62
implementing 62
Azure Private DNS zone 73
creating 63, 64
Azure private endpoint
configuring, for Azure WebApp 438
connectivity, testing to Azure WebApp
from external network 445
connectivity, testing to Azure
WebApp via 444

creating, for Azure WebApp 439-443

designing 437

implementing 437

resource group, deleting 446, 447

Azure Private Link

designing 437

implementing 437

Azure Private Link service

considerations 438

integrating, with DNS 438

Azure-provided DNS

used, for modifying VNet 69, 70

Azure-provided name resolution 44

exploring 46

Azure Public DNS

implementing 73

Azure Public DNS zone

creating 73, 74

Azure regions within geopolitical region

reference link 242

Azure Resource Manager (ARM) 358

Azure resources

cleaning up 118

deploying, via provided ARM template 254

provisioning 290-293, 419, 461-464

template deployment, initializing
    in GitHub 87, 89

WebVM, connecting with Cloud Shell 89

working with 86

Azure Route Server 110

BGP peering, configuring 115

BGP peering, configuring on
    NvaVM 113-115

configuration, validating 116

dedicated subnet, adding 112, 113

deploying, into RouteServerSubnet 113

learned routes, validating 116

used, for implementing BGP
    dynamic routing 111

Azure SQL Proxy mode 312

Azure Standard load balancer rules

Inbound Network Address
    Translation (NAT) rules 358

load-balancing rules 358

outbound rules 358

Azure subnet workloads routing

additional system routes, reviewing
    for network features 92-95

default system routes, reviewing 90, 91

exploring 90

Azure subscription

authorizing 303-307

Azure Traffic Manager service

designing 404, 405

endpoints, configuring 407

implementing 404, 405

traffic routing method, configuring 406, 407

Azure Virtual Network Gateway 152

Azure virtual network perimeter

securing 285, 286

Azure VNet 4

use cases 4

versus traditional networks 5

Azure VPN Gateway 152, 153

feature consideration 155, 156

generation, using 153, 154

performance considerations 154

point-to-site (P2S) VPN connection
    over SSTP (Secure Socket Tunneling
    Protocol) or IKE v2 153

scalability considerations 155

site-to-site (S2S) VPN connection over
    IPsec (IKE v1 and IKE v2) 152

SKU, using 153, 154

troubleshooting, with diagnostic logs 195

used, for implementing VPN
connection 164

VNet-to-VNet VPN connection over
IPsec (IKE v1 and IKE v2) 153

**Azure vWAN hub-and-spoke
topology 237, 238**

connectivity capabilities 238

virtual VWAN type, selecting 240

vWAN components 238, 239

B

backend targets 372

backend pools 372

redirections 372

Basic SKU

use cases 351

Basic VWAN

versus Standard VWAN 240

**Berkley Internet Naming
Daemon (BIND) 52**

BGP dynamic routing

implementing, with Azure Route Server 111

BGP-enabled VPN connection

Azure VNet connectivity, verifying 178-180

BGP peering status, verifying 177

configuring 174-176

gateway subnet, creating 168, 169

implementing, in Azure 168

local network gateway, creating 172, 173

on-premises network connectivity,
verifying 178-180

VPN connection status, verifying 177, 178

VPN gateway, deploying into
subnet 170, 171

BGP peering

implementing, between NVA and
virtual hub 251, 252

in ExpressRoute provider models 204

BGP peering, configuring to NVA

reference link 252

Bidirectional Forwarding Detection (BFD)

implementing 229-231

Border Gateway Protocol (BGP) 96, 203, 248

advertisements, propagated to subnets 109

advertisements, propagated via
custom route table 110

advertisements, through route server 110

advertisements, through VNet gateway 109

advertisements, via custom route table 109

used, for implementing dynamic
custom routing 108

BreakingPoint Cloud account

creating 303-307

C

central management

implementing, with Firewall
Manager 341, 342

Certificate Authority (CA) 378

CharisTech 17, 26, 38

CharisTech resource group

creating 18-20

CharisTechRG resource

cleaning up 36, 78

**Classless Inter-Domain Routing
(CIDR) 17, 217**

client address pool 180

cloud exchange co-location 202

Cloud Shell

used, for connecting to WebVM 41, 42, 89

connection monitor 452-454

use cases 454

connections per second (CPS) 218

connection troubleshoot tool 455

use cases 456

connectivity association key (CAK) 228

Content Delivery Network (CDN) 380

Core Rule Set (CRS) 375

CoreServicesVNet 17, 164, 254

subnets, creating 20-24

VNet, creating 20-24

CPU quota limits

determining, for recommended
    subscription regions 31-33

cross-network connectivity

designing, over ExpressRoute 222

enhancing, with ExpressRoute
    Global Reach 225-227

enhancing, with multiple ExpressRoute
    VNet connections 224

enhancing, with VNet peering 223

implementing, over ExpressRoute 222

cross-region load balancer

references 355

cross-region VNet connectivity

implementing, with vWAN 132

cross-site scripting (XSS) 369

cross-VNet connectivity options

comparing 146

VNet peering 120

VPN gateway connection 120

vWAN 120

custom DNS server

used, for modifying VNet 56

customer-managed DNS servers 50

implementing 51

customer-managed virtual network 237

custom routing

implementing, with user-defined routes 96

custom rule sets 332-336

**custom rules for Web Application Firewall
    v2 on Azure Application Gateway**

reference link 336

**custom rules for Web Application
    Firewall with Azure Front Door**

reference link 336

D

DatabaseSubnet 20

data centers (DCs) 200

data path performance

improving, with ExpressRoute
    FastPath 218, 219

Data tier Subnet 11

DDoS alerts

configuring 301-303

DDoS attack 286

application DDoS attacks 287

protocol DDoS attacks 287

volumetric DDoS attacks 286

DDoS diagnostic logs forwarding

configuring 299, 300

DDoS IP Protection

versus DDoS Network Protection 289

DDoS metrics

reviewing, for telemetry 298

DDoS protection

enabling, on virtual network 296, 297

implementing 286, 287

DDoS Protection plan

creating 294, 295

DDoS test

results, reviewing 309

running 308, 309

default name resolution option

reviewing 46-49

testing 46-49

**Destination Network Address
   Translation (DNAT) 315**

diagnostic logs

GatewayDiagnosticLog 195

IKEDiagnosticLog 195

P2SDiagnosticLog 195

RouteDiagnosticLog 195

TunnelDiagnosticLog 195

used, for troubleshooting Azure
   VPN Gateway 195

diagnostic tools, Azure Network Watcher

connection troubleshoot 455, 456

IP flow verify 456, 457

next hop tool 459, 460

NSG diagnostics 457, 458

Packet capture 460

VPN troubleshoot 460

disaster recovery (DR) 226

DNS forwarding

configuration 55, 56

DNS records

adding, for forward lookup zone 53, 54

adding, for reverse lookup zone 54, 55

adding, to DNS zone 67-77

verifying, to DNS zone 67, 68

DNS record types

reference link 61

DNS server configurations

applying 55, 56

Domain Name System (DNS) 29, 37

dual-stack 8

dual-stack EngineeringVNet subnets

creating 26, 27

dual-stack EngineeringVNet VNet

creating 26, 27

dual-stack subnets

creation, verifying 28

dual-stack VNet

creating, in Azure 26

creation, verifying 28

dynamic assignment 28

dynamic custom routing

implementing, with BGP 108

**Dynamic Host Configuration
   Protocol (DHCP) 28**

E

encryption

implementing, over ExpressRoute 228, 229

end-to-end encryption with IPsec 228

EngineeringVNet 26, 254

equal-cost multi-path routing (ECMP) 161

existing DNS server configuration

reviewing 51-53

ExpressRoute 198

components 200, 201

cross-network connectivity, designing 222

cross-network connectivity,
   implementing 222

encryption, implementing 228, 229

private peering 199

public peering 199

use case 199

ExpressRoute circuit

creating 232

deprovision 233

ExpressRoute gateway, connecting to 233

provisioning 232

ExpressRoute circuit SKU

selecting 206-211

ExpressRoute connectivity model

selecting 201

ExpressRoute direct model 201-206

ExpressRoute encryption

reference link 228

ExpressRoute FastPath

configuring, for new/existing
connections 221, 222

reference link 220

unsupported scenarios 220

used, for improving data path
performance 218, 219

ExpressRoute gateway

connecting, to ExpressRoute circuit 233

gateway subnet, creating 231

implementing 231

resources, cleaning up 233

service key, retrieving 232

serviceProviderProvisioningState
status, checking 232

VNet, creating 231

ExpressRoute gateway SKU

GatewaySubnet, implementing 217, 218

implementing, with zone
redundancy 215, 216

modifying 216, 217

reference link 213

selecting 211-215

ExpressRoute Global Reach

reference link 226

used, for enhancing cross-network
connectivity 225-227

ExpressRoute local mappings

reference link 208

**ExpressRoute locations, mapping
to Azure regions**

reference link 201

**ExpressRoute peering locations
and connectivity partners**

reference link 202

ExpressRoute provider models

BGP peering 204

ExpressRoute VNet gateway service

deploying 232

external name resolution

options 73

scenarios 73

external site 373

F

firewall

connectivity, testing through 328-330

Firewall Manager

central management, implementing
with 341, 342

firewall policy

reviewing 324-328

firewall service

reviewing 324-328

forward lookup zone

DNS records, adding 53, 54

FQDN filtering 312

Front Door endpoint

certificate support, for custom domains 385

custom domains 383

custom domains, adding to 382-385

Front Door profile 381

**fully qualified domain names
(FQDNs) 48, 372, 455**

G

GatewayDiagnosticLog 195

GatewaySubnet 16, 220

creating 231

implementing 217, 218

GCMAES256 261

Generic Routing Encapsulation (GRE) 5

geo-proximity load-balancing algorithm 355

GitHub

    template deployment, initializing

        39-41, 87-89, 130, 131, 254-258

global commercial Azure

    reference link 206

global load balancer

    configuring 361-368

    creating 361-368

global load-balancing/application

    delivery service

    versus regional load-balancing/

        application delivery service 348

global transit network architecture

    implementing, with VWAN 279, 280

guaranteed low latency 198

H

high availability (HA) 351

holdtime 229

hub-and-spoke architecture

    VNet peering, using 124-126

hub and spoke topology 236

I

IKEDiagnosticLog 195

IKEv2 VPN 182

infrastructure-as-a-service (IaaS) 15, 450

Integrated Service Environment (ISE) 477

internal name resolution

    options 44

    scenarios 43

internal name resolution, options

    advantage 45

    Azure Private DNS 61, 62

Azure Private DNS Resolver 73

Azure Private DNS zones 73

Azure-provided name resolution 44

customer-managed DNS servers 50

limitations 45

Internet Engineering Task Force (IETF) 10

internet SP (ISP) 203

Intrusion Detection and Prevention

    Service (IDPS) 310

intrusion detection systems/intrusion

    prevention systems (IDS/IPS) 96

IP address space

    selecting, for VWAN hub 242

IP flow verify tool 456, 457

IPsec 228

K

keep-alive time 229

L

listener 373

load balancing 348

M

managed rule sets 332, 333

Media Access Control Security

    (MACsec) 228

Microsoft_BotManagerRuleSet (BRS) 333

Microsoft cloud services 200

Microsoft_DefaultRuleSet (DRS) 333

Microsoft-managed virtual network 238

multiple ExpressRoute VNet connections

    used, for enhancing cross-

        network connectivity 224

Multiprotocol Label Switching (MPLS) 204

N

name resolution

scenarios 42

scenarios and options 42

testing, from internet client 77, 78

testing, from WebVM virtual machine 58-72

name server (NS) records 76

naming conventions

reference link 7

network interface card (NIC) 8

network monitoring tools, Azure Network Watcher

connection monitor 452-454

connection monitor, creating 466-474

connection monitor, reviewing 474, 475

implementing 465

network issue, triggering 474, 475

topology, visualizing 451-466

Network Security Group (NSG) 11, 122, 218, 358, 371, 438, 456

Network Virtual Appliance (NVA) 11, 81, 96, 123, 218, 243, 310

next hop tool 459, 460

non-zonal configuration 357

NSG diagnostics 457, 458

NSG flow logs 475, 476

downloading 480, 481

enabling 478-480

limitations 477

reference link 477

reviewing 480, 481

use cases 478

NVA and virtual hub

BGP peering, implementing between 251, 252

NvaVM 98

O

onprem-network 164

OnPremVM 164

Open Systems Interconnection (OSI) 350

OpenVPN 182

Open Worldwide Application Security Protocol (OWASP) 369

OWASP Core Rule Set (CRS) 333

P

P2SDiagnosticLog 195

P2S VPN connection

Azure VNet connectivity, verifying 194

gateway settings, configuration 189-191

gateway settings, configuration for VPN clients 192, 193

implementing, with Azure certificate authentication 184

remote PC connectivity, verifying 194

remote users PC, connecting via RDP 184-189

packets per second (PPS) 218

parameters

initializing 165-167

partners with integrated virtual hub offerings

reference link 253

pass-through network load balancer 350

peering 199

Personal Information Exchange (PFX) 377

Platform-as-a-Service (PaaS) 450

platform service firewall 412-415

Azure Private endpoint, configuring for Azure WebApp 438

Azure private endpoints, designing 437

Azure private endpoints, implementing 437

Azure Private Link, designing 437
Azure Private Link, implementing 437
exceptions 412-415
service endpoints 416-418
service endpoints, configuring
    for storage account 422

platform service network security
implementing 412
parameters, completing 420, 421
template, deploying to Azure 420, 421
template deployment, initializing
    in GitHub 420, 421

platform services
working with 15

points of presence (PoP) 379

point-to-point encryption with MACsec 228

point-to-point Ethernet 203

point-to-site connections 180
authentication type, selecting 183
connection pool, defining 181, 182
tunnel type, selecting 182

policy-based VPN types 156-158
limitations 157
versus route-based VPN types 156

private IP address assignment
dynamic assignment 28
exploring 33
for subnet workloads 28-30
static assignment 29
VMs, deploying with dynamic
    private IP assignments 33-35
VMs, deploying with static private
    IP assignments 33-35

private peering 199

private peering and public peering
selecting, between 199, 200

protocol DDoS attacks 287

provider model 201-205
public peering 199
PublicWebServiceSubnet 20

Q

Quagga 98

R

RADIUS authentication 183
redirections 373
**regional load-balancing/application
    delivery service**
versus global load-balancing/
    application delivery service 348

Remote PC 164
resources
cleaning up 147
providing 129
provisioning 38, 39

reverse lookup zone
DNS records, adding 54, 55

route-based VPN types 159
versus policy-based VPN types 156

RouteDiagnosticLog 195

route network traffic
NVA, reviewing 98-100
route table, associating to subnet 105
route table, creating 102, 103
user-defined route, creating in
    route table 104, 105
verifying, from subnet to
    through NVA 106-108
WebVM, connecting with Cloud Shell 98
with route table 97

route selection and priority 117
   longest prefix match 117
   route type match 117
routing 81
   for Azure VNet workloads 82, 83
   for dual-stack subnets 86
   in virtual hub 249
routing behavior
   modifying 96
routing infrastructure
   configuring, for VWAN hub 244, 245
routing infrastructure unit 244
routing rules, components
   backend setting 377-379
   HTTP/HTTPS listener 375, 376
rules 392
rule set 392
   configuration 393

S

scalable network topology
   designing, in Azure 236
SD-WAN configuration
   in virtual hub 249
SD-WAN connectivity architecture
   with Azure Virtual WAN
   reference link 253
secured hub 280
Secure Sockets Layer (SSL) 349
Secure Socket Tunneling
   Protocol (SSTP) 182
security associations (SAs) 156
server, connection policy
   reference link 312
service endpoints 418, 416, 419
   configuring 432-437

   configuring, for storage account 422
   configuring, to access storage
      account 424-428
   connectivity, testing to storage account
      from private subnet 428-430
   file share mounting information,
      obtaining 422-424
   reference link 416
   storage accounts connection, testing
      from external network to confirm
      denied access 430, 431
service key (s-key)
   retrieving 232
service-level agreement (SLA) 351
serviceProviderProvisioningState status
   checking 232
service providers (SPs) 201
SharedServicesSubnet 20
Simple Mail Transfer Protocol (SMTP) 350
single-stack 8
single-stack VNet
   creating, in Azure 17
   subnets creation, verifying 24, 25
   VNet creation, verifying 24, 25
Site-to-Site connectivity
   configuring, with VWAN 258, 259
site-to-site VPN connectivity,
   implementing with VWAN 262
   connectivity, verifying to on-premises
      site through VWAN 277, 278
   on-premises VPN device,
      configuring 274-276
   resources, cleaning up 279
   routes, verifying to on-premises site
      through VWAN 277, 278
   site-to-site gateway, adding
      to VWAN 263-265
   VPN configuration information,

obtaining 271, 272

VPN site, connecting with
   VWAN hub 268-271

VPN site, creating in VWAN 265-268

**small and medium-sized
   business (SMB) 310**

Software-as-a-Service (SaaS) 200

**Source Network Address Translation
   (SNAT) 315, 351**

SSL/Transport Layer Security (TLS) 368

standard hub-and-spoke topology 237, 238

Standard SKU

availability zone configuration
   option, selecting 355-357

backend pools, selecting 358

benefits 355

load balancer rules, defining 358

load balancer, selecting to implement 352

tier, selecting of load balancer 353-355

use cases 351

Standard tier 369

Standard V2 tier 369

Standard VWAN

versus Basic VWAN 240

static assignment 29

Stock-Keeping Unit (SKU) 350

Structured Query Language (SQL) 350

subdomain 383

subnet delegation 17

subnet workloads

private IP address assignment 28-30

system routes 82

for Azure Management public
   IP address ranges 85

for network traffic 83

for RFC 1918 private IP address ranges 85

for RFC 6598 address space 85

for unspecified addresses 84

T

telemetry

DDoS metrics, reviewing 298

template

deploying, to Azure 165, 167

template deployment

initializing, in GitHub 39-41,
   87-89, 165-167, 254-258

test with simulation partners

reference link 304

third-party device compatibility 163, 164

third-party network virtual appliance

deploying, in connected VNet to
   inspect network traffic 282

third-party SD-WAN NVA

implementing, in virtual hub 252, 253

third-party security virtual appliance

deploying, in virtual hub 282

topology visualization 451, 452

traditional networks

versus Azure VNet 5

Transmission Control Protocol (TCP) 350

Transport Layer Security (TLS) 310, 317

trusted services

reference link 416

TunnelDiagnosticLog 195

TXT record 384

U

uniform resource identifiers (URIs) 455

unique resource naming strategy 6

User Datagram Protocol (UDP) 350

User Defined Routes (UDRs) 96, 218, 371

reference link 220

V

V1 service tiers to V2 service tiers migration
reference link 369
virtual hub
Azure Firewall, deploying 280-282
routing 249
SD-WAN configuration 249
security considerations 280
third-party SD-WAN NVA,
    implementing 252, 253
third-party security virtual
    appliance, deploying 282
virtual hub NVA deployment options
comparing 283, 284
virtual LANs (vLANs) 5
virtual machine scale sets (VMSSs) 4
virtual machines (VMs) 3, 82, 352, 451
virtual network, for Azure services
reference link 412
virtual network subnet
linking, for auto-registration 65, 66, 67
Virtual Network (VNet) 3, 81, 198, 352
connecting, to regional virtual hubs 140-143
connecting, VPN gateway
    connection used 126
connecting, with VNet peering 121
connecting, with vWAN 128
connectivity, verifying 145, 146
creating 231
DDoS protection, enabling on 296, 297
effective routes, verifying 143, 144
modifying, to use Azure-
    provided DNS 69, 70
modifying, to use custom DNS server 56
virtual VWAN type

selecting 240
Virtual WAN hub 239
**virtual WAN, upgrading from
    Basic to Standard**
reference link 241
virtual WAN (vWAN) 235, 239
creating 132-135
used, for configuring Site-to-Site
    connectivity 258, 259
used, for implementing cross-region
    VNet connectivity 132
used, for implementing global transit
    network architecture 279, 280
virtual hub, creating in VNET 135-138
VNets, connecting with 128
VM location
determining 30
VM sizes
determining 30
VNet connection route propagation 250, 251
VNet connection route table association 249
Vnet injection 15
VNet integration 15
reference link 15
VNet IP address spaces
planning 8-11
VNet location
business compliance requirements 7
planning 7, 8
resiliency requirements 8
user proximity 7
Vnet naming
planning 6, 7
Vnet naming restrictions
reference link 6

VNet peering 11

advantages 121

and transitive routing 123

architecture considerations 122

configuring 124

implementation, planning 121, 122

used, for enhancing cross-
    network connectivity 223

using, in hub-and-spoke
    architecture 124-126

VNets, connecting with 121

Vnet subnet segmentation

planning 11-14

platform services, working with 15-17

volumetric DDoS attacks 286

VPN connection

implementing, with Azure
    VPN Gateway 164

VPN connection, high-availability options

active-active mode 161, 162

active-passive mode 160

selecting 159

VPN gateway connection

architecture considerations 128

Site-to-Site (IPsec) connection 126, 127

used, for connecting VNets 126, 127

VNet-to-VNet connection 126, 127

VPN troubleshoot tool 460

supported gateway types 460

unsupported gateway types 460

VWAN hub connections 239

vWAN hub, design considerations

IP address space, selecting 242

regions, selecting 241

routing infrastructure, configuring 244, 245

routing preference, configuring 245-248

VNets, connecting with VWAN 248

VWAN hub S2S VPN

availability considerations 260

performance considerations 261, 262

scalability considerations 259

W

WAF policy

limitations 341

WAF policy associations 339, 340

WAF policy associations, options

Application Gateway 339

HTTP listener 339

route path 339

WAF tier 369

WAF V2 tier 369

Web Application Firewall (WAF) 318, 349

custom rule sets 334-336

implementing, in Azure 331, 332

managed rule sets 332, 333

policy mode 337-339

rule actions 337-339

Web tier Subnet 11

WebVM 254

connecting, with Cloud Shell 41, 42, 89

WebVM virtual machine

name resolutions, testing 58-72

wide area networks (WANs) 199

wildcard domain 383

Z

zonal configuration 356

zone redundancy

used, for implementing
    ExpressRoute 215, 216

zone-redundant configuration 356

www.packtpub.com

Subscribe to our online digital library for full access to over 7,000 books and videos, as well as industry leading tools to help you plan your personal development and advance your career. For more information, please visit our website.

Why subscribe?

- Spend less time learning and more time coding with practical eBooks and Videos from over 4,000 industry professionals

- Improve your learning with Skill Plans built especially for you

- Get a free eBook or video every month

- Fully searchable for easy access to vital information

- Copy and paste, print, and bookmark content

Did you know that Packt offers eBook versions of every book published, with PDF and ePub files available? You can upgrade to the eBook version at www.packtpub.com and as a print book customer, you are entitled to a discount on the eBook copy. Get in touch with us at customercare@packtpub.com for more details.

At www.packtpub.com, you can also read a collection of free technical articles, sign up for a range of free newsletters, and receive exclusive discounts and offers on Packt books and eBooks.

Other Books You May Enjoy

If you enjoyed this book, you may be interested in these other books by Packt:

Cloud Auditing Best Practices

Shinesa Cambric, Michael Ratemo

ISBN: 9781803243771

- Understand the cloud shared responsibility and role of an IT auditor
- Explore change management and integrate it with DevSecOps processes
- Understand the value of performing cloud control assessments
- Learn tips and tricks to perform an advanced and effective auditing program
- Enhance visibility by monitoring and assessing cloud environments
- Examine IAM, network, infrastructure, and logging controls
- Use policy and compliance automation with tools such as Terraform

Mastering Python Networking - Fourth Edition

Eric Chou

ISBN: 9781803234618

- Use Python to interact with network devices
- Understand Docker as a tool that you can use for the development and deployment
- Use Python and various other tools to obtain information from the network
- Learn how to use ELK for network data analysis
- Utilize Flask and construct high-level API to interact with in-house applications
- Discover the new AsyncIO feature and its concepts in Python 3
- Explore test-driven development concepts and use PyTest to drive code test coverage
- Understand how GitLab can be used with DevOps practices in networking

Packt is searching for authors like you

If you're interested in becoming an author for Packt, please visit `authors.packtpub.com` and apply today. We have worked with thousands of developers and tech professionals, just like you, to help them share their insight with the global tech community. You can make a general application, apply for a specific hot topic that we are recruiting an author for, or submit your own idea.

Share your thoughts

Now you've finished *Designing and Implementing Microsoft Azure Networking Solutions*, we'd love to hear your thoughts! Scan the QR code below to go straight to the Amazon review page for this book and share your feedback or leave a review on the site that you purchased it from.

https://packt.link/r/1803242035

Your review is important to us and the tech community and will help us make sure we're delivering excellent quality content.

Download a free PDF copy of this book

Thanks for purchasing this book!

Do you like to read on the go but are unable to carry your print books everywhere?

Is your eBook purchase not compatible with the device of your choice?

Don't worry, now with every Packt book you get a DRM-free PDF version of that book at no cost.

Read anywhere, any place, on any device. Search, copy, and paste code from your favorite technical books directly into your application.

The perks don't stop there, you can get exclusive access to discounts, newsletters, and great free content in your inbox daily

Follow these simple steps to get the benefits:

1. Scan the QR code or visit the link below

https://packt.link/free-ebook/9781803242033

2. Submit your proof of purchase
3. That's it! We'll send your free PDF and other benefits to your email directly

www.ingramcontent.com/pod-product-compliance
Lightning Source LLC
Chambersburg PA
CBHW081452050326
40690CB00015B/2775